Traité complet de la théorie et de la pratique de l'harmonie (1844)

Complete Treatise on the Theory and Practice of Harmony

Portrait of François-Joseph Fétis. Lithograph by J.B. Madou.

Traité complet de la théorie et de la pratique de l'harmonie (1844)

Complete Treatise on the Theory and Practice of Harmony

by François-Joseph Fétis

Translated with introduction and commentary
by Peter M. Landey

HARMONOLOGIA: STUDIES IN MUSIC THEORY No. 13
Thomas Christensen, General Editor

PENDRAGON PRESS
HILLSDALE, NY

Other Titles in the series
HARMONOLOGIA: STUDIES IN MUSIC THEORY

No.1 *Heinrich Schenker: An Annotated Index To His Analyses of Musical Works* by Larry Laskowski
No. 2 *Marpurg's Thoroughbass and Composition Handbook: A Narrative Translation and Critical Study* by David A. Sheldon
No. 3 *Between Modes and Keys: German Theory 1592-1802* by Joel Lester
No. 4 *Music Theory from Zarlino to Schenker: A Bibliography and Guide* by David A. Damschroder and David Russell Williams
No. 5 *Musical Time: The Sense of Order* by Barbara Barry
No. 6 *Formalized Music Thought and Mathematics in Composition* (revised edition) by Iannis Xenakis
No. 7 *Esquisse de l'histoire de l'harmonie: An English-Language Translation of the François-Joseph Fétis* History of Harmony by Mary I. Arlin
No. 8 *Analyzing Fugue: A Schenkerian Approach* by William Renwick
No. 9 *Bach's Modal Chorales* by Lori Burns
No. 10 *Treatise on Melody* by Anton Reicha, translated by Peter Landey
No. 11 *A Topical Guide to Schenkerian Literature: An Annotated Bibliography with Indices* by David Carson Berry
No. 12 *Structure and Meaning in Tonal Music: A Festschrift for Carl Schachter* edited by Poundie Burstein and David Gagne
No. 14 *Music Theory from Boethius to Zarlino: A Bibliography and Guide* by David Russell Williams and C. Matthew Balensuela

Library of Congress Cataloging-in-Publication Data

Fétis, François-Joseph, 1784-1871.
[Traité complet de la théorie et de la pratique de l'harmonie. English]
Traité complete de la théorie et de la pratique de harmonie (1844) = Complete treatise on the theory and practice of harmony / by François-Joseph Fétis ; translated with introduction and commentary by Peter M. Landey.
p. cm. -- (Harmonologia : studies in music theory ; no. 13)

TABLE OF CONTENTS

INTRODUCTION

BOOK ONE

BOOK TWO

FIRST SECTION

SECOND SECTION

THIRD SECTION

BOOK FOUR

TRANSLATOR'S INTRODUCTION

When the *Traité complet de la théorie et de la pratique de l'harmonie* was first published in 1844,[1] François-Joseph Fétis (1784-1871) was at the height of his influence as a theorist, pedagogue, and biographer.[2] A towering figure in the history of music theory, his prodigious knowledge of both repertory and theoretical sources was unsurpassed in his time. Few theorists, before or since, have attained such an extensive and profound command of philosophy and musical aesthetics, and applied that knowledge to a general theory of music.[3] The *Traité complet* remains one of the most influential, yet controversial treatises of the nineteenth century, and many of the ideas set forth there are a matter of common parlance in music theory today. Many subsequent theorists were swayed by his thought, or railed against it. Hugo Riemann (1849-1919) remarks: "To his meditations we are indebted for the modern concept of tonality... He found himself emancipated from the spirit of any particular age, and able to render justice to all the various styles of music."[4] Matthew Shirlaw (1873-1961) was not so charitable: "Anything more ill-considered, more inadequate than Fétis' "metaphysical" theory of harmony based on the principle of *tonality* which he himself does not understand, and is unable to explain, it would be difficult to conceive."[5]

---

[1]Hereafter abbreviated as *Traité complet*. One of the longest running treatises in music theory, it exhausted twenty editions, the most recent dating from 1903. Upon publication it was immediately translated into two separate Italian editions by Emanuele Gambale, *Trattato completo della teoria e della practica dell'armonia* (Milan: Lucca, 1844), and Alberto Mazzucato, *Trattato completo della teoria e della practica dell'armonia* (Milan: Ricordi, 1844). A Spanish translation appeared by F. Gil de Asis, *Tratado completo de la teoria y practica de la armonia* (Madrid: M. Salazar, 1850).

[2]I have attempted to provide a wider context for some of Fétis' ideas with supplemental material from various primary sources, including the *Biographie universelle des musiciens*, the *Revue musicale* and the *Revue et Gazette musicale de Paris*. These are abbreviated *FétisB, Rm*, and *RgmP* respectively.

[3]Under the entry on himself in the *Biographie universelle*, Fétis argues that the study of philosophy is "indispensable for the exposition of the principles of the theory of music and for the analysis of the facts of the history of this art." *FétisB,* 4:106.

[4]Hugo Riemann, *Musik-Lexicon* (Leipzig, 1882), Eng. trans. J. S. Shedlock (1893-7), (Da Capo Press, 1970), 235.

[5]Matthew Shirlaw, *The Theory of Harmony* (London: Novello and Co., Ltd., 1917), 351.

The final shape of Fétis' theory of harmony as set forth in the *Traité complet* is partly an assemblage of his writings and deliberations on the subject during a period of nearly half a century. His thoughts on the works of numerous theorists are found practically verbatim in the *Biographie universelle* (1835-44/1860-65) and his ideas on music theory appear throughout the *Revue musicale* (1827-35), the *Revue et Gazette musicale de Paris* (1835-80) and various other journals. On his own account, he had already written a monograph on the theory of harmony by 1816, but after sending the first few pages to the publisher in 1819 he decided to withhold publication out of consideration for Catel (1773-1830), not wishing to offend the older theorist by criticisms of his theory.[6] It was not until 1823 that the book was published as the *Méthode élémentaire d'harmonie et d'accompagnement*, which, he says, was only an abridged version of the earlier work "without any discussion of theory." Written in a succinct and didactic style, Fétis claims that it became an important harmony textbook in France and Belgium as a result of its straightforward presentation of ideas. Fétis considers that he had already established his theory of harmony in the *Méthode*, and that he had spent the twenty years leading up to the *Traité complet* merely perfecting it.[7]

The main body of Fétis' theory is contained in the first three books of the *Traité complet*. A modified version of his *Esquisse de l'histoire de l'harmonie* comprises Book Four in which he offers an account of the history of music theory leading up to his formulation of the four orders of tonality.[8] An appendix was later added in which he counters criticism of his theory of substitution by the revered French pianist, theorist, composer and piano pedagogue, Pierre-Joseph Zimmerman (1785-1853). The 1849 third edition brings in the famous philosophical Preface, and a new Foreword introduces the ninth edition of 1867, the last to appear before his death. Clearly, despite the late date of the publication of the *Traité complet* in Fétis' career, much of its content is the result of a long period of gestation and represents his mature thought.

In the philosophical Preface, Fétis begins by describing some of the events that first shaped his theoretical outlook. As a student at the Paris Conservatory around the turn of the century he was exposed to the intense controversies surrounding the theories of Jean-Philippe Rameau (1683-1764) and Catel. This encounter cultivated in Fétis a critical attitude that

[6]Charles-Simon Catel's *Traité d'harmonie* (Paris, 1802) exerted considerable influence during the first quarter of the nineteenth century, having been adopted as the official harmony textbook at the Paris Conservatory.

[7]*FétisB*, 4: 103, 108.

[8]The *Esquisse*, published in 1841 in a limited edition of 50 copies, was compiled from its earlier serialization in the *Revue et Gazette musicale* in 1840. See *Esquisse de l'histoire de l'harmonie: An English-Language Translation of the François-Joseph Fétis History of Harmony,* translated by Mary Arlin (Stuyvesant, NY, Pendragon Press, 1994).

led to his dissatisfaction with the work of both theorists. Rameau's writings, he thinks, although more methodical, force art into a system, and Catel's theory, while offering a more practical explanation of musical processes, is nevertheless based on the specious division of the monochord. His attempt to reconcile these opposing methods resulted in two epiphanic experiences. The first happened following a meeting with Étienne Méhul (1763-1817), an ardent supporter of Catel. After leaving the house of this illustrious composer one day, Fétis recalls: "an idea came to me like a beam of light, and which placed me on the road to the doctrine that I have since developed in all my works."[9] This was the notion that explanations of harmony by divisions of the monochord, numerical progressions, and arbitrary classifications of chords are basically flawed. Rather, Fétis focuses on how sounds succeed each other in the scale of the two modes, which, he thinks, unites the horizontal and vertical domains, with tonality as the "regulating principle." He further concludes that there can be only two fundamental chords—the perfect chord and the dominant seventh. The former is a chord of repose because it does not require continuation, whereas the second has "tendencies of resolution" and "characterizes movement in harmony."[10] Convinced that these two chords constitute the totality of "natural" harmony he comes to the belief that all other chords are simply their modifications.

Fétis reports that he spent the next twenty years immersed in the careful analysis of musical works and in the examination of theoretical treatises, which numbered in the hundreds. His second epiphany happens at the end of this period of intensive study. In May 1831, while strolling through the *Bois de Boulogne*, he has a profound revelation that all musical experience is metaphysical, where nature provides the elements, but human understanding, sensibility, and will determine particular tonalities.[11] He is now certain that the divisions of the monochord cannot serve as explanations of harmonic processes, for we are not aware of them. Fétis believes that if consonances and dissonances were governed externally by the "resonances of sonorous bodies," then this would result in a uniformity of musical organization across cultures, which is clearly not the case. Furthermore, Fétis claims that he has discovered the principles of tonal transformations, and "devised the classification of the various orders of tonality that succeeded one another over three centuries through the affinities between tones that were brought in by harmony."[12]

[9]*Traité complet,* xlviii. Fétis reports that shortly thereafter he moved from Paris to the Ardennes, which places this event around the year 1810.

[10]*Traité complet*, xlviii.

[11]Ibid., lii.

[12]Ibid., lii.

Fétis is also dissatisfied with ideas about musical organization based on numerological mysticism. He describes the musical customs of oriental pantheism, tracing the belief in "the identity of universal harmony and the harmony of musical tones" through Indian, Hebrew, and oriental cultures to the philosophy of Pythagoras, Plato, and its transmission into modern Europe. This idea, however, removes "freedom in the conception of art," and denies the "intellectual and emotional faculties the possibility of modifying the elements therein."[13] Nor does Fétis tolerate the view that musical understanding is rooted in physiology,[14] arguing that any attempt to attribute it to the structure of the ear reduces musical perception to a mere play of sensations.[15] In a final blow to prescriptive philosophies he rejects the theory of vitalism that infuses matter with a mysterious life force, and challenges the notion that life is only a mechanical arrangement of physical and chemical processes.

Fétis proceeds to demonstrate how the human spirit has conceived and modified the elements of music. He begins with the observation that various scale systems exist in different cultures, from which he draws two chief conclusions; first, that scale formations are the product of particular cultural preferences and individual sensibilities, and second, that they perforce give rise to different systems of tonality. He devotes the remainder of the Preface to the evolution of tonal systems, manifested in the four orders of tonality. He examines these systems not just in technical terms, but also as the corollary of the expressive needs of their time.

---

[13]Ibid., lvi.

[14]In an article published by the Académie Royale de Belgique in the same year that Fétis added his philosophical Preface to the third edition of the *Traité complet*, he further expounds upon the idea that musical understanding is not physiologically determined: "The imagination awakes; not this imitative imagination that is only a kind of memory of the sensibility, but transcendent imagination, creator of the idea, producer of sonic images not furnished by any exterior model, the character of which is found only in itself." He continues: "From there the particular character of art that makes up these sonic images called music; from there the sublimity of this art and its supremacy over all the others as the manifestation of the creative power of humankind; from there, finally, is the absolute ideality that is associated with the notion of beauty with regard to the products of this art." "NOTE SUR LES VERITABLES FONCTIONS DE L'OREILLE DANS LA MUSIQUE," Académie Royale de Belgique, extrait du tome xvi, no. 3, des Bulletins (1849), 11-14.

[15]Fétis takes issue with the view that all knowledge originates in sensation, advocated by the French philosopher Étienne Bonnet de Condillac (1715-1780). In his *Traité des sensations* (1754) Condillac imagines a statue that has not yet received any sense impressions. The first sense that it experiences is smell, which results in either pleasure or pain, and the pleasure/pain dichotomy forms the basis for all future judgment. The next stage involves memory as the statue compares one smell to another, which brings about the process of judgment. Fétis rejects this reduction of the understanding to pure sensation arguing that there exists an *a priori* musical sense.

In Book One, Fétis sets out to establish that the laws of tonality find their origin in the intervallic relationships of the notes of the scale. The special functions of each scale degree determine the kinds of intervals that accompany them. This melodic/harmonic complex results in "a quality of necessity that is generally designated by the term tonality."[16] Perfect consonances of the octave and fifth are "consonances of conclusion" because they provide a sense of repose. Consonant thirds and sixths are imperfect because they require continuation. The perfect fourth is a "mixed consonance" because it has consonant characteristics, yet also lacks repose. The tritone between scale-degrees 4 and 7 is not, according to Fétis, a diminished interval, for it occurs diatonically. He calls it an "appellative consonance," with the fourth degree and leading tone being summoned by scale-degrees 3 and 1.[17] He contends that the appellative consonance is activated by the presence of scale degree 5, whereas in other contexts (vii^6—I^6, for example), obligatory resolutions are relaxed.[18] This seemingly innocuous point is pivotal for the distinction that he draws between old and modern tonality, for it is only through the combination of the appellative consonance and the fifth degree that the dominant seventh becomes a fully functional key-defining chord. It is the law of tonality that thus shapes the nature of dissonance, which is either tonal, arising naturally within the scale (2nds, 7ths, and 9ths), or altered, resulting from the combination of different scales forming augmented and diminished intervals. These alterations set up new tendencies towards other keys and are therefore "attractive" intervals. Multiple interpretations of augmented and diminished intervals (for example, an augmented second may sound to the ear like a minor third) Fétis calls "variably attractive," a distinction that constitutes the basis for his subsequent treatment of altered chords.

The juxtaposition of scale degrees 4 and 5 from which Fétis obtains the dominant seventh is a clear departure from Rameau's derivation of the seventh from the superposition of thirds. The notion that the dominant seventh arises naturally from the "clash of boundaries" between the two tetrachords that make up the scale is the prime justification for its not having to be prepared. Fétis argues that "this dissonance is inherent in tonality, like consonant harmony,"[19] and in response to Zimmerman's criticism that there is no theoretical proof of this assumption he declares that "some substances and primary causes will be an eternal mystery for us."[20] Fétis proclaims that this clash of boundaries resulting in the

[16]*Traité complet*, 2.

[17]Fétis earlier refers to this interval as a "weak consonance" because of its "natural movement." *Rm*, No. 13 (1827), 332-333.

[18]*Traité complet*, 257.

[19]Ibid., 38.

[20]Ibid., 257.

dissonant dominant seventh forms a constant that "fixes consequently the place of the other notes." This leads him to the critical notion that the essence of modern tonality resides in the unprepared dissonance of the dominant seventh chord.[21] Sevenths on other scale degrees arise from prolongation, substitution, or their combination, and are the product of incidental dissonance.

Fétis observes that scale-degree 6 may support both stable and unstable chords. Momentary repose on this degree is established by the accompaniment of the fifth, resulting in the tonic chord of the relative minor, or a deceptive cadence. He considers that the sixth is the best interval to accompany scale-degree 6 because it removes all ambiguity concerning its tonal nature. In the strict context of the tendencies of scale degrees following his system of tonality, a chord of conclusion on this scale degree challenges the hegemony of the tonic. Similarly, the second degree cannot constitute a point of repose, for when it is accompanied by the fifth the possibility of establishing other keys arises, destroying its "tonal character." The intervals that best suit the second degree are the sixth, third (with sixth), and fourth (with sixth), which ensure its function as a support for passing chords. Fétis is not consistent, however, in his opinion of the second and sixth scale degrees presented in the *Traité complet*. In the *Traité du contrepoint*, he admits a wider use of these degrees: "The second and sixth degrees are able to support all the intervals, for they result neither in the relation of the tritone [false relation], or in the sensation of keys foreign to the principal key."[22]

Fétis deems the third scale degree to be "completely opposed to any feeling of repose," for its fifth is the leading tone which has a natural attraction toward the tonic. The best harmonies for scale-degree 3 are the sixth, which avoids repose, and the third, "the character of which determines the mode because of its minor or major quality."[23] Likewise, the seventh degree also lacks repose, as it is impossible to form a fifth above it (Fétis does not mention the natural minor here). He considers, however, that the chord of the minor fifth and sixth (six-five chord) preserves the tonal character of the seventh degree, the minor fifth forming an appellative consonance that causes it to rise to the tonic. All other successions of the seventh degree involve the sixth.

With these ideas concerning imperfect and equivocal intervals, Fétis believes to have set forth the foundational principles of the laws of modern tonality: "*Tonality is formed from the aggregation of necessary relations, successive or simultaneous, of the tones of the scale*."[24] Furthermore, the

---

[21]*Traité du contrepoint et de la fugue* (Paris, 1824/46), 71.

[22]Ibid., 3.

[23]Ibid., 21.

[24]*Traité complet*, 23.

reciprocal connection between the tendencies of scale degrees and the intervals they support ensures the union of melody and harmony.

Having examined the nature of intervals in the context of the scale, in Book Two Fétis turns to the subject of chords. Five-three chords are "perfect" because they create a sense of repose. They are supported by scale-degrees 1, 4, 5 and 6, and their "fixed position on certain notes of the scale is the necessary result of the laws of tonality."[25] Root position chords on other scale degrees result from harmonic sequences whose symmetrical movement suspends the sense of tonality until their moment of conclusion, causing the ear to accept apparent anomalies in the tonal hierarchy. Perhaps the most notable anomaly is the minor fifth chord on scale-degree 7. The suspension of its appellative tendency when the chord belongs to a symmetrical sequence represents for Fétis "the solution to one of the greatest metaphysical difficulties in the theory of harmony," for he proves that the conditions that override the surface demands of tonality do not invalidate its fundamental laws.[26]

Following the principles established in the treatment of scale degrees, Fétis contends that inversions of consonant chords are entirely different sonorities than when in root position because they are no longer perfect. These chords, which by definition lack repose, are supported by scale-degrees 2, 3, 6, which are characterized by their tendency toward stable chords. His recognition that inversions are a type of modification demonstrates sensitivity to various tonal nuances that are to some extent flattened out by the reductive aspect of fundamental bass theory.

Fétis then turns his attention to dissonant chords. The dominant seventh forms a natural dissonance arising from the tetrachordal "clash of boundaries" and the appellative consonance, to which is added the fifth above the dominant. The intervallic structure of the natural dissonant seventh chord can only appear diatonically over a single note, that of the dominant, which gives this chord its unique key-defining quality. The dominant seventh may resolve as a perfect or interrupted cadence. If the necessary movements of the fourth and seventh degrees are not fulfilled, a change of key results. This involves the enharmonic respelling of the dominant seventh, discussion of which Fétis reserves for Book Three.

The thorough-bass nomenclature that Fétis uses for the inversions of the dominant seventh reflects the obligatory resolutions of the appellative consonance. In first inversion, or chord of the fifth and sixth, scale-degrees 4 and 7 are obliged to resolve to scale-degrees 3 and 1. The second inversion, called leading-tone sixth (*sixte sensible*) because the sixth above the bass is the leading tone, resolves the appellative consonance to either a root position or a sixth chord. The third inversion, or chord of the tritone,

[25]Ibid., 25.

[26]Ibid., 31.

signals the tritone that is found between the bass and an upper voice. Fétis always resolves its appellative consonance onto a tonic sixth chord. In the dominant seventh chord and its inversions, scale-degree 4 is doubly inflected toward scale-degree 3 as the seventh of the dominant and as part of the appellative consonance.

Now that Fétis has established the role of consonant and natural dissonant chords he can address the various forms of their modification. These include substitution, prolongation, chromatic alteration, passing tones (*notes de passage*),[27] and their combinations. All modifications serve to vary natural harmony (the perfect chord, dominant seventh, and their inversions) or to establish contact with other keys.

Fétis' concept of substitution lies at the heart of his theory of tonality. He introduces it dramatically as "one of the most delicate questions in the theory of harmony." It is formed by replacing scale-degree 5 with that of scale-degree 6 in the dominant seventh chord. The substituted note, like the dominant seventh, does not require preparation and it must always return to the note that it displaces.[28] It arises melodically and thus occurs in the highest voice regardless of the inversion of the dominant seventh. If the dominant seventh is in root position a dominant ninth chord results (see example 1 below). The most significant outcome of the substitution is the creation of the leading-tone seventh derived from the first inversion of the dominant seventh, with the fully diminished leading-tone seventh resulting from substitution in the minor mode (see example 2).

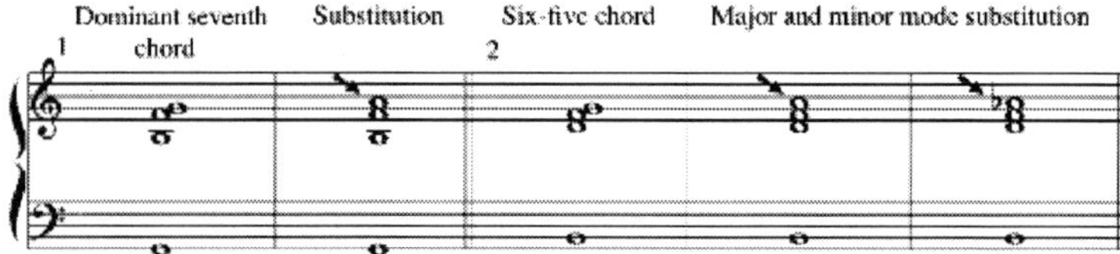

An exception to the placement of substitution in the melody happens in minor mode substitution, where the substituted flat sixth may appear in any voice because the augmented second between the substituted note and the leading tone is enharmonic with the minor third, and therefore does not offend the musical sense (*sens musicale*).[29] On the contrary, the pleasure

[27]In Fétis' terminology, passing tones include the all types of non-chord tones. Those that occur off the beat are called real passing tones, while those that occur on the beat are called appoggiaturas.

[28]The notion that a dissonant note may "stand for" a consonant note comes from a long-standing music-theoretic tradition. For discussion on the background of this debate, see Albert Cohen, "*La Supposition* and the Changing Concept of Dissonance in Baroque Theory," *Journal of the American Musicological Society*, vol. XXIV (Spring, 1971), 64-84.

[29]For discussion of Fétis' notion of *le sens musicale* see D. Martin Jenni, "Fétis and *Le sens musicale*," in *Convention in Eighteenth- and Nineteenth-Century Music: Essays in*

afforded by the attraction between the leading tone and the substituted note (which forms a minor or diminished seventh) creates an "impassioned accent." Other seventh chords do not have this quality, for they lack the attractive power of the leading-tone seventh. This leads Fétis to conclude: "The leading-tone seventh is, in the order of dissonances, what the major fourth and minor fifth are in the order of consonances."[30]

Whereas chords modified by substitution and the dominant seventh do not require preparation, all other dissonant clashes are brought about by prolongation. True modification of natural chords happens only when they introduce dissonances, resulting in 2-3, 7-6, and 9-8 prolongations, which Fétis refers to as retardations. While he recognizes the 4-3 retardation, he thinks that the dissonant fourth is not a result of a clash against the bass, but a clash of a second or seventh in the upper voices. He argues that a fourth against the bass, without a clash between the upper voices, does not always form a dissonance. These are the only retardations that operate within the context of modern tonality, and while they must be prepared, Fétis demonstrates insight into how the preparation is effected. In a perceptive analysis of a passage from Mozart's *Cosi fan tutti* he claims that both Gottfried Weber (1779-1839) and A. B. Marx (1795-1866) are in error for declaring that Mozart fails to prepare a prolongation that Fétis correctly contends is implied by the preceding harmony.[31]

Fétis is careful to establish that substitution and prolongation may be used in combination without confounding their individual effects. The following example shows the combined modification beginning with the dominant seventh chord, followed by substitution, prolongation and their combination, resulting in a subdominant chord over a dominant pedal.

Natural harmony Substitution Prolongation Substitution and prolongation combined

Fétis then sets forth his explanation of the origin of the supertonic seventh chord and its inversions. The modification of the first, second, and third inversions of the dominant seventh chord by substitution and prolongation results in the third inversion, root position, and first inversion of the supertonic seventh chord respectively (examples 1, 2, and 3 below). The second inversion of the supertonic seventh is made possible by substitution in the bass. The requirement that the substitution be placed in

---

Honor of Leonard G. Ratner, ed. Wye J. Allenbrook, Janet M. Levy, and William P. Mahrt (Stuvvesant, N.Y: Pendragon, 1992), 447-72.

[30]*Traité complet,* 51.

[31]Ibid., 64.

the melody is here relaxed because the prolongation of the C, delaying the B, forms a minor third with the A in the bass, thus avoiding the clash between scale-degrees 6 and 7 (see example 4).

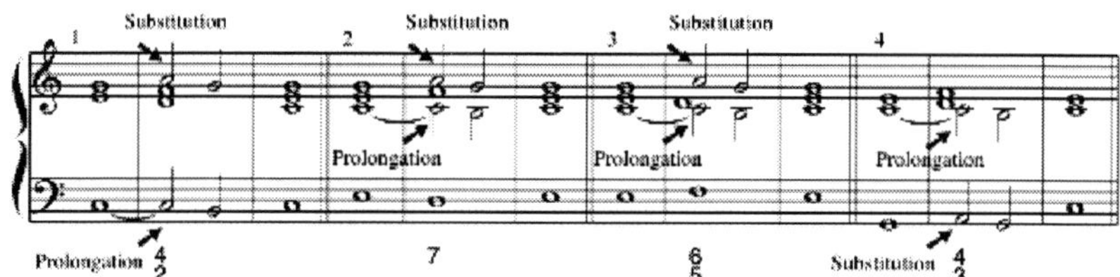

Fétis does not regard these substitutions and prolongations as non-chord tones that delay subsequent chords, but as independent entities that he calls artificial chords. On this point, however, he wants to have it both ways. Having created the linear derivation of chords with substitution and prolongation, he removes them from their voice-leading context in order to establish them as independent verticalities, the artificiality of which he must nevertheless insist in order to remain faithful to his view that they cannot function as tonally stable chords. Other theorists, he says, falsely consider these chords as fundamental, and think that they may be inverted. In Fétis' system only natural chords are inverted, and so inversions of artificial chords must be derived from the inversions of the natural chords from which they originate. Taking secondary sevenths as fundamental chords causes them to be isolated, resulting in a lack of hierarchical disposition essential for his system of tonality.

Fétis' theory of chord placement and succession is clearly influenced by the tradition of the *règle de l'octave* which he acknowledges at the very beginning of the *Traité complet*: "The scale is both the rule of the order (*règle de l'ordre*) of the succession of tones, because they have the closest affinities, and is the measure of distances that separate them."[32] He returns to the subject after he has established the relations that "make up the harmony of which every scale of a major or minor key may be accompanied, without introducing relationships with foreign scales," and offers the following paradigmatic scale harmonization:[33]

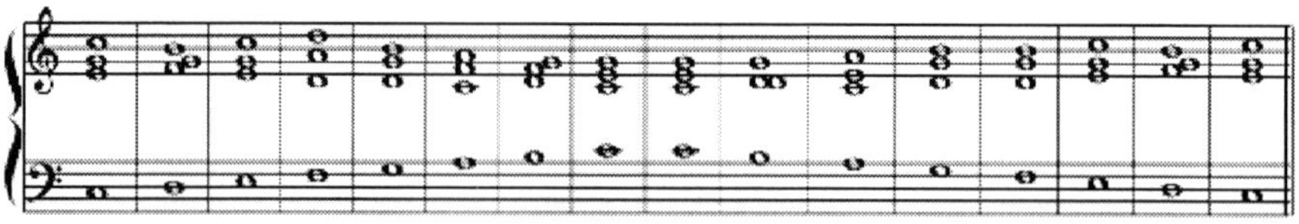

Interestingly, Fétis uses the perfect chord on descending scale-degree 6, despite his former assertion that "the sixth removes all ambiguity concerning the tonal nature of the sixth degree."

[32]*Traité complet,* 2.

[33]Ibid., 84.

Fétis notes that modulations resulting from natural dissonant chords have invoked the leading-tone sixth chord on descending scale-degree 6, and he remarks: "The old French harmonists called this formula the *règle de l'octave*; the Italians call it the *scala armonica*, or simply *scala*:"

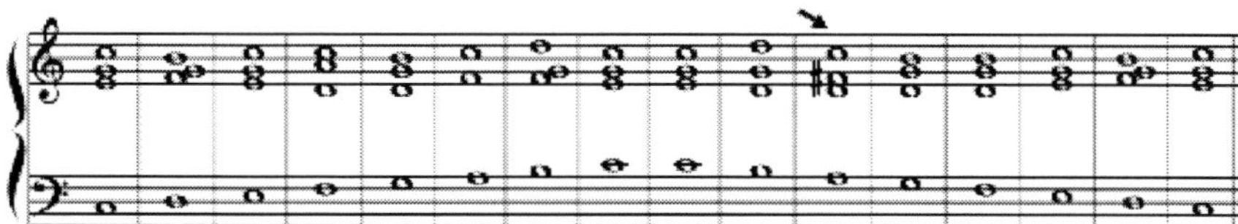

Fétis takes exception to this form of the *règle,* however, for he thinks the leading-tone sixth chord disrupts tonal unity by setting up the dominant as a temporary tonic.[34] He suggests that the minor scale version of the *règle* is better because it uses the "simple sixth" on this degree:

He continues with a form of the *règle* with modification by substitution:

Substitution Substitution

Here the substitution on ascending scale-degree 2 results in an unprepared VII 6/5 chord. Fétis, however, regards it is an artificial sonority derived from, and representing, the V 4/3 chord. The substituted A is melodically motivated, which standing for G, does not require preparation.

Fétis also offers a version of the *règle* that combines prolongation and substitution on the ascending fourth degree:

Prolongation

Substitution

Although this is the same II 6/5 chord found on ascending scale-degree 4 in the *règle* devised by the French harmonists cited above, Fétis regards it as an artificial chord derived from the third inversion of the dominant

[34]Following the conventional form of the *règle*, Catel also uses V 4/3 of V on this degree.

seventh. Curiously, the voicing that he uses in this instance runs contrary to his dictum that the substitution must occur in the upper voice![35]

Fétis' idea of tonality is thus largely an outgrowth of the fundamental principles of the *règle* where root position perfect chords occur primarily on scale-degrees 1 and 5, with the other scale degrees relegated to some form of sixth or applied chords.[36] Moreover, Fétis contends that various scale degrees may be associated with a specific harmony even when removed from the context of the scale:

> We have thus arrived at the complete constitution of tonal unity in modern music. All consonant and dissonant relationships of a single scale are established and demonstrated, as much in successive as in simultaneous order: each note of the scale, whatever the circumstances of its connection with the others, has in each instance its own particular harmonies.[37]

Having demonstrated the foundation of tonality in the structure of the scale, established principles of chord succession (including surface anomalies), and shown various types of chord modification, Fétis thinks that he has accounted for all the possibilities of diatonic harmony. Next he considers modifications that alter natural intervals through chromatic inflection, including modifications to the substitution and prolongation. Fétis can now designate altered notes forming the tritone by the terms diminished fifth and augmented fourth, because, unlike the minor fifth/ major fourth of the appellative consonance, they do not occur diatonically. The dominant seventh modified by substitution may also be altered. In this case scale-degree 2 in the upper voice (the fifth of the dominant seventh) is raised, and ascends to scale-degree 3. The substitution here occurs in an inner voice and forms an augmented fourth with the altered note that mimics the appellative consonance, resulting in a dominant ninth chord with raised fifth, demonstrated in the following example.

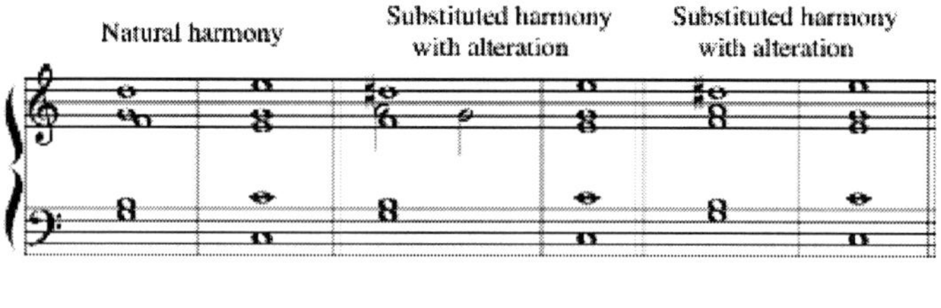

Natural harmony

Substituted harmony with alteration

Substituted harmony with alteration

---

[35]Given Fétis' notion that the substituted II 6/5 chord represents the V 4/2 chord, it seems problematic that the seventh in the bass should resolve upwards in this instance, if the theory is to have any basis in perception. Elsewhere in the treatise, Fétis leads this chord of substitution to a tonic first inversion chord, thus resolving the implied seventh. See his remarks on page 45.

[36]For a comprehensive discussion of the history of the rule of the octave, see Thomas Christensen, "The *Règle de l'Octave* in Thorough-Bass Theory and Practice," *Acta Musicologica*, vol. LXIV (1992), 91-117, and Joel Lester, *Compositional Theory in the Eighteenth Century* (Cambridge and London: Harvard University Press, 1992), 72-82.

[37]*Traité complet*, 46.

The modifications of alteration, prolongation, and substitution are often combined, and may be simple, double, or triple.[38] Simple alteration involves ascending or descending movements of one degree. Ascending alteration results in a natural dissonant chord of another key (secondary dominant), and descending alteration in the shift from the major to minor mode (modal mixture). Fétis likens the effect of the ascending alteration to that of the leading tone, and of the descending alteration to that of the descending fourth degree of natural dissonant harmony. In the following example the ascending alteration F-sharp in the bass of the supertonic 6/5 chord forms a first inversion dominant seventh chord in G major (No. 1), and the descending alteration A-flat in the tenor creates a change of mode (No. 2). Fétis argues that these are not true alterations because each can be understood in a diatonic context (in a new key or in a different mode).

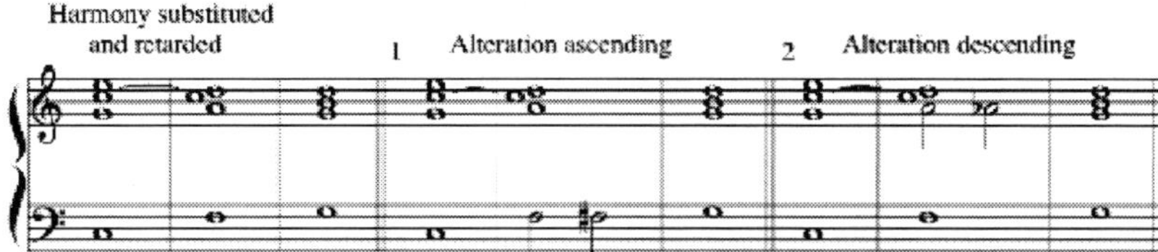

In the minor mode the descending alteration is a true alteration because it does not result in just a change of key or mode. It must resolve on the natural chord before the bass moves, and may include the substitution. In the following example, with a triple modification of alteration, substitution, and prolongation, the B-flat descending alteration of the second degree moves to the B-natural in the V 4/2 chord before the movement of the bass leads to the A minor sixth chord. The origin of the chord is the II 6/5, itself a modification of the V 4/2 chord to which it resolves. This configuration, with lowered scale-degree 2, is as close to Fétis gets to describing the Neapolitan sixth chord.

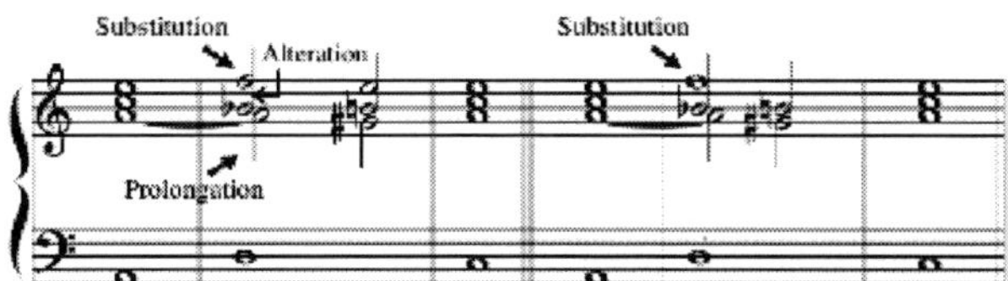

In Fétis' system, what today are called the Italian, French, and German augmented sixth chords constitute true alterations. The Italian sixth derives from the IV^6—V progression in the minor mode with raised scale-degree 4. The French sixth finds its origin in the leading-tone sixth chord (V 4/3), with lowered fifth, leading to the tonic chord. Fétis treats the German sixth as a doubly augmented fourth chord, which he gets from the II 4/3 chord with triple alteration. In each case the altered harmony

[38]Fétis' discussion of these chords is found in Book Two, chapter VIII.

arises out of voice-leading activity, and stands for the function of the diatonic harmony that it displaces. The following example shows Fétis' derivation of the augmented sixth chords.

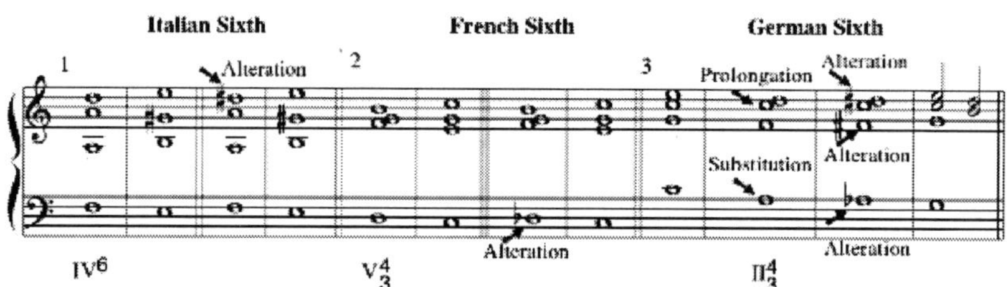

Fétis thus establishes a paradigm of pitch hierarchy where chord successions must follow the rules of succession from which they originate, and may be modified by substitution, retardation, and alteration of pitches. He is now able to prescribe a method for harmonizing a melody. First, the melody is stripped of ornaments and modifications. Modulations must be identified, which in Fétis' time include what today are called tonicizations. Perfect chords on the tonic, subdominant, dominant, and dominant seventh chords in keys to which the melody modulates are found, and inversions, modifications to natural harmony, and decoration of the bass and inner parts may then take place. This procedure resembles those in modern harmony textbooks where basic chord progressions are found before inversions, substitutions and voice-leading modifications are added.[39]

Having defined the fundamentals of diatonic and chromatic harmony Fétis turns to the subject of tonality and modulation in Book Three where he lays out his theory of the four orders of tonality. The first order, which he calls unitonic, refers chiefly to modal music, and consists of consonant sonorities prolonged by the "artificial" dissonance of the retardation, which "was only a means to vary the form, without consequences for the feeling of repose, inherent in the structure of the tonality."[40] This diatonic tonality was for Fétis the ideal manifestation of the peaceful serenity of Christian sentiment. It is distinguished from modern tonality by the appearance of perfect chords on each scale degree resulting in what is for Fétis a perspectiveless succession of chords. It should not be imagined, however, that Fétis' conception of the unitonic order represents a criticism of this style of music. In fact, nowhere is Fétis more eloquent than in his praise of sixteenth-century vocal polyphony. He does not limit unitonic harmony to plainchant but applies it to common practice harmony with examples from Mozart and Rossini consisting of tonal adjacencies that create the free succession of two perfect chords.

---

[39]See, for example, Allen Forte, *Tonal Harmony in Concept and Practice* (Holt, Reinhart and Winston, 1978), 231.

[40]*Traité complet,* lxx.

One of the most controversial claims of Fétis is his insistence that a second order of tonality that he calls transitonic is established by the emergence the dominant seventh chord. Formed by the clash of boundaries between the two tetrachords of the scale and combined with the appellative consonance, it engenders a sense of the special character of each scale degree that is an essential distinction between the unitonic and transitonic orders. Fétis attributes the advent of the transitonic order to Monteverdi who "found the means of transition from one scale to another," which creates a heightened sense of drama that is "inseparable from the attraction of tones."[41] It is principally the unique quality of the leading tone, however, which ushers in the modern era:

> If we examine what actually distinguishes the tonality of our modern music from that of plainchant, we will see that the attraction of the fourth degree and the leading tone, this interval, which, added to the dominant, is the principal constituent of the dominant seventh that determines the character of the *leading-tone* (*note sensible*), and this note alone makes all the difference between our tonality and that of plainchant. Now, the leading tone is precisely what I call the *expressive accent*, because on its account or by the attractive note of the fourth degree the impassioned character of all music is manifested.[42]

The modern translation of *note sensible* as leading tone does not appear to do justice to its expressive power as described by Fétis. Its literal translation is "sensitive note," which implies receptivity, and, more generally, that which can be perceived by sense. Rameau quotes Gioseffo Zarlino (1517-90) on its significance: "The semitone is the salt (if I may thus express myself), the ornament, and the cause of beautiful harmony and good modulation."[43] Referring to the *note sensible*, Rameau adds: "This name is thus eminently suitable for the sound which leads us to that sound which is the center of all modulation."[44] Fétis' view of the distinctive role of the *note sensible* in the formation of modern tonality thus emerges from a well-established music-theoretic tradition.

Fétis considers that the transitonic order lasted up to the third quarter of the eighteenth century, as composers were more concerned with "the distribution of ideas and their periodic return than in the search for new tonal attractions."[45] Once the resources of transitonic tonality were exhausted natural dissonant harmony acquired a multidimensional aspect,

---

[41]Ibid., lxxv.

[42]See Fétis' article, "Of the fundamental distinction between the various eras of modern music," *RgmP*, No. 56 (1840), 482.

[43]Jean-Philippe Rameau, *Traité de l'harmonie réduite à ses principes naturels* (Paris, 1722), translated as the *Treatise on Harmony* by Philip Gossett (New York, 1971), 64. The passage is from Zarlino's *Institutioni*, Part III, Ch. 10, 182.

[44]Ibid., 65.

[45]*Traité complet*, 174.

for just as "the attraction of two notes of the same scale was able to place in relation two different keys, the attraction of notes which belonged to diverse scales would establish multiple relationships between keys."[46] This he calls the pluritonic order—the multiplicity of tonal tendencies of certain notes created by modification of the dominant seventh by substitution in the minor mode (diminished seventh), the enharmonic dominant seventh/augmented sixth exchange, and the respelling of an isolated note. Pluritonic enharmony produces "the effect of surprise through unexpected successions of chords," which creates in the mind "the satisfaction of grasping and analyzing instantaneously the principle of transformation of the relations between keys."[47] Fétis calls this a new kind of "expressive accent" in which the musical sense seeks to rationalize the paradox of the simultaneous allusion to different keys.

The harmonic ambiguity of the pluritonic order blends into the final order of tonality that Fétis calls omnitonic. The distinction between the pluritonic and omnitonic orders is that in the former "one of the tones of a chord is alternately considered as the point of contact between diverse keys," whereas in the latter, modulation is the "result of multiple alterations of the intervals of chords."[48] The omnitonic order involves the enharmonic respelling of the melodic modifications of substitution, prolongation and alteration, their combination allowing the possibility of "resolving at will into one key or another."[49] This order arises "from the universality of the tonal relations of melody, through the joining of the simple transition to simple enharmony and to the transcendent enharmony of the alterations of the intervals of chords."[50] Although Fétis thinks that "the mind grasps perfectly the connections between the altered tones, and the sensibility, far from being offended, receives from it distinct pleasure,"[51] he cautions: "the frequent use of multiple attractions of tonalities has the serious drawback of incessantly exciting nervous emotions, and removing from music the simple character and purity of idea, in order to transform it into a sensual art."[52] Fétis predicted that the overuse of implied modulations would saturate the expectations of the listener and eventually lead to the decline of tonality, as he understood it.

---

[46]Ibid., lxxvi.

[47]Ibid., lxxvii.

[48]Ibid., 181.

[49]Ibid., 185.

[50]Ibid., 180.

[51]Ibid., 194.

[52]Ibid, 194. Anton Reicha (1770-1836) gives a similar opinion: "Modulations are not the goal of music .... bad composers believe that heterogeneous modulations may make up for what is lacking in ideas." *Treatise on Melody* (1814), translated by Peter M. Landey (Hillsdale, N.Y: Pendragon, 2000), 49.

In Book Four Fétis presents a thematically organized history of music theory. Although a reworking of his *Esquisse*, it flows naturally from the rest of the *Traité complet*, tracing the development of ideas that influenced his thought while also criticizing what he thinks are the faults of various systems. Starting with Rameau, Fétis claims that his superposition and subposition of thirds led him to consider chords in isolation, at least with respect to the "natural laws of tonality" understood as the placing of particular chords on specific scale degrees. Fétis claims that aurally-based rules of succession were replaced by an "order of generation," appealing because of its consistency. He refers here to the regularity of fifth movement in the fundamental bass, which left "all the harmonic groups isolated and unconnected," for the function of secondary chords organized hierarchically around the tonic/dominant axis was thereby destroyed.[53] Marpurg, he notes, falls into the same error, confusing natural dissonant chords with those resulting from prolongation and substitution.

The important discovery that the dissonant minor seventh may exist by itself, without preparation, Fétis attributes to Georg Andreas Sorge (1703-78) who derives this chord through "the notes of the trumpet and the geometric progression." Fétis does not here object to this procedure even though he elsewhere declares canonist methodology arbitrary and invalid. (Recall that Fétis derives the unprepared dominant seventh from the tetrachordal clash of boundaries between the fourth and fifth scale degrees.) Although he thinks that Sorge was the first to view "consonant harmony and the dominant seventh as forming the class of natural chords," he considers that Sorge "was mistaken in placing in the same category the minor seventh chord on the second degree."[54]

Fétis dismisses Abbé Georg Joseph Vogler (1749-1814) and Daniel Jelensperger (1787-1831) for allowing perfect chords on all scale degrees, but commends Christoph Gottlieb Schröter (1699-1782) for recognizing that all chords are the product of the perfect chord through inversion, substitution of the seventh for the octave in V^7, and for taking II^7 as a prolongation. Schröter further understood "the elements of the alterations of intervals of natural chords and the new characteristics that these alterations give to them."[55]

Fétis also applauds Johann Philipp Kirnberger (1721-83) for weighing the relative stability of chords according to the scale-degrees on which they occur, seen in his classification of the level of dissonance in seventh chords according to their distance from the tonic. Fétis accepts his resolution of the prolongation into a sixth chord on the second degree, but questions the case where he adds the fifth of the chord, resulting in a root

[53]Ibid., 201.

[54]Ibid., 244.

[55]Ibid., 245.

position supertonic seventh that in Fétis' view runs contrary to the principle of tonality.

Fétis credits Rameau, Catel and Abbé Roussier (c. 1716-1792) with the discovery of substitution, although they were not, he thinks, aware of its melodic motivation. Rameau "grasped the fact of the substitution only in the inversions of the seventh chord in the minor mode [and] called modifications of this kind borrowed chords."[56] Catel points out the correlation between the dominant ninth and the leading-tone seventh, and the similarity between diminished and dominant seventh chords. Abbé Roussier observes, "The substitution, or borrowed chord, consists of employing, in the minor modes only, the diminished seventh chord on the leading tone, in place of that of the dominant," which he illustrates with the following example:[57]

Basse fondamental

It is the relatively unknown Jean-François Boëly (1739-1814), however, whom Fétis thinks comes closest to the discovery of true substitution. He noticed that the diminished seventh was a "*chord by substitution or borrowing*, to be used at will in place of the leading-tone chord of the minor mode that it always represents, whichever form it takes in its inversions."[58] Fétis takes the idea of substitution and bends it to fit his theory of tonality according to scale-step harmonic norms. Treating the substituted sixth degree as a "melodic accent," he uses it to show how chords of substitution belong to the class of artificial modified chords. Moreover, substitution combined with prolongation gives rise to the supertonic seventh chord, which in turn may be subjected to alteration in the creation of various chromatic chords.

In contrast to those theoretical systems that Fétis recognizes as having influenced his thought stand the empirical approaches of Weber and Reicha. Fétis views this new empiricism as no better than the aprioristic speculations of canonist methods. Weber's disdain for the slightest theoretical generality results in an "overly-minute analysis of particular cases," and while his approach may offer useful insights, its explanatory power is compromised, for only in the context of a general theory can the distinctive features of individual cases be fully appreciated. Fétis reserves the greatest contempt for Anton Reicha, proclaiming his system the "most

[56]Ibid., 49.

[57]Abbé Roussier, *Traité des accords* (Paris, 1775), 46.

[58]*Traité complet,* 49.

deplorable return toward the crude empiricism of the old methods of the early eighteenth century."[59] Frustrated by the influence that his theories exerted during the first half of the nineteenth century Fétis takes him to task on his thirteen fundamental chords, arguing that their arbitrary determination and lack of coherent relationship results in a "multitude of particular facts."

Fétis concludes the *Traité complet* with a summary of his theory of harmony. Tonality emanates from the relative degree of repose and activity of the notes in the scale from which all melodic and harmonic configurations are derived. The natural fundamental chords are the tonic, dominant seventh (in which is contained the appellative consonance), and their inversions. All other chords result from prolongation, substitution, alteration, and their various combinations. The substitution is a melodic accent of scale-degree 6 for scale-degree 5. It generates the leading-tone and diminished seventh chords as well as other chromatic chords. Prolongation and substitution do not change the goal of the natural chords they modify, whereas alterations inflect the harmony toward different keys. Alterations, combined with substitution and prolongation produce "multiple affinities," allowing a note to resolve in any key, which eventually leads to the dissolution of tonality. Anomalies to the system are found in sequential progressions where symmetrical patterning suspends tonal expectations until the sequence comes to an end. Scale-step harmonic norms, and with them, the tendency toward repose and activity of each chord, unite the melodic and harmonic domains.

In his outline of the history of harmony Fétis weaves a golden thread from the theories of Rameau, Sorge, Schröter, Kirnberger, and Catel to his own, leaving the reader with the impression that he has fully taken into account the influences of his predecessors on his thought. Yet he fails to mention aspects of his theory that were anticipated in the works of former theorists, some of whose efforts he is in other respects highly critical.

Contrary to popular belief, the concept of *tonalité* did not originate with Fétis. Brian Hyer notes that Alexandre Choron (1771-1834) may have been the first to coin the term in his *Sommaire de l'histoire de la musique* of 1810,[60] although Catel uses it as early as 1802 in his treatment of enharmonic modulation, albeit only in the narrow sense of a change of key.[61] Although Fétis commends Catel for recognizing the difference between chords arising form natural and artificial harmony, he is curiously silent on Catel's use of the *règle* and his normative harmonization of the chromatic scale similar to Vogler's "omnibus" sequence, neither of which

[59]Ibid., 241.

[60]See Brian Hyer, "Tonality," *The Cambridge History of Western Music Theory*, ed. Thomas Christensen (Cambridge: Cambridge University Press, 2002), 730.

[61]Catel, 100, 102.

he acknowledges.[62] Nor does he draw attention to the definition of tonality offered by Castil-Blaze (1784-1857) who observes that, "the octave, fifth, and fourth notes of the mode are tonal intervals, but they cease to have this property the moment they are used on the second, third, and sixth notes of the mode," for this would give "an implicit idea of a new mode."[63] Castil-Blaze further asserts that perfect chords, when inverted, assume a melodic character rather than a purely harmonic function, thus anticipating Fétis' opinion of these chords as a type of modification.

Concerning the critical concept of the appellative consonance, Hyer notes that it was already identified by Choron, and Christensen finds what is perhaps the earliest reference to the idea of appellation in the work of Anton Bemetzrieder (1739-1808), who speaks of the propensity for dissonance to return to a consonant state by a process he calls the *loi des appels*.[64] Also predating aspects of Fétis' ideas about tonality, Choron distinguishes between *tonalité ancienne* and *moderne,* attributes the discovery of the dominant seventh to Monteverdi, and insists that the division of the sonorous body has no relevance for actual music.[65]

Fétis is also reluctant to recognize the work of theorists who consider ambiguities that result from possible reinterpretations of chords. Vogler, in his *Handbuch zur Harmonielehre* (1802) examines multiple function chords (*Mehrdeutigkeit*), including diatonic and enharmonic pivot chords.[66] Reicha, in his unpublished *Praktishe Beispiele* (1803) notes that complex modulations create "unexpected" (*unerwartet*) events that "hold the attention of the listener."[67] Catel, speaking with reference to listener expectations, gives copious examples of modulation using the diminished seventh chord and dominant seventh/augmented sixth exchange.[68] Weber explores continuity in terms of *Mehrdeutigkeit*, famously exemplified in

---

[62]Abbé Vogler, *Kurhpfälzische Tonschule* (Mannheim, 1778). For further discussion of the omnibus, see Robert Wason, *Viennese Harmonic Theory from Albrechtsberger to Schenker and Schoenberg* (Ann Arbor, 1985), 16-19.

[63]See the entry under *Tonalité* in his *Dictionnaire de musique moderne* (Paris, 1821/25), 529-30.

[64]See Thomas Christensen, "Bemetzrieder's Dream: Diderot and the Pathology of Tonal Sensibility in the *Leçons de clavecin*," in *Music, Sensation, and Sensibility*, ed. Linda Phyllis Austern (New York and London: Routledge, 2002), 39-56.

[65]Concerning Fétis' debt to Choron, see Bryan Simms, "Choron, Fétis, and the Theory of Tonality," *Journal of Music Theory*, 19/1: (Spring, 1975), 112-138.

[66]For discussion of Vogler's concept of multiple function chords see Floyd K. Grave and Margaret G. Grave, *In Praise of Harmony: The Teachings of Abbé Georg Joseph Vogler* (Lincoln and London, University of Nebraska Press, 1987).

[67]*Praktische Beispiele, ein Beitrag zur Geistkulture des Tonsetzers ... mit Philosphisch-praktischen Anmerkungen zu den praktishen Beispielen* (Vienna, 1803), 12. (Paris: Bibliothèque nationale, Mss. 2496, 2510.)

[68]Catel, 38-39; 97-102.

his analysis of the slow movement of Mozart's Quartet K. 465, and challenged by Fétis as the result of a spurious empirical methodology.[69] Interestingly, one of Fétis' most perceptive musical analyses is of a section from the slow movement of Beethoven's Fifth Symphony where he adopts an analytical stance strikingly similar to Weber's Mozart analysis![70]

An important strand of music theory that does not figure in Fétis' system is the emerging concept of the musical idea, seen chiefly in the works of Reicha and Choron. Reicha presents an early description of motivic procedures in the *Traité de mélodie,* where he says, "It is not always necessary to state the entire motif (theme) in the course of a piece in order for it to be appreciated, but to recall here or there a member or a figure, which may be repeated many times in succession, and developed with different notes."[71] In the *Traité de haute composition musicale* he speaks of *idées mères* and *idées accessoires,* and declares: "To develop one's ideas .... is to combine them in several interesting ways; it is in a word to produce new and interesting effects from previously heard ideas."[72] Reicha identifies seven categories of musical idea: key ideas (*idées mères*), accessory ideas, phrases, periods, ideas that are only melodically interesting, ideas that are only harmonically interesting, and those which combine both harmony and melody.[73] He then shows how a composer might invent variations on a musical idea, collecting them in a table before organizing the material into a suitable form.[74] In a similar vein, Choron declares: "In music, and in the arts in general, one calls idea that which in a more exact language one calls thought. Whatever it may

---

[69]Under the entry on Weber in the *Biographie universelle,* Fétis notes that his analysis of Mozart's String Quartet K. 465 caused such controversy at the Paris Conservatory that a special meeting was convened that included Luigi Cherubini (1760-1842), Ferdinando Paer (1771-1839), François-Adrien Boieldieu (1775-1834), Jean-François Lesueur (1760-1837), Reicha, Henri-Montan Berton (1767-1844), and Fétis. Lesueur, Fétis reports, was silent. Boieldieu, Paer, and Berton condemned the passage. Reicha, however, dared to defend it, causing Cherubini to declare: "*You do not know what you say: Fétis is right. His rule comes from the correct school: it condemns this passage*." Fétis chides that the author of the polemic, writing under the pseudonym of M. C. E. Leduc, is ignorant of even the simplest notions of harmony and counterpoint. He refuses to enter into further debate with him, and closes with the remark that Weber's analysis is inconclusive. *FétisB,* 8:522. See Fétis' article "Sur un passage singulier d'un quatuor de Mozart," *Rm* (1829), 601-606. For a discussion and reproduction of Weber's analysis, see *Music Analysis in the Nineteenth Century*, Volume I, ed. Ian Bent (Cambridge: Cambridge University Press, 1993). For a history of the polemic surrounding the analysis, see Julie Anne Vertress, "Mozart's String Quartet K. 465: the History of a Controversy," *Current Musicology*, 17 (1974), 96-114.

[70]*Traité complet*, 127.

[71]Landey, 72.

[72]*Traité de haute composition musicale* (Paris, 1824-26), 240.

[73]Ibid., 234-35.

[74]Ibid., 263.

be, the thought or musical idea arises in the mind of the composer, with all the accessory ideas that it requires."[75] These early notions of motivic-thematic procedures, however, are ill-suited to a system that treats melody as inextricably embedded in tonal processes. In Fétis' opinion, melody is subsumed by the relative weighting of chords, derived from the tendencies of scale-degree harmonic norms projected through the rule of the octave, creating a "depth of field" that is the essence of his concept of tonality.[76] Whereas Reicha recognizes that a narrative musical subject may exist apart from the constraints of consonance and dissonance, in Fétis' estimation it is the legitimization of non-harmonic dissonance that produces the centrifugal force that propels harmony into the omnitonic order that eventually heralds the demise of tonality.[77] Fétis' reluctance to consider the thought content of music as a developing melodic idea is further illustrated in his criticism of Reicha, after he heard him "seriously question" Cherubini on the value of simple counterpoint. Fétis quips: "He [Reicha] had arrived at the end of his career without understanding that simple counterpoint contains the entire art of writing, and there is no other useful means of learning this art."[78] This remark reflects the viewpoint that rules of counterpoint are harmonically derived, and is consistent with a non-motivic view of musical process. Moreover, Fétis did not seem to notice that some of his contemporaries were developing a theory that could account for interactions of melody, harmony, and phrase rhythm, as evidenced by Reicha's observation regarding the perception of melodic and harmonic closure in relation to the formal disposition of thematic material,[79] and by Momigny's (1762-1842) concept of *le phrasé*—the subordination of phrases according to the relative strengths of cadential points of articulation, creating spans of varying degrees of tension.[80]

---

[75]*Principes de composition des écoles d'Italie* (Paris, 1808-09), Book Six, 9.

[76]Hyer, 732, notes that Donald Francis Tovey (1875-1940) observed the similarity between the idea of perspective and tonality, and likened the tonic to the vanishing point.

[77]Despite the position that Fétis takes on the unity of melody and harmony in the *Traité complet*, he is fully cognizant of the nature of thematic development. Paraphrasing Karl Heinrich Ludwig Pölitz (1772-1838), Fétis reports that he argues that once a theme has been heard, the mind uses it "as the rule by which it judges . . . there being an identity between a theme and its development." See "L'état actuel de l'esthétique musicale" *RgmP* (1838), translated in *Music and Aesthetics in the Eighteenth and Early Nineteenth Centuries*, ed. Peter le Huray and James Day (Cambridge: Cambridge University Press, 1981), 506.

[78]*RgmP* (1840, No. 2). For further discussion of this remark, see page 28.

[79]Landey, 15.

[80]Jérôme-Joseph de Momigny, *Cours complet d'harmonie et de composition* (Paris, 1803-6), 424. In the language of our time, Dahlhaus points out: "the inner coherence that takes place between the sections of a movement can consist in the developing variation of melodic elements or motives, but it can also take the form of the recurrence and transformation of harmonic and rhythmic attributes, which, in accordance with the

While Fétis' explanation of tonality may appear to be only a synthesis of various theoretical systems, he organizes its elements into a coherent theory fortified within a historical, philosophical and cultural context that takes into account psychological and sociological determinants.[81] This leads to an appreciation of the music of the past on its own terms rather than in the context of, or as a means to, some future end. Fétis proclaims it erroneous to think that music exists only

> in an incessant state of progress ... which inevitably results in rejecting as outdated all that is not of the present time, of shaking the artist's faith in the legitimacy of his art, presenting the emotions of bygone generations as puerile illusions, and finally, offering the history of the monuments of music as but the pitiful remnants of an already forgotten world.[82]

Although Fétis believes that tonality is the product of experience, he does not mean to imply that music theory is subjective. Rather, he wishes to determine the precise nature of judgment in the perception of musical structure.[83] On this point he seeks guidance from Kantian philosophy, which acknowledges "the action of the external world upon our senses," but "also recognizes that the assessment of this acquired knowledge depends on the working of an inner sense. It thus reconciles and brings together the advantages of the empirical and the *a priori* systems."[84] While Fétis faults Kant's primitive views on music, the influence of Kantian philosophy is clearly reflected in his comment on the way we listen to music:

> How beautiful that is, we say: how great, how sublime! In so doing we judge; we express the results of the workings of our reasoning powers.

---

premise that an affect or character forms the 'real' theme, are every bit as thematic as a melodic figure, but in a different way." Carl Dahlhaus (1928-89), *Ludwig van Beethoven, Approaches to his Music*, trans. Mary Whittall (Oxford: Clarendon Press, 1991), 121.

[81]For an overview of Fétis' aesthetics, see Robert S. Nichols, "Fétis' Theories of *Tonalité* and the Aesthetics of Music," *Revue belge de Musicologie/ Belgisch Tijdschrift voor Muziekwetenschap*, vol. 26 (1972-73).

[82]*FétisB*, 4: 111.

[83]Fétis was not the only theorist of the first half of the nineteenth century to attempt to ground his thought in philosophy. In his unpublished treatise *Sur la musique comme art purement sentimental*, Reicha examines in some detail the relationship between mind and feeling in musical cognition: "The intellect can only compare ideas and draw the consequences of this comparison . . . On the other hand, feeling is more passive; it approves or rejects without comparison. Its entire criticism is limited to saying, this pleases me, this displeases me, without being concerned for why it is pleasing."* Reicha thus distinguishes between abstract intellectual activity and the empirical sensation of feeling.

**Sur la musique comme art purement sentimental, avec remarques philosophiques et critiques sur les operations morales de notre être* (1814), 74. (Paris: Bibliothèque nationale, Res. F. 1646.)

[84]"L'état actuel de l'esthétique musicale," le Huray and Day, 503.

> Something then has revealed to us abstract and general ideas of beauty, grandeur, and sublimity, created by successions of sounds.[85]

This reasoning power Fétis calls *le sens musicale*, although he was not the first to coin the expression.[86] He further grounds musical cognition in the process of judgment itself, the structural correlative of which he reveals at the beginning of the *Résumé philosophique*: "Music never makes a more profound impression than when it resembles absolutely nothing that has been heard, when it creates at the same time both the principal idea and the accessory means to develop it."[87] This is not to say that musical intellection should be fished out of abstraction. Fétis' metaphysics unites the apperception of musical process and the predispositions of the perceiver, by which necessary truths about our subjective experience of music may be ascertained.[88]

Fétis' appropriation of Kantian ideas is further seen at the conclusion of his analysis of the modifications of natural harmony, where he remarks: "Such is the synthetic and analytic theory of dissonant chords through prolongation."[89] This is an allusion to Kant's distinction between synthetic judgments that are founded on experience *a posteriori*, and analytic judgments that do not depend on experience for their confirmation, but "indicate another peculiar source of knowledge, namely, a faculty of cognition *a priori*."[90] Just as Kant reconciles pure *a priori* knowledge with that based on experience *a posteriori*, Fétis mediates between theoretical

---

[85]Ibid., 504.

[86]As Fétis himself points out, Christian Friedrich Michaelis (1770-1834) "established the fact that there must be a musical sense; without it, indeed, the ear would only perceive a succession of meaningless sounds" (le Huray and Day, 505). In concrete musical terms, Catel also recognizes the idea of a musical sense whereby the listener is able to make implicit judgments while perceiving complex modulations (Catel, 38-39).

[87]The *Résumé philosophique de l'histoire de la musique* is found in the first edition of the *Biographie universelle* (1835), 1: xxxvii-ccliv. Fétis' writings on the philosophy of music appear in the *Revue et gazette musicale* over a twenty-year period, from 1838-1858, and include: "Sur l'harmonie," III (1836), 299-305; "Etat actuel de l'esthétique musicale," V (1838), No. 1, 4-7; No. 5, 44-47; No. 14, 149-52: "Des Tendences de l'art musicale à l'époque actuelle, et de l'avenir," VI (1839), No. 17, 129-32; "De la Philosophie de la musique," VII (1840), 2-5, 13-15; "Mon testament musicale," XX (1853), 281-84, 297-300, 313-16, 321-24, 347-50; and "La Nature et la musique," XXV (1858), 277-78.

[88]On the influence of nineteenth-century idealist philosophy on Fétis' theory, see Rosalie Schellhous, "Fétis' Tonality as a Metaphysical Principle: Hypothesis for a New Science," *Music Theory Spectrum* 13 (1991), 219-40. See also Thomas Christensen, "Fétis and emerging tonal consciousness," in *Music Theory in the Age of Romanticism*, ed. Ian Bent (Cambridge: Cambridge University Press, 1996), 37-56.

[89]*Traité complet*, 72.

[90]Immanuel Kant, *Critique of Pure Reason* (1787), trans. J. M. D. Meiklejohn (New York, Continuum, 1986), 23.

tenets that are aprioristically determined and those that arise empirically. Fétis actualizes this reconciliation with the following declaration:

> Now, if modern tonality is complete with the perfect chord, the dominant seventh and their derivatives, all the other harmonies are just their modifications; all that remains is to discover what kinds of modifications these are. To use the language of philosophy, I would say that the initial chords are the general and the essential in music, and that the others are only the contingent.[91]

Fétis drives the point home when he insists that perfect chords with added sevenths and ninths cannot be placed on each scale degree because "most of these chords do not exist *a priori*."[92] By basing the tonic/dominant seventh axis in abstraction, and relegating all other chords to the level of the sensuous particular, Fétis appears to resolve the dichotomy between *a priori* and *a posteriori* musical judgment within his concept of the structure of tonality itself. It should be noted, however, that the form of *a priori* knowledge that Fétis invokes resembles what Kant calls "synthetic knowledge *a priori*," where "impure" elements of the sensuous particular are assimilated into general, abstract concepts.[93]

Fétis thinks that it is precisely the complex interrelationships between "essential" (natural) and "contingent" (modifying) musical elements that result in music's expressivity. The increasing use of chromaticism throughout the ages challenges the musical sense to ever more complex responses, and the twists and turns of musical perception are bound to expressive imperatives that are an inescapable fact of his thought:

> Having arrived at this point of transfusion of scales, art realizes in its most complete sense unity within variety and variety within unity. It is quite free to remain within the absolute unity of tonality, if the aesthetic feeling of the music must be calm, sweet or religious. If it requires transition, it can be

---

[91]*Traité complet,* 256.

[92]Ibid., 265.

[93]Kant asserts: "Knowledge *a priori* is either pure or impure. Pure knowledge *a priori* is that in which no empirical element is mixed up." Impure knowledge *a priori*, he says, is not derived "immediately from experience, but from a general rule, which, however, we have borrowed from experience." This process Kant calls "synthetic knowledge *a priori*," a similar notion to Fétis' "metaphysical" theory where abstract rules are initially derived from experience. Kant's notion of pure knowledge *a priori* is more closely approximated by the idea of a *sens musicale,* which situates musical understanding in the process of judgment, for on this view it is the pre-existing structure of the mind that conditions how and what it perceives. (See Kant, 22). On a purely objective level, Fétis appears to accept uncritically the notion of a tonic/dominant seventh *a priori* axis from which all other chords are derived, although he rejects the idea that it is grounded in *a priori* canonist principles. Perhaps the most direct correspondence between Kant's postulate of pure knowledge *a priori* and a music-theoretic concept can be seen in Reicha's comprehensive theory of phrase rhythm which considers periodicity as an abstraction, where *a priori* notions of space and time form intangible yet essential material that exists independently of sensuous melodic content. (See the *Traité de mélodie*).

> found in natural dissonant harmony, free from any alteration. But if the simple modulation does not suffice, and a more powerful shock is required, through the effect of an unexpected change in tonality, pluritonic enharmony provides the means. Finally, if ardent passions must be aroused, or the expression of feelings of profound melancholy is desired, the omnitonic order opens up infinite resources.[94]

If Fétis has been criticized for his conservative posture with respect to harmonic procedures and the music of his time, his insight that the orders of tonality had entered a new phase of dramatic coexistence has gone unnoticed. And while his view of the expressive import of these tonal categories may seem prescriptive, their transfigurations are a fundamental component of the musical language of composers of the modern era.

From an epistemological perspective, Fétis' notion of the orders of tonality mediates between the particular and the general, taking as a premise the empirical origins of the orders of tonality before resolving them into a set of dematerialized abstractions that demonstrates their processes of transformation.[95] Expressive and cognitive factors are united in a metaphysical network that is as relevant for the creative act of composition as it is for the musical sense that judges it. While Fétis' ideas are not free from bias, his capacity for historical synthesis challenges contemporary theorists to consider the orthodoxies of the present, be it through the resolution of complex mathematical modeling and musical perception, the reconciliation of conflicting theoretical systems, or the appraisal of sociological approaches as a precondition for musical understanding. Fétis' contribution to music theory is fittingly eulogized in the words of his Spanish translator, Francis Gil de Assis, whose remarks are as relevant today as they were in the middle of the nineteenth century:

> The philosophical spirit that reigns, as much in this work as in the majority of this illustrious author, combined with his great erudition, vast interests, and wide and deep study of musical phenomena, result in both a rational and sensitive exposition of the fundamental principles of the science and the history of the development of art.[96]

---

[94]*Traité complet,* lxxviii.

[95]Fétis applied the idea of the orders of tonality to rhythm, establishing the unirhythmic, transirhythmic, plurirhythmic and omnirhythmic orders. The analogy, however, is misleading, for he does not consider harmony and rhythm interparametrically, which results in an unfortunate compartmentalization of the two domains. His opinion, for example, that the music of his time was still in the unirhythmic stage is immaterial, for it ignored the fact that so-called unitonic music already demonstrated a wealth of rhythmic complexity! For an exposition of Fétis' theory of rhythm, see Mary Arlin, "Metric Mutation and Modulation: The Nineteenth-Century Speculations of F. J. Fétis," *Journal of Music Theory* 44/2 (2000): 261-322.

[96]Francis Gil de Asis, 3.

AKNOWLEDGEMENTS

During the preparation of this book I have benefited from discussions about theory and translation with many colleagues and students whose insights have been stimulating and helpful. I am grateful to Jeanette Amprimoz for her careful proofreading of the translation, and to Professor Thomas Christensen for his reading of the entire text and for numerous helpful suggestions. I would also like to acknowledge the kind help of library staff at the Sibley Library, Eastman School of Music; the Music Library, SUNY, Buffalo; the British Library; the Fonds Fétis, Bibliothèque royale Albert Ier, Brussels; the Bibliothèque nationale, Paris; the Bodleian Library, Oxford; and Senate House Library, University of London. Finally, to my wife Anne, and children Benjamin and Danielle, I give my appreciation for their endless support and inspiration during the long and winding preparation of this text.

FOREWORD

After the multitude of systems set forth concerning the formation of a science of harmony, after the publication of a great number of books on this science, what is the significance of this one, and from what principle is it the development? These are the questions that shall be asked, no doubt, by those who will delve into a reading of this work. I shall try to respond to them briefly.

The first one, conceived by Rameau at the beginning of the eighteenth century, considered the possibility of coordinating isolated harmonic occurrences in a systematic science. He sought this principle in the coincidence of the numerical proportions of intervals of tones with the phenomenon of the production of harmonics from a principal tone, in the resonance of a low string stretched by a weight proportional to its dimensions. From these two series of facts, he deduced a theory of the formation of chords through quite ingenious mechanical procedures, but which had the inconvenience of neglecting the important consideration of the relations of these chords to each other in their succession. Nevertheless, if this celebrated man erred in the choice of principle which led him to arrive at results so contrary to the nature of art, he nonetheless merits our admiration for the idea, great in itself, of the possibility of a rational theory of harmony, and for the general law of the inversion of chords, the discovery of which is his due. Many theorists have reproduced his system, diversely modified, in different forms.

Others, taking as a base the harmonics of the horn and trumpet, represented by the arithmetical progression 1, 1/2, 1/3, 1/4, 1/5, etc., were led to consider the principle of music, and consequently of harmony, as residing, not in the major and minor scales, but in the chromatic scale. They persuaded themselves that the consonant and dissonant chords, such as there are, belong to all the degrees of this scale, and thus the special destination of the notes of the scale and the chords is completely destroyed, and consequently tonality as well.

A third principle was sought in the systematic division of the string, and from this an ascending progression of thirds has been derived, in which one finds all the consonant and dissonant chords which were called *natural*. The other chords were considered as having been formed from these through artificial procedures. In the theories derived from this system, new truths have come to arrive at a complete and rational doctrine of the science. But these truths taken from mechanical procedures, foreign to the art itself, have remained without a link, and have only been able to resolve some of the problems of the science.

Finally, other theorists, adopting an empirical system, have pushed aside the difficulties concerning the origin of chords which are frequently found together in harmonic combinations, and have considered them as facts of experience; isolated facts for which nothing reveals the use, or the connection in a given key. In this system, some have limited the chords to a small number, others have extended the nomenclature. All were directed in their classifications by the particular views of their minds, and not by considerations relative to the art.

The immense quantity of treatises and methods of harmony published during the last approximately one hundred and twenty years are derived from these four systems. The only thing that has not been thought of, is to examine whether the natural constitution of the art, in its relations to our organization, does not provide a more real basis than acoustical facts and calculations of proportions, of which we have no consciousness, or of mechanical procedures, which are only a game of the mind, or finally of isolated empirical facts, which are not connected to any general law. Now this research, about which no other theorist has been concerned, has occupied my attention for forty years.

Abandoning all ideas of a system, I asked myself if the secret laws which govern the relations of the successions of tones in our major and minor keys were not the same as those which determine relations of simultaneity in chords; in other words, if the principle of melody was not identical to that of harmony. Before long, I acquired the conviction of this identity. I saw that amongst the multitude of combinations which compose the harmony of our music, there are two which our musical instinct accepts as existing by themselves, independently of all previous circumstances and all preparation, namely: the consonant harmony called the *perfect chord*, which has the character of repose and conclusion, and dissonant harmony, designated under the name *chord of the dominant seventh*, which determines the tendency, the attraction and the movement. The necessary resolution of the attractive notes of the latter, and the position of these notes within the scale, provide the laws of succession of five degrees of the scale; the position of the two other degrees determines itself. In this manner the necessary connection of tones is found, which one generally designates under the name of *tonality*.

In possession of these givens, I have thus seen that all harmony resides in these alternating necessities: repose, tendency or attraction, and resolution of these tendencies in a new repose. I have also seen that the two chords of which I have just spoken provide all the necessary elements for the accomplishment of the requirements of these two laws of all music. I have concluded from this that all other harmonies are only modifications of these, and I have classed these modifications in the following order: (1)

inversion of natural consonant and dissonant chords; (2) substitution of one note for another in the dissonant chord and in its derivations through inversion; (3) the prolongation of a note of a chord into the following chord; (4) the alteration of the natural notes of chords by signs belonging to various keys; (5) the combinations of these modifications.

Wishing to assure myself that these considerations had led me to irrefutable truths, without exceptions, and that there does not exist in music, given a specific key, other necessary chords than those of which I have just spoken, I took all kinds of compositions, and successively removing from them all the modifications which the feeling or fantasy of the composer had introduced into the natural harmonies, I saw that the latter sufficed to preserve in their works their tonal, melodic, and harmonic significance. From this I have concluded with certainty that the two consonant and dissonant chords are the only ones necessary.

Twenty years ago since I published a summary of these ideas in a *Methode élémentaire et abrégée d'harmonie et d'accompagnement*, which has since had three editions in Paris, two Italian translations, one of which was printed in Naples, the second in Turin, and an English translation by the composer, Bishop. Constantly concerned with perfecting my theory, I have, since that time, read everything that has been written concerning the science of harmony, and pondered upon and generalized my principles more and more. In publishing today the fruit of such long and conscientious studies, I believe that there will be nothing left for me to do concerning this subject.

The first book of this work contains an analysis of the relations of tones and tonality. The second offers a complete theory of natural chords and all their modifications. The third has as its object modulation considered from an absolutely new point of view. One will find there a new order of modulating formulae that has not yet been introduced into the art. The fourth book contains a critical analysis of the principal harmonic systems that originated in the works of Rameau. In these four divisions, the entire science of harmony appears to me to be contained.

The series of lectures that I recently gave on my theory in Paris, in a course divided into four sessions, and the success that it obtained with my audience, seems to me to augur well for the reception of my book.

The Author

Paris, March 3rd, 1844.

FOREWORD

TO THE NINTH EDITION

In concluding the preface to the third edition of this work, I said, despite the good reception that it had from its first publication, that it still remained to stand the test of time in order to be established as a doctrine. Since I last reread this same book, nearly a quarter of a century has passed; eight editions of the work gone out of print; thousands of harmonists have been instructed in the theory established there, who themselves have become teachers and propagate it; finally, from all parts the most learned men in the science of harmony have congratulated me. Many, endowed with the spirit of philosophy, have understood that the doctrine set forth in my work is none other than the revelation of the secret of the art, the fundamental law without which the works of this art, produced over practically the last four centuries, would not exist. I have not invented anything: I have discovered everything in the monumental history of music. The certainty of this truth is gradually spreading.

This is not to say that the entire musical world has rallied around the doctrine of harmony based on tonality, and that there are not other doctrines admitted in teaching; it is not in the nature of human affairs to give way to such a unanimity of views and opinions. Never has any other science seen the production of such extravagant fantasies than that of harmony; recently I have seen new ones spring up that are no less absurd than the old ones; it is unlikely that there will be any fewer in the future.

In Germany, treatises on composition and harmony increase year by year; there is nothing new but their titles or rather the author's names, for the basis of them all is found in the old works of Vogler and Friedrich Schneider. There are always the same errors of chords of every nature placed on all degrees of the scale, without regard for their laws of succession.

In France, especially in Paris, every harmony professor who attaches importance to certain teaching procedures, which fundamentally do not stray from Catel's system; every harmony professor, I say, wishes to bring to light a treatise, a method that carries his name and makes it known to the public. From the point of view of the science, these works are nonexistent; but, in consequence, they are obstacles to the propagation of the sound doctrine of the science intimately connected to the art; obstacles which, nonetheless, are only momentary.

To explain in a few words the principles that have directed me in the conception of my theory of harmony, I will say that abandoning any idea of system, I asked myself if the secret laws that govern the relationships of the succession of the notes of our major and minor scales were not the same that determine the relationships of simultaneity in chords; in other words, if the principle of melody is not identical with that of harmony; and I soon became convinced of this identity. I saw that among the multitude of combinations that make up the harmony of our music, there are two that our musical instinct accepts as existing by themselves, independently of any preceding circumstance and any preparation, namely: the consonant harmony called the *perfect chord*, which has the character of repose and conclusion, and the dissonant harmony designated by the term *dominant seventh chord*, which determines tendency, attraction and movement. The necessary resolution of the attractive notes of the latter, and the position of these notes in the scale, provide the laws of succession for five degrees of this scale; the position of the other two degrees is self-evident. In this way the necessary connections of sounds are found, which one designates in general by the term *tonality*.

With these givens, I thus saw that all harmony resides in these necessary oppositions: repose, tendency or attraction, and resolution of these tendencies in a new repose. I also saw that these two above-mentioned chords provide all the necessary elements for the accomplishment of the exigencies of these two laws of all music. I concluded from this that all the other harmonies are only modifications of those, and I classed these modifications in the following order: (1) inversion of natural consonant and dissonant chords; (2) substitution of one note for another in the dissonant chord, and in its derivatives through inversion; (3) prolongation of a note of a chord into the following chord; (4) alteration of natural notes of chords by accidentals belonging to various keys; (5) combinations of these modifications.

Wishing to assure myself that these considerations had led me to irrefutable truths, without any exception, and that there does not exist in music, a key being given, other necessary chords than those just mentioned, I took compositions of all genres, and removing successively all the modifications that the sentiment or the imagination of the composer had introduced into the natural harmonies, I saw that these suffice to retain the tonal, melodic, and harmonic meaning in their works; from which I concluded with certainty that the two consonant and dissonant chords are the only ones necessary.

There is no philosopher of some worth, no scholar with the habit of generalizing, who has not wished to arrive at the definitive solution to problems that have long remained incomprehensible: I admit that I find myself in an analogous position, and that my conviction that I have placed the science of harmony upon its natural foundation is unshakable. During sixty years of study and research on all that has been published on this very subject, my ideas have not wavered with regard to the principle of this science, namely, the *law of tonality*. I paid as much attention as I am able to objections that have been raised against me, and I believe to have successfully refuted those that appeared to have any substance; the others did not seem to me worthy of attention. Today, therefore, I declare, without any interest in self-importance, and solely for love of the science and the art, that I believe to have set forth in this book the *definitive foundation of the theory of harmony*.

The Author

Brussels, 25 February 1867

PREFACE

TO THE THIRD EDITION

A harmonist by instinct, from the age of nine I have written sonatas, concertos, and masses, without having the first idea about the theory of the art. Admitted as a student at the Paris Conservatory in my sixteenth year, I attended the harmony course given by the venerable Rey,[1] and there I learned Rameau's fundamental bass system, the only one known to my long-standing master. Shortly afterward Catel published his *Traité d'harmonie*, the foundations of which had been debated amongst a group of professors at the Conservatory.[2] A battle began between the supporters of the old system and those of the new doctrine. Because of my serious nature I was interested in these questions of theory, despite my youth and inexperience. I devoted myself to the examination of the two rival systems, and through the comparison that I made thereof, I sought to determine the degree of certainty of their fundamental principle. Discouragement was the first result of my efforts; for if, on one hand, I discovered a more philosophical method in Rameau's writings, I observed there the natural phenomena of art forced to be in tune with the principle of a system; and on the other hand, if Catel presented to me an arrangement of facts more in keeping with the feeling of harmony and the

[1]Jean-Baptiste Rey (1734-1810) was appointed professor of harmony at the Paris Conservatory in 1795. A staunch follower of Rameau, Fétis reports that he was bitterly opposed to Catel's system, which, combined with the support that he expressed for Jean-François Lesueur (1763-1837) in his quarrels with the Conservatory, resulted in his dismissal in 1802. *FétisB*, 7:410. [PL]

[2]According to Fétis, Charles-Simon Catel's (1773-1830) *Traité d'harmonie* (1802) was the first harmony treatise to challenge the hegemony of Rameau's thought in France. Catel, Fétis reports, derives a major ninth chord from the first nine divisions of the monochord, from which he extracts the perfect major and minor chords, the minor fifth (diminished) chord, the dominant seventh chord, and the leading-tone seventh chord. He considers these chords to be "natural" and the remaining chords simply the product of "artificial modifications." Fétis grumbles that Catel needlessly adopted canonist methods, thus leaving his system open to speculative debate. He considers that, quite apart from the aprioristic disputes amongst the canonists, Catel's distinction between natural and artificial chords makes good musical sense because the ear accepts the former as independent entities, while the latter can only be conceived as the product of anterior events. *FétisB*, 3:75. [PL]

practical processes of art, this advantage was offset by the faults of a purely empirical method of which the illusory foundation rested on the arbitrary divisions of a *corde sonore*.

Years elapsed, and during this time, chance having successively placed in my hands the treatises on harmony by Roussier[3], Langlé[4], the Chevalier de Lirou[5], Marpurg[6], Kirnberger[7], and Sabbatini[8], I read them

---

[3]Pierre-Joseph Roussier (c. 1716-1792) is known primarily for his *Traité des accords et de leur succession, selon le système de la basse fondamentale, pour servir de principes d'harmonie à ceux qui étudient l'accompagnement du clavecin avec une méthode d'accompagnement* (Paris, 1764), and *Observations sur différent points de l'harmonie* (Geneva and Paris 1765). Fétis demonstrates his own partiality with respect to Rameau, asserting that although Roussier followed closely Rameau's principles, he "had the merit of being the first in France who took into consideration the succession of harmonies." He commends Roussier for recognizing that certain chords are the result of combinations of prolongations, substitutions, and alterations, although he hastens to point out the intense criticism leveled against him for the "impertinence with which he treated the most distinguished authors" and the many errors in his writings. *FétisB*, 7:499. [PL]

[4]Honoré-François-Marie Langlé (1741-1807) is best known for his *Traité d'harmonie et de modulation* (Paris, 1797). While Fétis praises Langlé's attack on former harmonists who considered chords in isolation, he dismisses his idea that all chords are derived from one chord, that of the "third," by which he means the perfect chord. *FétisB*, 6:42. [PL]

[5]According to Fétis, Jean-François Lirou's (1740-1806) most important work is his *Explication du système de l'harmonie, pour abréger l'étude de la composition, et accorder la pratique avec la théorie* (Paris, 1785). Fétis claims that Lirou was the first French author to set aside completely Rameau's fundamental bass system and to seek the laws of harmonic succession in tonality, although he is disappointed that Lirou considers tonality as a scale derived from the resonance of sonorous bodies. Quoting Lirou, he writes: "C produces E, G; G creates B, D; moreover, C may be considered as the fifth of F, from F, A, C. Thus, C being placed in the middle, we find in the harmonic resonances of F, C, and G the succession of sounds, E, F, G, A, B, C, D, E, which contain all the intervals of our major scale, and which correspond to the two tetrachords of Greek music, E, A, G, A; B, C, D, E." Fétis, of course, considers any appeal to the harmonic resonance of sonorous bodies in support of harmonic systems to be purely arbitrary and mechanical. *FétisB*, 6:455. [PL]

[6]Friedrich Wilhelm Marpurg (1718-1795). See Fétis' critique of Marpurg's theory of harmony in Book Four of this work.

[7]Johann Philipp Kirnberger (1721-1783). In the *Biographie universelle* Fétis casts doubt on Kirnberger's claim that (like Rameau) he had reduced harmony to two fundamental chords, the perfect chord and the seventh, noting that Kirnberger's point of departure for the consonant chord is the perfect chord with major third, minor third, and minor fifth (on the seventh degree), and that, moreover, Kirnberger "considered as essential the four seventh chords G-B-D-F; A-C-E-G; B-D-F-A; C-E-G-B, which to him appeared to differ only by the quality of their intervals." Although Kirnberger considers these seventh chords to be increasingly perfect the closer their proximity to tonic harmony, Fétis recognizes only the first as an essential chord approached without preparation, and the others, being always prepared, as arising from prolongation and substitution. This leads him to claim that Kirnberger discovered "the mechanism of the prolongation of chords that are not modified by other circumstances." Fétis makes no mention of Kirnberger's concept of the ascending and descending leading tones on scale degrees seven and four respectively, an idea that would surely have influenced his own theory of tonality. *FétisB*, 5:339. [PL]

with care, and my uncertainties grew. For a long time I still asked myself the question: *What is the real foundation of harmony?* without finding a satisfactory answer. A new work by Momigny that appeared in 1806 did not further enlighten me, in spite of the promises of its author.[9]

Thus, believing to find more resources in the writings of mathematicians relating to the subject of my research, I read the works of Ballière[10], Jamard[11], Suremain de Missery[12], Tartini[13], Euler's *Essai*[14], and

---

[8]Luigi Antonio Sabbatini, (c. 1732-1809). According to Fétis, Sabbatini's principal work on harmony, *La vera idea delle musicali numeriche segnature diretta al giovane studiosò dell' armonica* (Venice, 1799), is only a description of Francesco-Antonio Vallotti's (1697-1780) harmonic system. Vallotti and the school of Padua are discussed in Book Four of this work. *FétisB*, 8:2. [PL]

[9]Jérôme-Joseph de Momigny (1762-1842). *Cours complet d'harmonie et de composition, d'après une théorie neuve et générale de la musique, basée sur les principes incontestables pùisé dans la nature,* etc. (Paris, 1806), 3 vols. Fétis critiques Momigny's theory in Book Four of this work. [PL]

[10]Fétis notes that Charles-Louis Ballière de Laissement (1729-1800) was a man of considerable distinction, studying music, literature, chemistry, and mathematics, and who associated with eminent Enlightenment figures such as J. J. Rousseau, d'Alembert, Diderot, and Voltaire. He nevertheless contends that Ballière's *Théorie de la musique* (Paris, 1764) goes astray by basing the scale on the harmonic series of the horn and trumpet, which displaces the semitone of the scale, and thus destroys the essential characteristic of modern tonality, introducing a note foreign to it. *FétisB*, 2:51. [PL]

[11]T. Jamard's (1734-1815) principal work is *Recherches sur la théorie de la musique* (Paris, 1769). Fétis points out that it is only a development of Ballière's theory, "no less false, arithmetic relations being substituted for geometric relations in the calculations of the intervals between sounds." *FétisB*, 5:248. [PL]

[12]Antoine Suremain de Missery's (1767-c.1840) principal work on music is *Théorie acoustico-musicale, ou De la doctrine des sons rapportée aux principes de leurs combinaisons* (Paris, 1795). In 1816 he also submitted a treatise to the *Académie des sciences* entitled *Géométrie des sons, ou Principes d'acoustique pure et de musique scientifique.* It was, however, vetoed by Jean-Baptiste Biot (1774-1862), one of the examiners and an eminent French scientist who had just published his own *Traité de physique expérimentale et mathématique,* in which, according to Fétis, he had reproduced all the former errors concerning the formation of the scale through the arithmetic proportions of sounds, errors which Suremain de Misery had apparently corrected. In retaliation, Suremain de Missery launched a scathing confutation of Biot's work in his *Méprises d'un géomètre de l'Institute, manifestées par un provincial; ou Observations critiques sur le traité de physique expérimentale et mathématique de M. Biot, en ce qui concerne certaines points d'acoustique et de musique* (Paris, 1816). Fétis reports that Noël-Mathieu Brossard, a prominent French legal expert with a keen interest in music theory later published a 265 page monograph based largely on Suremain de Misery's unpublished treatise, demonstrating that the numerical relationships adopted by the geometricians have multiple attractive tendencies, and as Fétis happily points out cannot therefore constitute the scale of modern tonality. Suremain de Misery provided most of the articles on acoustics in the *Dictionnaire de musique de l'Encyclopédie méthodique. FétisB*, 8:312. [PL]

[13]Under the entry on Giuseppi Tartini (1692-1770) in the *Biographie universelle,* Fétis writes that Tartini's harmonic system set forth in the *Trattato di Musica secondo la vera scienza dell'armonia* (1754) "is exactly the opposite of Rameau's, for he divides the harmonics back to the fundamental sound, by means of the phenomenon of the third

Catalisano's harmonic and physical-mathematical Grammar[15]; but here I found myself even further from my purpose than in the books of musicians; for at least the latter had been directed in their work by the feeling for the art, while the geometricians offered me only abstract speculations, without direct application to music.

I occasionally spoke about my confusion with the distinguished composer [Etienne-Nicolas] Méhul [1763-1817], but far from receiving encouragement, I found in him only incredulity about the possibility, and even the usefulness of a rational theory of music. "All that a musician must know about this science," he would tell me, "is found in the *Treatise* by Catel; the rest is useless." It must be acknowledged that these words were the sincere expression of an opinion shared by most artists. Since they do not imagine that art could be the subject of a science, they attach importance only to the processes of execution, and in general prefer empirical methods to those that require reasoning. Men of feeling, for that is the very reason they are artists, have difficulty fixing their attention upon serious things that they consider to undermine the activity of the imagination. They are unaware of how a true theory of the science of art can give elevation and clarity to ideas; and the small interest that they take in it is precisely the effect of this unawareness.

Notwithstanding the respect I felt for Méhul's renowned achievement, his objections did not shake my faith in the existence of a principle of harmony that was different from the hypotheses of the scholars, and not restricted to the sole physical pleasure of the effect of sounds. Upon leaving the house one day of this famous artist, following a conversation

---

sound, while the French harmonist proceeds in the opposite direction." Criticizing Fétis' critique of Tartini as "very inadequate," Shirlaw asserts that, on the contrary, Tartini's system both affirms and complements Rameau's, for Tartini considers the third sound to be nothing other than the fundamental bass itself. See Matthew Shirlaw, *The Theory of Harmony*, 293. [PL]

[14]Fétis here refers to Leonhard Euler's (1707-1783) *Tentamen novae theoriae musicae ex certissimis harmoniae principiis dilucide expositae* (*An attempt at a new theory of music, clearly set forth according to the most well-founded principles of harmony*) (St. Petersburg, 1739), translated into French as *Essai d'une nouvelle théorie de la musique* (1839). A preeminent mathematician, Euler sought to rationalize music according to mathematical processes. Fétis writes, "This learned man has shown in his *Tentamen novae theoriae musicae* that a profound knowledge of mathematics does not preclude error, when the assumptions that form the basis of the calculations are unsound." Fétis argues that the methodology Euler uses to establish the agreeableness of various combinations of sounds runs contrary to the perception of consonance and dissonance in practice. See Fétis' lengthy discussion of the *Tentamen* in his *Esquisse de l'Histoire de l'harmonie. FétisB*, 4:53. [PL]

[15]Fétis reports that in his *Grammatica-Armonica fisico mattematica ragionata su i veri principi fondamentali teoricopratici, per uso della gioventù studiosa, e di qualunque musicale radunanza* (Rome, 1781), Gennaro Catalisano (1728-1793) follows Rameau and Tartini by using the harmonic, arithmetic, and geometric proportions to account for the generation of consonances and dissonances, subjecting these proportions to what he calls "a labyrinth of puerile calculations." *FétisB*, 3:74. [PL]

on this very subject, an idea came to me like a beam of light, and which placed me on the road to the doctrine that I have since developed in all my works. The principle of harmony (I said to myself) has been sought in acoustical phenomena, in various systems of numerical progressions, in the more or less ingenious processes of the aggregation of sounds, and in the arbitrary classification of chords; but it is obvious, through examination of the monuments of the history of music, that it is not through these things that art was formed. Every kind of phenomena that modern experience has established, the stacking of thirds ascending or descending, and other elements that served as the foundation for theorists, have not been the guiding principles that, from the beginning, have directed musicians. A more active, more immediate cause must have influenced them in the formation of chords and in the progressions they gave to them. This cause, or in other words, this principle of harmony, both as art and as science, can only have been that which controls the relationship between sounds and the order in which they succeed each other in the scale of the two modes; for it is impossible that there be two principles in art, where one would control the successions of melody, and the other the aggregations of harmony, since these two things are closely linked.

Now, the regulating principle of the relationship of sounds, in their successive and simultaneous orders, is in general designated by the term *tonality*. Everything in harmony which is an immediate consequence of the tonal order is called *diatonic,* and may be considered the absolute expression of it, leaving aside all extraneous circumstances, and therefore necessarily has a native and natural existence; while that which does not conform to this tonal constitution, and does not immediately satisfy the sensibility and the understanding, has only a momentary and artificial existence.

One understands that from this point of view, I sought the principle of harmony in the music itself, and that I discarded all considerations foreign to human nature, that is to say, the divisions of the monochord, the numerical progressions and mechanical formations of chords according to certain systems, because we are not conscious of these things either in composing or in hearing music; they are not integral parts of the art, and have not consequently contributed to its formation. I asked myself which chords exist on their own as a result of present-day tonality, independently of all modifying circumstances, and I discovered only two: the first is *consonant,* composed of three tones, and is called the *perfect chord* (*accord parfait*); the second is *dissonant,* composed of four tones placed at intervals of a third, and is called *dominant seventh chord*. I saw that the first chord constitutes repose in harmony, because when it is heard nothing indicates the necessity for continuation; the other chord, on the contrary, is attractive, in its relationship to certain notes of the scale; it thus has tendencies of resolution, and it characterizes movement in harmony.

I had arrived at these initial and important fundamental ideas, when family interests obliged me to move away from Paris and settle in the country, in the Ardennes region. During my stay of three years in this land of mountains and solitary woods, I often took long excursions where complete isolation allowed me to indulge in uninterrupted musings about the theory of harmony. After having determined the character and functions of the two consonant and dissonant chords, I carefully considered whether any other harmonic aggregation was necessary to constitute tonality; but I could discover none, and I became convinced that all other chords are the modifications of these two, and that their purpose is to cast variety into the forms of harmony, or to establish different relationships between modes. Since I was in possession of this basic truth, it only remained for me to research the nature and the mechanism of various genres of modifications. The long meditations of my solitary wanderings were thus occupied.

In 1816, the manuscript for my *Traité de l'harmonie* was completed. I have stated elsewhere the reasons that prevented me from publishing it at this time.[16] Nevertheless, in 1823 I made known a summary of its fundamental ideas in a *Méthode élémentaire et abrégée d'harmonie et d'accompagnement,* the success of which was encouraging, for it saw three editions in a short period of time, and was translated into several foreign languages.[17]

When I had allowed the enthusiasm which almost always seizes the author of a new theory to cool down, I experienced the need to assure myself, on the one hand, that I had not been preceded by any other author on the road that I had embarked upon, and on the other, that the history of the art would be in agreement with my system. To remove my scruples concerning the first point, I surrounded myself with all the books in which harmony had been treated more or less directly, in greater or lesser depth. The number of works of this kind that I have read over a twenty-year period amounts to more than eight hundred. With respect to the composers of every kind that I have analyzed, I have arranged them according to epoch and to transformations in the art. It would be difficult for me to give an accurate idea of the inexhaustible source of instruction that I found in

[16]Under the entry on himself, Fétis reports that when he submitted his new theory of harmony to the French Academy for approval, the Minister of the Interior and the Secretary of the Academy of Fine Arts decided that the public should judge the merit of his work. In 1819 he therefore began publication with Eberhardt, but after only five pages had been printed, Catel asked him to obtain some poetry for the Opera. This renewed contact with Catel evidently awakened Fétis' sympathy, for he decided to cease publication of his book so as not to upset his older colleague by challenging principles relating to his work. *FétisB*, 4:103. [PL]

[17]*Méthode élémentaire et abrégée d'harmonie et d'accompagnement* (Paris, 1824). Fétis writes that this work, written in a succinct and didactic style without any discussion of theory, became the only work that was used to teach harmony in France and Belgium. *FétisB*, 4:103. [PL]

this relentless work, the results of which led me to the conviction of the infallibility of my principles. My *Esquisse de l'histoire de l'harmonie, considérée comme art et comme science systématique*[18] has made known to the public the care with which I have carried out my research concerning this subject.[19]

In 1822, Luigi Cherubini [1760-1842], who had just been appointed director of the Paris Conservatory, proposed to entrust me, in my capacity as professor of composition at this school, with the writing of an introductory book on the forms of the art of musical composition, under the title of *Traité du contrepoint et de la Fugue*,[20] to replace outmoded or inadequate works by Fux,[21] Martini,[22] Paoli,[23] and Albrechtsberger.[24] I spent two years of assiduous effort on this large work, of which the second

---

[18]Published by Bourgogne and Martinet, Paris, 1840, 1 vol, 178 pages. See also the *Gazette musicale de Paris,* 1840, nos. 9, 20, 24, 35, 40, 52, 63, 67, 68, 72, 73, 75, 76, 77.

[19]Part of the *Esquisse* is reproduced in Book Four of the *Traité de l'harmonie*. See Mary Arlin's translation, *Esquisse De L'Histoire De L'Harmonie: An English-Language Translation of the François-Joseph Fétis History of Harmony* (Stuyvesant, NY, Pendragon Press, 1994). [PL]

[20]*Traité du contrepoint et de la Fugue* (Paris, 1824). Fétis quotes Cherubini's praise of this treatise as "... the only work of this kind where the rules of its technical compositions, particularly those of the fugue, are explained clearly and systematically. *FétisB*, 4:103. [PL]

[21]Concerning Johann Joseph Fux's (1660-1741) *Gradus ad parnassum* (Vienna, 1725) Fétis writes, "the progression of the studies is excellent, rational, and founded on an excellent analytical system on the art of writing." He goes on to say, "The most important and just criticism that can be made of this master, is that he lacked any criticism and evaluation in the analysis of the rules he has given; rules taken from a very good feeling for practice, but in which there is almost never any perception of their true origin." *FétisB*, 4:220. [PL]

[22]Fétis considers Giovanni Battista Martini (1706-1784) to be the most learned musician of the eighteenth century. He defends Martini against criticism that he wrote in an outdated tonality claiming that better models of this style could not be found. *FétisB*, 8:296 [PL]

[23]Fétis almost certainly refers to Giuseppe Paolucci (1726-1776), a composer and theorist whose treatise *Arte pratica di contrappunto dimostrata con esempli di vari autori, e con osservazioni* (Venice, 1765-72), served as the plan for Martini's *Esemplare ossia Saggio fondamnetale pratico di contrappunto* (Bologna, 1774-75). Fétis notes that whereas Martini uses musical examples taken mostly from the sixteenth century, Paolucci draws from the seventeenth and eighteenth centuries as well. His consideration of genre and style as factors in the determination of tonal organization may have influenced, if only tangentially, Fétis' concept of the orders of tonality. *FétisB*, 7:158. [PL]

[24] Fétis criticizes Johann Georg Albrechtsberger's (1736-1809) treatment of fugue in the *Anweisung zur composition* (Leipzig, 1790), remarking: "The most difficult parts of fugue, the *answer* and the *countersubjects*, are only touched upon, and the examples are not varied enough." He nevertheless thinks the treatise to be an improvement on Fux's *Gradus*, "which, based on the tonality of plainchant, is too far removed from modern methods." *FétisB*, 1:41. [PL]

edition appeared in 1846,[25] and the new considerations, to which I had to surrender myself in order to discover the reasons for the rules and which had only been presented by my predecessors in an empirical manner and through the authority of tradition, forced me to discover new and innumerable applications of the law of tonality, which proved to me, with a new and greater force, the absolute identity of the principles that regulate the melodic succession of tones, and of those that are the foundation of harmony. Therefore, I no longer had any doubt, and was certain that a single law governs the relationships of tones, both in the order of succession and in simultaneous aggregations.

But what is the law of tonality itself, and from where does it arise? If I were to keep to the unanimous opinion of theorists and historians of music, nature has fixed the order of tones in the scale, and we find elements of this in the multiple resonances of certain bodies, in the methodical division of the string, and even in certain numerical progressions which are the inverse expression of string lengths corresponding to each tone of the scale, or of the number of their vibrations. But what! Do we not have proof that tonality has not everywhere been the same in every age? Do we not know that even today it is not the same with all peoples, and that in Europe it is formed in a very different manner in the music of the church and in that of the theater? Moreover, these tones given by nature are indeed the elements of a scale, but do not determine its form, upon which the character of all music depends. It is therefore necessary to recognize that the mysterious law that guides the affinities of tones has another origin; in fact I could find it only in human organization; but the latter's mode of action, which determines this or that tonal configuration, from which one draws all consequences, presented itself to my mind in only a confused manner. My uncertainties always caused me to postpone publication of my theory of harmony; for I realized that it would remain incomplete until my doubts were dissipated.

The moment finally arrived in which I could possess a doctrine of science and art where not a single point remained obscure or uncertain, in which all parts were a consequence of one another, and which alone could provide the complete solution to all problems. Here are the circumstances under which this was revealed to me:

On a beautiful day in the month of May, 1831, I was going from Passy to Paris, and, as usual, I was walking along a solitary road in the *Bois de Boulogne*, dreaming about this theory of music, always the object

[25]*Traité du contrepoint et de la fugue, ou Exposé analytique des règles de la composition musicale*, etc. (Paris, Troupenas, 1846), in two parts.*

*In the Preface to the 1846 edition Fétis notes that the treatise was written at Cherubini's request in order to supplant Anton Reicha's *Traité de haute composition* (1824-26), which, he says, because of its many errors and arbitrary principles "merits the oblivion into which it has already fallen." [PL]

of my thoughts, and of which I wished to create a science worthy of the name. Suddenly, the truth presents itself to my mind; the questions are clearly asked, the darkness dissipates; the false doctrines fall piece by piece around me; and all of this is the result of the following propositions, which are my point of departure:

Nature provides as the elements of music only a multitude of tones that differ from one another through pitch, duration, and intensity, through larger or smaller nuances.

Amongst these tones, those in which the differences are tangible enough to affect the sense of hearing in a well-defined manner become the object of our attention; the idea of relationships that exists amongst these tones arises in the understanding and from the sensibility on the one hand, and the will on the other, the mind arranging them in different classes where each corresponds to a particular order of emotions, feelings and ideas.

These series therefore become types of tonalities and rhythms that have necessary consequences, under the influence of which the imagination assumes its duties in the creation of beauty.

All of this came to me at once like a flash, and the emotion caused me to sit down at the foot of a tree. I spent six hours there absorbed in thought; but these hours were for me an entire lifetime, during which the historical tableau of all the conceptions of the art, of all tonal forms, from antiquity to the present day, unfolded before my eyes. I grasped the principles, the causes of transformations, and I thus arrived at what music would become, developing itself according to the final requirements of tonality, rhythm, and accent. At the same time I devised the classification of the various orders of tonality that succeeded one another over three centuries through the affinities between tones that were brought in by harmony. Finally, the examination of the determining causes of the attraction of tones in harmony made me discover the origin of the errors which have until now falsified the mathematical theory of music; for I saw that the attraction arose from the tendencies of the two minor semitones of the scale, which a hypothesis of Ptolemy, accepted without examination, had considered as major, from which arose a double error: (1) to assume the intervals of tones to be in different proportions, while they are all equal; (2) to give descending tones greater importance than ascending ones, when the contrary is precisely the case. Finally, I realized through intuition that the intonation of tones must be varied, due to tendencies determined by their harmonic aggregations; a conjecture which I have since verified through numerous experiments, and which, combined with previous observations, has led me to reform the mathematical theory of music.

After having spent about a year putting my new ideas in order, I thought I should submit them to the opinion of scholars and a few eminent artists; to this end, I opened, in July 1832, a free course where I presented my doctrine to an audience in which I had the honor to see members of the Academy of Sciences of the Institute, most of the professors of the Conservatory and the most famous artists.[26] The high praise that was given to me during and after this course, would have made me decide to bring to light my theories of art and science, if soon after I had not been called far from Paris to take up the position which I have occupied for fifteen years. The care required for the organization of a new school, and the immense work that I had to do to put in order, complete and publish my *Biographie universelle des musiciens,* long delayed the realization of my views concerning the philosophy of music.[27] Finally, in January 1844, I decided to bring out my *Traité de l'harmonie*, which contains a part of this body of my doctrine, and I returned to Paris where I opened a new free course, intended to explain to the public the ideas that had thrown me in a direction absolutely opposed to that of other theorists. My audience was considerable: a lively discussion occurred at the end of each session between the advocates of various systems taught in the schools and those in whom I had instilled my convictions. Spirited secret meetings sometimes went on for several hours in the surrounding area where I gave my lectures.

It was under these circumstances that the work appeared of which today I am bringing out the third edition. The good reception that it has had is verified by the prompt sale of the first two editions. Passionate polemics have nevertheless been raised by the theories that are set forth: specialized journals of music and others have been full of them, not only in France, but abroad. I believed it necessary to analyze, in the notes at the back of this edition, some objections that have been made to me concerning the classifications of chords where I have distanced myself from certain methods. But the most notable difficulties dwelt on the intellectual principle that I give to the formation of tonality; for if sensualism and fatalism have fallen into disrepute with philosophers, they have yet a lively existence in the preconceptions of artists. They absolutely want a scale given by nature, the chords the elements of which we find in the resonances of the sounding plates of cylinders, bells, and what not? Finally, they want that the ear be the judge and physical pleasure the goal.

The science of harmony is only part of a totality of which the philosophy of music must offer the complete system. Those of my readers who have not attended the verbal presentation that I made of it have not grasped the connection; I believed that there was no better response to

[26]In these lectures Fétis asserts that musical perception is subjective and based on specific habits, which accounts for the different kinds of scales used in different in various cultures. This leads him to conclude that the mathematical division of a string does not provide a real basis for the formation of scales, from which he further deduces that all scales are metaphysical entities, arising from unique circumstances. *FétisB*, 4:111. [PL]

[27]*Biographie universelle des musicians* (Brussels, Méline, Cans & Co, 1835-1844/1860-65), 8 vols.

their objections than the summary that I shall present in this preface. In all likelihood I will not convince all minds: but at least all misunderstanding should cease when I will have expressed all of my thoughts.

If we go back to the oldest ideas of oriental pantheism, we shall find all notions of the harmony of tones united with those of the organization of the universe. Among the peoples of India, it is in the Vedas themselves, or sacred books, that one must seek the origin, contemporaneous with creation, and inseparable from cosmogony, theogony and philosophical theology. Among the gods and the spirits, are counted those which preside over the different parts of music; ether is pure sound;[28] the seven nymphs called *Swaras* are personified notes of music (identified sounds). Sardja, the first note or tonic of the scale of tones, often manifests itself with the characteristics of *Saraswati*, daughter, wife and sister of Brahma. These nymphs are epitomized in the person of *Swaragrama*, Goddess of the scale, and the general scale of tones is deified in *Mahaswaragrama*, which is none other than *Saraswati*, in one of her forms. The light *Apsaras*, created to charm the court of the God *Indra*, king of the firmament, form concerts with the *Gandharbas*,[29] celestial musicians, seven in number, who preside over the harmony of the spheres cast into space. From the union of Brahma and Saraswati is born Nardja, who invents *vina*, a most excellent musical instrument, and forms it from a tortoise shell, which, according to Indian cosmogony, carries the world on its back. Six other children of Brahma and Saraswati, called *Ragas*, are the spirits that preside over the principal passions and the musical modes that are their expression. Daughters of Mahaswaragrama, the musical nymphs, called *Raginis*, are joined in groups of five for each of the Ragas, and personify secondary passions or modes.

Amongst them, four leaders each represent seven modes in four systems to which they give their names. The fifth, who is the general symbol for this, leads the way: it is Mahaswaragrama herself, that is to say, music, the concept of which contains all the systems and all the modes. From the union of the Ragas and the Raginis a multitude of children are born, who are as many derived modes. Their production has no limits, say the commentators of Vedas: like the waves of the sea, they may be multiplied to infinity. It is easy to understand how these children of the Ragas and Raginis, in infinite numbers, are but the melodies formed with the modes. Governors of the art of combining tones, the Raginis weigh them: their step is rhythmical, their motion is a harmony, their posture a cadence.

These ideas, concerning the celestial origin of music, from this primordial art which alone has enjoyed since the most distant antiquity, in

---

[28]See *Manava d'Harmasastra,* or *Book of the Laws of Manou*, concerning the civil and religious institutions of India, translated from Sanscrit by M. L'Oiseleur de Louchamps (Paris, 1833), 76.

[29]Ibid., 37.

all peoples, the privilege of being the work of the Gods, are found with certain modifications in various peoples of the Orient; but within these modifications, a principal idea crosses the centuries, namely: harmony produced by the movements of celestial bodies, of which the music of man is but an imperfect imitation. The Hebrews borrow it from the Chaldeans and the Saducuees who, attentive observers of the progression of the stars, concluded by attributing to them a direct, supreme, and eternal influence upon the entire universe. This principle, accepted by the Hebrews, brought them to the idea of particular abstract intelligences that presided over the harmony of the spheres. These intelligences are the *Angels*, and the movements of the celestial spheres form the concerts by which they glorify the Eternal. The Elohim (the Hebrew name for God prior to the name Yahweh) of Genesis, who is none other than Metatrone of the Talmud, and whose power is subject only to the author of all things, reigns over the spheres scattered through space, as over the angels which guide them.

It is also this same idea of an inferior power to that of the creator of the universe, but who gives life and movement to his works, which Pythagoras borrowed from the peoples of the Orient, with the idea of universal harmony. He made it the soul of the world, to which he attributed harmonic proportions that Plato made known in an obscure passage in the Timaeus, and which are those of the scale in the music of the Greeks. It is the soul of the world that gives birth to the particular souls that take from it their substance, life, movement and harmonic organization.

The tradition of the soul of the world and universal harmony does not stop there; handed down from century to century, recorded and modified by the Alexandrian school, reproduced in the writings of Plutarch,[30] Cicero,[31] Ptolemy,[32] Censorinus,[33] Macrobius,[34] Boethius,[35] and many others, it reappeared after the rebirth of letters in the works of Plato

---

[30]Mestrius Plutarchus [c46-127]. *The Creation of the Soul,* 12, 19, 21, 22. *De Musica,* 22, 44.

[31]Marcos Tullius Cicero [106 BC-43 BC]. *The Republic*, Book Six.

[32]Claudius Ptolemaeus [c90-c168]. *Harmony*, Book III, c. 4-16.

[33]*De die natali*, c. 13.*
*Censorinus. 3rd century Roman grammarian and writer. His only extant work is *Liber de die Natali* (*On the Day of Birth*), written in 238. [PL]

[34]*Commentary on the Dream of Scipio*, Book II, chs. 1-4.*
*Ambrosious Macrobius Theodosius, 5th century Roman philosopher and Latin philologist. *In Somnium Scipionis* contains the text of Cicero's *Dream of Scipio*, with Macrobius' commentary. Translated and edited by W. H. Stahl as *Macrobius, Commentary on the Dream of Scipio* (New York: Columbia University Press, 1952). [PL]

[35]Anicius Manlius Severinus Boethius (c470-525). *De [institutione] musica*, Book II.*
*Translated by C. Bower and C. Palisca as *Fundamentals of Music* (New Haven: Yale University Press, 1989). [PL]

scholars, gave birth to the bizarre musings of Robert Fludd,[36] and ended by misleading the powerful mind of Kepler[37] at the very moment that this learned man had just discovered the fundamental laws of astronomy.

Leaving aside what is wrong in the hypothesis of the identity of universal harmony and the harmony of musical tones, one may say that its existence resulted in taking away from man his freedom in the conception of art, in imposing conditions upon him in a fatal manner, and of prohibiting his intellectual and emotional faculties the possibility of modifying the elements therein. The theorists, who, in modern times, have tried to reproduce this hypothesis, have not understood that the result of their efforts is averse to human organization.[38] If one supposes, in fact, that Creation has ordered in an invariable manner the system of tones, and that man is conscious of its permanence, must it not therefore be admitted that variety in the character of music and harmony is impossible, and that the impressions produced by the combinations of these sounds must be identical in all individuals endowed with the auditory organ? But, this is not what takes place; for the history of the art, studied with intelligence, demonstrates that the intervals and the scales of tones have been conceived in different ways, according to time and place; and we know from experience that the impressions produced by music are not the same in all peoples.

Physiologists, whose opinions tend to substitute the action of the organism for that of intelligence, have wanted to attribute the determination of tones, their complete accuracy and their intervals, to the structure of the ear. Not to speak of Booerhave, who supposes that the semi-circular canals of the ear are composed of a series of arcs of different diameters, intended to produce as many definite tones as those of the chromatic scale;[39] of Lecat,[40] who conjectures that the cochlea is a keyboard instrument, fitted with many tiny stretched strings divided down the middle wall membrane, having varying lengths and widths arranged amongst themselves and intended to vibrate individually in unison with the tones that strike them;[41] of Dumas,[42] who claims that the ear drum is

---

[36]Robert Fludd [1574-1637]. *Utriusque Cosmi*, Book III – *De Musica Mundana.*

[37]Johannes Kepler (1571-1630). *Harmonices mundi*, Book IV, c. 6; Book V, c. 4-8.

[38]See Roussier, *Mémoire sur la musique des anciens,* 73, 87; *Letter touching on the division of the zodiac and the institution of the planetary week in relation to a geometric progression, upon which musical proportions depend.* (*Journal des beaux-arts et des sciences,* November, 1770).

[39]Hermann Booerhave [1668-1738]. In the notes of his edition of *Opuscules anatomiques* by Eustachi (Delft, 1726).*

*Bartolomeo Eustachi (c.1513-1574). His *Opuscula anatomica* (1564) is credited with the first description of the *tuba auditiva* that is still referred to by Eustachi's name. [PL]

[40]Claude-Nicolas Lecat (1700-1768). French anatomist and surgeon, founder of the *Académie royale des sciences, belles lettres et arts* in Rouen (1744). [PL]

[41]*Traité de l'ouïe,* following his *Traité des sensations et des passions en général, et des sens en particulier* (Paris, 1766), 2 vols.

elliptical and made up of diverse strings which correspond to as many particular tones.[43] And finally, of the many others who have hazarded the same kind of hypotheses, have we not read books where physicians and professors of mathematics undertake to found systems of tonality, of melody and harmony upon the structure of the auditory organ,[44] and whose objective is to demonstrate that the laws of succession and of aggregation of tones are based upon the phenomena of perception? What these authors have claimed to establish according to physiological considerations and assumptions of fact, the sensualist philosophers of the eighteenth century inserted in their metaphysics. "As for the actual tones, *the ear* (said Condillac) *structured in such a way to feel connections precisely, brings to bear a finer and more extensive judgment.* Its fibres appear to share the vibrations of the sonorous bodies, and it may detect several at once."[45] The conclusions of these doctrines are that music is given to us entirely through the mechanism and organization of the ear, under the impression of external information, and that the enjoyment it gives us is purely physical. It is not unsurprising that one sees these theories reproduced in our time in the anthropological lectures of an erudite professor at the University of Koenisberg, the same university in which Kant's voice brought forward quite different doctrines forty years earlier.[46] According to Mr. de Baer, the author of these lectures (§175), *the*

---

[42]Charles-Louis Dumas (1765-1813) was professor of anatomy and dean of the Faculty of Medicine at Montpellier. A member of the French Academy, his *Principes de physiologie* appeared between 1800-1806 in which he contributed to the development of the principle of vitalism, which insists, in contrast to the idea of mechanism, that life involves a special principle and cannot be explained only in terms of physical and chemical properties. [PL]

[43]*Principes de physiologie*, etc., 2nd edition, vol. III, 544.

[44]See Pierre Mengoli,* *Speculazioni di musica* (Bologna, 1670), *Specul.* 1, 2, 3, 4, 5, and Al. J. Morel,** *Principe acoustique nouveau et universel de la théorie musicale, ou Musique expliquée* (Paris, 1816).

*Pietro Mengoli (1626-1686), a prominent Italian mathematician, was a professor at the University of Bologna from 1648-86. [PL]
**Fétis appears to have conflated two of Alexander-Jean Morel's (1775-1825) works. The *Biographie Universelle Ancienne et Moderne* (Paris 1853) claims that there is another work entitled *Système acoustique, ou musique expliquée* (Paris, 1824). According to the same source, Morel "established his system after the structure of the ear, where he believed to find the principle of the feeling for tonality." [PL]

[45]*Traité des sensations*, part I, ch. viii, §4.*
*In his influential *Traité des sensations*, Étienne Bonnot de Condillac (1715-1780), the founder of absolute sensationalism, argues that all knowledge begins with sensations that create impressions, traces of which are then stored in the memory. It is from the comparison of these memories that judgments are formed and abstraction made possible. Thus, for Condillac all our ideas are ultimately derived from the senses. The application of this doctrine to the understanding of music clearly runs contrary to Fétis' contention that tonal systems are the result of active mental processes. [PL]

[46]*Vorlesungen über Anthropologie,* by Dr. Karl-Ernst von Baer, Koenisberg, 1824 (277 onwards).*

ear has the faculty to distinguish sounds, because of their low or high pitch (*die Foehigkeit unsers Ohrs die Toene nach ihrer-Hoehe und Tiefe su unterscheiden*); the relation of two tones is more agreeable *to the ear* as their numerical relationship is more simple (*Je einfacher die Zoehlenverhoeltnisse zweier Toene, um desto angenehmer ist ihre Verbindung für das Ohr*); and, finally, the ear has desires (*Begierden*), and demands (*Erforderungen*). If the ear has all this in its domain, what then is the role of intellect? Evidently, in this hypothesis, music is only a play of sensations; it could not become an art.

Nothing is more worthy of attention than the perseverance that has been given in all ages to the search for the origin of music, either in cosmological sources, or in natural phenomena, and to suppose that it was imposed upon man by the Creator under determined conditions, leaving him only the freedom to combine the elements. From this arises the idea of a scale or succession of tones given by nature, which one tried to find in universal harmony, or in the structure of the ear, or in that of the human voice,[47] or even in the acoustical divisions of certain tubes, or finally in geometrical and arithmetical progressions. Some people have even gone so far as to contest the spontaneous discovery of the simultaneous harmony of sounds by human intelligence and sensibility; and because experiments by modern physicists have found in the resonances of certain sonorous bodies phenomena that produce consonant harmonies, and others, more recently, are believed to have recognized the production of dissonances, one was persuaded that a more legitimate basis would be given to this part of the art by phenomena still unknown at the time of its creation, than by the instinct that had found it; so that generations whose toil and felicitous inspiration have developed harmonic combinations of sounds would have been relegated to the influence of the occult, while they believed only to be obeying the laws of their intuitive and intellectual faculties.[48]

In order to enlighten ourselves on the error of the majority of theorists and music historians in the assumption they have made of an invariant scale given by nature, we will take a quick look at the notion of scales that were the foundations of the art among different peoples in various eras.

Amongst the monuments of the Sanskrit language more than two thousand years prior to the Christian era, treatises on music are found where we see the exposition of a system of tonality in which intervals a

---

*Karl Ernst von Baer (1792-1876) was appointed professor at Königsberg in 1817 where he taught zoology and anatomy. [PL]

[47]*The Philosophy of the Human Voice,* etc., by James Rush (Philadelphia, 1827), 29-50.*

*James Rush (1786-1869) studied at Princeton and Edinburgh and obtained an M.D. from the University of Pennsylvania in 1809. Upon retirement as Treasurer of the United States Mint he published several books, including *The Philosophy of the Human Voice: Embracing its Physiological History; Together With a System of Principles*, which was published in six revised editions during his lifetime. [PL]

[48]See the fourth part of this work.

little larger than a quartertone entered into the composition and modifications of a large number of modes. These modes also had as a principle the variety of tones with which each scale began. Finally, there were modes in which the scales were incomplete and contained only five or six tones, and where the intervals had no relationship with those of the scale of modern music.

With the ancient inhabitants of Persia, the usual scale of tones was divided by quartertones, and these entered into combinations with a certain number of modes that were analogous to those of the music of the inhabitants of India. In spite of the great revolutions for which Persia had been the stage, this system of tonality was preserved until the seventeenth century of our era; for the Persian musicians which Amurat IV led into slavery at Constantinople after the capture of Bagdad, in 1638, introduced this system of tonality into Turkey where it was still in use at the end of the eighteenth century.[49]

With today's Arabs, where the Moors have preserved the character of antiquity, the tones are divided by thirds, and the semitones are equal to those of our music. These elements combine in a large number of modes analogous, in the variety of initial tones and occasional suppression of certain tones, to those of India and Persia. The divisions on the necks of their instruments provide us with sufficient proof of the existence of this system, which in all likelihood was that of all Semitic peoples.

The aesthetic principle of the art based on these scales of small variable intervals that is found in all peoples of the Orient is that of a languid and sensual music, conforming to the customs of the nations where they were conceived. One does not see, in fact, any other use of music by these peoples apart from that of amorous songs and lascivious dances.

On the other hand, among the rugged and serious populations descended from the yellow or Mongolian race, the music, serious and monotonous, strange and austere for Europeans, is the product of a system of tonality where the semitone very often disappears, and in which the incomplete scale is composed of only five tones placed next to each other at intervals of a tone, with gaps where there are the semitones of the so-called *diatonic* scale. Such is the musical system of the Chinese, Japanese, Cochin-Chinese, Koreans, Manchurians, and of the real Mongolians. The soft accent cannot be heard because it can only be found with the use of the semitone.

---

[49] See the *Letteratura turchesca,* of Toderini, vol. 1, 243-252.*

*Giambattista Toderini (1728-1799) was a Jesuit scholar who studied archeology and physics. A noted Ottomantist he published several books, including *Della Letteratura turchesa* (Venice, 1787), 3 vols. [PL]

If we carry the examination of the organization of tonality to the Pelasgian peoples of Greece and Asia-Minor, we become aware of transformations, which, in the space of about six centuries, completely change its nature. A part of the Pelasgians was established in Thrace: amongst them were born Linus, Orpheus, and Thamyris, famous poet-musicians, who probably made use of the same tonalities as the Pelasgians of Asia-Minor. Prior to the siege of Troy, Olympia and other musicians of Phrygia and Lydia, composed hymns in a tonality called *enharmonic*, in which the notes were arranged in two intervals of a quarter-tone (called *dieses*), followed by a major third, this being succeeded by the interval of a tone; then came two more quarter-tones, followed by a major third. Such was the division of the octave in this system of enharmonic tonality, which would offend the musical sensibility of a modern European, but which has much in common with certain modes of the oldest music of India. Now, Olympia and the other musicians of Phrygia and Lydia, of whom we have just spoken, were of the same race as those who followed Pelops in Greece, and who brought with them their musical modes.[50] These companions of Pelops were Pelasgians, and the Pelasgians were Hindus or Hindu-Scythians.

Later, when the Hellenists, coming from Caucasian Scythia into Greece, under the leadership of Deucalion, had become powerful and had conquered the Peloponnesus, they replaced the ancient enharmonic tonality of the Pelasgians with the division of the tone by thirds, which they had taken from the scales of the Semitic peoples from whom they drew their origin. For example, three notes placed at a third of a tone apart, followed by a fourth a tone apart, then a fifth at the distance of a semitone from the latter, and finally three notes at intervals of a third of a tone, were the divisions of the octave in the enharmonic genre of one of the modes of Greek music, called the Lydian mode. Now, this disposition of notes is precisely that of one of the modes of Arab music today. This second form of enharmonic tonality was in use for many centuries. When other kinds, called *chromatic* and *diatonic*, had introduced easier forms of intonation into each mode, the small intervals of the enharmonic genre were abandoned, and this genre continued to exist only in theory in the chart of the modes. The chromatic genre was of many kinds, of which the easiest for the voice was the *chromatic tonic*. The scale of this genre was formed with a semitone, another semitone, then a minor third followed by a tone, which were succeeded by two semitones followed by a minor third. This new formation of tonality still felt the effects of oriental origins through the two consecutive semitones, and by the gap of the minor third. The perception of this root ceased only when the tonal form, called diatonic, was discovered, in which the semitone is isolated, before or after

[50]Fétis cites as his source Book xiv, ch. 21 of the *Deipnosophistae* by Athenaeus, a Greek rhetorician writing around the turn of the third century A.D. [PL]

two or three notes. This form ended up being the only one in use: it was applied to different modes.

In its origin, the modes of Greek music were only three in number, namely, the Phrygian, Lydian, and Dorian; but this number progressively increased to thirteen, and finally to fifteen. As in the modes of Hindu and Arab music, the principle of the diversity of Greek modes consisted in the ability to change the position of the intervals of the notes, by beginning each scale with a different note taken from the diatonic pattern. The difference of the position of tones and semitones constituted what was called *octave species*.[51]

Although we have only a vague notion of the state of Greek music based upon these elements of modes and genres, and upon poetic meters that applied to each particular mode, we know that its aesthetic qualities resulted primarily from the correctness of accent and rhythm in sung poetry. With regard to the question so often debated as to whether the Greeks considered the simultaneous harmony of sounds as a necessary deduction in the overall conception of music, it would have been simplified and clearly presented if it had been pointed out that harmony is only inherent in melody in as much as it consists of tonal unity; now, the small number of passages taken from authors of antiquity, upon which one relies to affirm that the Greeks had used harmony, only make reasonable sense in supposing that the melody of a mode was accompanied by the same melody transposed to another mode; this is obviously contrary to the true meaning of the word *harmony*. We note, in addition, that nothing similar appears to have existed in the golden age of the culture of the arts in Greece and that this tonal paradox is marked only by times of decadence.

We have just seen by what series of transformations the diatonic scale of sounds has separated itself from the enharmonic and chromatic intervals that had been mixed with its own in other tonal formulas; and we may now recognize what is wrong in the assumption that this scale is the necessary condition of all music, that it is given by nature, and that it does not rest with man to imagine another which might satisfy the needs of his sensibility. What nature gives are tones varied by an infinity of greater or smaller differences of intonation. With these elements man combines tonal successions in a certain systematic order that would not exist if the choice of elements were different and which would be replaced by another system. Modified by education and custom the sensibility produces its phenomena and the imagination gives birth to its works of art in the world of tonal order where these faculties operate; but this order is only part of an immense totality and man's faculties of feeling and intellect are

---

[51]For the development of the exposition of tonalities of all the systems see the work that I published in the *Gazette musicale de Paris* (1846) concerning the *General System of Music*.

susceptible to activity under the influence of infinitely varied impressions of the relationships of tones.

I anticipate the objection that one might use against me. If human freedom, one may say, to conceive systems of relationships of tones is as absolute as you claim, how is it that one was not able to give more regularity to the diatonic scale by allowing only equal intervals instead of the mixture of tones and semitones that one observes and of which we do not even know the cause? If I am not mistaken, this argument, far from destroying the free exercise of the faculties of man in the conception of the laws that regulate the relations of tones, provides me with precisely the means to demonstrate this complete freedom.

The possibility of an infinite multitude of tones of different pitch in the production of sonorous phenomena cannot be placed in doubt. Now, in this multitude the infinitely small differences between a tone and its lower or upper neighbor affect the sensibility in only a confused manner and the intellect consequently cannot determine the intervals. In order to arrive at the formation of a scale of perceptible and measurable differences the intellect must choose sounds in which the intervals are appreciable, and neglect the intermediary ones. In this operation it is obvious that it proceeds by elimination. It is thus that the ear is able to clearly perceive and the mind to discern and measure, for example, the differences between sounds placed at intervals of a quartertone. Experienced in the frequent perception of these relations of sounds the auditory organ may receive a pleasant impression and the mind may arrive at a conception of a tonal system in which this interval is one of its elements. This is precisely what took place in the ancient music of Persia and in the enharmonic genre of the Greeks. Further extending this operation to the elimination of quartertones the intellect reaches the concept of a chromatic scale composed of semitones in which it combines the elements in diverse systems, for example, in the chromatic tonic of the Greeks and in the various modes of the ancient and modern diatonic genre. The existence of the interval of a tone in music can only be comprehended therefore by the elimination of a multitude of smaller intervals, notably that of the semitone. If this last elimination takes place in the diatonic scale between certain determined tones and not elsewhere it is because these conditions respond to the needs of certain forms of art. Now, one cannot deny that the forms of art are the product of the man's faculties of feeling and intellect. One sees that the argument drawn from the inequality of intervals between tones of the diatonic scale, far from undermining our reasons for its formation, confirms them.

The tonal transformations that remain for me to discuss, and which have operated within the limits of the diatonic system, will render even more obvious the limitless faculty for creation that the human spirit possesses in the domain of art and in its elements.

The diatonic scale is composed of seven tones, of which five are placed at intervals of a tone, and two at intervals of a semitone. If one begins the scale with each of these notes, it is clear that it will present itself in as many forms as there are notes, for, in each, the arrangement of tones and semitones will be different. There is, therefore, in the elements of the diatonic scale, the possibility of forming seven different scales. These are the scales that are called *modes*. Because of the difference in the position of tones and semitones in the octave of each of these modes the mathematician and astronomer Ptolemy proposed that the number of scales be reduced to seven, for there are only seven possible forms with the elements of the diatonic genre. However, from the earliest times of Christianity, the use of chant for hymns, psalms, and prayers having been established in the assemblies of the Christians of the Orient, the number of modes was increased to eight in the tonal system of their religious melodies, according to considerations that will be explained.

The ancient Greeks divided the octave, or octachord, into two tetrachords, or series of four consecutive tones, between which there was the disjunction of a tone.[52] Another arrangement of the division of the octave governed the organization of the tonality of Church chant. It consisted in considering the four principal modes, namely, the dorian (scale of D), the phrygian (scale of E), the lydian (scale of F), and the mixolydian (scale of G), as *keys*, or *authentic modes*, by creating in the melodies the tonal division of the octave at the fifth note, while the inferior modes called *plagal*, that is, the hypodorian (scale of A), the hypophrygian (scale of B), the hypolydian (scale of C), the hypomixolydian (scale of D), had the tonal point of division of the octave at the fourth note, and the final of these melodies occurred on this note instead of on the first, as in the authentic modes. Now, it is precisely this that distinguishes the two scales of D, called the dorian and hypomixolydian modes. A new principle had therefore come to modify the Greek system of diatonic tonality.

This system was carried into Italy and Gaul with the first chants of the Oriental Christians, although the four authentic modes appear to have been the only ones that were used at first. But later, when the authors of melodies of the Catholic Church had adopted the distinction between authentic and plagal modes, they pushed the principle of the difference in the division of the octave to its ultimate conclusion, considering the seven modes that generate the diatonic genre in its direct order as authentic, having the tonal point of division of the octave on the fifth note of each scale, and the melodic final on the first. Then, placing at the lower fourth of each of these modes as many plagal modes, where the tonal point of

---

[52]Concerning the formation of the Greek musical system, see the work of Boeckh in his excellent edition by Pindare (vol.1); that of [François-Loius] Perne [1772-1832], in *Revue musicale* (vols. III, IV, V, VIII, IX); the series of articles that I have published in the *Gazette musicale de Paris* (1846); the notes of Henri Martin, in his *Etudes sur le Timée de Platon*; and the new *Mémoires* of Bellerman, Fortlage and Vincent.

division was the fourth note of the scale, as well as the melodic final. This produced in fact fourteen modes. The reality of the principle of these modes cannot be doubted, for the song books of the Catholic Church contain melodies that could only have been imagined by their authors to be in the ninth, tenth, thirteenth, and fourteenth modes. However, the Oriental doctrine of eight modes prevailed, and the custom was generally established.[53] But this custom introduced into the Church chant a singular anomaly, for the obligation to transpose, for example, the melodies of the thirteenth and fourteenth modes into the fifth and sixth, made necessary in notation, in order to preserve the tonal character, the use of certain signs of alteration of pitch which do not belong to the diatonic genre in which all the Church chant is conceived, but to the chromatic genre to which it is foreign. This observation is decisive and demonstrates incontrovertibly the existence of the fourteen modes.

Allow me to mention the importance of the transformation that was brought about in diatonic tonality, in passing from the chant of Greek poetry to that of the Church. In appearance, the modes were identical because the scales of tones were the same. But the character was different, because the division of the scales resided in another principle. To be sure, it is not an empty distinction that the same scale has as its melodic final either the first note or the fourth, and where the dominant note, that is, the one on which the melody pivots, is just as modular as the final. The considerable difference that established in this respect the constitution of the authentic and plagal modes of plainchant in comparison to Greek music does not appear to have caught the attention of any music historian. For they have all stated the identity of the scales in the modes of either music without attaching importance to the difference in divisions. However, from an aesthetic point of view, these two conceptions of an identical tonality have had consequences that cannot be placed in the same category. I have already remarked that the character of Greek music consisted of the characteristics of accent and rhythm. With Christianity, the art took a new and more elevated direction. For the first time, a sublime feeling, drawn from the ethics of the Gospel, manifested itself in the chants of the Christians in strains that were in turn solemn, grateful, resigned, or pervaded by a sweet joy, and always inspired by that which is most pure in the heart of man. Now, the diversity of character, which resides in the structure of the modes of plainchant, provided the authors of Church chants the natural means of expression for all these feelings. The variety of forms of plainchant was without doubt established by feeling and thought. But its realization could happen only through the variety of tonal forms.

---

[53]The modern Greeks also recognize the existence of fourteen modes, which they distinguish as *authentic, plagal, medial and derived*. But they use them only in secular music, and in the Church, they allow only eight.

The careful examination of ecclesiastical chant leaves no doubt about the fortunate choice of modes used by those who composed it, with respect to the feeling expressed in the texts. One is equally struck by the peculiar qualities that the modes have to respond to these sentiments, each through its particular character, and through the position more or less solemn, more or less exalted which it occupies in the scale of sounds. To cite only a few examples, let us first examine the quality of sweet joy that reigns in all the chant of the Christmas celebration, composed largely in the most exalted modes of the scale, which are remarkably analogous to the major keys of modern music. The seventh mode, where the harmonic division is on the fifth note, because it is authentic, is the most frequently used. It is in this mode that the following chants are written: *Puer natus est nobis, Magnificat, Rex pacificus, Angelus ad pastores ait, Facta est cum Angelo, Redemptionem misit Dominus, Exortum est in tenebris,* etc. Most of the other chants are composed in the eighth mode. What peacefulness in the hymn *Jesu Redemptor omnium,* resulting not only from the beauty of the chant itself, but from the choice of its tonality and its authentic mode! What enthusiasm, blended with gratitude and veneration in the *Te Deum laudamus,* where the tonality supports so well the intentions of the composer! Let us compare the chant of this solemnity with that of Holy Week, and we will have clear proof of the power of tonality, for in the latter chant, the quality of melancholy, of profound sadness, is the product of the four first modes, analogous to the keys which we call *minor*. It is in these modes that the authors of the chant found distinctive accents with which to convey the sentiments of their souls. This conception of tonal properties for the expression of sentiments, so well felt and so well applied by the Christians of the first centuries, was, as has just been said, a new and great manifestation of the beautiful in art, because it is completely independent of the effects of rhythm. Nothing analogous had existed in antiquity, because the feelings that had impressed their special character upon the tonality of plainchant could have awakened in humanity only under the influence of the law of Christ.

The more we advance in the examination into which we are delving, the more it becomes evident that the specific forms of the series of sounds generally designated by the names *modes*, *scales*, and *genres*, are the immediate products of the dual activity of feeling and intellect of the human species. Instinct and the influence of circumstances may direct us without our knowledge in the modifications or transformations that we cause them to undergo. But barely do these modifications or transformations manifest themselves to our feeling, when the mind takes hold of them and organizes them in a systematic form. Then our aesthetic faculties develop in the domain of the new tonal order that is offered to them; and it is only after they have exhausted the resources of the new tonal order that the necessity for another transformation is sensed.

Although the tonality of the chant of the Churches of the Orient and the Occident were based on the same principle, it was not long before their melodic character became different, for the Oriental penchant for rapid movements of the voice, the quivering and ornaments of all kinds in practice, had penetrated even the chants of their Church, while in Italy and Gaul the taste for chant was generally much more simple. This resulted in considerable differences that are recorded in the books of the two Churches.

Presented here, in chronological order, is one of the most important transformations that art has experienced since ancient times. It is understood that it is a matter of the introduction, in music, of the simultaneous harmony of sounds, which, in the present state of things, appears inseparable, although all antiquity had ignored this principle, and even today most of the nations of the world are insensitive to it. The first efforts to use this harmony could not foreshadow what it later became, for they were in manifest opposition to the principle that, alone, may order the relations of tones, namely, tonal unity.

The earliest periods in the history of harmony are enveloped in darkness. Isidore, Bishop of Seville,[54] who lived in the seventh century, is the first author to speak of it in clear terms. He defines harmony as: *The modulation of the voice and the concordance of many sounds heard simultaneously*.[55] Between the Bishop of Seville, who died in 636, and the monk Hucbald, of Saint-Amand, who wrote in the last years of the ninth century, no information is found concerning the use of harmony in the Middle Ages. But we see in the *Treatise on Music* of the latter that at that time there were already many ways to harmonize the chant of the Church, and this harmonized chant was called *organum*. The work of Hucbald contains examples of these diverse systems. The first one, which applied to melodies of the authentic modes, was called *symphonie*. It consisted in accompanying the chant by a harmony in which the fifth of each of these notes could be heard, such that the same chant was heard in two different modes at once. A third voice called the *antiphonie* was usually joined to the *symphonie*, that is to say, at the octave above. In the plagal modes, the harmony consisted in accompanying the chant at the fourth of each note, which also caused the chant to be heard in two different modes at once. This harmony at the fourth was called *diaphonie*, to which an *antiphonie* could also be added.[56] But in general, the terms *symphonie* and *diaphonie* were given to this mixture of different modes, whether or not they were accompanied by doubling the chant at the octave.

---

[54]Saint Isidore of Seville (c.560-636). Spanish prelate and scholar, considered the most learned man of his time and last of the Latin fathers of the Western Church. Known particularly for his vast encyclopedia *Etymologiae*, which remained a popular reference work through the Middle Ages. [PL]

[55]Harmonica (musica) est modulatio vocis, et concordantia plurimorum sonorum et coapiatio. *Sentent, de musica,* c. 6.

[56]See my work on *les époques caractéristiques de la musique d'église*, in the *Revue de la musique religieuse* (v. III, 169-73).

The fifth, considered separately, is a harmonic interval, consonant, without attraction, and which, consequently, produces a feeling of harmonic repose almost as satisfying as the octave. The joining of these intervals is therefore an element of harmony that the Greeks knew well, but from which they were unable to take anything that would have led them to true harmony, because in their musical system, the other elements were lacking. They also considered the fourth to be a consonance, and truly it has this character, because it is generated by the fifth in the division of the octave. But it is less harmonious than the fifth, because it does not provide, like the latter, the feeling of harmonic repose. These intervals were admitted by the Greeks amongst the consonances, because only they could be formed with the stable chords of the two disjunct tetrachords that constituted the octave. These stable chords were the first, the fourth, the fifth, and the eighth of each octave species or of each mode. The second, third, sixth, and seventh chords, changeable on account of the enharmonic, chromatic and diatonic genres, were given a lower priority, and considered incapable of participating in the formation of consonances. From this arose the opinion that refused this quality to thirds and sixths in the ancient musical system of the Greeks, and which prevented them from being admitted amongst those that could form simultaneous harmony. It is this false doctrine, without any doubt, which was opposed to the conception of true harmony in the music of antiquity.

Once on this path, if the Greeks have used another music than the chant and the accompaniment at the unison and octave, they could only imagine an accompaniment either of the fifth or the fourth, and they could only realize it by accompanying one mode with another. This is of course destructive of all feeling of harmony in the sense of *good relations*, for, either tonal unity is a necessity of our organization, or it is not. In the first case, everything must contribute to this unity; in the second, there would be no modes strictly speaking, no scales, no relations good or bad between the tones. The *symphonie* and the *diaphonie,* that is, the successions of fifths or of fourths, which seem to be introduced into Greek music toward the period of decadence, are in effect dreadful in their erroneous relations. These are the same things that writers of the Middle Ages reproduce under the same names, and of which they have left examples.

It would be useless to search in these forms, supposedly harmonic, for some element that could lead to true harmony, that is, to successive aggregations of tones that might contribute to the tonal unity of melodies. However, Hucbald shows us that as early as the end of the ninth century, there was, independently of *symphonie* and *diaphonie,* a system of *organum*, where unison, the major third, the fourth and the fifth were in turn employed in the harmonization of chant, by successions of parallel or contrary movements of voices, of which he has provided examples.[57]

[57]Hucbaldi Musica Enchiriadis, c. xviii, ap. Gerberti *Script eccles. de Musica,* vol. I, 170.*

Where did this beginning of art come from, and how was the third introduced amongst the consonances? I have mentioned elsewhere the motives which led us to believe that the harmony of the third joined with the fifth originated in the northern regions of Europe,[58] and that it was imported by popular chants into Germany, Italy, Gaul, and Spain, by the invasions of peoples from the North in the fifth and sixth centuries. The tonal arrangement of old melodies still in use by these nations, the principles which governed the construction of the rustic instruments that accompanied these melodies, and the penchant which the Slavic peasants have for harmonizing in chorus on the thirds of certain notes of their simple chants, appear to be sufficient proof that it is from this source that the first element of harmony came, and from this part of music which has become in modern times so complete and so fine an art! This seed, deposited by the Gothic nations in the Southern and Western parts of Europe, in all likelihood passed from popular traditions to the *organum* of Church chant.

Be that as it may, we may conclude that at the end of the ninth century the idea of tonal harmony based on successions of diverse kinds of intervals was brought about and that it tended to further develop. The practice of *diaphonie* and *symphonie* did not disappear immediately. But the art slowly and progressively emerged from it and toward the end of the fourteenth century consonant and tonal harmony was definitively constructed in a regular manner that conformed to its diatonic nature.

Then a singular phenomenon appeared. For musicians seduced by the charms of harmony and by the plentitude of its chords directed all the resources of their talents toward the mechanical development of these forms, posing problems of combination of which the solution was not in the best interest of art, and forgetting that the simultaneous harmony of tones, when separated from melodic thought, is only a part of a whole in which only the totality may awaken in the soul and the mind the feeling and conception of beauty. Yet such is the influence of example and custom that for more than one hundred and fifty years, music, either religious or profane, had no other base than the chants of the Church, or the common melodies of popular songs, these being only a pretext for ingenious research into the art of grouping sounds. The subject, the object to be expressed, the feeling to be aroused, in accordance with the meaning of the words, were equally disdained by the authors of the harmonic combinations, the performers, and even the listeners. The mind was fixed on one thing, namely, the comprehension of the physical work and the attractiveness of its effect. We nevertheless remark that this direction, so opposed to the aesthetic object of music, led artists to the knowledge of a

---

*English translation by W. Rabb, ed. C. Palisca in *Hucbald, Guido, and John on Music: Three Medieval Treatises* (New Haven: Yale University Press, 1978). [PL]

[58]*Resumé philosophique de l'histoire de la musique,* in the introduction to the *Biographie universelle des musiciens,* vol. I, cxxxvi onward.

multitude of characteristics of the aggregations of tones, and that the art of writing harmony with elegance and purity, under given conditions, owed it the greatest progress.

Toward the middle of the sixteenth century, some men of genius, at the head of which were Clément Janequin [c.1485-1558] in France, and Palestrina in Italy, directed art onto a better path, by the distinct expression that they gave their compositions, with respect for the subject and for the sense of the words. Janequin's instinct took him toward comic expression, but a loftier sentiment manifests itself in the Church music and madrigals of Palestrina [c. 1525-1594]. The sweet calm of the tonality of plainchant supported his devout inspirations. No one grasped the spirit better or had put so much majesty, veneration and love into the chant of the prayer. The masses, the lamentations and the *Stabat Mater* of this artist, are the highest manifestation of Christian feeling, and the perfect ideal of the form analogous to this feeling is pushed to the sublime in some of his works. Palestrina's slightly younger compatriot, Luca Marenzio [1553-1599], attained in his madrigals for several voices no less remarkable perfection, through a fortunate expression of tender and sweet feelings. His melancholy genius experienced the need to open new paths to find more touching accents. But his efforts did not lead to what he was searching for because the diatonic tonality of plainchant does not contain the elements of this kind of ardent expression.

The great musicians of the fifthteenth century and of the first half of the sixteenth century had exhausted all the resources that this tonality could offer for the mechanical and conventional harmonic combinations of tones. And the artists did not conceal, at the end of the sixteenth century, that it would be difficult to attain the grandeur combined with the simplicity that one admires in the chant of the Church, the perfection of Palestrina's forms and style, and finally, the elegance, the grace tinged with sweetness and melancholy that lend their charm to the madrigals of Marenzio. Instinctively they were forewarned that the time of a necessary transformation had arrived. A vague restlessness was making itself felt in their attempts at innovation. But what principle must have directed them? This is what no one knew. Consonant harmony, the elements of which they found in the diatonic tonality of plainchant, was composed of relations of tones without tendencies, which caused the feeling of repose to remain in all harmonic successions. With respect to the dissonances that they introduced by artificial means, they were only the product of the retardation of one of the tones of a chord through the immediate prolongation of one of the tones of the preceding chord. Now when this device comes to an end the natural tone must then be heard. This device was only a means to vary the form, without consequences for the feeling of repose, inherent in the structure of the tonality.

As early as 1555, a learned Italian musician, Nicola Vicentino [1511-c.1576], had understood that the diatonic tonality did not contain the variety of accents needed by the art to enter down the path of new forms, and his meditations had led him to conclude that the introduction of the chromatic genre of the ancients into modern music was the only means of attaining this end. With great conviction he wrote a voluminous book in which he attempted, not only to establish the solidity of his system through theory, but where he applied it through examples.[59] Captivated by a doctrine that responded to the needs of their genius, Marenzio, the Venetian [Giovanni] Croce [1557-1609], and [Carlo] Gesualdo [1560-1613], prince of Venosa, sought to put it into practice in several of their works, published before 1590, and to draw new effects from it. But none of these men, endowed with distinguished talent, nor Vicentino, succeeded in making a synthesis of the chromatic scale in which the semitones have tendencies of resolution with a harmony that, by nature of its aggregations, is essentially diatonic and devoid of attraction. The incompatibility of these things are conspicuous in works where the above-mentioned celebrated artists tried to make foreign modes follow one another through the semitones of the chromatic scale, sounding on each tone the harmony of the consonant chord, the character of which is absolute repose. The labored impression, I would say almost painful, which successions of this genre cause one to experience come from the lack of logic perceived by the mind in the association of heterogeneous elements.

To produce the chromatic genre in harmony it was necessary to find the formula for an aggregation of tones, a chord that had the same character of attraction as the scale of semitones. The musical instinct of [Claudio] Monteverdi [1567-1643], an eminent Venetian composer, led him to this discovery in the final years of the sixteenth century. Before him all dissonance introduced in harmony had been, as we have already seen, only a device whereby a note of a chord, prolonged onto the following chord, caused a foreign note to be heard there, and retarded the hearing of the natural, or consonant note. But Monteverdi with no other guide than his inner feeling perceived the possibility of hearing as pleasurable a chord in which there would be a dissonance, independent of the prolongation, under certain conditions of which he himself was not clearly aware. To understand these conditions let us first point out that dissonance only occurs in the clash of two neighboring tones, which form the interval of a second, or by inversion the interval of a seventh, or finally, in doubling the second an octave higher which produces the interval of a ninth. Suppose now that a tone is accompanied by another, with which it forms the dissonance of a seventh. This dissonance, in order to be immediately heard, as a consonant harmony, must be grouped with the major third and perfect fifth. But such a harmonic combination can only exist with a scale arranged as follows: tone, tone, semitone, tone, tone, tone, semitone. And the fifth note of this scale is the only one that,

[59]*L'Antica musica ridotta alla moderna pratica*, etc. (Rome, 1555), trans. Rika Maniates as *Ancient Music Adapted to Modern Practice* (New Haven, Yale University Press, 1996).

through the arrangement of tones, may be harmonized with the major third, the perfect fifth, and the minor seventh, such as G-B-D-F. Now, the note that forms the major third (B) against the fifth (G) is the seventh of the scale. It is separated from the eighth only by a semitone, and the dissonance of the seventh (F) is formed by the fourth note, which is separated from the third by a semitone. These two notes (B, F), placed in contact, form an attractive harmony that can only satisfy the musical sensibility and the understanding by the resolution of these same notes to those separated from them by only a semitone, as B followed by C, and F followed by E. This happens in such a way that the seventh note ascends to the eighth, and the fourth note descends to the third, and the attractive tendency of the two notes is satisfied in drawing them towards each other.

In order to construct all the scales such that the two semitones occur between the third and fourth notes, and the seventh and eighth notes, while all the other notes are a tone apart, the diatonic scale is insufficient, for it does not provide all the notes which can fulfill these conditions. One must therefore have recourse to the chromatic scale of semitones, and borrow from it the notes that are needed to construct all the scales following the model of C, D, E, F, G, A, B, C. Suppose, for example, that D is the first note of the scale. In order to place the third note at the interval of a semitone from the fourth, F must be replaced by a higher tone called F-sharp in the language of musicians. And in order for the eighth note to be a semitone from the seventh note, C must be replaced another note a semitone higher, commonly called C-sharp. By means of these transformations, the scale of D will be constructed exactly like the scale of C, that is to say, tone, tone, semitone, tone, tone, tone, semitone. If the scale has F for its first note, there will be a tone between the first and second notes, a tone between the second and third, and finally a tone between the third and fourth. The latter note will therefore be a semitone too high, and this note (B) must be replaced by another note a semitone lower, taken from the chromatic scale, called B-flat. This done, the rest of the scale is as it should be, for, from the B-flat to the fifth note there is a tone, from the fifth to the sixth, a tone, from the sixth to the seventh, a tone, and from the seventh to the eighth, a semitone.

If all the scales of the tonality generated by the natural dissonant chord are uniform in their construction, all, however, have two modes, which are called *major* and *minor*. The arrangement that has just been explained is that of the major mode. In the minor mode, the scales have the first semitone placed between the second and third notes, and the second semitone between the fifth and sixth notes, so that two semitones are found within the first six notes of the scale, while in the major scale they are found within the compass of the octave. But the dissonant chord, being placed on the fifth note in this mode, as in the major, can only be realized when the third above this note is major; now, this is possible only if the seventh note is raised a semitone. As a result, the seventh note is separated from the eighth by only a semitone, as in the major mode. There are in fact therefore three semitones in the minor mode of each scale, where the ascending and descending elements may be arranged in the following pattern:

Ascending — A, B, C, D, E, F, | Descending — E, D, C, B, A, | Ascending — G-sharp, A.

The attraction of the natural dissonant harmony renders obligatory the ascending resolution of the semitone between the seventh and eighth notes. The euphony of pitch and the requirements of the diatonic genre, which cannot admit an interval larger than a tone between two neighboring notes, lead to also raising the sixth degree by a semitone in the scale of the ascending mode. The form of this scale is the following:

A, B, C, D, E, F-sharp, G-sharp, A.

But the harmonic attraction does not exist in the descending scale. The semitone from the seventh to the eighth note is removed, and the semitone characteristic of the fifth to the sixth notes is reestablished. The form of the scale is thus as follows:

A, G, F, E, D, C, B, A.

Note that the harmonic attractions of semitones form the tender, melancholy, and passionate accents of music. Now, in the minor mode there are two such attractions, one between the fourth degree and the seventh in the ascending scale, and another between the second degree and the sixth. Thus the tonality of the minor mode is particularly suited to the expression of the feelings in question.[60]

Such is the system of tonality to which the unexpected introduction of natural dissonant harmony in art gave birth. Let us take a quick glance at the very considerable consequences of Monteverdi's discovery.

(1) In its broadest conception, the tonality of plainchant had fourteen modes or scales, of which only twelve had been employed. Through

[60]Through a coincidence very worthy of attention, all nations both ancient and modern have expressed, in their national songs, their customary tendencies for sadness or joy, through the character of the tonality that they used. The free nations, those that enjoy without constraint the fruits of their labour, compose their popular songs in the major mode. In looking over the collections of songs of this type that belong to the countries of Gaul, of ancient Ireland, of Switzerland, of the Tyrol, one notices that their tonality, although often uncommon, is analogous to the major mode. But enslaved peoples drained of their original energy generally express in their songs a feeling of melancholy and sadness that is characterized by a mode of minor tonality. This is the tonality of most of the popular songs of the Slavic peoples of Russia, Gallicia, Poland, and the peasants of part of Silesia. An exception must be made of the Bohemians, where the songs are almost always in the major mode, because slavery in all rights did not weigh upon them.

transposition of the chants of the ninth mode to the first, the tenth to the second, the thirteenth to the fifth, and the fourteenth to the sixth, the number of modes and scales had been reduced to eight. Under these circumstances, the tonality of plainchant generates itself, and all the scales differ according to the placement of the semitones. This is not the case in the new tonality created by natural dissonant harmony. For although the form of these scales is diatonic, this tonality allies itself with the chromatic scale and borrows from it the means to transform tones into semitones, and semitones into tones, for the uniformity of its scales. The diatonic genre also allies itself with the chromatic scale by taking for the first note of its scales each of the semitones of this chromatic scale. But the chromatic scale has a double tendency that coincides with the attractions of dissonant harmony; one ascending through *sharped* tones, the other descending through *flatted* tones. Now, all diatonic scales necessarily having seven different notes, seeing that the eighth is only the doubling of the first at the octave, it follows that the tones contained within the compass of the octave number twenty-one, of which seven are independent of sharps or flats, seven are sharp, and seven flat. Each of these tones may be the first of a diatonic scale constructed according to the scale C, D, E, F, G, A, B, C. Consequently, there are twenty-one similar scales. On the other hand, each scale has two modes, one major, the other minor. The number of scales or tonalities is therefore in fact increased to forty-two.[61]

(2) Consonant harmony, the only kind that was able to exist in the tonality of plainchant, did not provide a means for introducing *modulation* into music, that is to say, to relate keys to each other. This is because, conforming with the tonality from which consonant harmony derived its principle, it was without tendency or attraction, and consequently constituted music that was *unitonic*. Through the discovery of natural dissonant harmony, which is essentially attractive, Monteverdi, having related the diatonic and chromatic scales, found the means of transition from one scale to another. *Modulation* came into existence, and in this way music passed from the unitonic order into the *transitonic* order.

(3) Through this innovation, the nature of the art was changed, and the transformation was complete. For the accent which is expressive, passionate, dramatic, is inseparable from the attraction of tones, and cannot exist without it. Unitonic tonality and harmony, excellent for the expression of pious sentiments, for impressing upon the soul sweet and calm affections, and finally to give the music of the Church a solemn and majestic character, were, by their very nature, incapable of arousing impassioned emotions. On the other hand, the attractive harmony and new tonality found themselves suddenly richly empowered with the qualities

[61]Musical language is deficient in having only one word for two very different things, one being the interval between two sounds, the other the form of a scale. It is to the latter that the noun *tonality* applies.

that were lacking in ancient music. But it was feared that, issuing from their special domain, that is to say the expression of passions, the tendencies of the new art would break into religious music, and change the nature of its character. This was, in fact, what happened. Barely had the artists been in possession of the emotional accent, when musical drama was invented. The old concert music, so calm and full of meticulous harmonies, the genre of madrigal arranged for four, five, or six voices, were succeeded by airs for solo voice or duets, in which feelings and words were obviously the focus of what the musicians intended to express. Uncertain of what they should call these new forms of compositions, they conceived bizarre names, such as *Scherzi amorosi*, *Grazie ed affetti*, *Nuove musiche*, and many other similar names. A little later the *cantata* emerged, a kind of small monologue drama. The song for solo voice, accompanied by one or many instruments, had replaced the ensemble of many voices. The feeling (*sentiment*), moved by harmonic attraction, had experienced new joys in the variety of sonorities that combined in the mixture of instruments. Monteverdi, who was the great innovator of this era, did not only discover natural dissonant harmony, the source of all these novelties, for he was the first to have given dramatic expression to the recitative, a good example of which can be seen in the *Battle of Tancredi and Clorinda*, in the words: *Amico*; *hai vinto, io ti perdona*. He was really the first to express true emotion in his airs, which he distinguished from recitative in a clearer manner than other composers of his time. Nothing, in fact, is more touching than Arianna's sorrowful melody (*Lasciate mi morire*), in *Theseus*.[62] Finally, Monteverdi demonstrated, considering the times in which he lived, a prodigious understanding of the use of the resources of orchestration, to increase the expression of the song.[63]

In these transformations, everything was a conquest. But the desire to innovate in all aspects of the art had taken over the spirit of artists. It led them astray when they wanted the aesthetic feeling of religious music to be modified by the consequences of natural dissonant harmony and its tonality. For, just as the tonality of plainchant is powerless to express the passions, so the passionate character of the tonality of modern harmony is antipathetic to religious feeling. We have just seen that with the latter were born dramatic forms and elaborate effects of instrumentation. Now, all this was gradually introduced into the music of the Church, from which Christian and Catholic fervor were imperceptibly banished to make way for worldly accents.

---

[62]Fétis here refers to Monteverdi's lost opera *L'Arianna*, of which only the famous *Arianna's Lament* survives, both as a solo song and as a madrigal. [PL]

[63]Many people, including Alexander Oliïbïcshev [1794-1858], author of a *New Biography of Mozart*, (Moscow, 1843), 3 vols., have objected to me that Palestrina and other composers who preceded Monteverdi, used the chord of the dissonant seventh before him. Concerning this, see Note A at the end of this volume.

We touch upon one of the most remarkable mysteries, one of the most delicate, most unique in the theory of music. I entreat the reader to accord me his complete attention. After the great tonal transformation that was brought about by dissonant harmony, which has just been analyzed, it was believed that the art would henceforth take all its harmonic creations from the relations between sounds that were established by this great revolution. The entire seventeenth century, and the first half of the eighteenth in fact only gave birth to compositions conceived under the influence of this tonal order. But, a little later, there were musicians who, guided by their instinct, as Monteverdi had been, recognized that if the attraction of two notes of the same scale was able to place in relation two different keys, the attraction of notes which belonged to diverse scales would establish multiple relationships between keys, and that these relationships would result in more abundant expressive accents. A new kind of emotions, moreover, must have resulted from harmonic associations of unrelated keys. For tonal unity, which is the law of all music, does not permit two keys or two modes to be perceived at the same time by musical feeling and understanding. The association can only take place in their succession, when the raised tone of a scale, for example, may be taken for the non-raised tone of another scale, and where its true character only manifests itself at the moment of resolution. Suppose, to further clarify, that there are joined in a single harmonic aggregation the two attractions of the minor mode, namely, the seventh note raised a semitone with the fourth, and the second note with the sixth, such that the association is: G-sharp-B-D-F. The natural resolution of this chord would be the perfect chord of the tonic of the mode A-C-E, for the tendencies of the double attraction lead it there. One sees that the dissonant chord and the one that resolves its attractions contain all the notes of the scale. But if, at the moment of succession, the note F changes to E-sharp, which only differs by the minimal interval of a ninth of a tone (a difference which disappears in the chord of keyboard instruments through a procedure called *temperament*), the E-sharp, instead of having a descending tendency, like F, will have a tendency to ascend toward the F-sharp. Now, a scale in which E-sharp and F-sharp are components, can only have F-sharp as the tonic, so that the resolution of the dissonant chord occurs in the major or minor modes of this scale, and that two totally foreign keys will have been placed in contact by the single fact of the enharmonic tonality of one of the notes of the dissonant chord.

We now see what would happen if, at the moment of the resolution of the chord of G-sharp-B-D-F, the G-sharp were changed to A-flat, which differs only by a ninth of a tone. A-flat, through an attraction opposite to that of G-sharp, will be called to descend towards G, and through this change of tendency, the note D will take on an attractive character toward E-flat, while B preserves its tendency toward C. The resolution of the chord, by the single act of changing enharmonically the G-sharp to A-flat, will therefore occur on the consonant chord of G-C-E-flat, and the scale of C-minor, will follow immediately that of A-minor.

Finally, if at the moment when G-sharp changes to A-flat, B changes to C-flat, which only differs from it by a minimal interval of about a ninth of a tone, the attractive tendency of this C-flat, instead of ascending toward C, will descend toward B-flat, while the other notes will preserve their tendencies as in the preceding transformation, so that the resolution of the chord thus transformed or modified will be made on the consonant chord of G-B-flat-E-flat-G, and that the scale of E-flat major will follow that of A-minor.

From these remarkable harmonic transformations springs a new order of development in tonality, in which many scales are placed in contact through a single chord. I call this the *pluritonic* order. It introduces, amongst the emotions excited by music, the effect of surprise, through unexpected successions of chords, which not only affect the sensibility in a very vivid manner, but also bring to the mind the satisfaction of grasping and analyzing instantaneously the principle of transformation of the relations between keys.

Once engaged on this path, the art developed accordingly and arrived at the final limit of the problem of the attraction of tones, which may be set forth as follows: *To find harmonic formulas such that a single note, (that is to say, a definite given tone), may be placed in immediate relationship with all the scales of the two modes*. Without dwelling on the problem, some celebrated musicians of recent times, amongst whom one notices Mozart, Beethoven and Rossini, have instinctively resolved it in particular cases. In the fourth part of this work, I have treated the question in a general manner, and I believe exhaustively. Let us point out the principle that leads to the solution of the problem.

In harmonic aggregations, all association of tones that, without betraying the feeling of the prevailing tonality, establishes tendencies towards other tonalities is normal. This principle, by virtue of which natural dissonant harmony has become prominent in the art, and which has made possible the harmonic transformations of which I have just spoken, sufficiently justifies, with respect to the feeling and the intellect, the replacement of certain natural notes in a scale, in consonant and dissonant chords, with notes borrowed from other keys. This operation is known in schools as *alteration*. In ordinary application, the alteration consists only of an attractive accent of a semitone that does not lead into the scale from which it was borrowed, but which resolves as would the natural note whose place it has taken. Yet the tendency of a note borrowed from a scale nonetheless exists towards that scale, and the natural resolution of the chord may, by means of such a foreign note, be diverted from its destination. If the alterations of this chord are numerous, some will be attracted upwards, others downwards. In this case, the possibilities for diverse resolutions will multiply according to the manner of aggregation.

In these combinations, the will of the composer solely determines the choice of the attraction that will prevail over others. But a remarkable phenomenon is produced in the soul of the well-organized performer, whose vocal or instrumental part of a harmonic ensemble has the attractive note that determines the resolution and dominates the other parts. For if the note is ascending, the artist instinctively raises the intonation to render the resolution more perceptible. Conversely, he lowers it as much as possible when the attraction is descending, if it is the note that brings about the resolution of the chord. In these peculiar tonal fluctuations, the variations in intonation sometimes exceed a sixth of a tone, according to repeated experiments that I have done with Scheibler's instrument.[64] The multiplicity of alterations resulting from a chord modified by collective alterations, permit this chord, as I have demonstrated during the course of this work, to be placed in tonal relation with all the scales in both modes. Thus it is evident that the music has, through harmony, entered the final order of tonality that I call *omnitonic*. Tonal unity always exists at the moment when the chord is heard, because the mind grasps perfectly the connections between the altered tones, and the sensibility, far from being offended, receives from it distinct pleasure. But the affinities of the chord, thus altered with all the scales, only manifest themselves at the moment when one of these resolutions is heard. Now the uncertainty disappears, and this succession of chords and tonalities which has remained the secret of the artist up to the moment it is heard, causes a feeling of surprise mixed with pleasing sensibility on the one hand, and on the other, satisfies the intellect, which immediately grasps all the points of contact through which the tonal transformation has taken place. Having arrived at this point of transfusion of scales, the art realizes in its most complete sense the unity within variety and the variety within unity. It is quite free to remain within the absolute unity of tonality, if the aesthetic feeling of the music must be calm, sweet or religious. If it requires transition, it can be found in natural dissonant harmony, free from any alteration. But if the simple modulation does not suffice, and a more powerful shock is required, through the effect of an unexpected change in tonality, pluritonic enharmony provides the means. Finally, if ardent passions must be aroused, or the expression of feelings of profound melancholy is desired, the omnitonic order opens up infinite resources.

If we now glance at the diversity of conceptions of tonality, from the most distant antiquity to the present day, we will see with astonishment the art beginning with enharmony, gradually arriving at diatonic tonality, then, by means of harmony, returning, through the transition of scales, to the small attractive intervals, without which the strong tendencies of scales toward each other could not manifest themselves, and satisfy either the feeling or the intellect.

---

[64]Johann Heinrich Scheibler (1777-1837) developed an instrument called a tonometer with which he was able to demonstrate different approaches to equal temperament. [PL]

Such is the history of tonalities, to which is intimately linked that of harmony, a history long neglected by musicians, but which alone can guide the theorist in his search for a complete and rational theory of harmony. In vain, men distinguished by real merit have deluded themselves that they had arrived at a formulation of a similar system by other paths. In vain they have outlined various routes. In vain have they called to their aid mathematical calculations, physics experiments, the particular properties of various aggregations of sounds and all the most daring resources of the imagination. The history of their efforts is only that of their errors. The fourth part of this work provides information and analyses concerning this subject for which one would search elsewhere in vain and gives the most clear demonstration of the inability of the human mind to found a theory of the science of harmony upon other premises than that of the art, namely, the laws of tonality and its transformations; for tonality is music in its entirety according to its harmonic and melodic attributes.

Anyone reading this preface with care will easily understand how my work is completely different from all those that have been published on the same subject. Instead of establishing *a priori* rules taken from subjects foreign to the art in order to subdue it, I have begun from the art itself in order to deduce the theory. The fine reception given to my book appears to have justified my enterprise so far. But it yet needs to be subjected to the test of time, which alone is decisive. For other systems have also obtained brilliant success at first, only to fall later into discredit. Fully confident in the principle that has guided me, I will await this final test, of which others apart from myself will be called upon to ascertain the results.

The Author.

Brussels, January 13, 1849.

TREATISE

ON THE THEORY AND PRACTICE OF

HARMONY

INTRODUCTION

THE PURPOSE OF HARMONY AS ART AND SCIENCE

1. Music is the product of the successive and simultaneous combinations of sounds.

Successive combinations of tones are designated by the term *melody*; simultaneous combinations, by that of *harmony* in general, and by that of *chords* in particular.

EXAMPLES

2. Tones heard successively or simultaneously are in certain relationships. The purpose of art is to arrange tones into relationships that develop feelings and ideas that are more or less striking, more or less grand, more or less pleasing, more or less able to fulfill the views of the artist; to discover the laws of these relationships is the purpose of science.

Harmony, therefore, is both an art and a science.

3. There must be a succession between groups of tones or chords that make up the harmony; now, the consideration of the relationships of each group on its own would not serve to uncover those of the successive order: these are thus one of the elements of the art and science of harmony.

4. If the laws of the relationships of harmonic succession were different from those of melodic succession, the effect of the harmony would spoil the melody, and one could not accompany the other: the laws of harmony and melody are therefore identical with respect to succession.

5. All laws of relation are expressed in one way or another: in modern music the formula for the melodic and harmonic law of succession resides in the major and minor modes of the scale.

The scale is both the rule of the order (*règle de l'ordre*)[1] of the succession of tones, because they have the closest affinities, and is the measure of distances that separate them.[2]

6. The results of the harmonic and melodic affinities of the major and minor scales give the successions of each genre a quality of necessity that is generally designated by the term *tonality*.

7. The order of the tones of the scale is so well determined by the nature of the mode, that this being given, there is no doubt for an experienced ear about the degree of the scale to which each tone belongs, nor about the normal succession of tones on all degrees.

8. The degrees of the scale are called by names, some of which indicate the melodic or harmonic character of the tones that constitute it.

Thus the first note of the scale of any given key is called the *tonic,* because it gives its name to the key; the second is called the *second degree* (and, in the language of some early harmonists, the *supertonic*); the third, the *third degree* (formerly the *mediant*, because it is midway between the first tone and the fifth in the chord which is called *perfect*); the fourth, the *fourth degree* (formerly the *subdominant*); the fifth, *dominant*, because it is found in a great number of harmonic combinations; the sixth, the *sixth degree* (formerly the *superdominant*); the seventh, the *leading tone (note sensible)*, when it has a tendency to ascend towards the tonic, and *seventh degree* in other cases.

TABLE

DEGREES OF THE SCALE IN C IN THE MAJOR AND MINOR MODES

MAJOR MODE

Tonic — Second degree — Third degree — Fourth degree

Dominant — Sixth degree — Leading tone — Tonic

[1]Fétis describes here what is generally known as the *règle de l'octave*. [PL]

[2]I do not feel I must explain here what the term scale means, for this belongs to the elementary study of music, knowledge of which is assumed of all who would commit themselves to the study harmony.

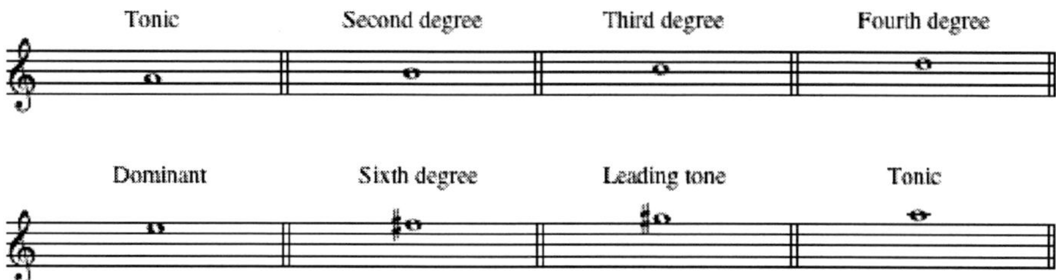

The sixth and seventh notes of the descending minor scale, having other affinities than in the ascending scale, are lowered by a semitone.

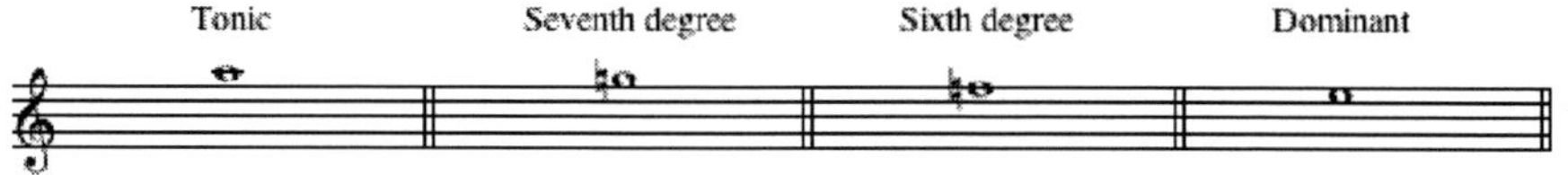

9. Each tone of a scale, having a particular character, and fulfilling a special function in the music, is accompanied by a harmony in keeping with this character and function. The collection of harmonies belonging to each degree of the scale determines the tonality.

To give one of the tones of the scale another harmony than what is intended by the nature of this tonality would be betraying the very objective of the harmony and offending the musical sense (*sens musicale*), which can be satisfied only by the logical use of chords.

10. Harmonic combinations that conform to the conditions of the tonality of a scale are said to be *natural*.

Those that join the elements of several scales into a single group are said to be altered.

11. Natural harmonies often present themselves with modifications that change their direction. These modifications are of two kinds, namely: those that do not alter the character of the affinity of the natural notes of the chords, and those that establish new affinities. In the first case, they do not change the tonality and serve only to introduce variety into unity; in the second, they give rise to *modulation*, that is, the passing from one scale to another.

12. Consequently, the art of harmony consists of: (1) accompanying each note of the scale of a key by natural or modified harmonies that belong to it, and in practicing the succession of these harmonies, according to certain laws that will be set forth in this book; (2) creating a succession of harmonies in one key to harmonies of another through modulation, in which the laws are derived from the affinities that will also be explained.

Any given harmonic combination is necessarily contained in these two operations.

13. It follows as well from the above that the science of harmony consists of: (1) finding in individual harmonies the elements of which they are composed, and the origins of the aggregations of these elements; (2) discovering and expounding the laws of affinity that determine the characteristics of tonality; (3) establishing the laws of succession, in keeping with these affinities.

All science that is real and free from hypothesis is contained in these conditions.

14. The purpose of this book is to set forth both the artistic processes and the scientific facts.

BOOK ONE

THE RELATIONSHIPS OF TONES, OR OF INTERVALS CONSIDERED AS ELEMENTS OF HARMONY

Chapter I

THE NATURE AND NAMES OF INTERVALS

15. The difference in pitch between two tones establishes between them a relationship to which one gives, in general, the name *interval*, because this difference is measured by the position where each of the two tones is found on the monochord.

16. In measuring an interval, the point of departure is always the lowest tone: the distance from the lower to the higher sound is the name of the interval.

17. The smallest measurable distance that is admitted by harmony is the *semitone*:[1] this interval is found, for example, between the tones C and D-flat. It is called a *minor second*; the *major second* is composed of a tone or two semitones; the *minor third* consists of a tone and a half; the *major third,* two tones; the *perfect fourth* (*quarte juste*), two tones and a half; the *major fourth*, three tones: this interval is sometimes called the *tritone*, because of the number of tones of which it is composed;[2] the minor fifth (*quinte mineure*) contains two tones and two semitones;[3] the perfect fifth (*quinte juste*), three tones and a half, the *minor sixth*, three tones and two semitones; the *major sixth*, four tones and a half; the *minor seventh*, four tones and two semitones; the *major seventh*, five tones and a half; the *octave*, five tones and two semitones.

---

[1]I do not mention here the difference in major and minor semitones, because it is of no use in the theory of harmony.

[2]One must not confuse the meaning of the word *tritone*, as it is here used, with that of the chord of three tones, also called the *tritone* by certain German scholars, because a defined sound is called *tone* in the German language, while it is called *note* in the language of French musicians.

[3]I say here *two tones and two semitones*, instead of the simpler expression of *three tones*, because the minor fifth is found between the leading tone and the fourth degree, and the two semitones are separated.

Although the intervals that exceed the limits of the octave are only the repetition at one, two, or three octaves above, etc., of those which are contained in the first octave, one counts, for reasons that will be explained later, the *minor ninth*, composed of five tones and three semitones, and the *major ninth*, formed by six tones and two semitones, as distinct intervals, although in fact their constitution resembles that of the minor and major seconds.

TABLE

NATURAL INTERVALS IN THE MAJOR AND MINOR MODES

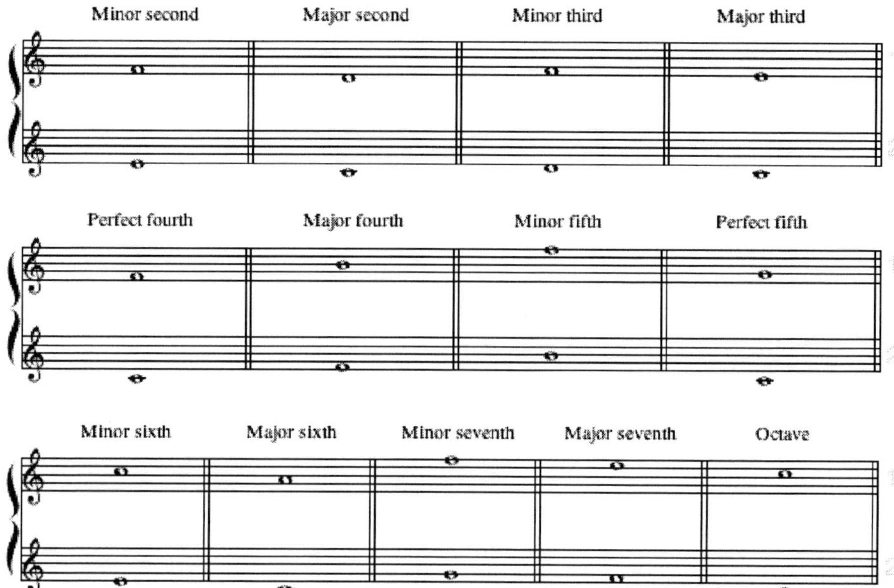

18. Sometimes the natural intervals of a key and of a mode are altered through the imagination of the composer, who seeks in these momentary alterations accents that are more expressive than those of the natural intervals.

19. The adjectives *diminished* or *augmented* are added to the names of the altered intervals, according to whether the alteration contracts or expands the natural interval; thus, one says a *diminished third*, or an *augmented fifth*.[4]

The diminished interval is always a semitone smaller than the minor interval of the same name; the augmented interval is always a semitone larger than the major interval of the same name.

20. The alterations connect tones that are naturally foreign to one another.

[4]The French harmonists of the eighteenth century gave the augmented intervals the term *superfluous* (*superflus*). This expression has no rational meaning, and may give rise to false interpretations. There can be nothing superfluous in an art.

A foreign relationship of tones happens when the notes that form the altered interval have accidentals that cannot be found together in a given key. For example, the *diminished third*

is made up of the two notes D-sharp and F-natural, which cannot exist in any key simultaneously, for in all the keys in which D-sharp is found, F is also sharp. Thus, the *augmented sixth*

places in relation two tones foreign to each other, for no key contains both E-flat and C-sharp.

TABLE[5]

ALTERED INTERVALS ADMISSIBLE IN HARMONY, TAKING THE KEY OF C.[6]

Augmented second	Diminished third	Augmented third	Diminished fourth	Augmented fifth*
Diminished sixth	Augmented sixth	Diminished seventh**	Diminished octave	Augmented octave

21. Considered alone, many altered intervals offend the ear, because it cannot understand their tonal relationship; but in succession, these relationships establish themselves with respect to the hearing in a perceptible and logical manner.

---

[5]Catel introduced into the nomenclature the term *diminished fifth* (*) for the fifth on the seventh degree of the scale: he should have called it the *minor fifth*; for there is nothing diminished about an interval where the two notes are in a natural state in the key.

[6]The *augmented second* and the *diminished seventh* (**) are alterations only in the major mode; for in the minor mode, they are made up of the leading tone and the sixth degree of this mode.

The *augmented seventh* does not figure in this table, because this alteration, converging with the octave, cannot be used, since it needs to be resolved on the latter interval.

Chapter II

CONSONANCES AND DISSONANCES; CLASSIFICATION OF INTERVALS IN THESE TWO ORDERS OF HARMONY

22. Certain intervals immediately please the ear, because their essence grasps the spirit of a perfect connection with tonality, and at the same time develops in us a feeling of repose or a sense of completion: these intervals are the *fifth* and the *octave*. They are called *perfect consonances*, that is to say, *consonances of conclusion*.

The *unison* is also a *perfect consonance*, because it is the result of identical tones; but it is clearly not an interval.

23. Other intervals please us also through the harmonic and tonal relations of their constituent tones. They determine the mode by their major or minor quality: these intervals are the *thirds* and *sixths*. They are called *imperfect consonances*, because they do not give a feeling of repose.[7] The lack of a sense of completion is particularly noted with the sixth. It is possible that in the composer's mind, and in order to leave a certain sense of indefiniteness in the spirit, the conclusion of a phrase, or even of a piece of music, is made with the third, particularly a major third: but one may never finish with a sixth on the principal note of the key, that is, on the first note of the scale, because the ear desires a more definite conclusion.

24. The fourth has been the object of long disagreements and lively debates among harmonists. Considered first as an excellent consonance, it then gave rise to misgivings that have been debated in specialized books. But from the second part of the fifteenth century, musicians have treated it as a dissonance, and this usage continued until the beginning of the eighteenth century. Then, through a remarkable error, the origin of which will be explained later, it was believed that in certain cases it is a consonance, and in others a dissonance.

In fact, the perfect fourth is a consonance, because it is not in itself subject to be resolved like the dissonances; but it is not a perfect consonance, for nothing gives less feeling of repose and sense of completion than this interval. Neither is it an imperfect consonance, such as thirds and sixths, for it is invariable in the two modes: it is a mixed consonance, the use of which is limited to a small number of cases that are indicated in the second book of this work.

25. Harmonists have been no less hampered, up to the present time, in determining the nature of the major fourth and the minor fifth. The

[7]Harmonists have given a quite ridiculous explanation of the term *imperfect consonance*, in saying that they are so called because they may be major or minor without ceasing to be consonant, while the perfect consonances have only one mode. As if there were greater imperfection in characterizing the mode than the key!

majority has called them dissonances, but without being able to deny that these dissonances are of another kind than those of which we shall shortly speak. Their error arose from the fact that the fourth degree, which enters into the composition of these intervals, is in fact in a state of dissonance in certain chords through its contact with the dominant; but this circumstance is foreign to the very nature of the major fourth and the minor fifth. The use of these intervals, in chords where this contact does not exist, is a source of contradictions and reservations for these same harmonists.

It is of note that these intervals characterize modern tonality by the dynamic tendencies of their two constituent notes, the leading tone, which calls for the tonic to follow, and the fourth degree, usually followed by the third. Now, this characteristic, eminently tonal, cannot constitute a state of dissonance: in fact, the major fourth and minor fifth are used as consonances in many harmonic successions.

The major fourth and the minor fifth are therefore consonances, but consonances of a particular kind, which I designate by the term *appellative consonances*.

TABLE

OF CONSONANT INTERVALS

Perfect consonances — Imperfect consonances

Octave | Perfect fifth | Major third | Minor third | Major sixth | Minor sixth

Mixed consonance — Appellative consonances

Perfect fourth | Major fourth | Minor fifth

26. There are intervals that, while conforming to the unity of the key, are not pleasing in themselves and satisfy the musical sense (*sens musicale*) only through their connection with consonances: they are called *dissonances*.

27. Two notes are dissonant because they are adjacent, either directly or indirectly. Thus, the notes C and D in whatever position they are found, form a dissonance. If the clash is direct and immediate, such as,

these two notes form a dissonance of a second. If the clash is inverted, that is, if D is the lower note and C the higher, such as,

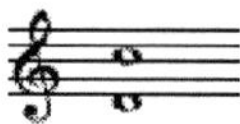

the interval is the dissonance of a *seventh*. Finally, if the clash is direct, but mediate, that is to say, if C is the lower note and if D is in a higher octave, such as,

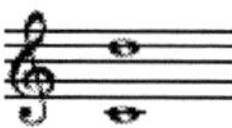

the interval is a dissonance of a *ninth*.

The *second*, *seventh*, and *ninth* are thus dissonances that have a major or minor quality according to whether the two notes that form the interval are closer together or farther apart by an interval of a tone or a semitone.

28. There is a question that has never been examined or resolved in a scientific manner, namely: what is the nature of altered intervals? To resolve this, it is important to remember that the purest state of pleasure for the musical sense resides in a perfect relationship of tonality between sounds, and that sensual pleasures found outside this condition result from restlessness, passionate impulses, and nervous outbursts, expressed by the contact of diverse tonalities and by the alternations of dissonances and consonances. Thus, for the musical sense, the sensation of consonance exists only in tonal unity, from which it follows that altered intervals are dissonances, but dissonances of a particular kind, which I believe must be designated by the term *attractive*.

What proves that most of these intervals have a dissonant quality only because their constituent notes have different tonal tendencies, which cause a kind of anxiety in the musical sense until the resolution, is that the ear finds the tones that enter into their construction to be synonymous with other tones, which, combined in a similar way, but having solely tonal tendencies, are true consonances. For example, the *augmented second,*

would sound to the ear like a *minor third,*

if the succession of harmonies did not hint at various types of resolution, which throw the mind into uncertainty until one of these resolutions occurs. The same with the augmented fifth,

which would give the sensation of a *minor sixth,*

if the tendencies of the different tonalities did not give it a dissonant character.

The altered intervals are thus dissonances that I refer to as being *variably attractive*, because they have tendencies toward different tonalities.[8] The dissonances of this kind are: (1) the *augmented second*, (2) the *diminished third*, (3) the *augmented third*, (4) the *diminished fourth*, (5) the *augmented fifth*, (6) the *augmented sixth*, (7) the *diminished seventh*, (8) the *diminished octave*, (9) the *augmented octave*.

TABLE OF DISSONANT INTERVALS

Tonal dissonances

Minor second — Major second — Minor seventh — Major seventh

Minor ninth — Major ninth

Variable attractive dissonances

Augmented second — Diminished third

Augmented third — Diminished fourth — Augmented fifth — Augmented sixth

Diminished seventh — Diminished octave — Augmented octave

[8]The classification of intervals contained in this chapter is very different, on many points, from ordinary classifications: it may cause surprise among harmonists. I myself was unable to make up my mind on this subject, until the law of tonality, having opened to me a treasure of undeniable theories, revealed to me the secret of all harmonic combinations.

Chapter III

THE INVERSION OF INTERVALS

29. The general scale of tones shows that they are arranged in an identical order from octave to octave, rising by degrees from low to high. Now, a note (considered as a determined *tone*), taken as the midpoint between two others an octave apart, and of the same denomination, forms, with respect to one and the other, different intervals. For example, G taken as the midpoint between low and high C, is the fifth of the first note, and the fourth of the second.

DEMONSTRATION

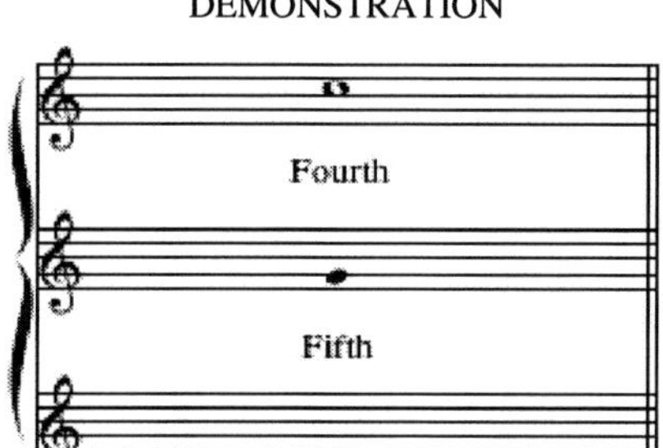

30. This granted, if we consider C and G in the abstract, that is, without making a distinction between the octaves, we see that these notes may be in different positions with respect to each other. This change in position of two given notes, by the transposition of one of them to another octave, is called *inversion of intervals*.

31. All the intervals between tones may be inverted. The inversion of the *second* produces the *seventh*; that of the *third*, a *sixth*; that of the *fourth*, a *fifth*; that of the *fifth*, a *fourth*; that of the *sixth*, a *third*, that of the *seventh*, a *second*.

32. Thus the inversion of consonances produces consonances, and that of dissonances generates dissonances.

33. But major intervals produce minor intervals through inversion, and *vice versa*.

Likewise, augmented intervals produce diminished intervals through inversion, and diminished intervals produce augmented ones.

34. It will be seen later that the inversion of intervals is a fruitful source of variety in harmony.

TABLE

OF THE INVERSION OF ALL INTERVALS

Major seventh	Minor seventh	Diminished seventh	Augmented sixth	Major sixth	Minor sixth	Diminished sixth
Minor second	Major second	Augmented second	Diminished third	Minor third	Major third	Augmented third

Augmented fifth	Perfect fifth	Minor fifth	Major fourth	Perfect fourth	Diminished fourth	Augmented third
Diminished fourth	Perfect fourth	Major fourth	Minor fifth	Perfect fifth	Augmented fifth	Diminished sixth

Major third	Minor third	Diminished third	Augmented second	Major second	Minor second	Unison
Minor sixth	Major sixth	Augmented sixth	Diminished seventh	Minor seventh	Major seventh	Octave

35. The intervals that exceed the limits of the octave are not susceptible to inversion, because the lower note, being transferred to a higher octave, is still found in the same position with regard to the lower note.

DEMONSTRATION

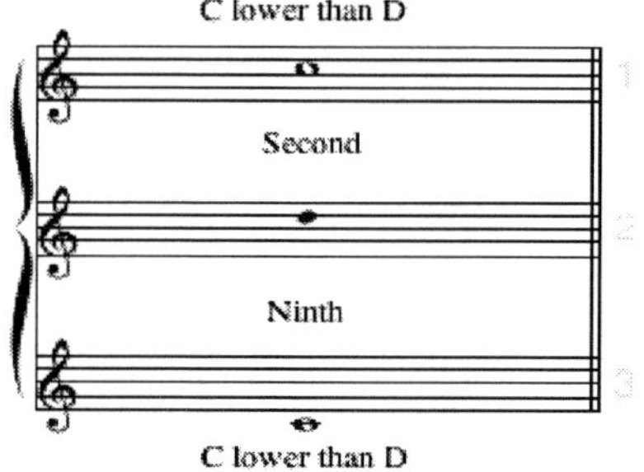

Chapter IV

THE SUCCESSION OF INTERVALS, CONSIDERED IN TERMS OF THEIR AFFINITIES AND IN THE DETERMINATION OF TONALITY

36. The subject of this chapter is the most important in the entire science of harmony, and even the whole art, for it arises from the mysterious laws that govern the connection of sounds, be it in the melodic conception, or in the harmonic combinations.

In fact, without entering into the philosophical considerations on the subject of the form of the scales of the two modes, considerations which cannot be developed here, it may be demonstrated that all music is based on the character of repose in certain intervals, the absence of this character in certain others, and finally of the appellative affinities of some.

This triple character, distributed amongst all the intervals that make up chords, contains the conditions that determine tonality, and assigns to each of these intervals the place it must occupy on the degrees of the scale of tones.

37. If it is the harmonies that give the ear the feeling of repose and conclusion, it is obvious that these harmonies can only be well placed on the notes of the scale that have the same character, through the position which they occupy in this scale or through the diverse circumstances of their connection with other notes.

In the same manner, if there are harmonies which exclude the sensation of repose and conclusion, they may only conserve their character as long as they are based on notes of the scale which do not imply in themselves, or in their relation to other notes, the idea of conclusion or repose.

Finally, it is no less evident that the attractive harmonies, which determine the attractions of certain other harmonies, can only be formed by means of notes of the scale which have among each other this relation of attraction, and consequently harmonies of this kind can only belong to these same notes.

38. This granted, it is only a matter of recognizing the notes of the scale in which may be observed one of these three above-mentioned characteristics. In order to proceed with the search for these notes, the observations contained in the following paragraphs are of the utmost importance.

OF THE FIRST NOTE OF THE SCALE

39. The first note of the scale of any given key is the only one in which the harmony itself gives both the feeling of repose and knowledge of the key and mode.

When it is accompanied by the fifth or the octave, it has the quality of absolute repose in which there is no sign of disturbance.

EXAMPLES

In the key of C

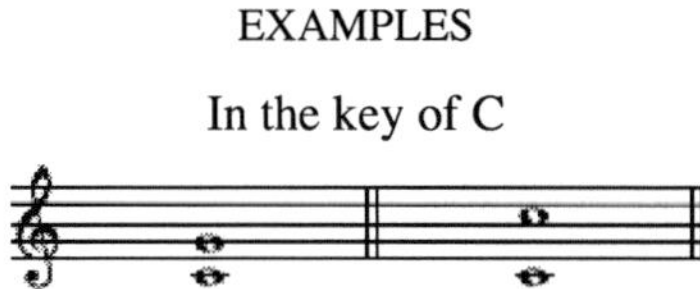

With the harmony of the third the tonic does not lose the quality of repose, but this harmony adds the information of the mode to that of the key (*ton*), for if the third note above the first note of the scale is major, the mode is major, and if the third is minor, the mode conforms to this third.

EXAMPLES

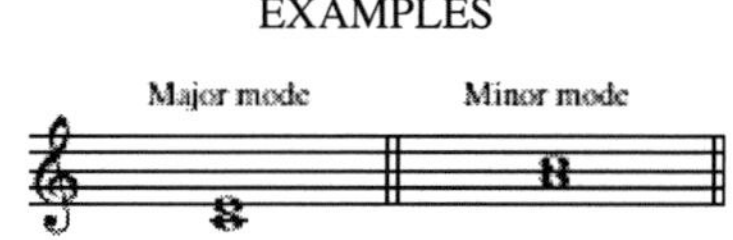

The properties of the first note of the scale, and the special harmonic features which belong to it, have given it the name *tonic*.

All other harmony where the fifth, octave and third, are not the elements, takes away from the tonic its quality of repose. For example, the fourth and the sixth, which are devoid of this quality, even though they are consonances, and which consequently attract other harmonies in order to conclude, cannot accompany the tonic without immediately removing its quality of repose and without suspending the idea of conclusion. This is why harmony composed of these two intervals can only occasionally be placed on the tonic in a transitory manner to lead the harmony to a final conclusion.

EXAMPLE

OF THE FOURTH NOTE OF THE SCALE

40. Although the fourth note of the scale does not have the character of absolute repose that belongs only to the tonic, it does not exclude the idea of momentary repose. But for this very reason that the repose on the fourth degree is only transitory, it is possible that this repose not take place; it follows that all the intervals, be they of repose or not, may accompany the fourth degree and determine by their nature either a momentary repose, or the necessity for immediate succession. Thus, the third, the fifth, the sixth and the octave may equally well accompany this note.

41. With regard to the fourth by which the fourth degree is sometimes accompanied, it is necessarily major, for it is formed with the leading tone. Now, it has been seen above (§25) that the fourth of this kind is an appellative consonance which resolves by an ascending movement of the higher note and by a descending movement of the lower note; from which it follows that every fourth degree, accompanied by the major fourth, must be followed by the third, if the harmony does not establish a change of key.

DEMONSTRATION

OF THE DOMINANT

42. The dominant, or fifth note of the scale, is an incidental point of repose, like the fourth degree: the third, the fifth and the octave are the only intervals in the harmony which give it this quality of repose.

With respect to the sixth, it provides the ear with a satisfying harmony on the dominant only when it is accompanied by the fourth which, formed with the tonic, retains for the harmony of the sixth the character of the tonality. But this harmony is only admissible on the dominant when it presents a transitory passage into repose (see example 1 below), or when the dominant, deprived of all quality of repose, resolves itself through ascending or descending movements of one degree (see examples 2 and 3).

The harmony of the fourth and sixth is also acceptable on the dominant in a succession that presents only the inversion of its own intervals, because this inversion is only a suspending of the real resolution.

DEMONSTRATION

But if the dominant is immediately followed by another note, at the interval of a third, fourth, fifth, etc., the harmony of the fourth and sixth cannot be suitable for it, because it is deprived of the qualities of resolution in the succession.

43. The fourth degree and the dominant, having a character of tonal repose, a quality which momentarily makes them similar to transitory tonics, offend the ear when the harmonies of the intervals that give the feeling of this repose immediately succeed each other on these two notes; for two immediate reposes, by harmonies which themselves do not have any point of contact, present the musical sense with the appearance of a tonal absurdity. Hence the rules that prohibit, in the art of writing, the succession of two fifths and two major thirds in the reciprocal passage from the fourth to the dominant, and from the dominant to the fourth degree, which may be seen in the following examples:

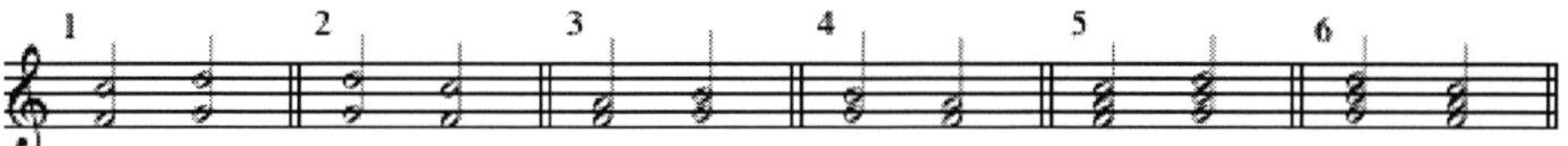

The succession of the two major thirds of examples 3, 4, 5, 6, is called a *false relation*, because the quality of the intervals of repose and of the mode place in immediate contact tonalities that have no connection. But if the third of the fourth degree is accompanied by the sixth, the succession becomes good, because the note of this sixth is at the same time the fifth of the dominant, and it establishes the contact.

DEMONSTRATION

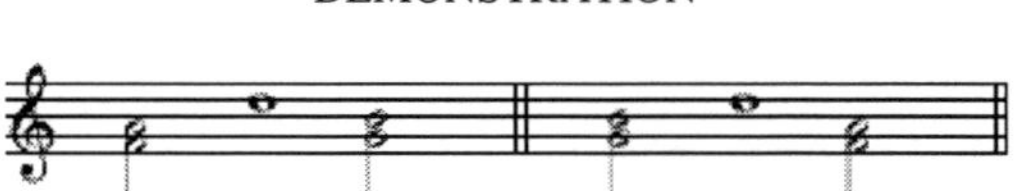

44. The dominant receives immediately and without preparation a dissonant interval of the seventh for accompaniment. This seventh is formed by the fourth degree, as in this example.

In the order of tonal unity, these two notes (the fourth degree and the dominant) are the only ones that are able to form a dissonance that the musical sense accepts hearing from the outset, and without a preceding consonance. Any other dissonance, resulting from the clash of two neighbouring tones or the inversion of these tones, is necessarily the product of the prolongation of a note heard first in a state of consonance, as in this example:

45. The fourth degree and the dominant are fully able to form a natural dissonance, as a result of the disposition of the notes of the scale, in two successions of four tones (called *tetrachords* by the Greeks), composed of two consecutive tones followed by a semitone.

DEMONSTRATION

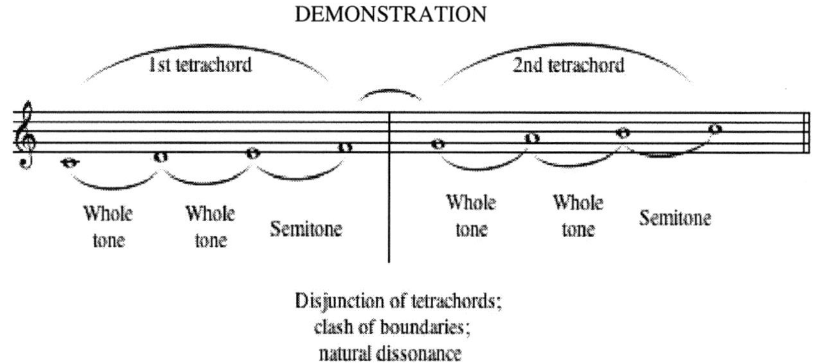

The natural dissonance of the fourth degree and of the dominant is therefore at the point of contact between the two equal parts of the scale.

In the minor mode, the disposition of the tones and semitones of the two tetrachords is not symmetrical. But the natural dissonance is also placed at the point of separation of the two tetrachords, between the fourth degree and the dominant.

46. Experience shows that the tonal dissonances satisfy the ear only when they are resolved by descending one degree to a consonance. In the interval of the second, the lower note is the dissonance, and in the seventh, which is its inversion, it is the upper note.

Now, the fourth degree being the lower note of the interval of a second, and the upper note of that of the seventh, it is clear that the natural dissonances are used only when the fourth degree is immediately followed by the third, either above or below.

DEMONSTRATION

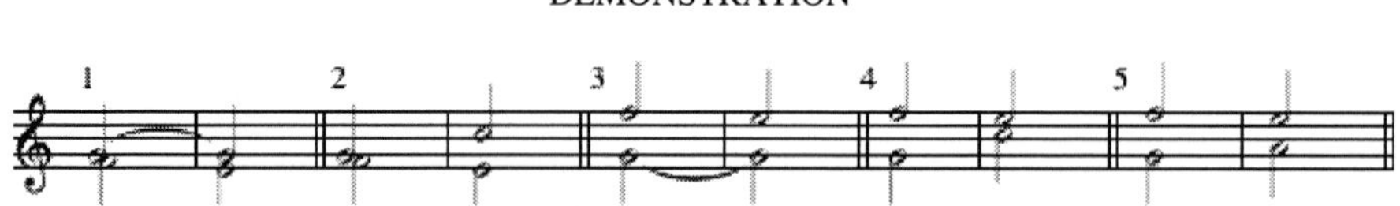

The latter two of these examples are called *cadences*. No. 4, which presents a conclusion on the tonic, is called a *perfect cadence*. No. 5 is a *broken cadence*. Later we will see what is the nature of the sixth degree, when it is accompanied by a fifth, as in this example.

47. The natural dissonances of the fourth and dominant degrees, combined with the appellative consonances that arise from the connection of the fourth degree with the leading tone, uniquely characterize modern tonality, and stamp it with a completely different quality from that of the old tonalities.[9]

OF THE SIXTH NOTE OF THE SCALE

48. The sixth degree does not have the quality of repose like the tonic, the fourth degree and the dominant. It is, however, sometimes accompanied by the fifth, because it is the same note as the tonic of the minor mode relative to the major tonality to which it belongs, and because, in the minor tonality, it may be considered as the fourth degree of the relative major mode. Thus, in the tonality of C major, it represents the tonic of A minor, which is its relative. And in the tonality of C minor, it represents the fourth degree of E-flat, which is its relative major.

Now, the frequent alternation between major tonalities and relative minors, is cause for an incidental cadence made on the sixth degree, and it establishes there a momentary repose, because of its equivocal nature: this is what happens in the broken cadence seen above (§ 46, example 5), and in many other successions.

49. The sixth is not at all like the fifth; it removes all ambiguity concerning the tonal nature of the sixth degree, for this sixth could not accompany it if it were to be considered as the tonic of the relative minor mode. The harmony of the sixth therefore is that which best characterizes the sixth degree.

EXAMPLE

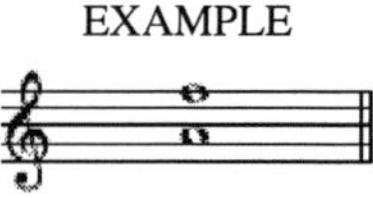

50. The third, by which one accompanies all the degrees of the scale, also belongs to the sixth, but determines neither its tonal character nor its modal signification, for it is minor on the sixth degree of the major mode of C, like on the tonic of the relative minor mode.

DEMONSTRATION

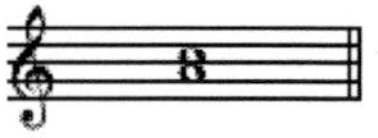

[9]On this subject, see the important observations in Chapter II of Book III of this *Traité de l'harmonie*, and in the second section of the second book of my *Philosophie de la musique*.*

*This work exists as an independent volume and in volume I, xxxvii-ccliv of the first edition of the *Biographie universelle* (1835-44). [PL]

OF THE SECOND NOTE OF THE SCALE

51. In modern tonality, the second degree is not a note of repose. If sometimes it is accompanied by the fifth, as in the succession of intervals in this example,

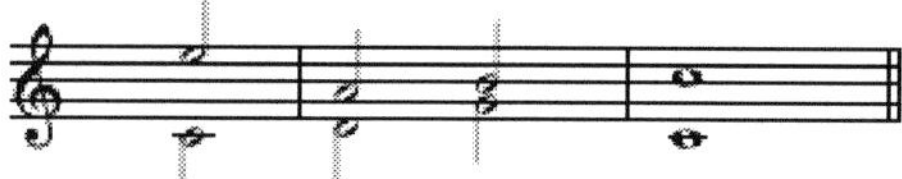

one takes away its tonal character, and brings about a vague change of tonality that opens the path to many endings in different keys, as in the following example.

52. The intervals that preserve the tonal character of the second degree are the sixth (ex. 1), the third (ex. 2), and the fourth (ex. 3), which combine in various ways in the harmonies of the chords.

53. Concerning the fourth, note that the suitability of this interval, in the accompaniment of certain notes of the scale, is a necessary consequence of the use of the fifth, as an interval of repose over the others; for the inversion of the fifth generates the fourth. Thus, the fifth of the tonic produces the fourth with which one accompanies the dominant when it is deprived of the character of repose (see example 1 below); the fifth of the fourth degree gives the fourth on the tonic (ex.2); finally, the fifth of the dominant produces the fourth on the second degree (ex. 3).

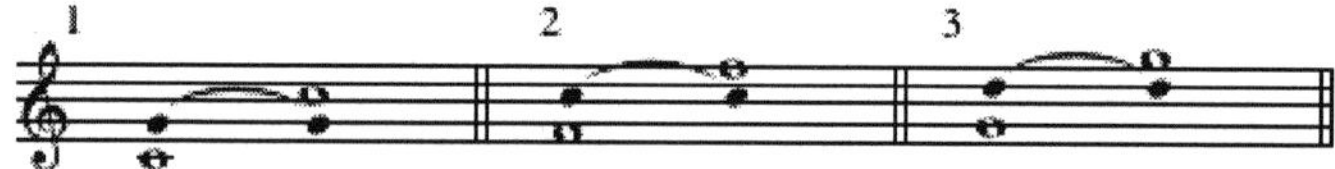

The use of the fourth on these notes, and only on these, is thus one of the conditions of tonality. Now, note that this is clear proof that the use of the fifth on the second degree and on the sixth is not tonal; for the fourth, which would be its inversion, is not used in any situation on the sixth degree, nor on the third.

OF THE THIRD NOTE OF THE SCALE

54. The tonal character of the third degree is completely opposed to any feeling of repose, and consequently excludes the harmony of the fifth. The reasons for this exclusion are: (1) that the fifth of this note would be formed with the seventh degree, of which the natural attraction toward the tonic could not satisfy the conditions of repose; (2) that this same seventh would establish a false relation of tonality with the fourth degree, toward which the third itself has an attractive tendency, being separated from it by only a semitone.

55. The harmonies that, alone, belong to the third degree are the sixth, because it excludes the idea of repose (ex. 1), and the third, the character of which determines the mode (ex. 2), because of its minor or major quality.

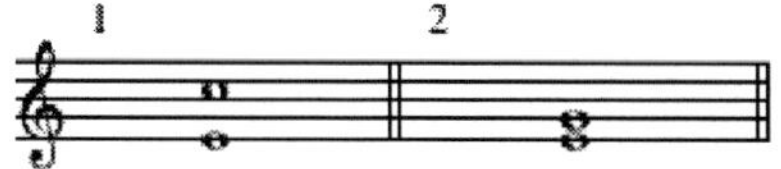

OF THE SEVENTH NOTE OF THE SCALE

56. The tonal character of the seventh degree is no less at variance with all feeling of repose than that of the third; even more so in that it is impossible to accompany it with the perfect fifth, since this interval does not exist between the seventh note and the fourth.

57. The harmonies that preserve the tonal character of the seventh are: (1) the minor fifth; (2) the sixth.

It is also accompanied by the third, which combines with the other intervals.

58. The minor fifth, an appellative and an attractive consonance, determines the ascending movement of the seventh degree on the tonic: this degree thus takes the name of *leading tone*.

EXAMPLE

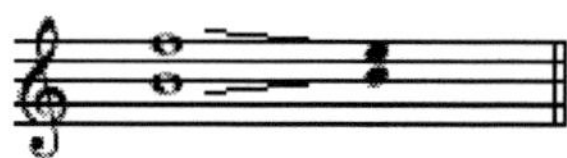

In all other successions, the sixth is the tonal harmony of the seventh degree.

EXAMPLE

SUMMARY OF THE ABOVE

59. Modern tonality resides in the attractions of certain intervals toward intervals of repose, and in the connection of these with others that, although lacking a character of attraction, nevertheless do not have one of conclusion.

60. The attractive intervals are the major fourth, the minor fifth and the natural dissonance of the dominant with the fourth degree.

61. The fifth and the octave are the only intervals of repose.

62. The intervals that lack a quality of conclusion, although not attractive, are the fourth and the sixth.

63. The third has a tonal character only on the dominant, where it is major in both modes, and on the second degree, when it forms a harmony with the sixth, for in that case the note of this third is in an attractive relation with the leading tone.

On all other notes of the scale the third does not have a tonal character, but its quality determines the mode on the tonic, the third, fourth, and sixth degrees.

64. The tonic, the fourth degree and the dominant, are the only notes of the scale able to assume the character of repose: they alone accede the harmony of the fifth.

65. The inversion of the fifth of the tonic, the fourth degree and the dominant, places tonally the fourth on the dominant, tonic and second degree, in transitory harmonies. When the fourth is used tonally on these notes, it is accompanied by the sixth, because it excludes the idea of conclusion.

66. The interval of the sixth is the only one that preserves the character of tonality for the second, third and sixth degrees. It is equally well placed on the seventh.

67. The appellative and attractive consonances of the major fourth and minor fifth that can only be formed by the joining of the fourth degree with the seventh, belong only to these notes.

The major fourth is placed on the fourth degree, when it is followed by the third; the minor fifth belongs to the leading tone, when it rises to the tonic.

These intervals, joined to the natural dissonance of the fourth degree and the dominant, are those that completely establish modern tonality.

68. The natural dissonance can be formed only by the clash of the fourth degree and the dominant; it resolves by descending one degree.

69. These precepts presume the unique tonality of a scale. Anything that would appear to bring about exceptions results from passing from the

tonality of one scale to another, from which arises another order of events that will be discussed in the second and third books.

70. In this summary is found the solution, long awaited for, of this question, in appearance so simple: *What is tonality*? Its explanation, in general terms, may be expressed thus: *Tonality is formed from the aggregation of necessary relations, successive or simultaneous, of the tones of the scale.*

In the tonal laws just expressed reside, therefore, not only all theory of tonal harmony, but also the unity of this harmony and of melody, in a word, of all music.

I will show, in the fourth book, how the incomplete conception of these laws led to a multitude of systems more or less ingenious, but more or less false: true abstract creations of the mind that are based only in the imagination of their authors, some of whom nevertheless were learned men.

END OF BOOK ONE

BOOK TWO

OF CHORDS

71. All harmony that is composed of more than two notes is called a *chord*.

72. Every complete chord, in keeping with tonal unity, which is formed with only three tones, contains only consonances and is called a *consonant chord*.

The chords that cannot be complete without four or more tones, belong to the class of *dissonant chords*, because they inevitably contain a clash of two neighboring tones, or the inversion of this clash.

FIRST SECTION

CONSONANT CHORDS

Chapter I

THE PERFECT CHORD, AND ITS USE IN THE HARMONIC PERIOD

73. A consonant chord formed from a note, its third and its perfect fifth, is called a *perfect chord*, because it gives us the feeling of repose and conclusion.

The character of conclusion and repose attached to this chord assigns it a position on the tonic, the fourth degree, the dominant and the sixth degree (in accordance with the considerations developed in §§39, 40, 42, and 48).

Examples in the key of C

1 Tonic

2 Fourth degree

3 Dominant

4 Sixth degree

74. When the third of the perfect chord is major, as in examples 1, 2, 3, above, the chord is major; when the chord has the minor third, it is minor.

In the major mode, the perfect chord is major on the tonic and on the fourth degree; in the minor mode, it is minor on the same degrees, for it is the third of these two notes that characterizes the mode (§39).

DEMONSTRATION

The perfect chord is major in the two modes on the dominant, because the third of this note is formed with the leading tone, the construction of which is invariable.

DEMONSTRATION

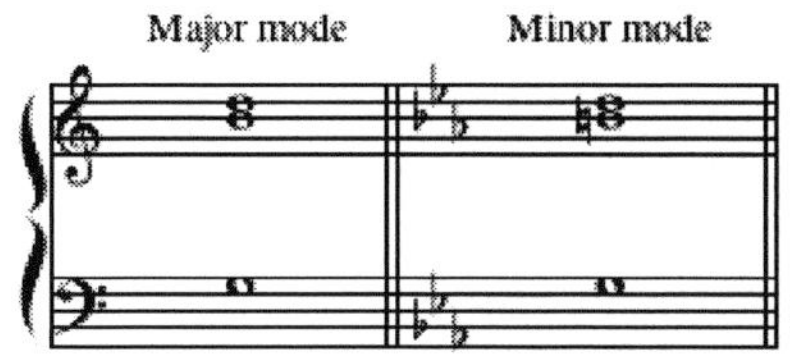

The perfect chord is minor on the sixth degree in the major mode; it is major in the minor mode.

DEMONSTRATION

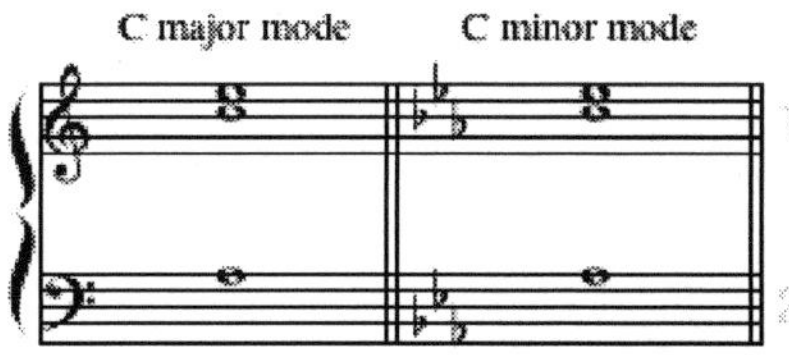

75. When the harmony is written for four voices or four instrumental parts, one of the three tones of the chord must be doubled, either at the unison or at the octave. The most harmonious doubling is that of the lower tone in one of the higher octaves:

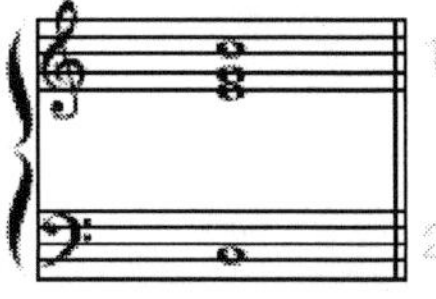

However, certain considerations of the ordered movement of voices sometimes requires the doubling of the third or fifth.

76. In the succession of harmonies, the intervals involved in the composition of the perfect chord are subject to various arrangements, which gives them a higher or lower position.

EXAMPLE

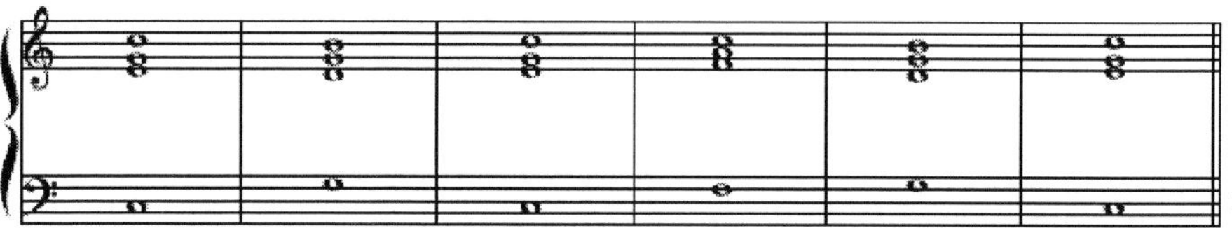

In the first chord of this harmonic phrase, the third is the lowest note; the fifth the middle, and the octave the highest note. In the second chord, it is the fifth that has the lowest position, the third the upper, and octave the middle. The third chord is similar to the first. In the fourth, the octave is the lowest note, the third the middle, and the fifth has the upper position. The fifth chord is similar to the second, and the sixth to the first. Such is the harmonic interlocking of voices in all pieces of music.

These different arrangements are called *positions*. The first position is where the third is the lower note and the octave is above (see example 1 below); the second is where the fifth is the lowest note, and the third the upper (ex. 2); the third is where the octave is the lowest note, and the fifth the upper (ex. 3).

EXAMPLE

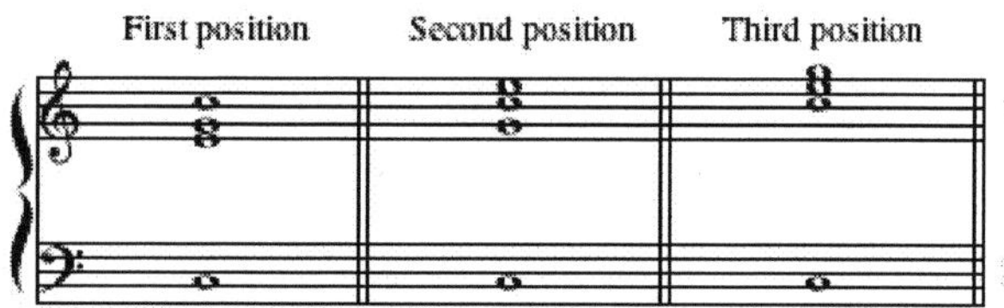

77. These arrangements of the intervals that make up the perfect chord are particularly appropriate because of the need to bring them together within the hand, in the organ or piano accompaniment. The different types of voice, and the different ranges of the instruments give rise to other groupings, more in keeping with the range of these voices and instruments, and in which the effect is more harmonious, because the distance bounded by the lowest note of the chord, and the highest, is divided in such a way that all the notes are found at more or less equal distances, as in the following example.

In this arrangement of the intervals of the perfect chord, the bass, tenor, contralto and soprano have notes that belong to the middle of their range, and the harmonic effect is more satisfying than any other harmonic arrangement.

78. I have tried to demonstrate above that the fixed position of the perfect chord on certain notes of the scale is the necessary result of the laws of tonality. But a phenomenon presents itself in certain harmonic formulas, for which the academic term is *bass sequences* (*marches de basse*), and more exactly, *progressions*, for the bass movements are only a part of the phenomenon. In these progressions, two chords follow each other in an ascending or descending movement: this succession and this movement fix the attention of the mind, which holds on to the form so strongly that any irregularity of tonality is not noticed. Now, the succession being accomplished, if the movement between two notes situated on higher or lower degrees resumes, and continues a series of similar successions, through an ascending or descending progression on all degrees of the scale, the mind, absorbed in the contemplation of the progressive series, momentarily loses the feeling of tonality, and regains it only at the final cadence, where the normal order is reestablished.

It follows that in progressions there are no fixed degrees, and that intervals and chords which, by their nature, belong to this or that scale, lose their special character, that the scale properly speaking is no more, and that the same chords may be placed on all the notes of the progressive series. The following examples of ascending and descending progressions of perfect chords will clarify what may be unclear to the reader about this theory.

In these progressions, the asterisk indicates the moment when the feeling of tonality is reestablished by the harmony of the dominant.

79. Considerations relevant to this kind of harmonic phenomenon are of the highest importance, for in these phenomena lies the cause of a multitude of errors spread throughout the majority of the theories of harmony. The harmonists not having seen that the law of uniformity in the progressions suspends the effects of the law of tonality up to the moment of the cadence, and noticing the perfect chord on all the degrees of the scale, decided on the general rule that this chord belongs in effect to all the notes of the tonal scale.[1] This resulted in a confusion of principles, where

---

[1]Rameau and the harmonists of his school did not make this error. This creator of the first harmonic system does not assign to the perfect chord any other place than the tonic, the fourth degree and the dominant; in fact, he does not deal with continuous progressions.

Catel, who did not know the law of tonality or the influence of progressions on the suspension of this law, said firmly that *all the notes of the scale are susceptible to receiving the perfect chord* (*Traité d'harmonie*, 9).

In the German School, [Johann Philipp] Kirnberger [1721-83] places the perfect chord on the tonic, dominant, second degree, fourth and sixth (*Grundsätze des Generalbasses,* 1er *Abschnitt,* 3, 4, 5, *Vorlesungen*). [Georg Andreas] Sorge [1703-1778] says that the scale naturally creates three perfect major chords, on the tonic, fourth degree and dominant, and three perfect minor chords, on the second, third, and sixth degrees (*Compendium harmonicum,* chapters 3, 7): he does not see that he thus confuses the tonality of plainchant with modern tonality.

Amongst the German harmonists of the present time, Abbé Vogler [1749-1814], [Gottfried] Weber [1779-1839], [Johann Christian Friedrich] Schneider [1786-1853], and Johann Anton André [1775-1842]* place the perfect chord on all notes of the scale. Anton Reicha [1770-1836] and A. B. Marx [1795-1866], as well as Sorge limit its use to the first six degrees.***

*A respected composer and music publisher, André produced a number of fine editions of Mozart's works from the composer's original manuscripts. Entrusted by Constanze and her husband Nissen with creating a chronological catalogue, he was unable to complete the immense project, although it helped lay the foundation for Ludwig von Köchel's catalogue. The theoretical work to which Fétis refers is André's proposed six-volume *Lehrbuch der Tonkunst*, although only two volumes were completed, the first dealing with harmony, and the second with counterpoint and fugue. [PL]

**Fétis asserts that a young composer would be better advised to study the treatises of the old Italian school than to follow Marx's theories, claiming that he falls into Marpurg's error and that of other German theorists by laying too much emphasis on canon and double counterpoint, which are only exceptions, and do not touch upon the real matter of counterpoint for the art of writing. Always ready to take a stab at Reicha, in the same article Fétis reports that he once overheard him "seriously question" Cherubini (1760-1842) about the purpose of the study of simple counterpoint, adding: "He [Reicha] had arrived at the end of his career without understanding that simple counterpoint contains the entire art of writing, and that there is no other useful means of learning this art." While this is certainly an unfair criticism, especially in view of the preeminent position Reicha assigns to fugue in the study of composition, the remark is instructive, for it shows that Fétis considers counterpoint an essential element of musical processes. See the *RgmP*, 1840, No. 2. [PL]

one was unaware that modern tonality had been absorbed into that of plainchant, by removing from it the distinctiveness of each of the notes of its scale.

80. One of the more striking consequences of the suspension of the feeling of tonality, by progressions that cover the length of the entire scale, or at least a part of this length, is found in the chord that accompanies the seventh degree. This chord, like the perfect chord, is composed of the third and fifth; but this fifth is minor, because there is nothing else to accompany the seventh degree.

DEMONSTRATION

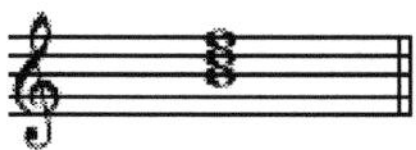

This chord has plagued modern harmonists. Rameau, not having noticcd it, did not account for it in his classifications; but, aftcr him, thosc who spoke of it did not know to what category it belonged, because of the uncertainty that prevailed amongst scholars about the nature of the minor fifth. Those who admitted the perfect chord on all notes of the scale made it a consonant chord. Reicha, who did not want the minor fifth, as well as the major fourth, to be consonant intervals of a particular kind, and who had not noticed that there is a dissonance only in the clash between two neighbouring tones or in their inversion, put this chord in the class of dissonant chords, under the name of *chord of the diminished fifth*.[2]

Catel, of all the harmonists, distinguished himself by the most peculiar confusion of ideas, for after having made the *diminished fifth* (minor) a dissonance, he places the chord, of which this interval is one of its elements, amongst the consonant ones, and even claims that it can serve as a momentary repose. The passage in his book where he sets forth this opinion is worth noting.

"Although the interval of the diminished fifth (he says) is not consonant, one cannot, however, classify this chord among the dissonant chords, since none of its constituent notes have a set progression (as have all dissonances), and that they may all ascend, descend, or stay in place: from which we may conclude that if this chord is less perfect than the other two, *it may nevertheless be used to make a momentary repose before arriving at a more perfect repose: thus, it must be classified amongst the consonant chords*."[3]

***Fétis examines the theories of Vogler, Weber, Schneider, Reicha, and Sorge in Book Four of this work and in the *Esquisse*. [PL]

[2]*Cours de composition musicale*, 8.

[3]*Traité d'harmonie*, 9.

Thus, here is a consonant chord in which one of its intervals is a dissonance! It is to such manifest contradictions, and to such confusion of principles that false premises lead.

In fact, it is clear that the *chord of the minor fifth*, which is being considered, is a consonant chord, in accordance with the nature of its intervals; but it can be used only by analogy in set progressions, because its resolution does not conform to the rules of tonality.

With regard to Catel's assertion that this chord may mark a momentary repose, clearly this is absolutely false; for the attractive quality of one of its intervals clearly renders it the least of consonant chords to be used in this way.

81. Nothing proves better how much the attention of the musical sense is diverted from the feeling of tonality by symmetry of movement and succession, than the tacit consent given by the mind to the use of the inflected consonance of the minor fifth, without its attractive resolution being carried out. In fact, in this succession

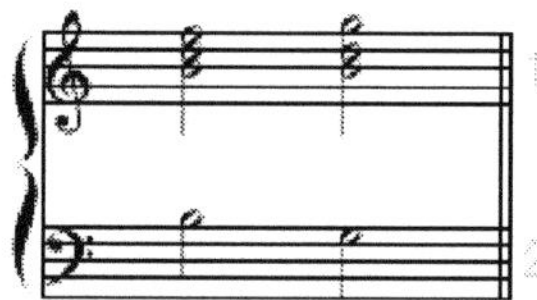

the movement of the parts, marked out by the progression, leads the minor fifth to ascend, instead of resolving it downward, conforming to the law of tonality.

82. Finally, such is the overpowering effect of the symmetry of movement and succession on the mind, in these particular progressions, that the false relation of the passing of the fourth degree to the seventh in the bass, everywhere else so disagreeable, is hardly noticed in these formulae:

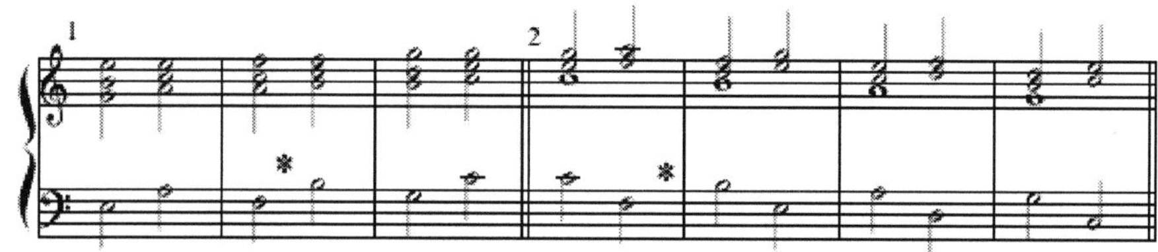

83. Note that the mind's tacit consent to the suspension of the feeling of tonality can be complete only when the regularity of the progression is perfect in all voices. For only this regularity can distract the attention from the feeling of tonality. Thus the progression always leads the voices that accompany it in keeping with the sense of its motion, as one sees in the preceding examples. If the progression is ascending, all the voices ascend by regular movements; if it is descending, all the voices descend.

There would consequently be something offensive to the ear in an irregular progression like the following:

The musical sense can only be satisfied when the movement used in the succession of the two first chords is reproduced symmetrically throughout the rest of the progression, as in the following example:

A single example of non-modulating progression, in an opposite motion, is found in a bass that descends by thirds; but the regularity of movement exists no less in all the parts. Here is this progression:

84. All interruption to the symmetry of movement in the voices is not only a cause of annoyance to the mind's attention to the order of progression: it also generates unruly successions of intervals, with respect to the art of writing, as can be seen in the second book of the first part of my *Traité du countrepoint et de la fugue*.[4]

85. If I am not mistaken, I have just resolved one of the greatest metaphysical difficulties in the theory of harmony. This solution removes the cause of serious errors where harmonists have fallen, and the anomalies that appeared to contradict the law of tonality; it also prepares easy pathways for the remainder of our journey.

---

[4]Paris, Troupenas, 1846; 2 parts, 2nd edition.

Chapter II

INVERSIONS OF THE CONSTITUENT INTERVALS OF THE PERFECT CHORD — THE CHORDS THAT RESULT — THE USE OF THESE CHORDS

86. As we saw in the preceding chapter, the perfect chord is made up of three essential notes that form the intervals of the third and fifth. If we apply to these notes the procedures of inversion explained in the third chapter of the first book, we derive two other combinations of the consonant chord.

87. The first of these combinations consists of transposing the low note of the perfect chord to one of the upper octaves, such that the third inverts to a sixth.

In this combination, the fifth of the perfect chord becomes the third of the inverted chord, which is thus made up of the lower note, its third, and its sixth, and which is called the *sixth chord.*

EXAMPLE

88. We see in this example that the lowest note of the sixth chord is the third of the lowest note of the perfect chord, as a result of the inversion. It follows that the third of any note that supports the perfect chord, according to the laws of tonality, may be the bass of a sixth chord. Now, the perfect chord being placed on the tonic, the fourth degree and the dominant, it is clear that the sixth chord may have as a bass the third, sixth, and seventh degrees.

DEMONSTRATION

1st inversion of the perfect chord of the tonic	1st inversion of the perfect chord of the fourth degree	1st inversion of the perfect chord of the dominant
Sixth chord on the 3rd degree	Sixth chord on the 6th degree	Sixth chord on the 7th degree

The third and the sixth of the sixth chords that are derived from the perfect chords of the tonic, fourth degree, and dominant, are minor in the major mode, and major in the minor mode.

89. We have seen the circumstances (§80) that may lead to placing on the seventh degree a chord made up of a third and minor fifth. This chord

has derived through inversion a sixth chord in which the bass note is the second degree. This harmony is quite characteristic of tonality, because the third and the sixth form an interval of a major fourth that resolves tonally, through the natural tendency of its constituent notes.

DEMONSTRATION

90. I have explained (§45) how one avoids the false relation that results from the succession of two major thirds on the fourth degree and the dominant, by means of the accompaniment of the sixth on the third of the fourth degree. If one seeks the origin of this sixth chord, it can only be found in the perfect chord placed on the second degree in progressions that suspend the feeling of tonality. The use of this sixth chord on the fourth degree can be seen in the following example:

It is also a suspension of tonal feeling that admits the sixth chord on the tonic, as derived from the perfect chord of the sixth degree, a chord that itself is only a suspension of this feeling. However, the total absence of tonal character in the sixth chord on the tonic is the reason why this chord is used only when it is preceded or followed by the perfect chord on the same degree.

EXAMPLES

91. In harmony for four voices or instruments, one of the intervals of the sixth chord must be doubled at the octave or unison. One of the doubled notes should be the bass, the third or the sixth: the choice of this note depends on the position of the preceding chord, or of the chord that follows that of the sixth.

One may set forth in general the rules concerning the doubling of intervals of the sixth chord as follows: (1) the sixth chord of the third degree and that of the seventh degree, both followed by a perfect chord rising one degree, must not double the bass note at the octave, but the third or the sixth, as in the following examples:

1 Doubled sixth 2 Doubled third 3 Doubled third 4 Doubled sixth

The reason for this rule, as with all rules in the science of harmony, is in the laws of tonality. In fact, the ascending tendencies that result from the semitone between the third and fourth degrees of the scale, and between the seventh and the eighth, do not permit the lower notes of these semitones to descend in the movement of one of the parts while they ascend in the other, because the musical sense would thereby be disturbed by a fault in the logical succession. The following successions would thus affect our tonal feeling in a disagreeable way:

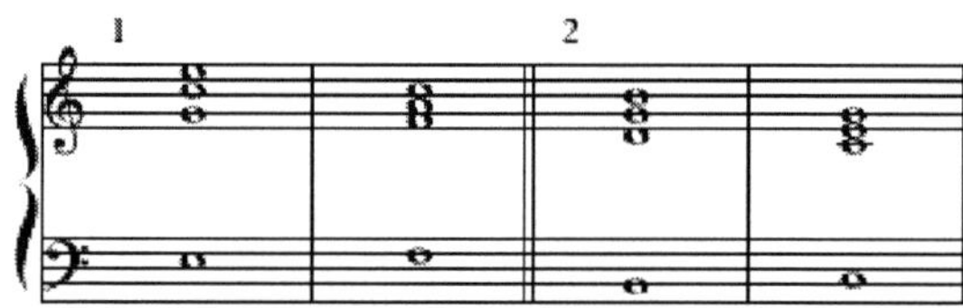

When the upper voice reaches the octave, in similar successions, and when the descending doubled note stemming from the bass note is in an inner voice, the feeling of conclusion, which is awakened by this disposition, weakens the unpleasant sensation that results from the transgression of the law of tendency.

DEMONSTRATION

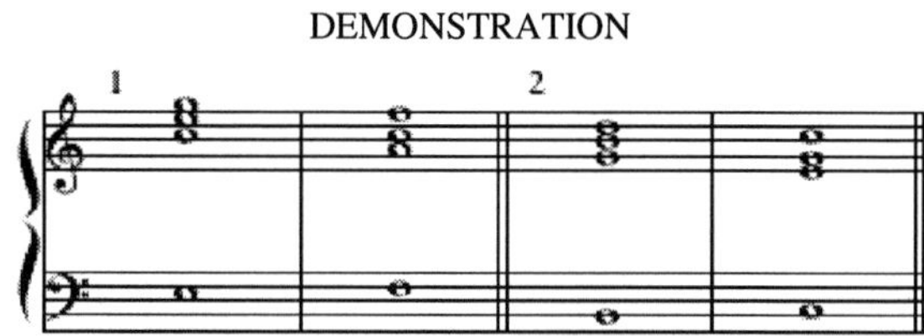

However, the doubling of the third and the sixth, of which I have given examples, are much more satisfying, and will always be preferred by harmonists in whom the feeling for tonal tendencies is well cultivated.

(2) The successions of a sixth chord to another sixth chord, through ascending movement of one degree, and that of a sixth chord to a perfect chord, through a descending movement of a second, or by a leap of a

given interval, allow the doubling of the bass of the sixth chord, without disturbing the feeling of tonality.[5]

EXAMPLES OF THESE SUCCESSIONS:

Successions from one sixth chord to another

Successions from a sixth chord to a perfect chord

1 2 3 4 5 6

92. Progressions where sixth chords are used have on them the same effect as on perfect chords, by suspending the feeling of tonality up to the tonal cadence. It is only in these circumstances that the characteristic position of these chords on certain notes of the scale disappears, and that they take place on all degrees. The following formulae represent some of these progressions.

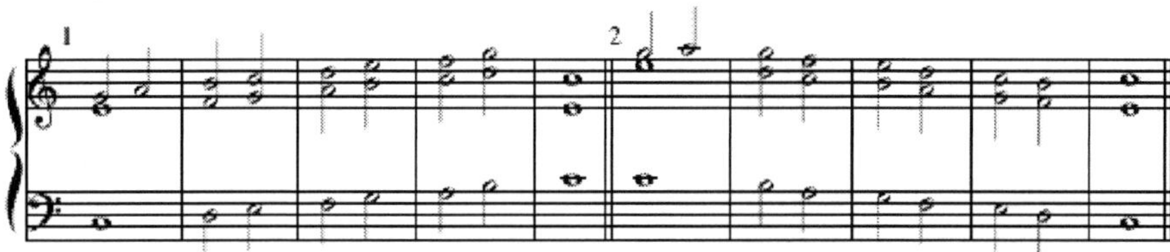

In all these formulae, the symmetry of movement alone holds the attention.

93. The second combination of the inversion of the intervals of the perfect chord consists of taking as the low note the fifth of this perfect chord, while moving the other two notes to higher octaves. This results in a chord composed of intervals of a fourth and sixth, called, from the name of these intervals, the *six-four chord*.

EXAMPLE

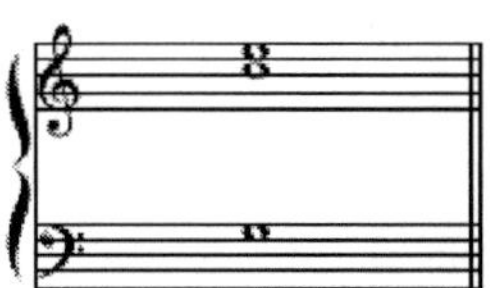

This chord completes the order of combinations of the three notes that enter into the formation of consonant chords.

[5]Fétis inadvertently writes "from a perfect chord to a sixth chord" for examples 5 and 6. I have amended this to agree with the written examples.

DEMONSTRATION

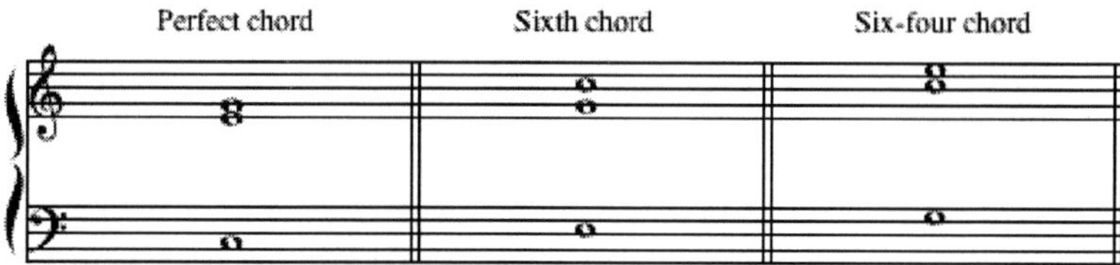

After the third combination, all three appear in the same order, an octave higher.

94. The interval of the fourth, deprived of equilibrium, is the least satisfying of all the consonant intervals, and of limited use in less common circumstances than the others: this also results in the six-four chord being used less frequently. It is primarily intended to precede the repose of the perfect chord on the note where it is placed.

EXAMPLE

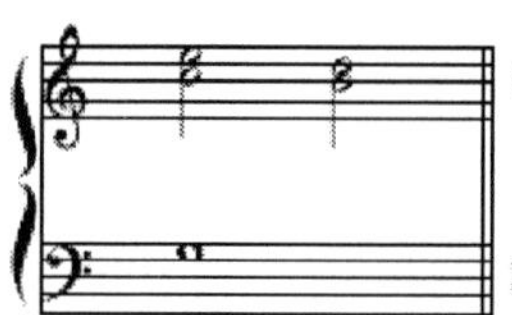

Sometimes it resolves on a sixth chord, when the bass makes an ascending movement of a second.

EXAMPLE

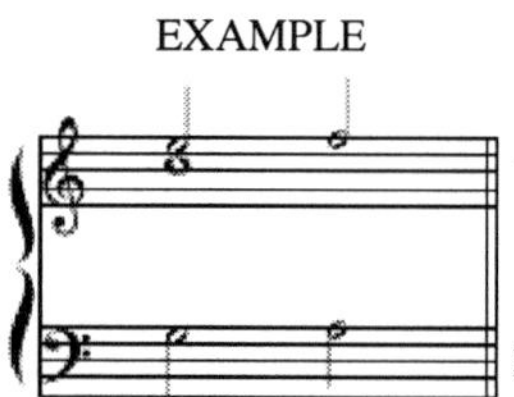

95. The inversion of the perfect chord of the tonic produces the six-four chord on the dominant; that of the perfect chord of the fourth degree gives rise to the six-four chord on the tonic; finally, the inversion of the perfect chord on the dominant produces the six-four chord on the second degree. The dominant, the tonic and the second degree are the only notes where the six-four chord is used, in circumstances similar to those discussed in §94. Here are examples of the tonal use of the chord on these three notes:

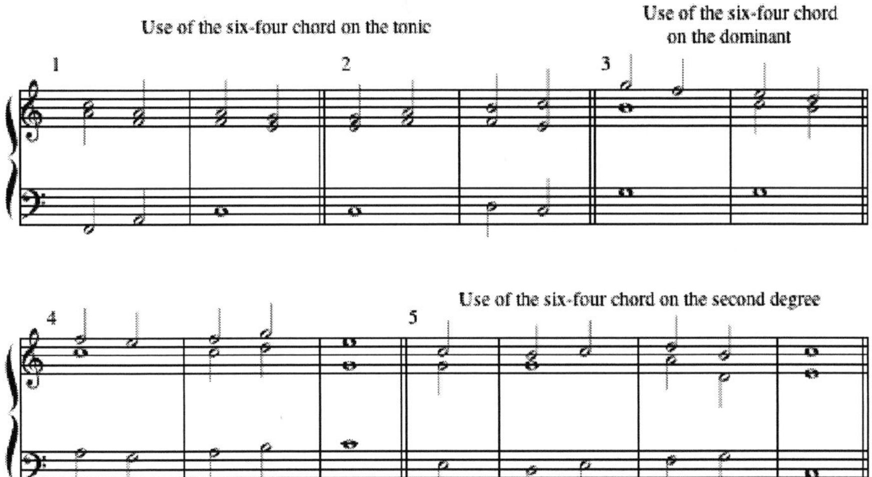

96. When one writes for four voices or instruments, one doubles the bass note at the octave (see example 1 below). One only doubles the sixth in music for five voices (see example 2); but the fourth is not doubled, because of its tonal weakness.

EXAMPLES

97. Such are all the possible consonant harmonies that result from tonal unity; such also are the circumstances of the use of these harmonies, based on the supreme law of tonality. No matter what combinations of this genre of chords are used in music, nothing else can be found, unless modifications are introduced that give them a new appearance, as will be seen in the third section of this book.

BOOK TWO

SECOND SECTION

DISSONANT CHORDS

Chapter III

THE NATURAL DISSONANT CHORD CALLED THE DOMINANT SEVENTH, AND ITS USE IN THE HARMONIC PERIOD

98. I have said previously (§§44 and 45) that, by nature of the division of the scale into two tetrachords, the boundaries of which clash with each other, the fourth degree forms with the dominant a dissonance of a seventh or second, because of the lower or higher disposition of its notes, and this dissonance is inherent in tonality, like consonant harmony.

Furthermore, I have shown (§§41 and 58) that the relationship of the fourth degree and the leading tone establishes between these degrees of the scale an attractive consonance that resolves, by the descending movement of the fourth degree, and the ascending[6] movement of the leading tone, into the order of tonal unity.

Now, if we join in a single harmony the natural dissonance of the seventh and the leading tone, which establishes with the fourth degree the relationship of attraction that characterizes modern tonality; if, moreover, we add to it the fifth of the dominant, formed with the second degree, we will have a natural dissonant chord, made up of four tones, in the following form:

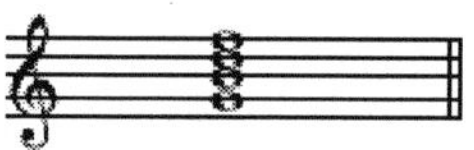

This harmony is called the *chord of the dominant seventh*, because it has as the low note or support, the dominant, and because the constituent intervals are found only on this note. These intervals are: (1) the major third; (2) the perfect fifth; (3) the minor seventh. The nature of these intervals is exactly the same in the two modes.

99. The consonant chords, which may belong to different degrees of the scale, do not have as pronounced a character of tonal determination as this natural dissonant chord, which acquires its make-up on only a single note. When it is heard, there is no further doubt as to the key; the entire

---

[6]Fétis inadvertently writes "descending" here. [PL]

secret of tonality is revealed by the relationship of the fourth degree with the dominant, and by the attractive relationship of this fourth degree with the leading tone.

100. The arrangement of intervals of the dominant seventh chord can be made, when it is complete, in five different ways, in four-part harmony.

DEMONSTRATION

1 2 3 4 5

The choice of these arrangements is governed by the need for the most natural and easy movement for the voices in the succession of chords.

101. The obligation to resolve the dissonance, by making it descend a degree, and raising the leading tone to the tonic, in tonal unity (see §§41 and 46), gives the connection of the dominant seventh chord with consonant chords a character of final resolution and cadence which the perfect chord of the dominant does not have, where all the notes move in a free direction.

When there is no change of key, the seventh chord must be followed by a *perfect cadence* on the tonic, or an *interrupted cadence* on the sixth degree, or finally by a harmony derived from the perfect chord of the tonic, which forms a *suspension of the cadence*, but which establishes the tonal resolution.

EXAMPLES

Perfect cadence Interrupted cadence Suspension of cadence

1 2 3

Every regular succession in which the two necessary movements of the fourth degree and the leading tone are not performed, leads to a change of key, as will be seen in the third book of this work.

It is true that certain harmonists, with the intention of completing the perfect chord that follows the seventh in the perfect cadence (see example 1 above), resolve only the dissonance, by making it fall, and do not cause the leading tone to ascend, which they thus write:

But, although this manner of writing has been frequently used in music composed since the end of the eighteenth century, it is no less unruly, in that it does not satisfy all the requirements of tonal feeling.

102. The purpose of the preceding paragraph led us to examine by what means one may complete the harmony of the perfect chord of the tonic, which follows that of the seventh in the perfect cadence, without transgressing the laws of tonality, with regard to the movement of the intervals of the latter chord.

This cadence shows us (§101, example 1) that the harmony of the seventh being complete, the compulsory movement of its notes does not allow the harmony of the perfect chord to be completed. However, a three-note chord, where one is obliged to omit a note, produces only a very weak harmony. This serious disadvantage can be avoided only by the omission of the fifth of the seventh chord, when one writes for four voices or instrumental parts, and by doubling the lowest note of the chord. This doubled note provides the means of conserving the fifth of the perfect chord that follows that of the seventh, without spoiling the movements of resolution of the fourth degree and the leading tone.

DEMONSTRATION

The fifth not being one of the intervals of tonal make-up in the seventh chord, and this chord being composed of four notes, its omission is not essentially harmful to the harmony.

One may, however, avoid this omission, in the passage from the fifth of the first chord to the fifth of the second, by means of contrary motion, when the arrangement of the voices that precede it permits.

DEMONSTRATION

In five-part harmony, no omission is necessary, and all the voices have regular movements, according to the requirements of tonality.

DEMONSTRATION

Chapter IV

THE INVERSION OF THE INTERVALS OF THE SEVENTH CHORD, THE CHORDS THAT RESULT, AND THE USE OF THESE CHORDS

103. In consonant chords, the three notes of the perfect chord combine, through inversion, in three different ways; in dissonant chords the four notes of the seventh chord provide four combinations by the same process.

104. If we take as the lowest note of one of these combinations the third of the seventh chord, by moving the dominant to one of the upper octaves, we have a chord composed of the leading tone in the bass, its minor third, minor fifth, and minor sixth.

DEMONSTRATION

This harmony is called the *chord of the minor fifth and sixth.*[7] As in the seventh chord, and in all its other inversions, the dissonance is here formed by the clash of the fourth degree with the dominant.

105. The intervals of this chord may be arranged, for voices or instrumental parts, in four different ways.

[7]The old French harmonists called this chord the *false fifth*. Catel and his school called it the *diminished fifth chord*. These designations are not precise; for there is nothing false or diminished in harmonies in keeping with the constitution of a unique and rational tonality. Reicha, who does not give names to derivations of perfect and seventh chords, calls them simply *first, second, third inversion,* etc.

DEMONSTRATION

As in the seventh chord, as in all chords, the most natural movement of voices determines the choice of these arrangements.

106. In keeping with the law of tonality, when there is no modulation, the minor fifth and sixth chord can have only one resolution, which consists of being followed by the perfect chord of the tonic; for the attractive tendency of the minor fifth compels the leading tone in the bass to ascend a degree, and the fourth to descend. The following examples offer this resolution in the various positions of the intervals.

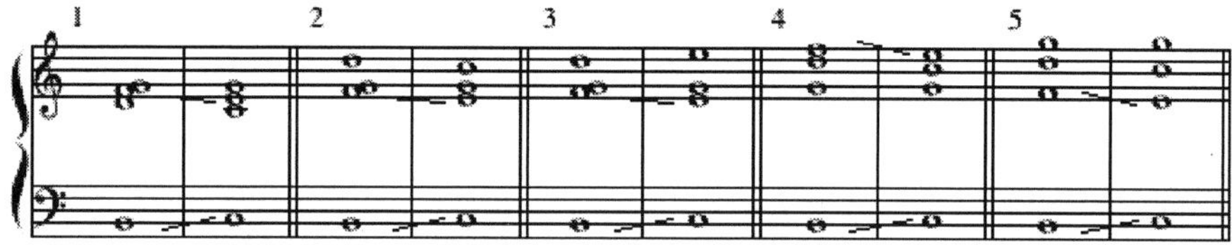

This obligatory resolution of the minor fifth and sixth chord shows that this chord can be employed on the seventh degree only when this note is followed by the tonic, and that, if the sixth degree follows it, it must be accompanied by a sixth chord, in which all the notes move freely. One does not, therefore, write as in example 1 below, but as in example 2.

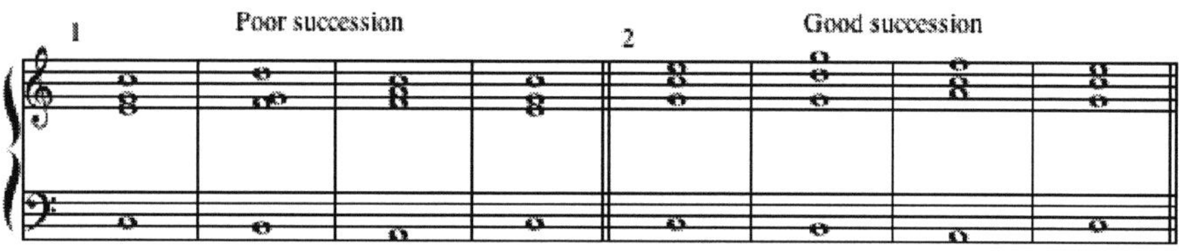

107. If we take as the lowest note of the dissonant chord the fifth of the seventh chord, by moving the other notes to upper octaves, we have as a third combination a chord made up of a minor third, perfect fourth and major sixth, which has the second degree as a bass.

DEMONSTRATION

This arrangement of the dissonant chord is called the *leading-tone sixth,*[8] because the interval of the sixth, which is a part of its make-up, is formed with the *leading tone*.

108. The intervals of the leading-tone sixth chord may be arranged in four different ways.

DEMONSTRATION

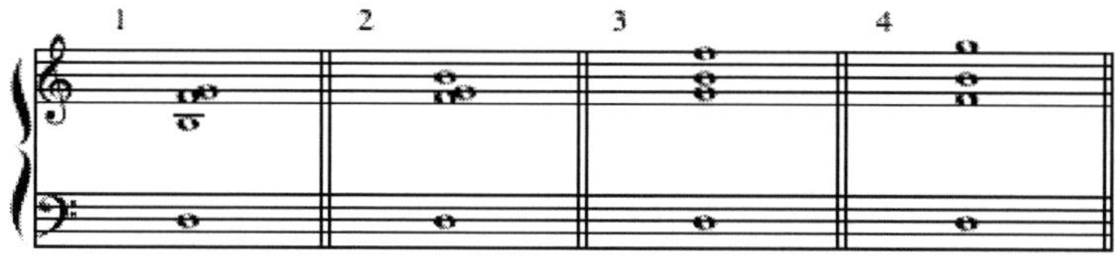

1 2 3 4

109. In keeping with the law of tonality, the leading-tone sixth chord may have two natural resolutions: the first, on the third degree using a sixth chord; the other, on the tonic carrying the perfect chord. The following examples offer resolutions in various positions of the chords.

RESOLUTIONS ON THE THIRD DEGREE

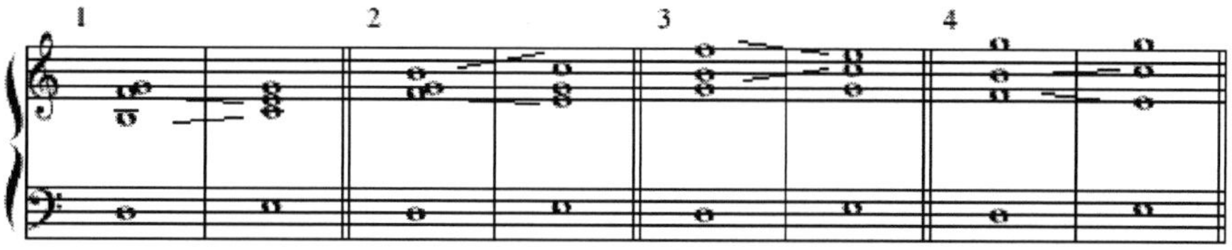

1 2 3 4

RESOLUTIONS ON THE TONIC

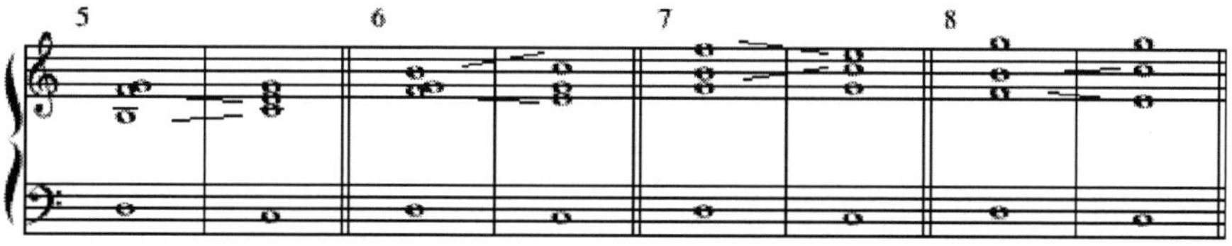

5 6 7 8

In these examples we see that the movements of the intervals are the same in the two resolutions of the dissonant chord, and that they differ only in the bass movement.

Any other succession after the leading-tone sixth chord would hinder the resolution of the attractive and dissonant intervals of this chord. For example, in a movement of the bass from the second degree to the sixth, the dissonance could not have a resolution, for its dissonant note must remain stationary. In a similar case, one must not accompany the second

[8]Rameau called this the *chord of the small major sixth*. The absurdity of such a designation is self-evident; for how can an interval be *major* and *small* at the same time? The fact is that this interval of the sixth is the largest that can be formed with the natural notes of a scale, because it is formed with the leading tone, which has an ascending tendency.

degree with the leading-tone sixth chord, but with the consonant sixth chord, in which the intervals behave freely. One would not, therefore, write as in the first example below, but as in the second.

1 Poor succession 2 Good succession

110. If we take as the lowest note of the dissonant chord the fourth degree, in moving the other notes to upper octaves, we have the fourth and last combination of the these elements. The harmony that results is composed of the second, major fourth and major sixth. Its bass note is the dissonance in the chord, for we are reminded that the dissonance results from the clash of the fourth degree against the dominant.

DEMONSTRATION

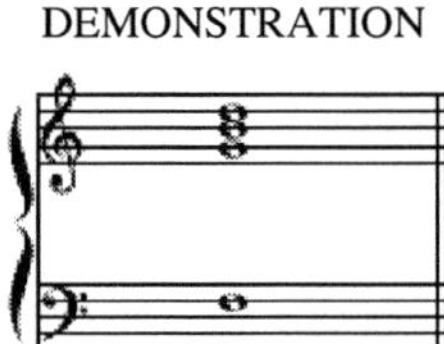

We call this harmony the chord of the *tritone*, because the major fourth, joined to the dissonance of the second, is its characteristic interval.

111. The chord of the tritone completes the order of combinations of the four notes of the dissonant chord.

DEMONSTRATION

Seventh chord Minor fifth and sixth chord Leading-tone sixth chord Chord of the tritone

Following the fourth combination, all four are presented in the same order, an octave higher.

112. The intervals of the chord of the tritone may be arranged in five different ways.

DEMONSTRATION

1 2 3 4 5

113. In keeping with the law of tonality, the chord of the tritone accompanies the fourth degree only when this note descends to the third of the scale, because it has a double descending tendency through its dissonant quality and its relationship with the leading tone. It thus follows that the fourth degree ascending must be accompanied by a harmony other than the tritone. The following examples offer the resolution of this chord in its various arrangements and according to the requirements of tonal feeling.

1 2 3 4

5 6 7

Any other use of the chord of the tritone would violate the feeling of tonality, even though the consonant harmony of the tonic would follow it, for the reasons explained above: the leap from the lowest note of this chord onto the tonic is therefore a serious error, or its ascent to the dominant, of which one finds examples in many compositions, otherwise meritorious, and even in the works of some distinguished musicians.

EXAMPLES

IMPROPER RESOLUTIONS OF THE CHORD OF THE TRITONE

1 2

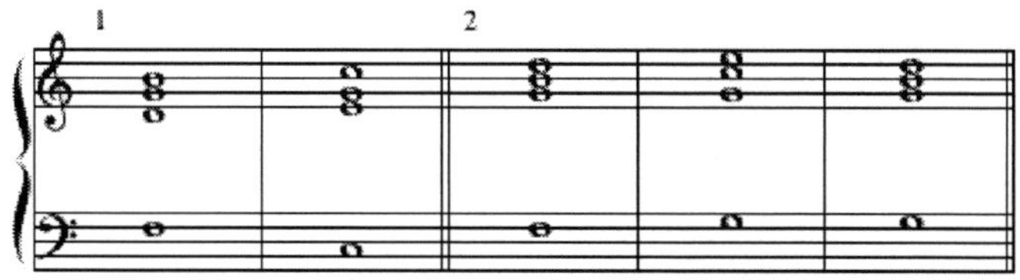

114. A fact of harmony, of which many examples are found, seems at first sight to contradict what I have said about the need for the descent of the fourth degree, and the ascent of the leading tone, in the resolutions of various combinations of the dissonant chord in keeping with tonal unity: this fact consists in the immediate succession of one to the other of these combinations, and without an intermediary consonant harmony. Here are examples of these successions.

1 2 3 4 5

But it is clear that these direct changes in the combinations of the same harmony only suspend the necessity of the tonal resolution, and that all these examples must conclude with the double resolution of the fourth degree and the leading tone on consonant harmony, at the risk of disturbing the feeling of tonality.

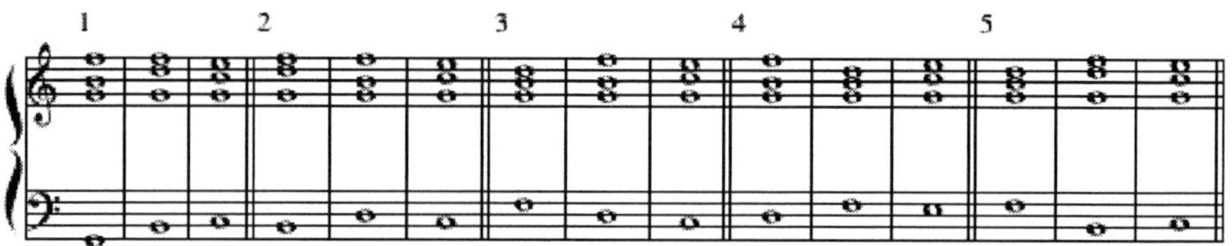

115. We have thus arrived at the complete constitution of tonal unity in modern music. All consonant and dissonant relationships of a single scale are established and demonstrated, as much in successive as in simultaneous order: each note of the scale, whatever the circumstances of its connection with the others, has in each instance its own particular harmonies.

Examples of harmonic periods, in the two modes of modern tonality, will round out the demonstration of this truth.

MAJOR MODE

MINOR MODE

116. These examples demonstrate that the perfect chord and the seventh chord comprise, with their derivatives, all natural harmony. The purpose of the rest of this book will be to give absolute proof, until it is perfectly clear, that all the other harmonic aggregations are only their modifications, classed as follows: (1) artificial and arbitrary substitution of one note for another; (2) retardation of the natural notes of the chords through prolongation of the notes of preceding chords; (3) chromatic alterations of the natural intervals of the chords; (4) combinations of these diverse kinds of modifications; (5) passing notes foreign to the harmony; (6) *appoggiaturas*; (7) anticipations; (8) pedal points.

BOOK TWO

THIRD SECTION

THE MODIFICATIONS OF NATURAL CHORDS

Chapter V

MODIFICATION OF NATURAL DISSONANT CHORDS BY THE SUBSTITUTION OF ONE NOTE FOR ANOTHER – THE RESULTANT CHORDS

117. We touch on one of the most delicate questions in the theory of harmony, one of the most peculiar facts of the art that science has explained. Here I must try harder to show clearly the consequences of the law of tonality in the phenomenon at hand. But I cannot hope to attain the end that I propose, unless the reader, granting me complete attention, divests himself of preoccupations with theories based on considerations other than those of tonality.

118. I have shown (§101) that in the resolution of the seventh chord, which leads to the perfect cadence, the best arrangement of this chord, either of four voices, or of five, doubles the octave of its lowest voice, and thus provides the way to complete the harmony of the perfect chord. Now, a harmonic fact, contemporaneous with the introduction of the natural dissonant chord in music, and with the formation of modern tonality, has shown that the ear admits the substitution of the sixth degree for the dominant, which forms this octave of the seventh chord, from which results the double dissonance of the seventh and the ninth in the chord.

In this state, the dissonant chord presents itself in this form:

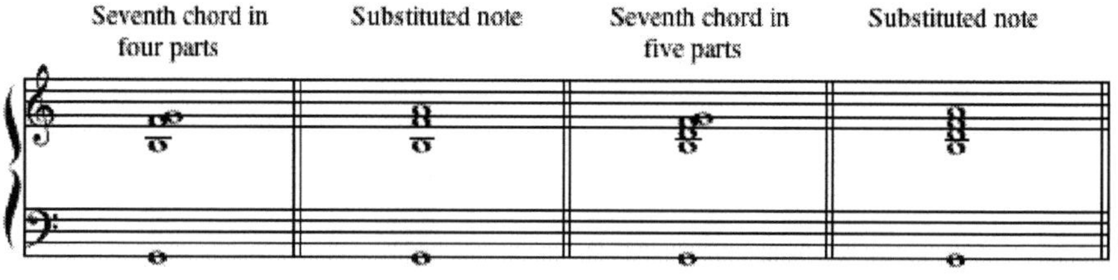

Seventh chord in four parts | Substituted note | Seventh chord in five parts | Substituted note

The dissonant chord with the substituted note is called the *dominant ninth chord*.

119. The modification of the dissonant chord, by the substitution of one note for another, has not been understood by harmonists who have considered the construction only of individual chords, and without regard for laws of succession and tonal structure. Only two theorists have been on the path of this important truth, where harmonic facts depend on a very delicate analysis, which it alone can elucidate; but they only caught a

glimpse of it through clouds that they could not break. The first of these harmonists is Rameau, who, having grasped the fact of the substitution only in the inversions of the seventh chord in the minor mode, called these kinds of modification, borrowed chords.[9] The other is Catel, who, without clearly perceiving the mechanism of the substitution, nevertheless saw the analogy of the use of chords modified by this substitution with natural dissonant chords, for he says: "The similarity that exists between these two chords (those of the seventh and ninth) proves their identity and clearly demonstrates that they have the same origin."[10]

120. The substitution of the sixth degree for the dominant, which is made in the seventh chord and in its inversions, is a melodic accent always placed, for this reason, on the highest note, in the major mode, and which often resolves on the replaced note, before the cadence.

DEMONSTRATION

The two ways of resolving the substituted note

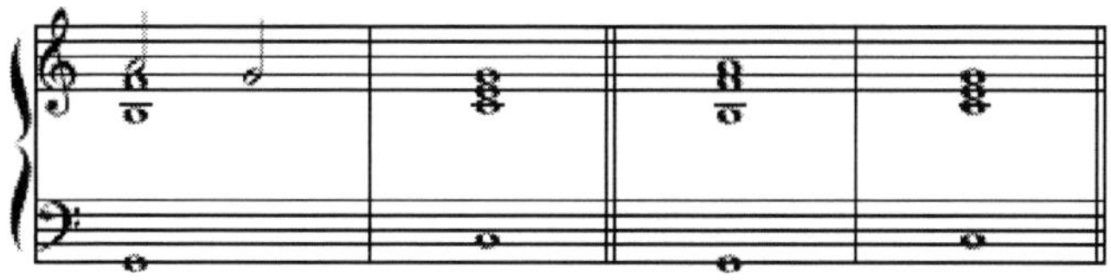

121. The same substitution of the sixth degree for the dominant is made in inversions the seventh chord. The first inversion, thus modified, produces a seventh chord in which the leading tone is the bass, and which is called, because of this, the *leading-tone seventh chord* (see example 1 below). In second inversion, the substitution replaces the fourth by the fifth, and produces a *fifth and leading-tone sixth chord* (see example 2). In third inversion, the substitution replaces the second by the major third. This chord thus modified is called the *tritone and major third* chord (see example 3).

Thus, as shown above, the substituted note is always the sixth degree, which takes the place of the dominant; it is a melodic accent in the inversions just as in the fundamental chord, and, so it is always placed in the upper voice, and at the distance of a seventh from the leading tone.

[9]*Traité de l'harmonie*, Bk. II, ch. xii, 79 onward.

[10]Catel, *Traité d'harmonie*, 11.

DEMONSTRATION[11]

1 Leading-tone six-five chord

Leading-tone seventh chord — Same as the preceding chord with the substituted note

2 Leading-tone sixth chord

Leading-tone six-five chord — Same as the preceding chord with the substituted note

3 Chord of the tritone

Chord of the tritone and major third — Same as the preceding chord with the substituted note

[11]The genius of the most sublime artist cannot break the laws of tonality without a blemish resulting in his work: an occurrence that refers to the rule set forth in this paragraph, on the necessity of placing the substituted note at the distance of a seventh from the leading tone, has provided a remarkable proof. It is this:

The first time that Beethoven's Symphony in C minor was performed in Paris, in the concerts of the Conservatory, and there obtained an enthusiastic welcome, the audience was struck by a most disagreeable sensation, when it heard, in a phrase in the adagio, the complete inversion of the leading-tone seventh with the substitution placed in the lower part. Artists and amateurs looked at each other with astonishment, in a kind of stupor. To be sure, with the exception of two or three harmonists, there was no one in the room who knew what it was, or if any rule of harmony had been violated; but instinct and tonal feeling alerted everyone to this fault, or, if you will, to the boldness of the composer.

Here is this unfortunate phrase that spoils one of Beethoven's most beautiful conceptions; the inversion that creates such a bad effect is marked with an asterisk.

Since the time of which I speak, one has become accustomed to this harmonic effect, as one becomes accustomed to faults of language that one hears often repeated; but to accustom the musical feeling to violations that have been made against it will never be considered great art by people of thought and taste.

122. The substitution resolves by descending onto the replaced note in the inversions of the seventh chord, as in the fundamental chord.

DEMONSTRATION

1 2 3 4 5 6

As one sees, these successions have the same destination as the natural dissonant chords, and fulfill the same functions in the harmonic period. They are optional and used only when the composer's thought needs a more energetic accent than that which may be provided by the natural note of the chord.

When the second degree descends to the tonic, the substitution must resolve on the natural note of the chord before the latter resolves on the perfect chord; without this precaution, there would be a succession of two fifths in parallel motion between the bass and the upper voice. Now, I have shown (§43) that this succession accentuates two different tonalities, without any contact, which must be forbidden. One must not write as in example 1, but as in example 2.

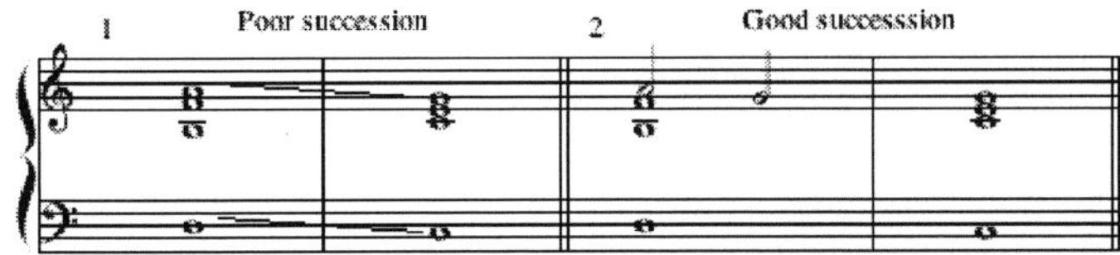

123. The phenomenon of the substitution of the sixth degree for the dominant, and of the agreeable sensation that it brings to the musical sense, can only be explained by the attraction that the leading tone creates with the ensuing dissonance. It is this attraction that results in a quality of impassioned accent in the substituted note, and the absence of harshness in its dissonant nature. Tonality here again makes its influence known; for every seventh chord, placed on other notes of the scale, develops different sensations in the musical sense from that of the leading tone, and does not have its attractive character. The leading-tone seventh is, in the order of dissonances, what the major fourth and minor fifth are in the order of consonances.

It suffices to show that the substitution establishes in harmony a melodic accent, in order to demonstrate that it must always be placed in the upper voice; but the consideration of the attractive interval that results is a further argument for the necessity of this arrangement; for if the leading tone were placed above the substituted note, there would not be an attraction between them, but repulsion.

DEMONSTRATION

124. When writing harmony in five parts, one conserves, in the inversions of the dissonant chord modified by the substitution, the dominant at the interval of the ninth from the substituted note: this dominant remains stationary in the resolution of the dissonant chord onto the consonant chord.

DEMONSTRATION

1 2 3

If the dissonance that results from the clash of the substituted note with the dominant were not at the distance of a ninth, it would be harsh and would develop an unpleasant sensation in the musical sense; for three tones, placed at a distance of a second from each other, collide; moreover, the resolution of the substituted note, taking place at the unison on the dominant, would not be heard; we would not be aware of it.

DEMONSTRATION

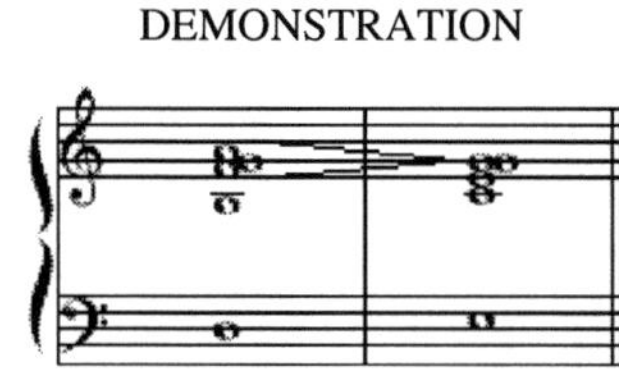

This would be much worse if the substituted note were not maintained at the attractive distance from the leading tone, and if it were not the upper note, for the ear would be struck by the intolerable harmonic confusion of four consecutive tones colliding in a succession of seconds, and the consonant chord that followed it would not suffice to satisfy the musical sense; for the resolution of all the dissonances, crushed up against each other, would not be clearly perceivable by the mind.

DEMONSTRATION

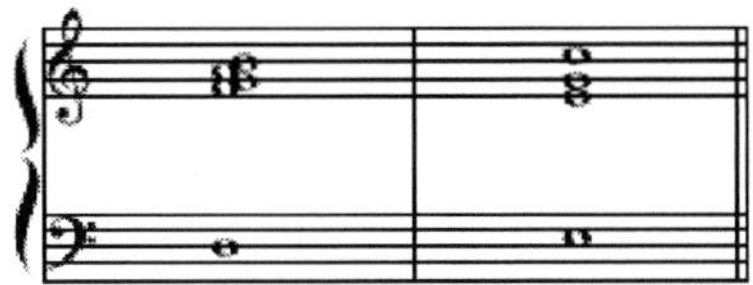

This analysis appears to me to demonstrate absolute proof of the power of tonal laws, which admits the substitution of the sixth degree for the dominant only on condition that this note be the ninth in relation to this dominant, because the substitution replaces the octave of this note; and in another connection the seventh with the leading tone, since in taking the place of the dominant, at the distance of the ninth, the substituted note replaces the sixth of the leading tone a degree higher, and establishes with this leading tone an attractive dissonance. Finally, I believe to have shown that, through these laws of tonality, thc resolution of dissonances becomes clear to the mind, while their transgression leads to horrible cacophonies, the cessation of which, through the return to the normal state of the consonant chord, does not even satisfy the mind, because it does not perceive the resolution of so many accumulated dissonances.

125. By not having made a close study of these laws of tonality, harmonists have fallen into strange errors and have injected a curious confusion into the explanation of the facts of the science. It would take too long and would be outside the plan of my work to analyze all these errors; but I must address two facts that have created doubt amongst scholars.

The first of these facts is the error that Catel and many other harmonists have made in seeing the dominant ninth chord and that of the leading-tone seventh as two different fundamental chords, each having their derivatives through inversion. These authors of harmony treatises did not see that the leading-tone seventh chord, that of the fifth and leading-tone sixth, and that of the tritone with the third, are the modifications of natural dissonant chords of four voices, through substitution, while those which I have just analyzed are the same modifications in five voices.

The result was that, taking the leading-tone seventh chord as a fundamental chord, Catel and his followers gave it three inversions that they arranged in this way:

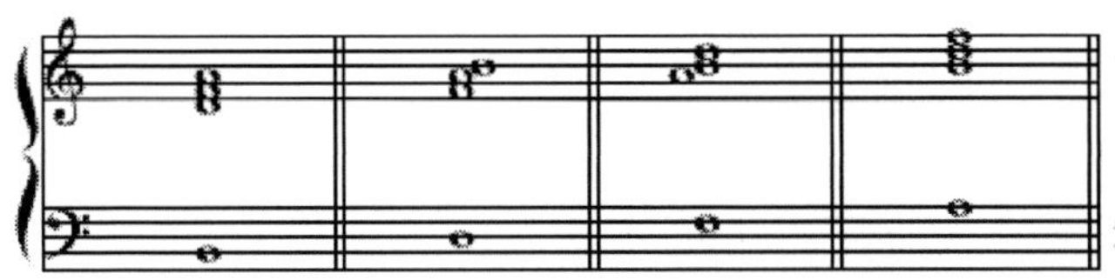

However, too good a musician in practice not to know that these chords have, in such a form, an abrasive harmony that does not allow their use, Catel adds the remark:

"In order to use the first and second inversions of this chord in a more pleasant way, the interval of the second that is found there must be presented in inversion as a seventh." He gives the following examples of these transformations, which are in fact the only way of writing these harmonies:[12]

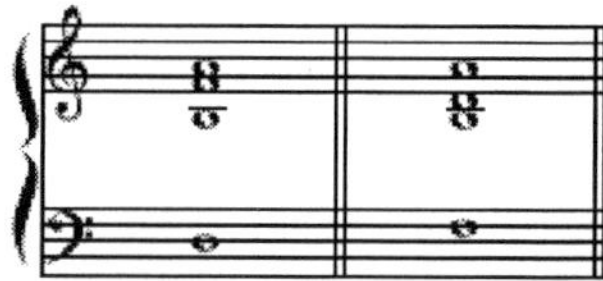

Here then, are some unworkable chords in Catel's so-called basic form.

With regard to the third derivative, which was firmly guided by the logic of inversion, he must acknowledge[13] *that it is not used without the preparation*, of which the following is an example:

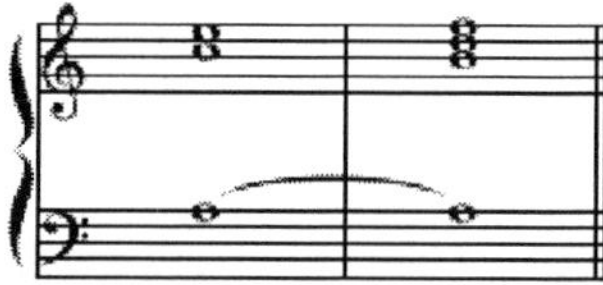

Catel did not see that the obligation to make this preparation constitutes a type of modification of natural chords that has no relationship to this one. In fact, what this master and the harmonists of his school took as a third inversion of the leading-tone seventh chord is only the fundamental dominant seventh chord, with the substitution of the sixth degree in the lowest note.

DEMONSTRATION

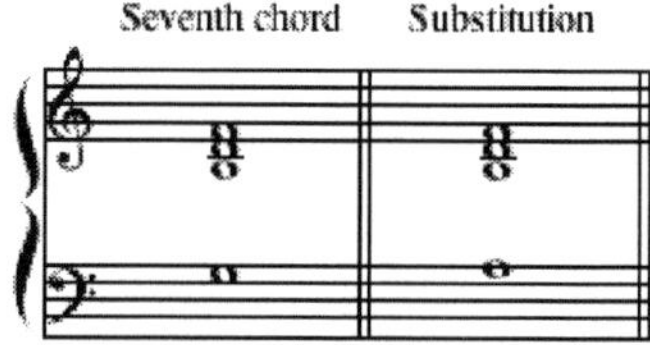

Now, this substitution is inadmissible, because the attraction of the leading tone and the sixth degree, required by the law of tonality, is not there; in a word, because the substitution is not allowed by the musical sense in the form of a second, in the major mode.

---

[12]*Traité d'harmonie*, 13.

[13]Ibid., 11.

Reicha, who is completely misguided in his system of harmony, as I will show in the fourth book of this work, nevertheless clearly saw that the leading-tone seventh chord comes from the same source as that of the dominant ninth; he established its derivation thus:[14]

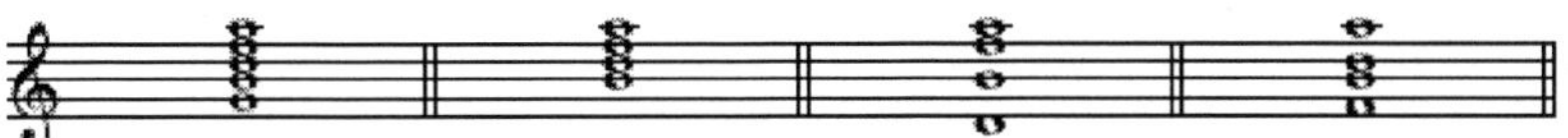

We see that he is not drawn to the so-called third inversion of Catel, and that he arranges the intervals as they should be, but without explaining the reason for this arrangement.

126. The second harmonic fact of which I wish to speak is provided by the theories of Calegari, Vallotti, Sabbatini, and the entire Paduan school. According to this theory, there is no modification of the natural harmony that cannot be overturned in practice, no interval governed by tonality that is not condensed at will through inversions. Applying this principle to the dominant ninth chord written in four parts, the above masters give as its last inversion a chord constructed as in example 2.[15]

1 Dominant ninth chord 2 Last inversion

Here the spirit of system claims to triumph over tonal and harmonic feeling, which has always rejected this inversion, because it cannot connect in a satisfactory way with the other chords, and because the interval of the seventh that is found there can be resolved only by a descending movement in the bass, which is in direct opposition to the laws of tonality previously explained.

DEMONSTRATION

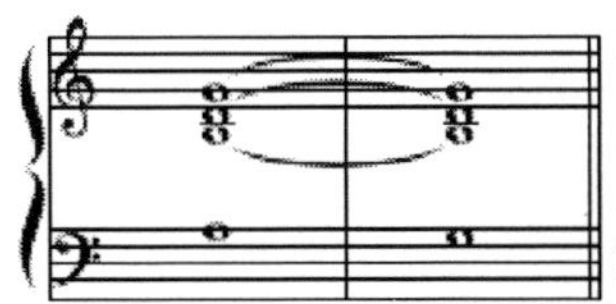

But we have occupied ourselves enough with erroneous systems: let us return to the harmony of nature.

127. The substitution of the sixth for the dominant is as much in harmony with tonal feeling in the minor mode as it is in the major. It

[14]*Cours de composition musicale*, 12.

[15]See the book entitled, *La vera idea delle musicali numeriche segnature*, by Sabbatini, CLIV.

produces the same results; but, because of the nature of the minor mode, the sixth degree being less high by a semitone than in the major mode, its substitution produces minor intervals, and the seventh that is formed with this degree and the leading tone is diminished.[16]

---

[16]Only one man, whose name and book are presently unknown, has observed the principle, so true, so fruitful and so lucid, of the modification of natural dissonant chords by substitution in chords of the minor mode. This musician, the father of a distinguished artist of our time, is Boëly. A declared advocate of Rameau's harmonic system, he hotly defended it against Catel's theory when it appeared, and in 1806 published a bitter critique of the latter in a book with the odd title: *Les véritables causes dévoilées de 'état d'ignorance des siècles reculés, dans lequel rentre visiblement aujourd'hui la théorie pratique de l'harmonie, notamment la profession* (l'enseignment) *de cette science* (Paris, 1806). (*Revelation of the True Causes of the State of Ignorance of Past Centuries, to which Today's Theoretical Practice of Harmony has Visibly Returned, Notably the Teaching Profession of this Science*).*

With much ranting, false perceptions and prejudices, Boëly indignantly rejects the major ninth and leading-tone seventh chords, because he did not find them in Rameau's *Traité de l'harmonie*; but he admits the diminished seventh chord, according to the principles of this harmonist, and makes the following observations about this chord, which are absolutely correct, although they are not expressed very clearly (page 125 of his book):

"He (Catel) would say: (1) That this seventh (diminished) is not a basic chord, and that it is only secondarily fundamental;

(2) That it takes its origin from the dominant-tonic G, for which art has substituted the sixth note A-flat, to have through inversion a seventh chord made up of three minor thirds in the following form, B-D-F-A-flat, where the note A-flat replaces the G which normally is a part of the false fifth chord (minor fifth and sixth), the first inversion of the dominant-tonic;**

(3) That for this reason one calls it in this case the *chord by substitution or borrowing*, to be used at will in place of the leading-tone chord of the minor mode that it always represents, whichever form it takes in its inversions."

One could not have been closer to a general and useful truth; but Boëly did not go further.

*In 1802 Jean-François Boëly (1739-1814) wrote a bitter attack against Catel (the same year that the Rameauian Jean-Baptiste Rey was dismissed from the Conservatory for his support of Lesueur) under the title: *Le partisan zélé du célèbre fondateur de l'harmonie aux antagonistes réformateurs de son système fondamentale, ou observations rigoureuses sur les principaux articles d'un nouveau traité, soi-disant d'harmonie, substitué par le conservatoire de Paris, à l'unique chef-d'oeuvre de l'art musical*. (*The Zealous Advocate of the Celebrated Founder of Harmony to the Rival Reformers of his Original System, or, Thorough Observations on the Principal Points of a New Would-be Treatise on Harmony, Substituted by the Paris Conservatory for the Irreplaceable Masterwork on Musical Art.*) Boëly sent his manuscript to François-Joseph Gossec (1734-1829) for his advice, only to receive a curt rebuke, which led him to publish his invective of 1806. *FétisB*, 2:243. [PL]

**Catel recognizes the similarity between the dominant seventh and leading-tone seventh chords, and asserts that they have the same fundamental: "The similarity that exists between these two chords proves their identity and clearly demonstrates that they have the same origin. One may therefore regard the generative sound of the dominant

It follows that the *dominant minor ninth* chord results from the substitution of the sixth degree for the dominant in the seventh chord of the minor mode (see example 1 below); that the same substitution, in first inversion, produces a *diminished seventh* chord (example 2); that it transforms the second inversion into a *minor fifth and leading-tone sixth* chord (example 3); finally, that it produces a *tritone and minor third* chord in its last inversion (example 4).

1 Seventh chord — Dominant minor ninth (Substitution) — 2 Minor fifth and sixth — Diminished seventh (Substitution)

3 Leading-tone sixth — Minor fifth and leading-tone sixth (Substitution) — 4 Chord of the tritone — Tritone and minor third (Substitution)

128. I have shown (§34) that the inversion of the interval of the diminished seventh produces the augmented second; now, the augmented second sounds to the ear like a minor third.

DEMONSTRATION

It follows that the harsh sensation of the interval of the major second that would result from the inversion of the leading-tone seventh in the chords of the major mode, does not exist in the minor mode; from which it results that the leading tone and the substitution of the sixth degree of this mode may be arranged at will in intervals of the diminished seventh or augmented second, in the second and third inversions, and that the musical sense is uniformly satisfied.

DEMONSTRATION

1 Leading-tone sixth chord — Same as the preceding chord with the substitution — 2 Chord of the tritone — Same as the preceding chord with the substitution

---

seventh as being also that of the leading-tone seventh." (*Traité de l'harmonie*, 1802, 15). Catel extends this identity to the diminished seventh chord. [PL]

The same source gives rise to the substitution of the sixth degree of the minor mode in the lowest note of the seventh chord.

DEMONSTRATION

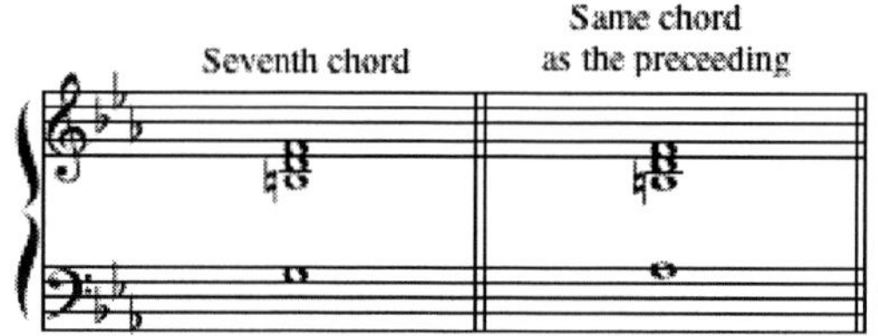

Such is the true origin of the so-called third inversion of the diminished seventh chord, called the *augmented second*.

129. The substitution of the minor mode resolves like that of the major mode, by descending a degree onto the natural note of the chord.

DEMONSTRATION

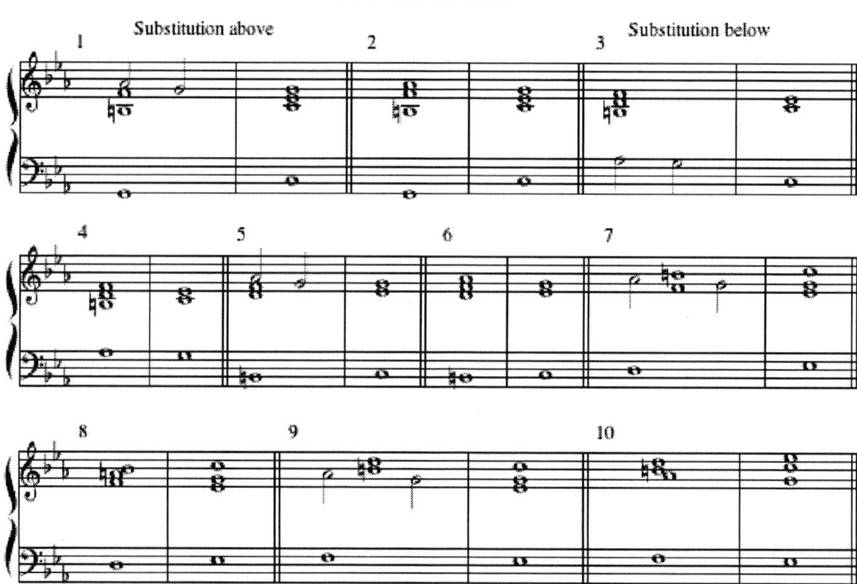

130. As in the major mode, the substitution is useful in harmony for five-part vocal or instrumental music, in causing the original note of the dissonant chord and the substituted note to be heard at the same time, in the case where these two notes are placed at the interval of the ninth, for the reasons explained earlier (§124).

DEMONSTRATION

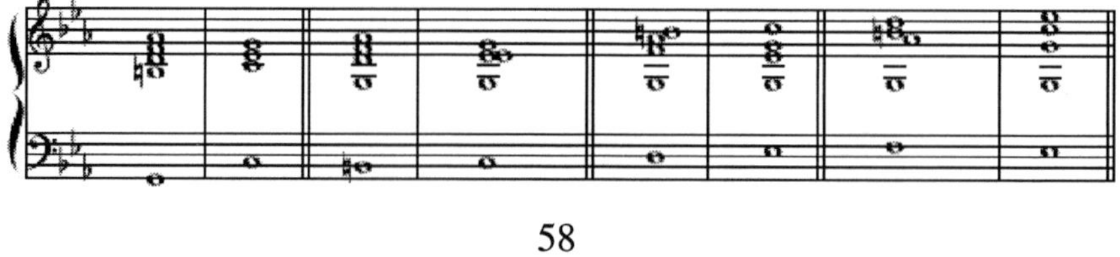

1 2 3 4

131. If I have imposed the order and clarity required in the analysis of the modification of natural dissonant chords by substitution, I had to show that the artificial chords that result introduce a variety of accents into the music, but do not create new instances of tonality; finally, that they do not require the harmonic period, like consonant and natural dissonant chords. At times they take the place of these, but always assume their existence; for, if one disregards these natural chords, their modifications are no longer possible.

It follows that the connection of harmonies modified by others may always be reduced to natural harmony; their use is discretionary, and the composer determines their use by considerations shaped by his thought, but not by tonal necessities. The following examples will conclude my demonstration of these evident truths.

MAJOR MODE

1 Harmony with natural chords

2 Same harmony with substitutions

MINOR MODE

3 Harmony with natural chords

4 Same harmony with substitutions

The simplest observation is sufficient to prove that the harmony of example No. 2 fulfils the same functions as that of No. 1, and that No. 4 has the same tonal signification as No. 3.

Chapter VI

THE EFFECTS OF THE RETARDATION OF CONSONANT AND DISSONANT INTERVALS THROUGH PROLONGATION; THE ARTIFICIAL CHORDS THAT RESULT

132. Our musical feeling has tonality as a first principle, which is nothing but the logical relations of sounds; the second principle, which is only a modification of the first, is the need for variety within unity. It is this need that has led to the modifications of natural chords. In the preceding chapter we saw an analysis of one of these modifications applicable only to combinations of the dissonant chord; there is another that finds its application in consonant and dissonant harmonies; *it consists in the retardation of the natural intervals of chords, by means of the prolongation of one or many notes of the chords that precede them.*

133. To understand the system of this kind of modification of natural chords, it must be noted that it is achieved through ascending, descending, or lateral movements, between the constituent notes, in their succession.

DEMONSTRATION

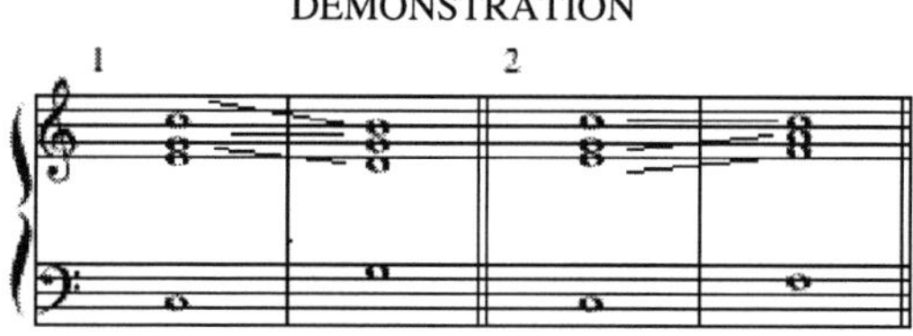

In example one, two of the upper parts have descending movement, and the middle voice remains stationary; in example two, the upper voice does not change pitch, and the other two have an ascending motion.

Now, all descending movement may bring about the prolongation of one or many notes of the first chord onto the second, and consequently retards the natural intervals of the latter, because if there results any dissonance of the second, seventh or ninth, this dissonance obeys the rule of tonality, and resolves by descending, thereby accomplishing the retarded movement.

DEMONSTRATION

1 Natural harmony 2 Retarded harmony

The prolongation that retards the third of the second perfect chord introduces into the latter an interval of a fourth against the bass, which has the relation of a seventh with one of the other notes of the chord; this dissonance resolves by descending one degree, and in doing this, it only serves to accomplish the retarded movement.

We note, in passing, that such is the origin of the error that has caused the fourth to be considered as a dissonance: concern with this fourth has been only with regard to the bass, and it has not been seen that it is the clash of the prolonged note against another, as a second or a seventh, which gives it its dissonant character, and obliges it to make a descending resolution. In the first of the following examples, the fourth produced by the prolongation is in the relation of a second to one of the upper voices; in the second, it is in the relation of a seventh:

EXAMPLE

The fourth which would not be in the relation of the second or seventh with one of the upper voices, would not have a dissonant character in a retarded harmony; it would be free in the succession of chords.

DEMONSTRATION

If the movement is ascending, in the succession of two chords, all prolongation that gives rise to dissonances is inadmissible, because these prolongations could not accomplish the retarded movement without violating the law of the resolution of dissonances.

DEMONSTRATION

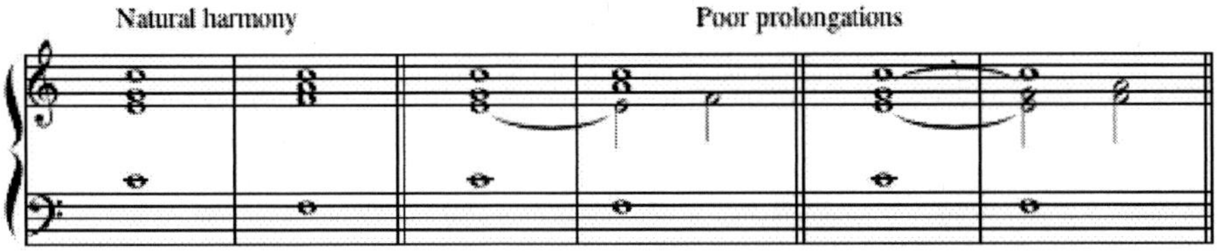

Natural harmony
Poor prolongations

It follows that prolongations are good in ascending movements only when they do not produce dissonances. The following is an example:

Natural harmony Same harmony retarded

However, if the ascending movement takes place from the leading tone to the tonic, the attraction of the first of these notes towards the second absorbs the sensation of dissonance, and the latter not only does not offend the ear in the ascending movement, but satisfies it through one of the most necessary consequences of the law of tonality.

DEMONSTRATION

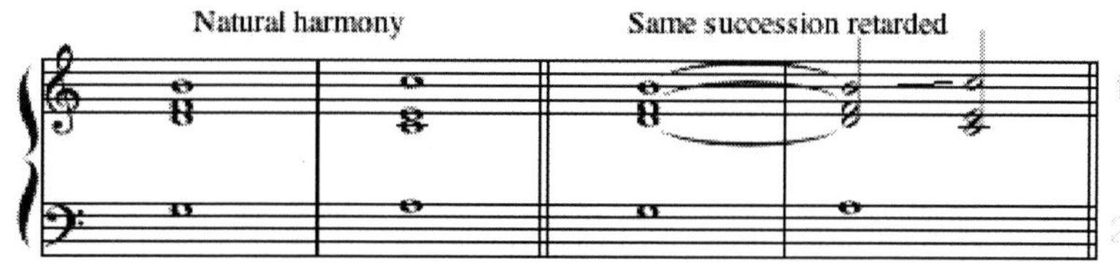

134. Every note that, before the dissonant prolongation, is heard in a state of consonance is called the *preparation of the dissonance*; and one says of every dissonance preceded by such a note that it is *prepared*.

The natural original dissonances, or those produced by substitution, are different from the dissonances that result from prolongation, in that the former satisfy the musical sense from the outset and without being prepared, while the others exist only through the very fact of the preparation. Now, the clash of the fourth degree and the dominant, combined with the attractive notes, alone has the ability to make itself heard without preparation, while the clash of any other two notes of the scale never does, and can only be the product of the prolongation. We will see, in the fourth book of this work, that by not having made this basic distinction, many harmonists have fallen into the errors of a system in direct opposition to the true principles of art and science.

135. The prolongations only modify natural chords insofar as they introduce dissonances. This kind of modification reduces itself to the following: (1) the retardation of the third by the prolongation of the lower note produces the second; (2) the retardation of the sixth produces the seventh, through the prolongation of the upper note; (3) the retardation of the octave, through the prolongation of the upper note, generates the ninth.

DEMONSTRATION

1 Natural harmony — Retarded harmony — 2 Natural harmony — Retarded harmony — 3 Natural harmony — Retarded harmony

Second — Seventh — Ninth

All chordal combinations, where prolongations are introduced, cannot contain other dissonances, either between the upper parts, or against the bass, for these are the only chordal combinations that are provided by the relations of tones in our tonality. It is therefore in error that certain unskilled composers have introduced into their works prolongations of the bass which give rise to retardations of the octave by the seventh, as in this example:

Natural harmony — Poor prolongation

To acquire proof that this retarded succession is in opposition to the law of tonality, it suffices to note that the seventh is not here the inversion of the second, as this law would require, but actually that of the ninth.

DEMONSTRATION

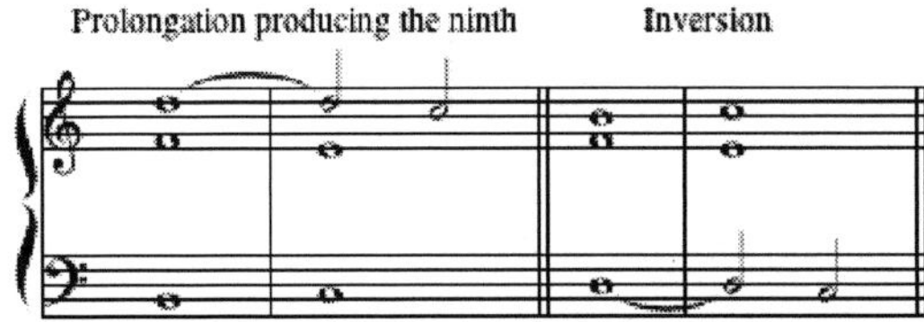

All the instances of tonal order are contained within the limits of the scale, that is, within the octave. In prolongations, one does not conceive the ninth as representing the second, but as having a particular and momentary significance of a tone beyond the limits of the octave; now, beyond this limit the intervals do not invert themselves: the prolongation of the seventh, retarding the octave, is thus not admissible.

136. The entire theory of the modification of natural chords, through prolongation, resides in the above stated principles: these will be seen applied to consonant and dissonant chords respectively.

137. Every descending succession of two chords of which the second is a perfect chord may result in prolongations that produce the retardation

of the third of the second chord by the fourth, and introduces into the upper parts a dissonance of a second or seventh. This dissonance resolves by descending one degree.[17]

---

[17]G. Weber and A. B. Marx, the former in his *Versuch einer geordneten Theorie der Tonsetzkunst*, vol. III, 50, 3rd ed., (*Essay Concerning an Ordered Theory of Music*), and the latter in his *Die Lehre von der musikalischen Composition*, vol. I, 237, (*Science of Musical Composition*), have cited a passage from the overture of *Cosi fan tutte*, by Mozart, where one sees a retardation of the third by the fourth that is not prepared, and which does not result from the prolongation of a note previously heard. Here is the passage:

Weber considered this passage as one of those that proves, according to him, that there are no absolute and general rules in music. For me, I see exactly the contrary, and the most delicate tonal feeling appears to me to have guided Mozart; for the harmony of the perfect chord of F appeared to Mozart implied and persistent during the three measures that precede the retardation of the perfect chord of G. This is so true that, later repeating the phrase, he places this harmony within it, and the succession becomes perfectly regular. Here is the entire passage:

It is evident that, in the first part of this passage, the C is conceived in the harmony of the previous three measures before the prolongation, since it is subsequently heard in the complete harmony.

If one supposes that in place of the first three measures, Mozart had composed these:

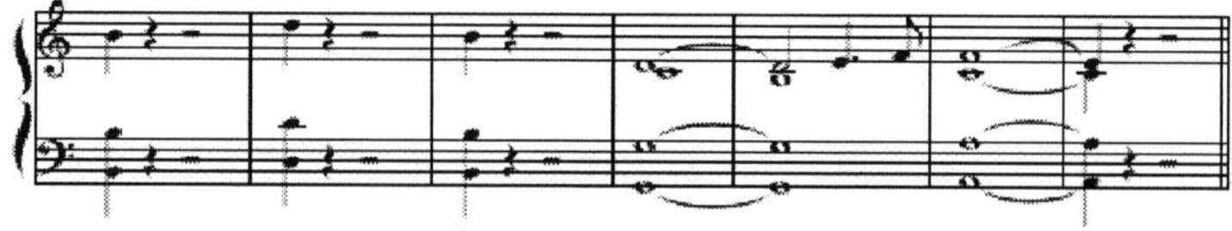

the retardation would become absurd, because nothing would be implied by the prolongation; this would offend the musical sense.

DEMONSTRATION

1 Natural harmony — Retarded succession — 2 Natural harmony — Retarded succession — 3 Natural harmony — Retarded succession — 4 Natural harmony — Retarded succession — 5 Natural harmony — Retarded succession

138. In every succession of two chords in which the second is perfect, the prolongation of a note that descends a degree onto the octave of this second chord produces a dissonance of a ninth, which resolves on the retarded octave.

DEMONSTRATION

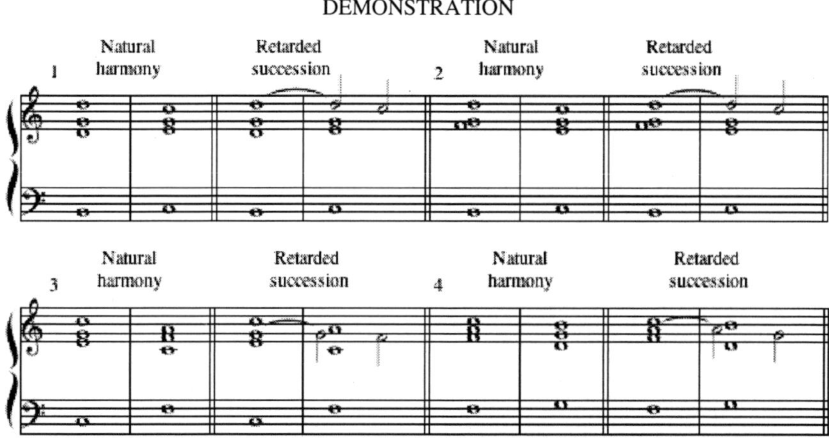

When two notes descend in the succession of two chords in which the latter is a perfect chord, the prolongation of these notes introduces into the second chord a double dissonance of a seventh in the upper parts, and a ninth against the bass, the resolution of which is the completion of the retarded movement, as in the following example:

Natural harmony — Retarded succession

139. Every descending succession of two chords, in which the second is a sixth chord, may give rise to prolongations that produce retardations

of the sixth by the seventh: this dissonance resolves by descending onto the retarded interval.

DEMONSTRATION

1 Natural harmony — Retarded succession — 2 Natural harmony — Retarded succession — 3 Natural harmony — Retarded succession

These prolongations, which retard the interval of the sixth, are those that were used by composers in times when consonant harmony was the only one in use, with artificial dissonances that introduced retardations of the natural intervals.

Modern harmonists, guided by the analogy of the dominant seventh chord, have believed that every seventh chord had to have the fifth in its composition, and introduced this interval into the retardations of the sixth, by means of a double prolongation, where one produces the fifth, which resolves ascending onto the sixth. They use this combination on the degrees where the sixth chord is placed.

EXAMPLES

1 Natural harmony — Retarded succession — 2 Natural harmony — Retarded succession — 3 Natural harmony — Retarded succession

Composers of former schools did not permit this double prolongation that produces the fifth in the retardation of the sixth chord: they were guided by a better feeling of tonality than modern harmonists, having understood that a retarded harmony should contain only the intervals that would compose it if there were no retardation. Now, the sixth chord being composed only of the third and the sixth, the prolongation that retards this sixth by the seventh must present only a seven-three chord. In general, when every retardation of a natural interval comes to an end, the chord should be in its original state. This rule is broken in the retardation of the sixth with the fifth; for if the fifth did not make an ascending movement onto the sixth when the seventh is resolved, one would not have a simple sixth chord, but a six-five chord.

DEMONSTRATION

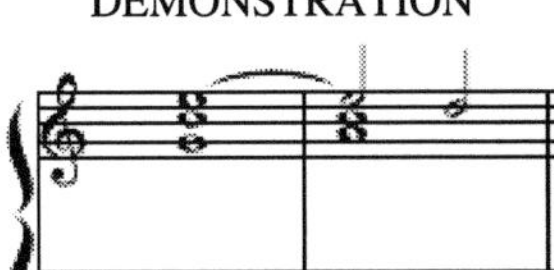

Thus, as I have just said, modern harmonists have been guided by the analogy of the dominant seventh chord, when they placed a fifth in the retardations of sixth chords, and this analogy caused them to forget the law of tonality.

Moreover, in the way they use the chord thus combined, the ascending movement of the fifth onto the sixth is not heard, because this sixth is in unison with the note upon which the prolongation of the seventh resolves: in order that the movement of the fifth be heard, it is necessary that this fifth be placed at a distance of a tenth from the dissonant interval of the seventh and ascend to the octave of the sixth.

DEMONSTRATION

Natural harmony

Double prolongation

It is important to note that the retardation of the sixth by the seventh with the fifth, used by modern harmonists on the third, fourth and sixth degrees, is the real origin of the seventh chords which the authors of certain harmonic systems consider as belonging entirely to these notes of the scale. I will discuss this subject in the fourth book of this work.

140. Some modern day composers present in their works examples of the simultaneous use of the non-retarded sixth, together with the retardation, by placing them at the distance of a ninth, as in this example:

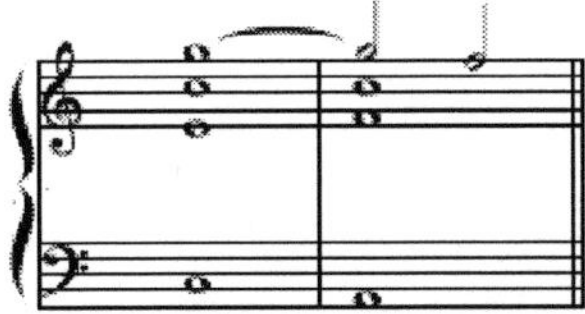

But the contradictory sensation that results from this aggregation disagreeably affects the musical sense.

141. According to the theory of the old Italian schools, the retardation of the octave by the prolongation of the ninth cannot accompany the sixth. This rule was based on a tonal consideration quite correct with regard to the harmony of the sixth on the seventh degree, because, as I have said (§91), the bass note cannot be doubled at the octave in this sixth chord,

without offending our tonal feeling with respect to the chords that must follow it, due to the tendency of the semitone between the leading tone and the tonic; therefore, the ninth must resolve precisely on this octave.

DEMONSTRATION

Natural harmony
Retarded succession

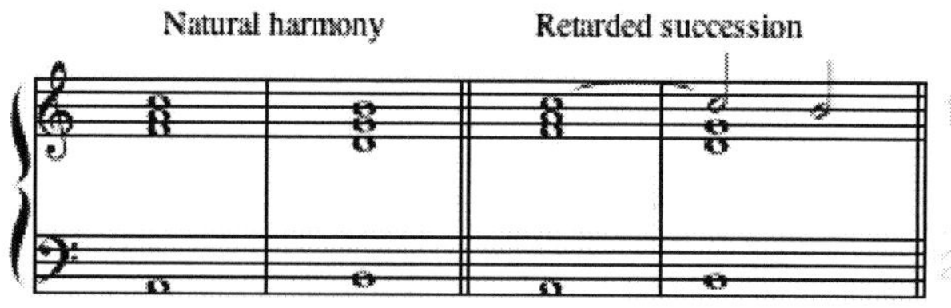

But by over generalizing this principle, the old masters erred, for the notes of the scale that do not have the tendency of the semitone and that carry the sixth chord accompanied by the octave, may certainly allow the prolongation of the ninth without offending our tonal feeling.

DEMONSTRATION

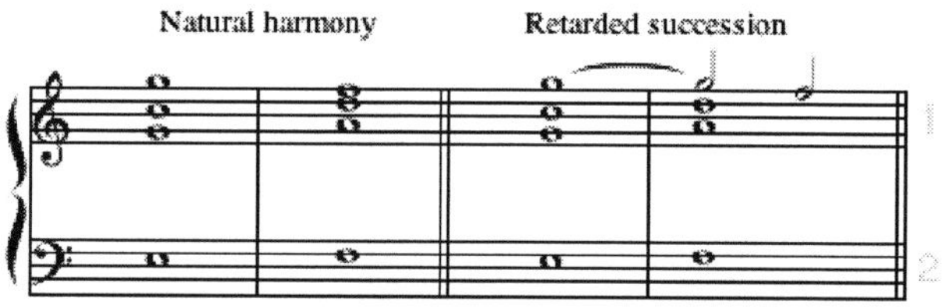

Natural harmony
Retarded succession

142. If two notes descend by one degree in the succession of two chords, in which the second is a sixth chord, these movements may be retarded and produce a double dissonance of a seventh and ninth.

DEMONSTRATION

Natural harmony
Retarded succession

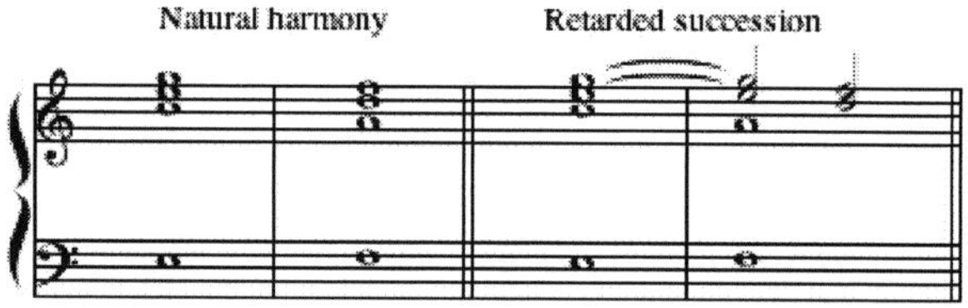

143. When the bass descends a degree in a succession of two chords in which the second is a sixth chord, the prolongation of the bass note of the first chord introduces into the second chord the dissonance of a second, which resolves by descending a degree.

DEMONSTRATION

1
Natural harmony
Retarded succession
2
Natural harmony
Retarded succession

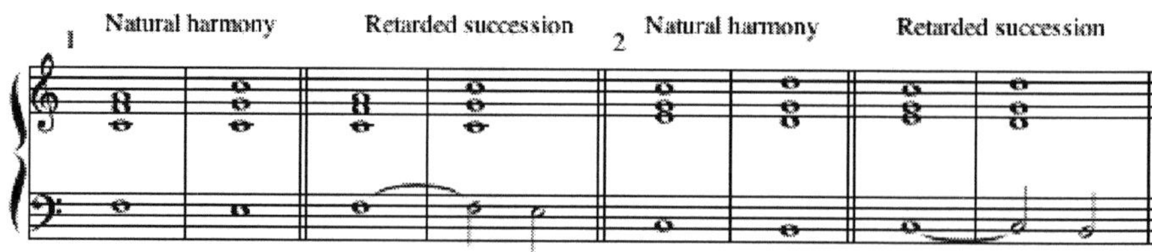

144. If the six-four chord follows the perfect chord or the sixth chord, through a descending movement of a degree onto the sixth, the prolongation retards this sixth, and produces a seven-four chord.

DEMONSTRATION

1 Natural harmony — Retarded succession — 2 Natural harmony — Retarded succession

3 Natural harmony — Retarded succession — 4 Natural harmony — Retarded succession

The tonal tendencies of the leading tone do not permit the use of this retardation of the six-four chord on the tonic; but the descending succession on the fourth may be retarded, and produce a dissonance of the fifth and sixth which resolves on the natural chord.

DEMONSTRATION

Natural harmony — Retarded succession

Some modern harmonists introduce into this retarded succession an interval of a third, to accompany the artificial six-five chord, as in this example:[18]

[18]Catel here provided a remarkable example of the confusion of ideas and the language into which one may fall in theories poorly conceived, upon simple perceptions; for, giving this example of the retardation introduced in the six-four chord (*Traité de l'harmonie*, 25), he thus declares: *double dissonance of the third and fifth, retarding the fourth in the six-four chord*. The third and fifth dissonances! Dissonances that retard the fourth, itself considered as a dissonance by Catel! What is there to say about such a jumble of errors? This recalls the *dissonant consonances* of Rameau (*Traité de l'harmonie*, 95)!

If they had better studied the logical connections of tones that derive from the law of tonality, they would not make this error, identical to that of the use of the fifth with the retardation of the sixth by the seventh. I see myself obliged once again to repeat here what I have said (§139): *A retarded harmony must contain only the notes which would make up the natural harmony if it did not have a prolongation.*

145. When a note descends a degree onto the octave that accompanies the six-four, in four-part harmony, the retardation of this movement produces an artificial nine-six-four chord.

DEMONSTRATION

Natural harmony — Retarded succession — Natural harmony — Retarded succession

This same succession may be retarded in the two descending movements; the double prolongation produces an artificial nine-seven-four chord.

DEMONSTRATION

146. The natural dissonant chords are sometimes prolonged in their entirety on the consonant chords that must succeed them; in this case, the bass note upon which the prolongation is made is the only one that belongs to the retarded chord, up to the moment of resolution.

DEMONSTRATION

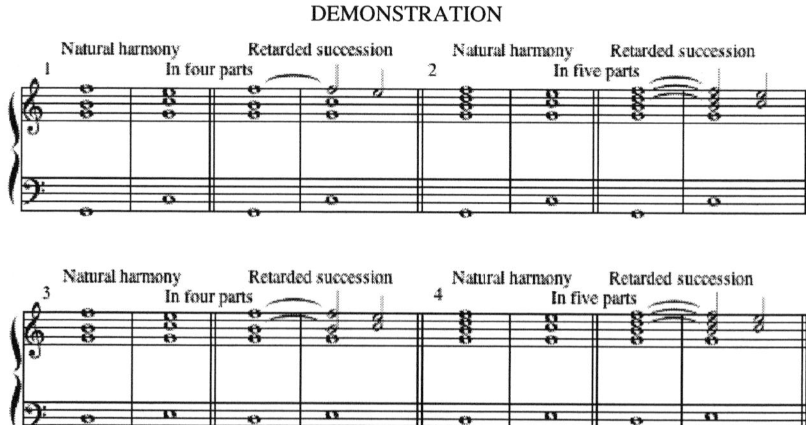

One sees that in these prolongations, the leading tone becomes a major seventh against the tonic; however, it resolves ascending, because, as I have said previously (§133, last example), its attraction toward the tonic absorbs the feeling of dissonance.

147. The dissonant chords in which the substitution is found may also be prolonged on the bass note of the consonant chord that must succeed them, as in the following examples.

The prolongation of the leading-tone seventh chord and that of the tritone with third cannot be made, because the second degree and the sixth form a fifth, which must be followed by another fifth in parallel motion in the resolution; for the second degree being in a state of dissonance, could not rise, and would be obliged to descend with the substituted note.

DEMONSTRATION

The substitutions of the dissonant chord may be prolonged in the minor mode as in the major mode; but the substituted note not having a determined position in the minor mode, as in the major mode, the substitutions of all combinations of the dissonant chord may be prolonged.

DEMONSTRATION

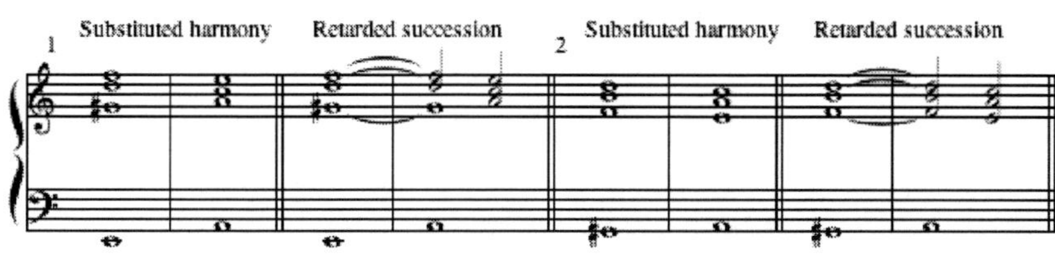

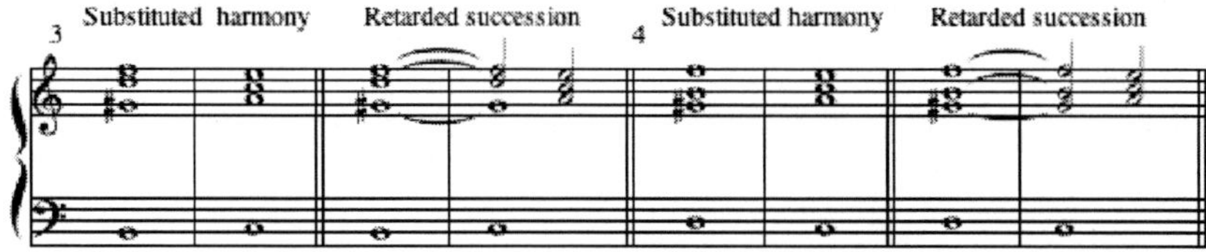

148. Such is the synthetic and analytic theory of dissonant chords through prolongation; a theory drawn from the relations of tones conforming to tonal laws, and in accord with the practice of the most celebrated composers. The application of this theory is found in the following exercises.

EXCERCISES

ON PROLONGATIONS IN CONSONANT CHORDS

We now proceed to examine the phenomena of the prolongation introduced into natural dissonant chords.

149. In the passage of a dissonant chord to a consonant chord, the descending movements of the tonic onto the seventh degree, and the third onto the second, produce prolongations that modify these chords.

150. The retardation of the leading tone through the prolongation of the tonic produces in the seventh chord, and in its inversions, a dissonance of a second or seventh, between the tonic and the second degree.

These chords thus modified, contain two dissonances, namely: (1) a natural dissonance between the fourth degree and the dominant; (2) an artificial dissonance, resulting from the prolongation; the two dissonances must descend by one degree.[19]

[19]An andante passage from Mozart's Quartet [K. 465, 2nd movement, mm. 26-31] offers an example of this genre of modification in the leading-tone sixth chord, where the prolongation does not precede the dissonance, as follows:

DEMONSTRATION

1 Natural harmony — Retarded succession — 2 Natural harmony — Retarded succession

3 Natural harmony — Retarded succession — 4 Natural harmony — Retarded succession

When writing in four parts, in suppressing the fifth of the seventh chord, the prolongation produces a retardation of the third by the fourth:

DEMONSTRATION

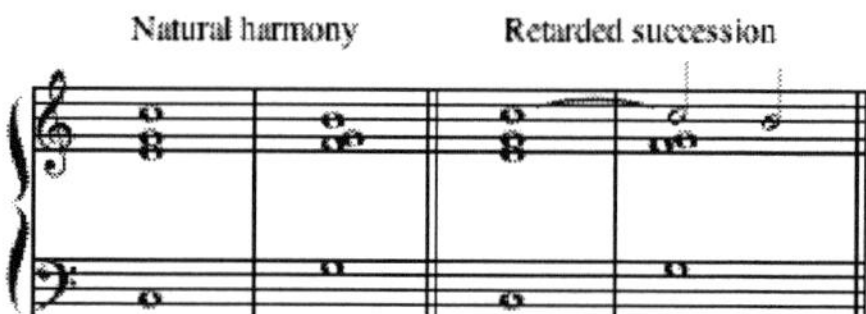

The motivation that led Mozart not to start in the first violin at the same time as the bass, the theme which is then heard in the other parts, in this manner:

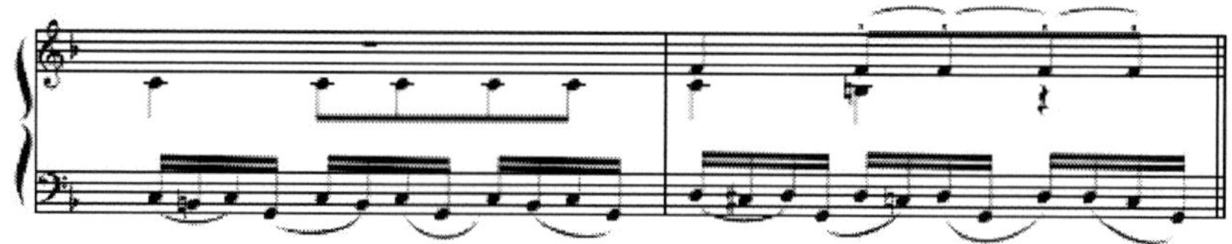

This motivation, I say, is that he wanted to give the entrance of the bass a more mysterious character, supposing correctly that the tonal feeling would make up for the implied prolongation.

The same circumstances happen in the minor mode.

151. The retardation of the second degree by the prolongation of the third, in the succession of a seventh chord, or of its inversions, to a consonant chord, produces a dissonance of a seventh between the fourth and third degrees. These two notes should in fact always be at a distance of a seventh, and never at the interval of a second, for if the natural dissonance of the fourth degree and the dominant were to collide with the dissonance through the prolongation of the third with the fourth, three notes would succeed each other at the distance of a second, for example, E, F, G, which would produce the harshest effect, except when the prolongation would be in the bass. These prolongations must therefore always be arranged as follows:

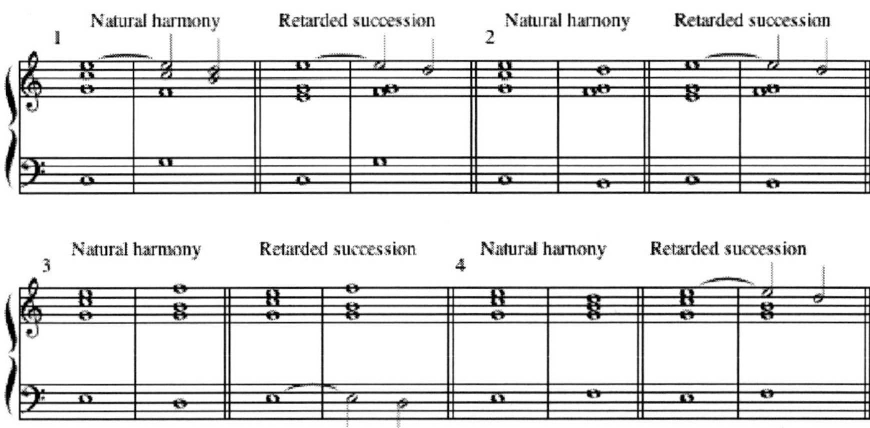

152. One sometimes joins two prolongations in the same chords, by keeping the same arrangement of the intervals.

DEMONSTRATION

As can be seen, the original chord appears in these successions as soon as the prolongations come to an end.

BOOK TWO

EXERCISES

PROLONGATIONS IN DISSONANT CHORDS

MAJOR MODE

MINOR MODE

Chapter VII

JOINING THE SUBSTITUTION TO THE RETARDATION OF INTERVALS IN THE SEVENTH CHORD AND ITS INVERSIONS—ARTIFICIAL CHORDS THAT RESULT

153. Each kind of modification of chords being independent of the other, and producing effects of a particular order, it is easy to understand that they may be used separately or conjointly, and that, in their joining, the mind does not confuse that which belongs to one or the other. In this way the effects of the substitution combine with those of the retardation in the use of dissonant chords, without mutually destroying their effect.

154. We know that, considered separately, the substitution of the sixth degree for the dominant, and the retardation of the leading tone by the prolongation do not change the tonal use of the dominant seventh and its inversions. The joining of the two kinds of modification of these chords does not take away from their destination or connection to consonant chords. Thus, the composer may write, for identical cases, one of the four following combinations of the same succession, guided solely by the imagination in the choice he makes.

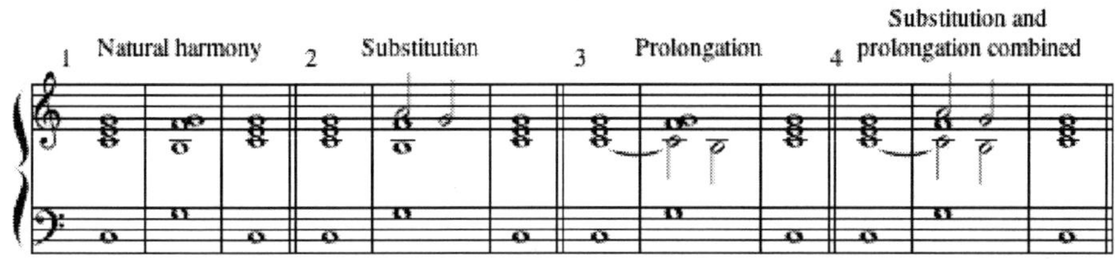

1 Natural harmony 2 Substitution 3 Prolongation 4 Substitution and prolongation combined

The identical circumstances happen in the inversions.

DEMONSTRATION

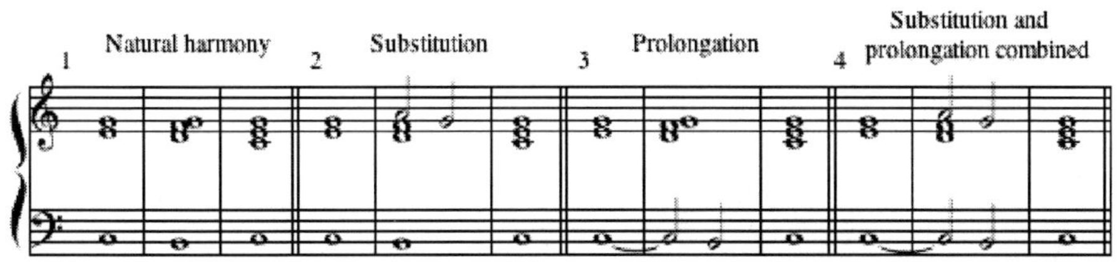

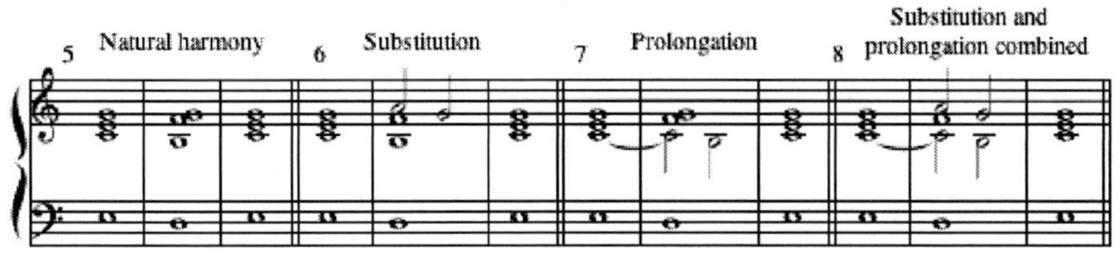

1 Natural harmony 2 Substitution 3 Prolongation 4 Substitution and prolongation combined

5 Natural harmony 6 Substitution 7 Prolongation 8 Substitution and prolongation combined

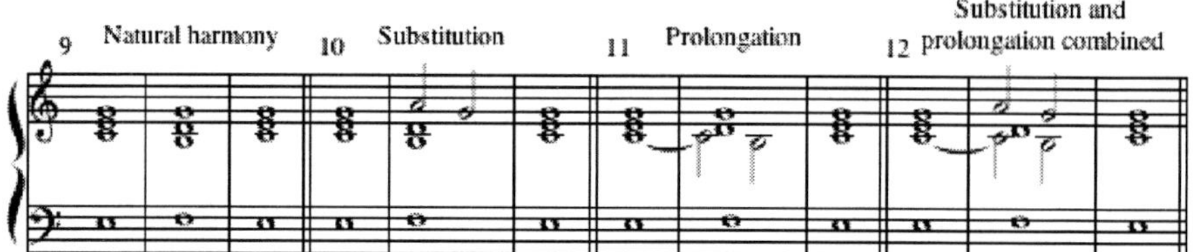

The substitution, which is not made on the lowest note of the seventh, in the major mode, for the reasons that we have seen above (§125), becomes possible with the prolongation, because the unpleasant clash of the sixth degree against the leading tone, as a second, no longer exists, the prolongation having replaced it with the third.

DEMONSTRATION

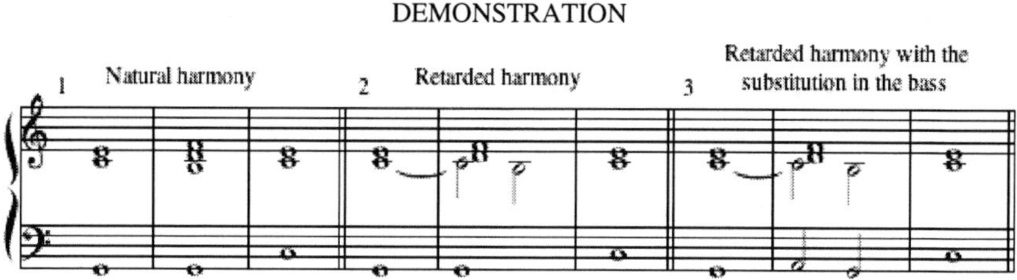

155. We have just seen that the prolongation causes the clash of a second between the sixth degree and the leading tone to disappear, which is the result of simple substitution; as a result the necessity of placing the substituted note as an upper note no longer exists, and the chords which are the product of the double modification may be arranged in various intervallic positions.

DEMONSTRATION

The disappearance of the double dissonance of the second between the fourth degree and the dominant, and between the sixth degree and the leading tone, which is the result of joining the substitution with the leading tone, is also the reason that the bass, becoming free in the chords of the second and fourth degrees, may make movements that place the resolution of the modified chords on other notes than those where they should be in a natural state, or with simple substitution, as in the following example.

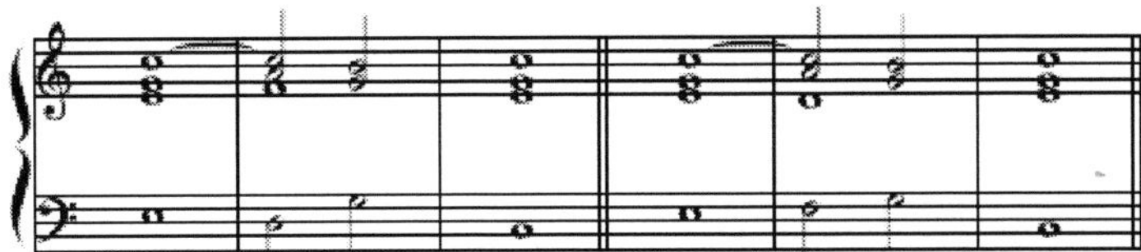

Sometimes the artificial dissonance of the six-five chord, instead of resolving immediately, is prolonged on the six-four chord of the dominant, and descends only onto the third of the following perfect chord: this suspension of the resolution is not lacking in charm.

156. The joining of the two kinds of modification in natural dissonant chords not having been perceived by harmonists, the artificial chords that result from them have plagued authors of a multitude of systems on the science of harmony. Some of them have considered the minor seventh chord with the minor third, for example, as a fundamental chord, composed of a minor third, perfect fifth and minor seventh, and have given it through inversion the other modifications of the dominant seventh chord and its derivatives, arranging them in the following order, and giving them the names placed above each one, as follows:[20]

---

[20]Rameau is the first to present these chords in this form. Catel, who had clearly seen that the seventh chord is not fundamental, and that it results from prolongation, went astray when he sought the harmonic mechanism of the formation of this chord. The minor seventh chord, he says, results from the prolongation of the tonic onto a perfect chord of the second degree. He demonstrates this proposition as follows (*Traité de l'harmonie*, 23):

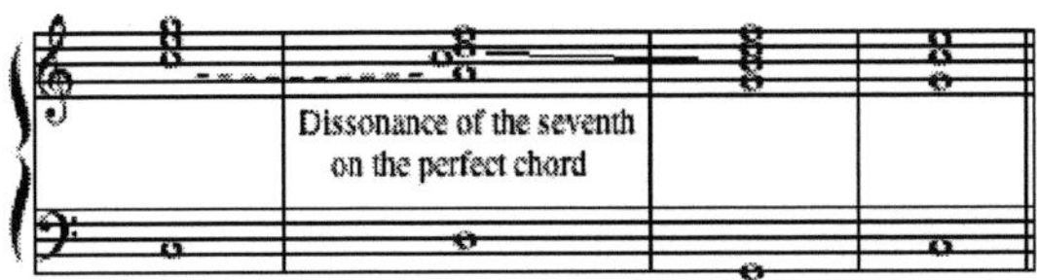

An analogous operation, that is, the prolongation of the tonic on the derivatives of the perfect chord of the second degree, provides him with the inversions of this seventh chord.

But the perfect chord does not belong to the second degree in our tonality; but every prolongation that produces a dissonance represents another natural note of a chord, a note which must be recovered in suppressing the prolongation, and which must be a

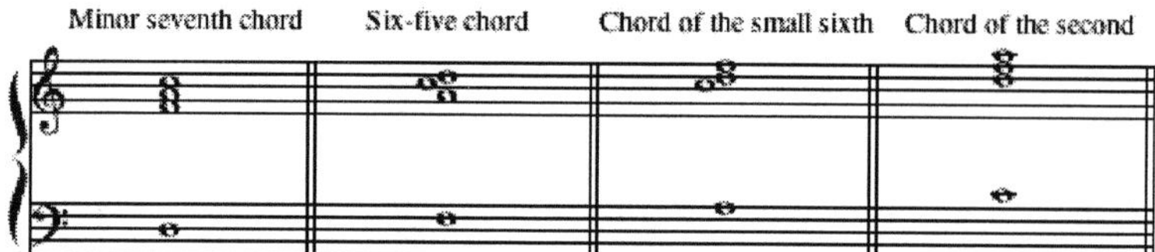

These chords, in isolation, reveal nothing to the mind about their use, and their origin disappears. All that the harmonists have been able to say, to distinguish them from natural dissonant chords, or those affected by substitution, is that the dissonance they contain *must be prepared*. But what is a prepared dissonance? What gives rise to the preparation? And from where comes this difference between the dissonances which require the preparation, and others which are not subject to it? These are insoluble questions for authors of systems based upon considerations of isolated chords, without the necessary connections through the law of tonality; finally, it is the source of poor reasoning, contradictory assertions, and cloudy theory found in all treatises on harmony.

157. The movement of the bass which causes the minor seventh chord to resolve on the dominant seventh chord, produced through substitution and prolongation, has given rise to progressions where each note is accompanied by a seventh chord, in which the nature of the intervals differ according to the degree of the scale where the chord is placed. So, on the dominant, it is made up of the major third, perfect fifth and minor seventh; on the second, third, and sixth degrees, it has the minor third, the perfect fifth, and the minor seventh; on the seventh degree the third, fifth, and seventh are minor; finally, on the tonic and on the fourth degree the third and the seventh are major, and the fifth is perfect.

---

consonance. The prolongation, of which Catel speaks, is therefore not made on a consonant chord, but on a six-five chord, since, in the example cited, C retards B.

DEMONSTRATION

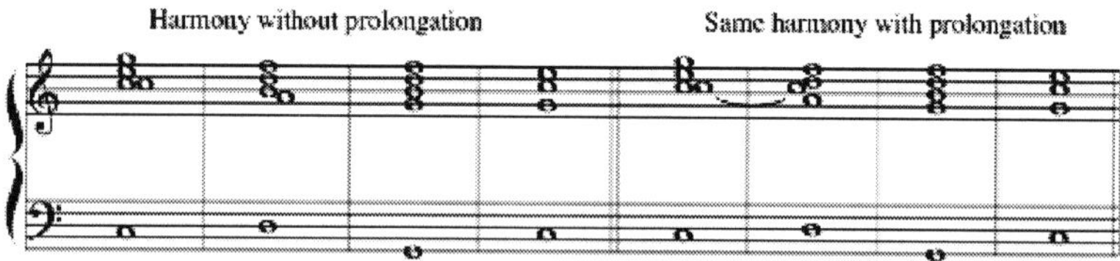

But the six-five chord is not a natural chord, and the one we see here on the second degree is precisely the product of the substitution arranged in another order than what is required by tonal attraction: the origin found by Catel is therefore false. As for the resolution of the chord onto the dominant seventh, I have shown from what it results (§156).

In Reicha's system, the minor seventh chord is the sixth chord in his arbitrary classification (*Cours de composition musicale*, 8).

As I have said and demonstrated (§78), the analogy of the movement fixes the attention in progressions of this kind, and suspends tonal feeling up to the cadence, such that in reality no degree is in fact determined until the moment of this cadence, which reveals the tonal feeling; we are only conscious of the uniform movement of the bass, and of the symmetrical composition of the chords that accompany these notes. Such is the phenomenon that manifests itself upon hearing this progression of seventh chords on movements of the bass rising a fourth and descending a fifth.

Progressions based on the same principles are also made with the other chords modified by both substitution and prolongation combined.

EXAMPLES:[21]

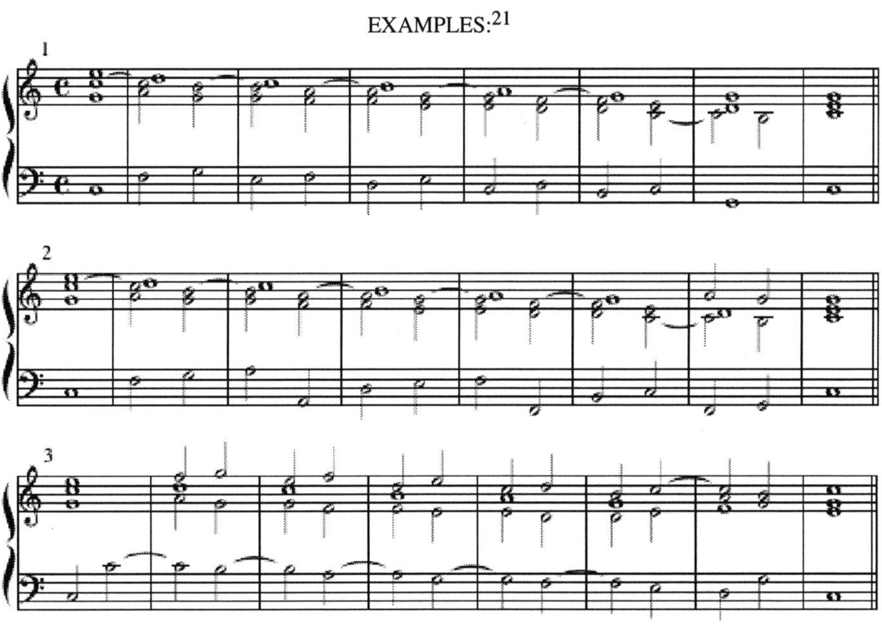

[21]A progression based on a combination of prolongation and substitution cannot be good unless the prolongation actually continues, and this is what generates the dissonance. This point must cause one to reject, as offending tonal feeling, the following progressions put forward by [Johann Christian] Frederic Schneider [1786-1840] (*Elementarbuch der Harmonie*, 15).

158. In the minor mode, one may use, as in the major mode, a combination of substitution and prolongation to modify the natural dissonant chords. The circumstances being similar for the use of these chords in the two modes, it would be pointless to speak of those of the minor mode, if the fifth of the minor seventh chord were not also minor, while it is perfect in the major mode.

DEMONSTRATION

Natural harmony — Substitution and prologation combined — Resolution on a different bass

---

1.

2.

3.

4.

Similar errors can be found only in a theory based on isolated seventh chords placed on all the notes of the scale.

Harmonists have regarded the chord thus constituted as a fundamental chord having inversions: they have arranged it in this way:

Now, the similarity of these chords with that of the leading-tone seventh and the other artificial chords of the major mode produced by simple substitution, presented in this order by Catel and many authors of harmonic systems, has been the source of many errors which I have already shown (§123). Here is what Catel said (*Traité d'harmonie*, 15):

"The leading-tone seventh chord does not belong exclusively to the major mode: *There are cases where one uses it without preparation on the second of the relative minor mode*. Thus it is called the chord of the second note of the minor mode. It resolves on the dominant."

After having given the following examples,

Seventh chord on the second in the minor mode — 1st derivation — 2nd derivation

Catel adds: "It is this double employment which has caused this chord to be called the *mixed seventh*."

"Since in the minor mode this chord is used much more often in preparing the seventh than without preparation, *it is nothing more than a diminished fifth chord* (minor fifth) *which receives a prolongation of the seventh. Thus, it returns to the series of simple chords that receive the prolongation of a foreign note*."

We see that this is again the false origin taken from the prolongation on a five-three chord on the second degree, of which I have just demonstrated the impossibility.

But if this chord is the product of a prolongation, its use without preparation is therefore not admissible; and if it does not have the same origin as the artificial leading-tone seventh chord, it is therefore not the same, and the idea of a *mixed chord*, belonging to two keys and two different modes, is therefore absolutely false!

It is into such errors that a musician, otherwise knowledgeable, and enjoying a deserved respect, may be drawn through faults of logic.

This clarification seemed to me necessary to dispel all doubts about the true origin of the harmonic combinations in question, and to complete the demonstration of this origin in the combination of substitution and prolongation.

159. We thus arrive at the end of all the harmonic combinations that can modify the natural chords in a regular way, in the form of a stable tonality. Every other modification establishes relations between diverse tonalities, or is irreducible to absolute forms, as will be seen later. It follows that all the chords previously analyzed make up the harmony of which every scale of a major or minor key may be accompanied, without introducing relationships with foreign scales. A review of some of these types of harmony will lead to some useful observations.

DIATONIC SCALES

ACCOMPANIED BY NATURAL CHORDS

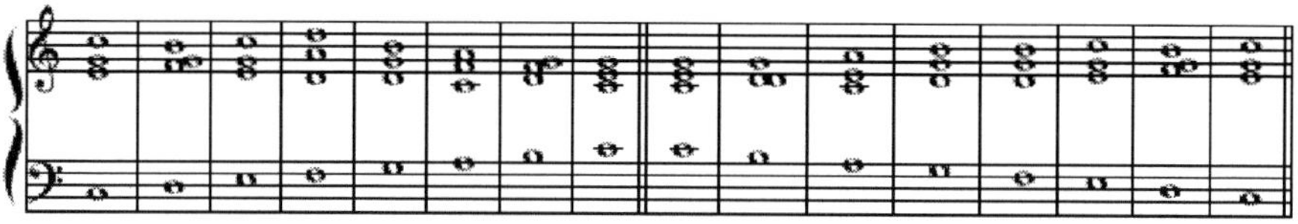

Same harmony modified by substitution

Same harmony modified by prologation

Same harmony with combined prologation and substitution of the fourth degree

The use of modulations that natural dissonant chords have introduced into music, in forming modern tonality, have given rise to a generally adopted formula of the harmonic scale, in which tonal unity is not preserved in descending; for there the leading-tone sixth is placed on the sixth degree, momentarily considering the dominant as a new tonic, and then returning to the key of the scale through the fourth degree, accompanied by the chord of the tritone. The old French harmonists called this formula the *rule of the octave* (*règle de l'octave*); the Italians call it the *scala armonica*, or simply *scala*. Here is this scale:[22]

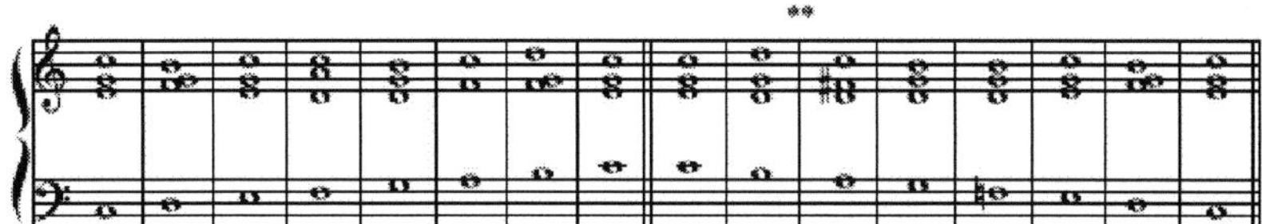

In the minor mode, the sixth degree being a semitone lower than in the major mode, one cannot accompany it with the leading-tone sixth: tonal unity permits only the sixth chord on this degree, as follows:

22**The two fifths between the upper parts that we see here, of which one is minor, have been the subject of controversy in various schools. Fenaroli‡ and the other Italian authors trained in the Naples school, wishing to avoid these fifths, write as follows:

But all the parts descending with the bass and forming amongst themselves lateral movements of the fourth in the succession from the second chord to the third, produces a tasteless and clumsy style. One may avoid it by writing thus:

The replacement of root position harmony in the tritone chord is only a change in the position of the notes in the perfect chord of the dominant, and is not unpleasant; but the problem with writing this way is the lack of all melodic shape in the first four chords.

As for me, I admit that I do not perceive any disadvantage in the two fifths, because they do not offend tonal feeling, which is the basis of all harmony.

‡Fétis reports that Fedele Fenaroli (1732-1818) provided a set of concise rules in a primer entitled *Regole per i principianti di cembalo nel sonar coi numeri e per principianti di contrappunto* (Naples, 1775). [PL]

This harmonic formula is unquestionably the best, the most consistent with the laws of tonality; however, it is not the one that is most generally used. The Italians and the old French harmonists use a six-four-three chord on the sixth degree of the descending scale, resulting from the prolongation of the tonic combined with the substitution of the sixth degree for the dominant in the bass (see §158, example 3).

EXAMPLE

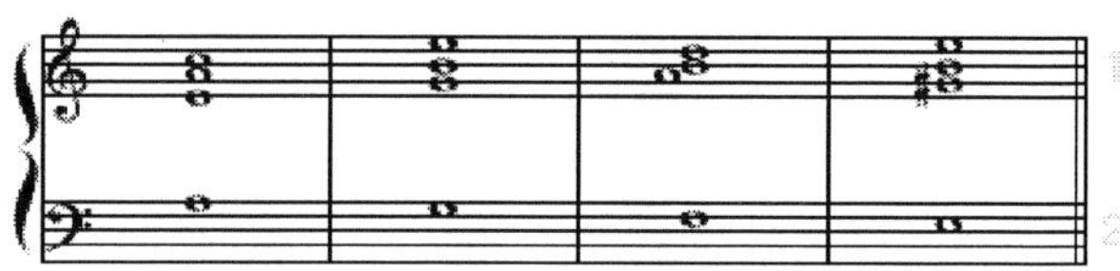

This harmony is clearly defective, in that the dissonance that is the result of the prolongation is not prepared in the chord of the sixth degree. It is, as will be seen, an application of the false theory of the mixed *seventh*, of which Catel speaks (see all of §158).

The German theorists have all evaded the fundamental difficulties of the determination of the tonality by the scale in the bass, by placing this scale only in the upper voice, where the harmonic accompaniment is easier, and in which they have not had any consideration for the laws of a singular tonality; but in particular cases where they have had to place on the descending sixth degree of the minor scale the harmony which appeared to them appropriate, they placed a chord of the third, fourth and augmented sixth, such as: (see Schneider's book, entitled *Elementarbuch der Harmonie*, 28, ex. b),[23]

in which ambiguous harmony becomes doubtful if it is a leading-tone sixth chord altered in the bass:

or the six-four-three chord of the Italian harmonists, altered in the upper part:

[23]Fétis reports that as a composer Schneider is regarded as one of the masters of the German school. His theory is discussed further in Book Four of the *Traité*. *FétisB*, 8:122. [PL]

Be that as it may, it is this harmony that, from Germany, has been introduced into France, and has been generally adopted for the accompaniment of the sixth degree of the descending scale of the minor mode, such that the formula of the scale is the following:

However, I repeat, the true tonal formula of this scale is that which places the chord of the simple sixth on the sixth degree.

160. Sometimes the scale progression is transformed by symmetrical forms of the harmony that accompanies it; so the notes of this scale lose their character of tonal determination, like all other non-modulating progressions.

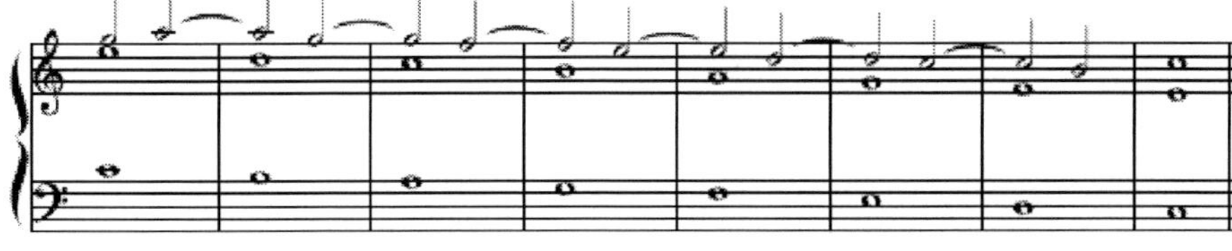

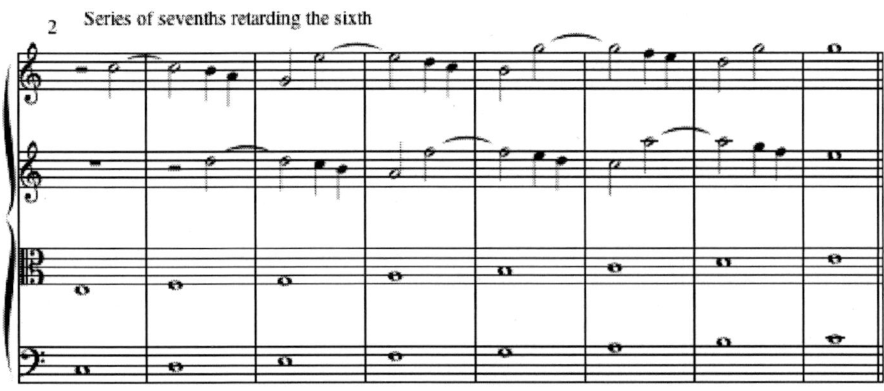

3 Series of ninths retarding the octave

Double prolongations of sevenths and ninths

Thirds retarded by the fourth

Chapter VIII

THE ALTERATION OF INTERVALS OF NATURAL CHORDS, AND THEIR MODIFICATIONS BY SUBSTITUTION AND PROLONGATION—THE HARMONIES THAT RESULT

161. As one advances in the science of harmony, one comes to believe that its absolute principle resides in the relations of the tonality of sounds, resulting from a certain necessary order among them, from which arises their functions, attractions, oppositions, and finally their laws of aggregation and succession.

The similarity of the principle of these two kinds of laws appears to me to have been demonstrated in what has preceded: what I have left to say will complete this demonstration, and will prove beyond any doubt that the consideration of isolated chords cannot arrive at any satisfactory result. It is in their succession that is found the origin of all kinds of modifications that are applicable to natural chords.

162. The last of these modifications is found in the arbitrary alteration of the natural intervals of chords, either original, brought about by substitution, or finally, by prolongations and retardations. The successive relationships are also the source of the latter kind of modification.

In fact, in every ascending succession of two notes separated by the interval of a tone, the first of these notes may be raised a semitone by an accidental foreign to the tonality of the chord, or by the suppression of a flat.

DEMONSTRATION

In the same way, in every descending succession of two notes separated by the interval of a tone, the first of these notes may be lowered a semitone by an accidental, a flat foreign to the tonality of the chord, or by the suppression of a sharp.

DEMONSTRATION

Chord of the tritone in C minor — Alteration of the sixth — Alteration without preparation — Minor fifth and sixth chord in the key of E — Alteration of the third — Alteration without preparation

3 4

163. Every alteration of an ascending succession has an ascending attraction; for, not only can it not change the succession that it modifies simply, but also, the effect of the alteration is to give to the altered note a tendency analogous to that of the leading tone in natural chords, and even more energy.

164. Every alteration of a descending succession has a descending attraction; for it cannot change the movement of which it is only a modification; besides, the flat, or the suppression of the sharp which constitute it, give it an analogy with the descending fourth degree of natural dissonant harmony, but with even more energy.

165. Sometimes the ascending and descending alterations are simultaneous: this happens when, in the succession of two chords, there are many ascending and descending movements of notes that are a tone apart.

DEMONSTRATION

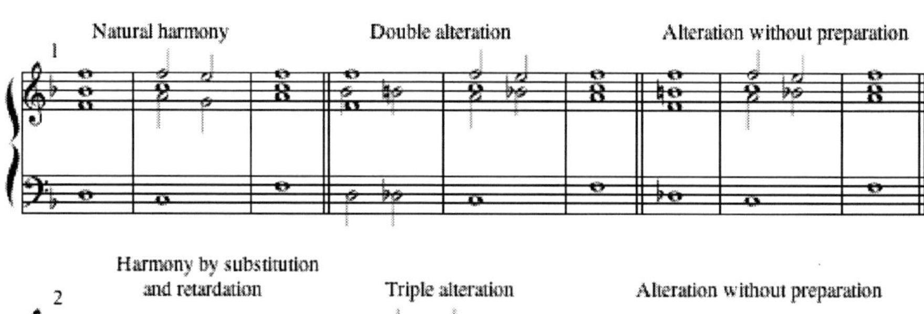

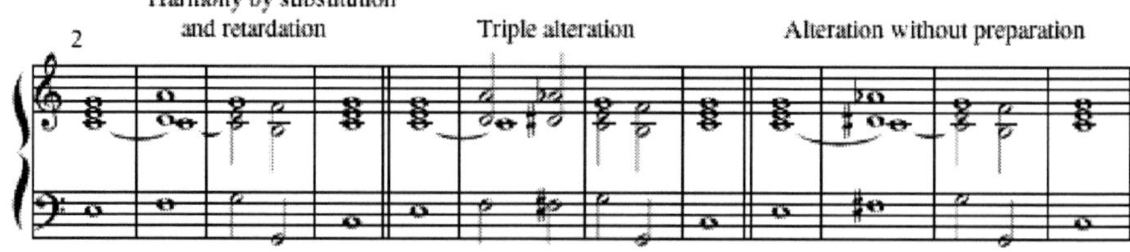

166. The alterations that consist solely in a change of mode, that is, in the substitution of a major interval for a minor one, and *vice versa*, are not considered true alterations. The following passages illustrate:

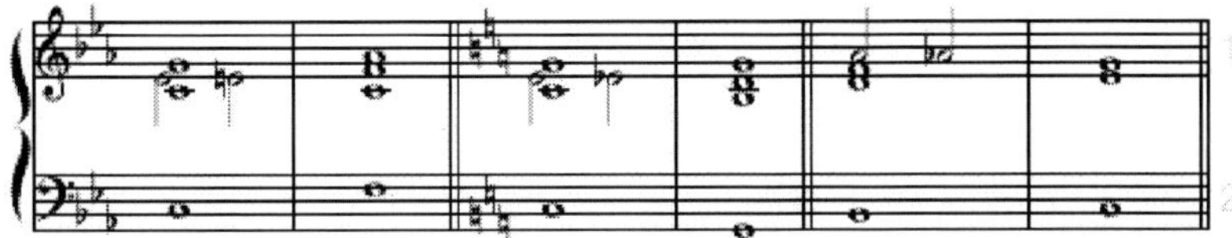

There can only be an alteration when using accidentals completely foreign to the tonality of a scale; this results in intervals that are not major or minor, but augmented or diminished.

167. The intervals that make up consonant chords are, as one knows, the third, fourth, fifth, sixth and octave: all may be altered, that is, augmented or diminished, in their connection with other harmonies.

168. The ascending alteration of the fifth happens only in the major mode: it produces the augmented fifth.

DEMONSTRATION

Natural harmony — Altered harmonmy — Alteration without preparation

The inversions of this alteration produce the major third, in the minor sixth chord, and the diminished fourth, in the six-four chord.

DEMONSTRATION

1 Natural harmony — Altered harmony — Alteration without preparation — 2 Natural harmony — Altered harmony — Alteration without preparation

169. The fifth of the perfect chord may also be augmented by the descending movement of the bass note of a chord of the sixth degree on the dominant.

DEMONSTRATION

Natural harmony — Altered harmony — Same without preparation

The inversions of this alteration produce the minor sixth with the major third, and the diminished fourth with the minor sixth.

DEMONSTRATION

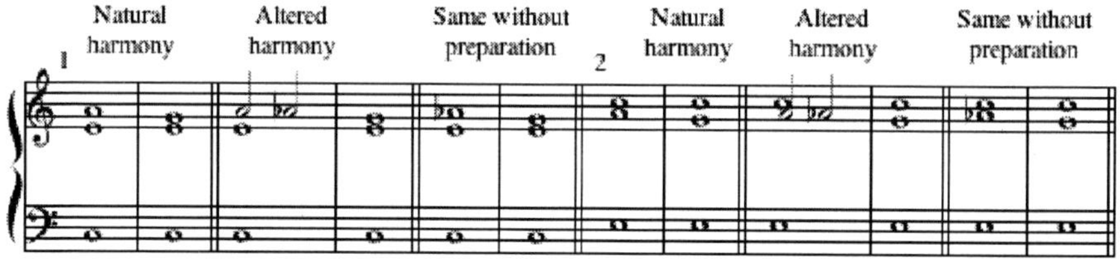

1 Natural harmony — Altered harmony — Same without preparation — 2 Natural harmony — Altered harmony — Same without preparation

170. The descending alteration of the fifth of a perfect chord is possible only in the passage from the tonic of a minor mode to the leading tone of another key. In this case, the altered fifth is called the *diminished fifth*, in accordance with the rule that classes amongst the augmented or diminished intervals all those that are not in the normal state of tonality, even though in fact this interval is the same size as the minor fifth of the leading tone.

DEMONSTRATION

Natural harmony — Altered harmony — Same without preparation

The inversions of this alteration produce the minor third with the major sixth (a combination that can only exist on the second degree, in the normal state of tonality, and which constitutes a true alteration on the tonic); finally, the sixth with *augmented fourth*, the designation of which is here founded on the same principle as that of the *diminished fifth*.

DEMONSTRATION

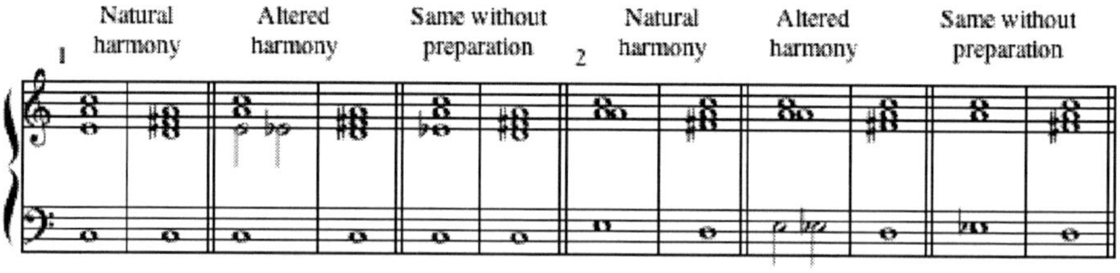

1 Natural harmony — Altered harmony — Same without preparation — 2 Natural harmony — Altered harmony — Same without preparation

171. The third of the perfect chord may be diminished in the passage from the perfect chord of the fourth degree of the minor mode to the dominant.

DEMONSTRATION

Natural harmony Altered harmony Same without preparation

The inversions of this alteration produce the augmented sixth with the third on the sixth degree of the minor mode, and the augmented fourth with the minor sixth on the tonic.

DEMONSTRATION

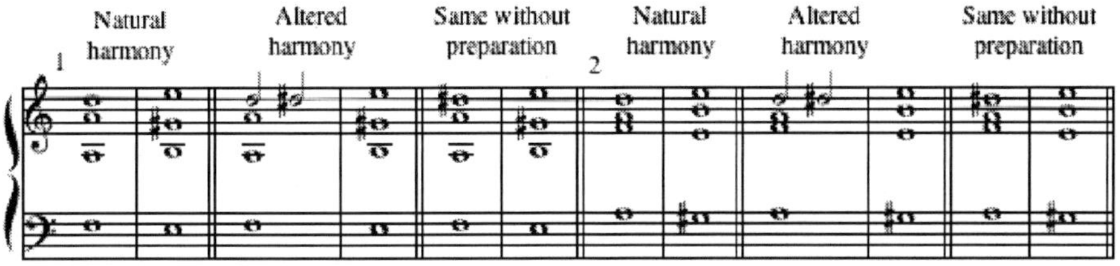

1 Natural harmony Altered harmony Same without preparation 2 Natural harmony Altered harmony Same without preparation

172. The ascending alteration of the third of the perfect chord is possible only in the passage from the tonic of a major key to one of the notes of the harmony of the dominant of another key.

DEMONSTRATION

Natural harmony Altered harmony Same without preparation

The inversions of this alteration produce the diminished third with the diminished sixth; and the augmented sixth with the perfect fourth.

DEMONSTRATION

1 Natural harmony Altered harmony Same without preparation

2 Natural harmony Altered harmony Same without preparation

173. Sometimes one uses simultaneous ascending and descending alterations in the perfect chord; for example, that of the augmented fifth of the major mode with a simple change of the major third to minor third. Although this is considered only a change of mode, it nevertheless creates a true alteration of the diminished sixth between the augmented fifth and the minor third.

DEMONSTRATION

Natural harmony Altered harmony Same without preparation

The first inversion of these alterations produces the major sixth with augmented third; the second inversion, leading from a six-four chord to another chord of the same kind, of which the effect would be dull and disagreeable, is used only when it is followed by the harmony of the dominant of another key.

DEMONSTRATION

1 Natural harmony Altered harmony Same without preparation 2 Natural harmony Altered harmony Same without preparation

173. (*bis*). The ascending alteration of the octave happens in the passage of a consonant chord to a natural dissonant chord: it produces the diminished octave when the alteration is in the lower note of the octave, and the augmented octave, when it is in the upper note.

DEMONSTRATION

1 2 3 4

This alteration should not be made without preparation because of its harshness.

174. The movement of the second degree, be it ascending or descending, is the only one that can be altered in the tonal resolution of natural dissonant chords, because the two other notes of these chords, namely, the fourth degree and leading tone, each have a forced movement of a semitone.

The ascending alteration produces, in the fundamental harmony, a seventh chord with augmented fifth. The effect of this alteration is pleasant only when the second altered degree is placed at the interval of the augmented sixth on the fourth degree.

DEMONSTRATION

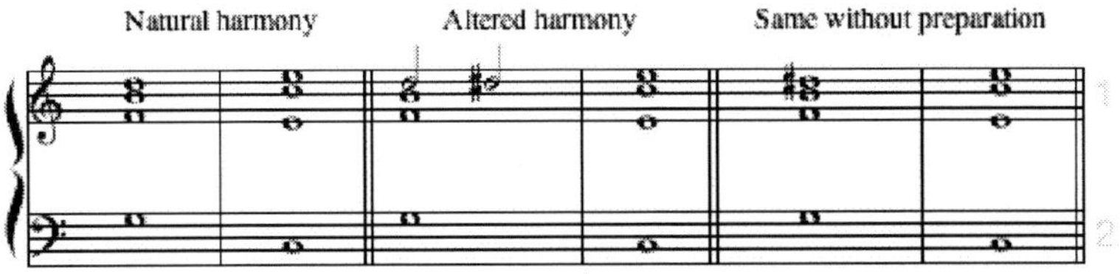

Natural harmony Altered harmony Same without preparation

The same alteration produces, in first inversion, a minor fifth and sixth chord with major third; in the second, a diminished third, diminished fourth, and minor sixth chord; in the third, a major second, major fourth and augmented sixth chord.

DEMONSTRATION

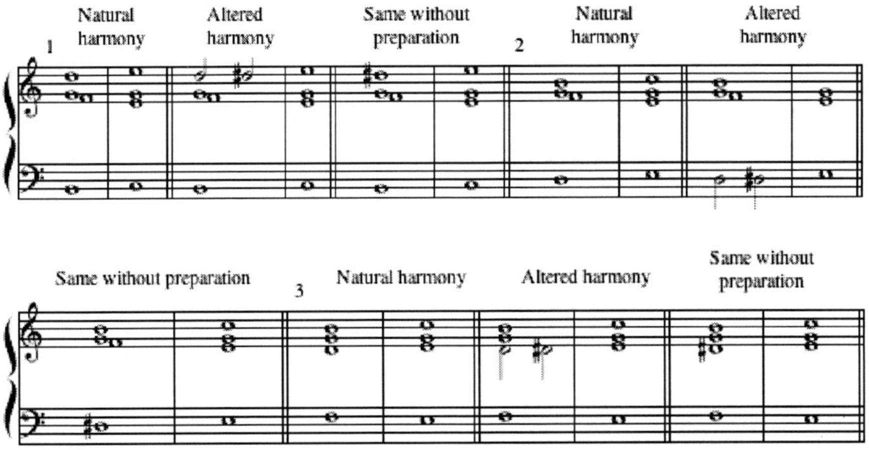

1 Natural harmony Altered harmony Same without preparation 2 Natural harmony Altered harmony

Same without preparation 3 Natural harmony Altered harmony Same without preparation

The descending alteration of the second degree produces, in the same fundamental harmony, a seventh chord with *diminished fifth* and major third.[24]

[24]Here the fifth is truly *diminished*, because the note that renders it does not belong to the key of this natural chord.

The same alteration produces, in the first inversion, a minor fifth and sixth chord with diminished third; in the second, a major third, major fourth and augmented sixth chord; in the last, a major second, major fourth and minor sixth chord.

DEMONSTRATION

1 Natural harmony | Altered harmony | Same without preparation | 2 Natural harmony | Altered harmony | Same without preparation

3 Natural harmony | Altered harmony | Same without preparation | 4 Natural harmony | Altered harmony | Same without preparation

When using this alteration, it is necessary to avoid the diminished third resolving on the unison, and to place, in the seventh chord and in its last inversion, the altered second degree and the leading tone an augmented sixth apart.

Sometimes composers use this descending alteration of the fifth of the seventh chord in reverse, that is, presenting first the altered note, then the natural note, as in the following examples:

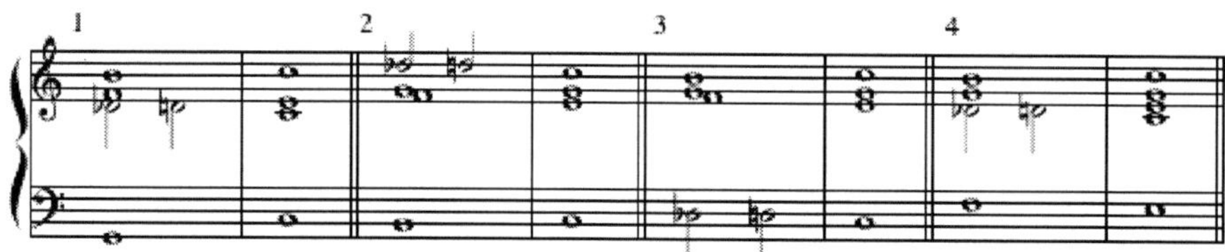

175. Two notes may be altered in the chords affected by the substitution of the major mode, namely: the substituted note, which descends a tone onto the dominant, in making its resolution, and the second degree, which rises a tone to the third.

The ascending alteration of the second degree gives, in the dominant ninth harmony, a chord composed of the major third, minor seventh, and major ninth.

In this combination, the necessity of having the altered note at the distance of the augmented sixth from the seventh, forces it to be placed in the upper part, but while maintaining the substituted note at the interval of a seventh from the leading tone.

DEMONSTRATION

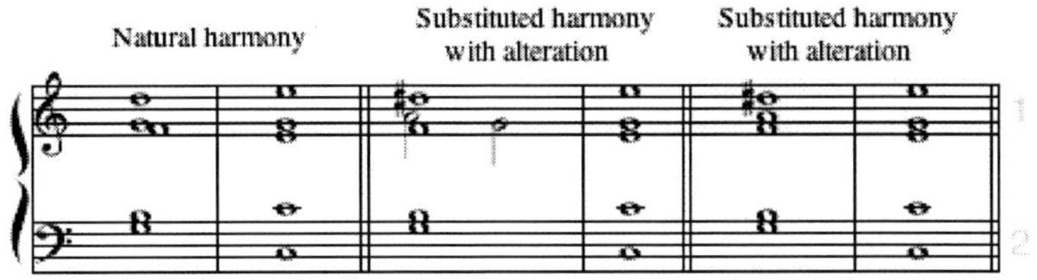

Natural harmony — Substituted harmony with alteration — Substituted harmony with alteration

This alteration produces in the harmony of the leading-tone seventh a chord made up of the major third, minor fifth and minor seventh; in the harmony of the fifth and leading-tone sixth, a chord composed of the diminished third, minor fifth and minor sixth; finally in the harmony of the tritone with third, a chord made up of the major third, major fourth and augmented sixth.

DEMONSTRATION

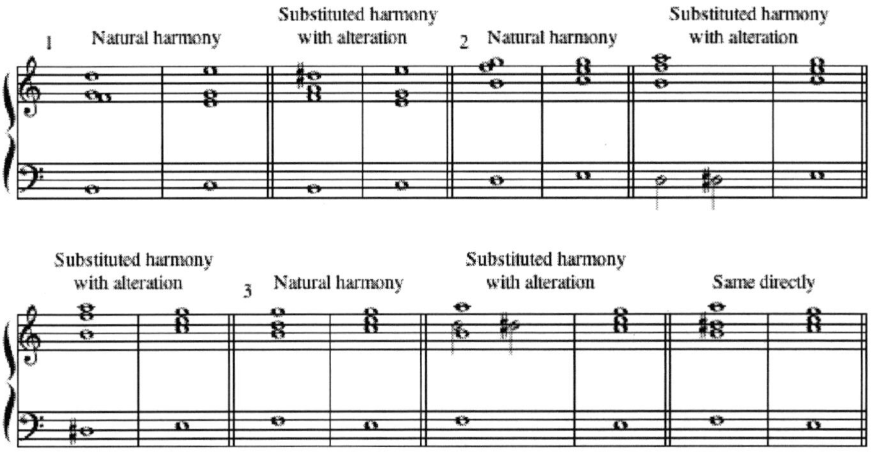

1 Natural harmony — Substituted harmony with alteration — 2 Natural harmony — Substituted harmony with alteration

Substituted harmony with alteration — 3 Natural harmony — Substituted harmony with alteration — Same directly

As one sees, the alteration is not prepared in the ninth chord nor in that of the leading-tone seventh, because the second degree can be admitted above the substituted note only in a state of alteration, in which the ascending attraction removes the harshness of this arrangement.

176. The alteration of the substituted note, in its descending motion, produces only a change of mode, for it simply transforms a major ninth chord into a minor ninth, a leading-tone seventh chord into a diminished seventh chord, etc:

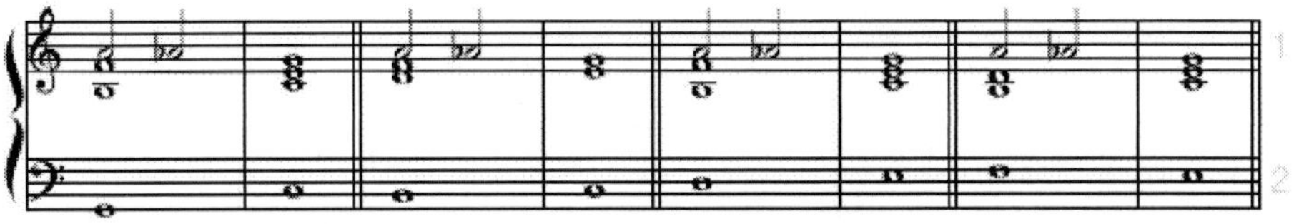

This would not therefore be considered a real alteration, if it could not combine with the ascending alteration of the second degree, so as to form with it a double alteration, of which the following are examples in all the combinations of the dissonant chord with substitution:

177. Chords with substitution in the minor mode sometimes combine with a descending alteration of the second degree. This alteration is fine in the fundamental chord, whether the substitution is in the upper or lower part. It is also fine in first inversion, that is, in the diminished seventh, and in the third, that is, in the tritone with minor third:

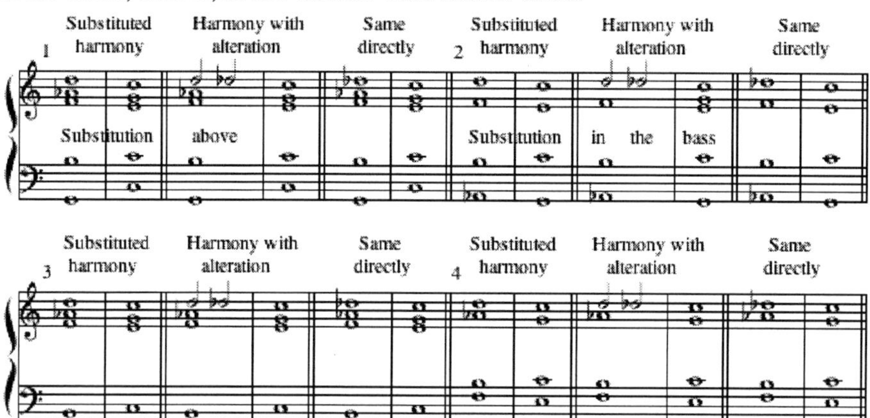

But the alteration of the second inversion, although more commonly used than the others, is a kind of tonal *contre-sens*;[25] for I have shown (§122) that this chord can be followed by the perfect chord of the tonic only when the substituted note resolves beforehand, in order to avoid the two successive fifths. Now, these two fifths being perfect, when the bass has a descending alteration, the harshness of this succession continues, notwithstanding the ascending attraction of the leading tone. It is therefore incorrect for many contemporary composers to write in this way:

[25]According to Rousseau, "Contrary-sense, in punctuation, is when a musical phrase is terminated by a perfect cadence in those places where the sense is suspended, or forms an imperfect stop where the sense is concluded." *A Complete Dictionary of Music* (1767), trans. William Waring (London, 1779), R. AMS Press Inc, 1975, 92. The analogy here is that the resolution of the chord when in second inversion to a root position chord where a first inversion chord is expected creates a tonal *contre-sens*. [PL]

The great masters, in whom tonal feeling was profound, such as Haydn, Mozart and Cherubini, never used this alteration in this way, which is called the *fifth and augmented sixth* chord. I will presently show how an alteration of analogous form, but which has another origin, may be used to advantage.

178. Composers sometimes use the alteration analyzed in the preceding paragraph in reverse, sounding it first, then resolving on the natural note of the chords, as in the following examples:

179. There is no real alteration that can combine with the retardation of intervals of consonant chords, because, on the one hand, those that are presented in the successions of these chords produce only changes of mode, and on the other, these ascending or descending motions are made between notes that are only an interval of a semitone apart.

180. In the succession of a dissonant to a consonant chord, modified by a prolongation, the second degree alone may be altered, because it is the only note of the chord that, in the succession, moves by a tone.

DEMONSTRATION

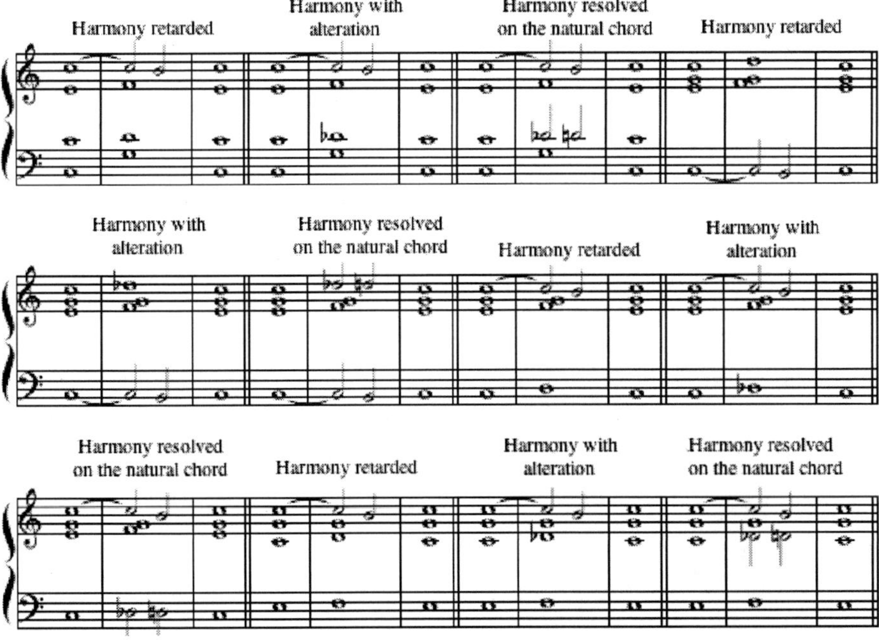

Although used less frequently, the ascending alteration of the second degree has nothing that repels tonal feeling.

DEMONSTRATION

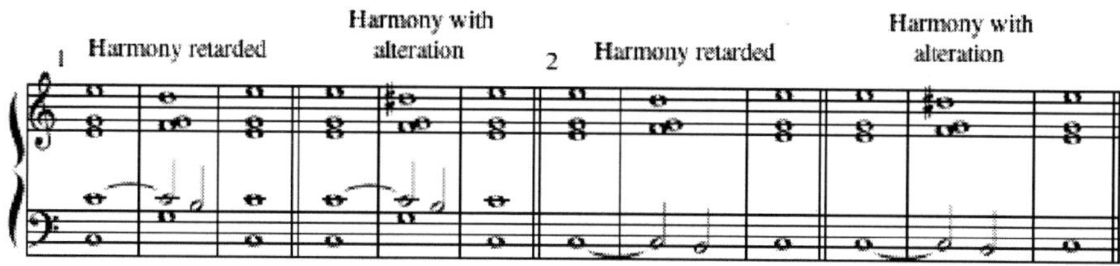

3 Harmony retarded
Harmony with alteration
4 Harmony retarded
Harmony with alteration

181. Alteration may also add a new modification to chords already modified by the combination of the prolongation and substitution.

If the alteration is simple, that is, if it happens only in ascending or descending motions of one degree, it changes the modified chords into natural dissonant chords of another key, when it is ascending (see ex. 1), or transforms the major mode into minor when it is descending (see ex. 2).

DEMONSTRATION

Harmony substituted and retarded
1 Alteration ascending
2 Alteration descending

In the minor mode the descending alteration of a single note does not bring about either a change of key or a change of mode, and consequently, is a true alteration; but it must resolve on the natural chord before the movement of the bass, or on the chord with substitution.

DEMONSTRATION

182. If the alteration is double, that is, both ascending and descending, it assumes the character of the true alteration, in that it places in relation notes that belong to different tonalities.

DEMONSTRATION

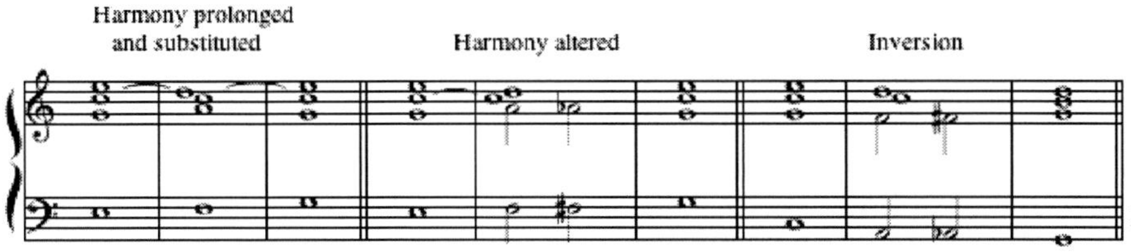

Harmony prolonged and substituted

Harmony altered

Inversion

Finally, if the alteration is triple, that is, if the three motions of the major second that are brought about in the succession of the two chords are altered, the tendencies to different tones multiply.

DEMONSTRATION

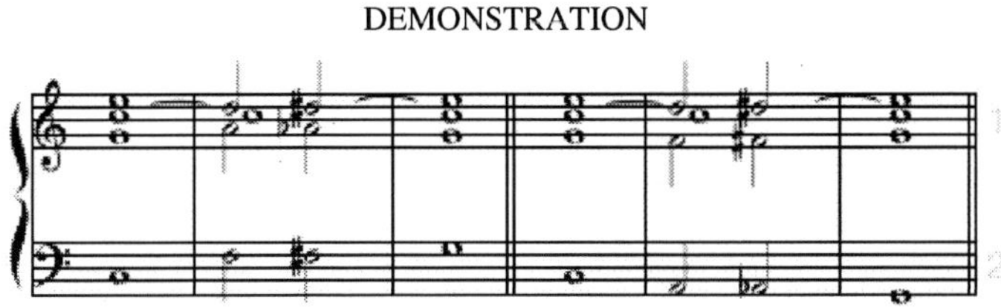

The peculiarity of the doubly augmented fourth has led most composers to replace this interval in the form of the fifth, writing it as follows:

Such is the true origin, such is the normal use of the fifth and augmented sixth chord: it must, as can be seen, resolve on the six-four chord of the dominant, because it takes the place of the six-four-three chord of the sixth degree, which is in fact followed by this six-four chord, in the normal order of tonality.

183. Note that harmonists often confuse the chords in which the interval of the augmented sixth is found and interchange them freely, although each of these chords is destined to fulfill the same functions as the unaltered chord from which it is derived: thus, when the augmented sixth chord should lead to a repose on the dominant of the minor mode, it takes the place of the chord of the simple sixth of the sixth degree of this mode, and must be made up of the doubled third and augmented sixth.

DEMONSTRATION

Natural harmony Altered harmony

When it must be followed by the perfect chord of the tonic, it is a modification of the leading-tone sixth chord of the second degree, and must be composed of the third, fourth and augmented sixth.

DEMONSTRATION

Natural harmony Altered harmony

Finally, when it is followed by the six-four chord of the dominant, it is a triple alteration of the six-four-three chord of the sixth degree, produced by the substitution combined with the prolongation.

DEMONSTRATION

In no case should the perfect chord of the dominant follow this chord. This would constitute a tonal *contre-sens*.

Chapter IX

THE PROLONGATION OF ALTERED NOTES

184. It has been seen above (§133) that all descending movement may lead to the prolongation of one or more notes of a chord onto another; but I have shown, in the same paragraph, that if the movement takes place from the leading tone to the tonic, the attraction of the first of these notes toward the second absorbs the sensation of the dissonance which results from the prolongation, and that this not only does not offend the ear in its ascending movement, but satisfies it, through one of the most necessary outcomes of the law of tonality.

Moreover, I have shown (§163) that the purpose of the ascending alteration is to give the altered note a tendency analogous to that of the leading tone of natural chords, and even more powerful.

The results of these facts are: (1) that the altered notes may be prolonged in their movement toward resolution; (2) that the dissonances produced by these prolongations must resolve by ascending, when they have the character of ascending alterations.

DEMONSTRATION

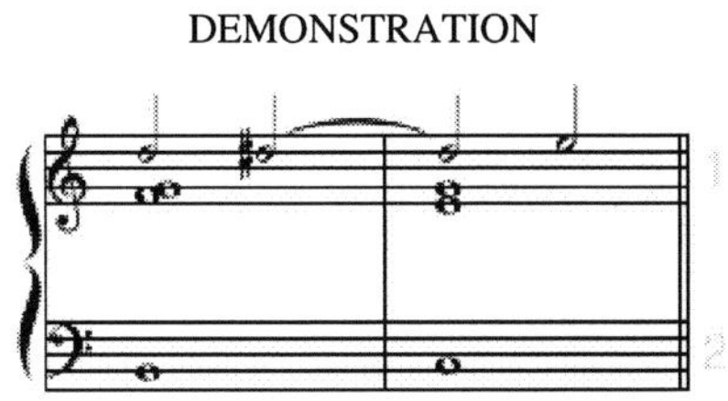

185. Every descending alteration in which the prolongation produces a dissonance follows the same law, and resolves descending.

DEMONSTRATION

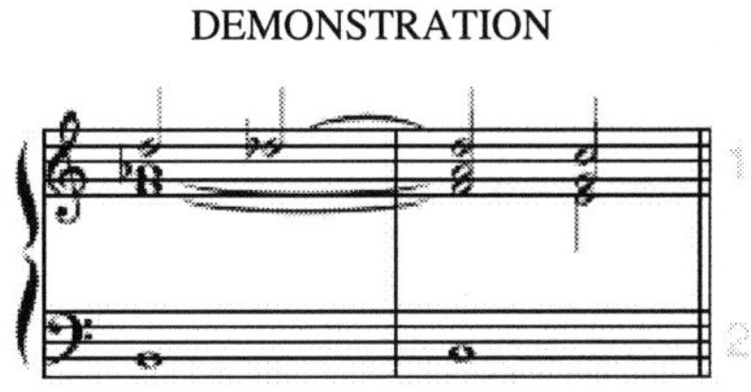

186. If the alteration is double, and both descending and ascending, the dissonances produced by the prolongations each follow the law that is particular to them for their resolution.

DEMONSTRATION

187. The prolongations of altered notes modify consonant chords, natural dissonant chords, dissonant chords with substitution, and dissonant chords with substitution and prolongation. They cannot all be inverted, because some of them have the character of a melodic accent rather than a harmonic combination: such are in general the prolongations of ascending alterations; such are in particular the examples that we have just seen (§184 and 186). In the same way, one may not invert the prolongations of descending alterations from which would result a dissonance of the seventh resolved by the movement of the bass, as in this example:

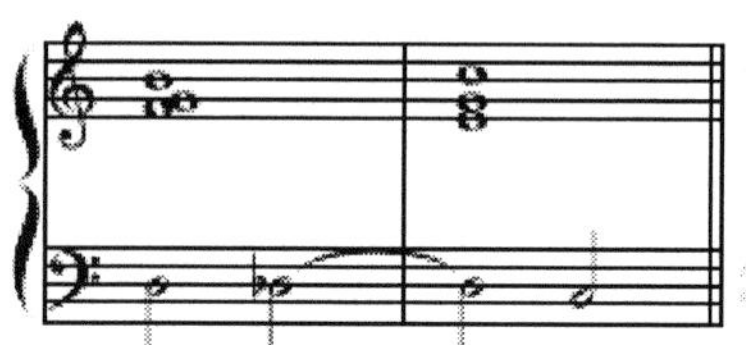

188. The prolongation of the augmented fifth of a perfect chord onto another chord of the same kind may be done in two ways, namely: (1) by the prolongation solely of the interval of the augmented fifth (see ex. 1 below); (2) by the prolongation of the entire chord (see ex. 2).

DEMONSTRATION

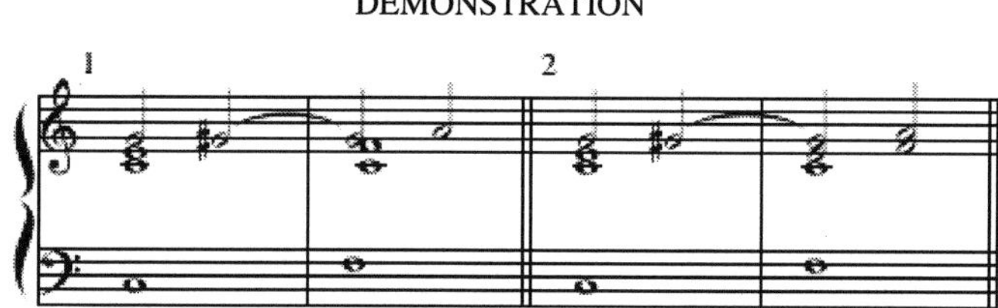

The inversions of the prolongation of the first example produce the following harmonies:

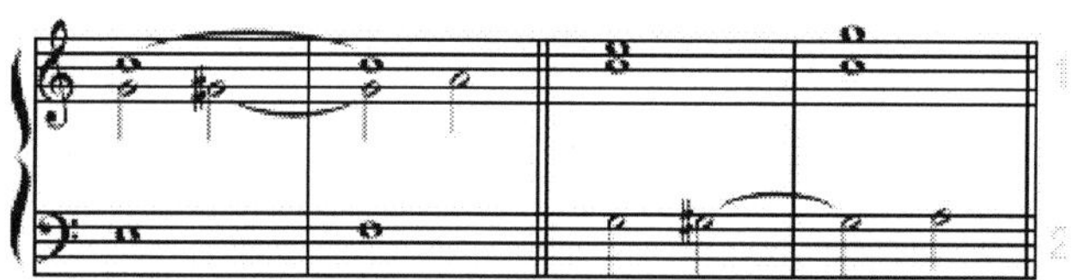

The inversions of the prolongations of the second example would not affect the variety of the harmony.

189. The prolongation of the augmented sixth onto the perfect chord of the dominant of the minor mode may be done in two ways, namely: (1) by the prolongation of the augmented sixth alone (see example 1 below); (2) by the same prolongation joined to the retardation of the third by the fourth (see example 2).

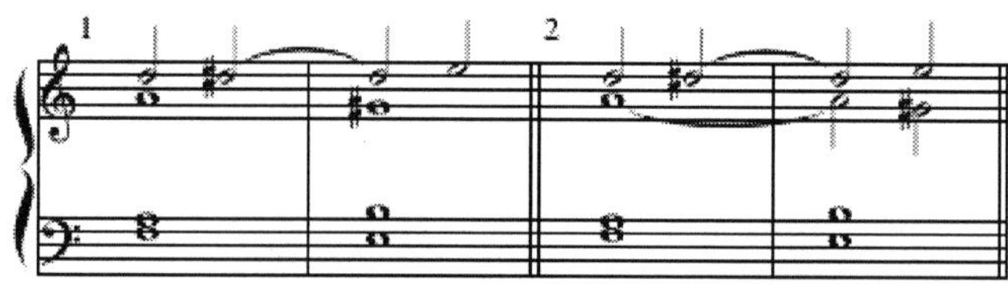

The inversion of the prolongation of the first example is fine on the sixth chord.

DEMONSTRATION

One may even combine this prolongation with the movement of the sixth degree toward the dominant.

DEMONSTRATION

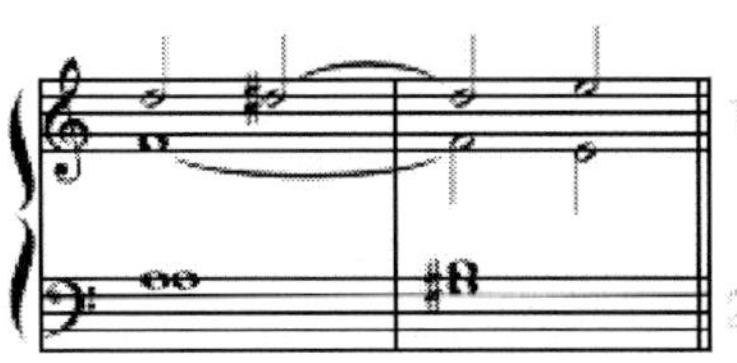

With regard to the prolongation of the alteration of the diminished third, from where these harmonies are derived, this is not done, because the prolongation has a melodic rather than a harmonic character, such that it produces an unpleasant effect in the bass.

190. The prolongation of the ascending alteration of the second degree in the dominant seventh chord and its inversions, onto the perfect chord of the tonic or its derivatives, may be made in two ways, namely: (1) by the prolongation of the altered note alone, as in examples 1, 2, 3, and 4 below; (2) by the prolongation of the entire chord thus altered, as in examples 5, 6, 7, and 8:[26]

[26]In example 7, one does not see the exact inversion of the preceding harmonies, because the retardation has much less attraction in the low note than in the leading tone.

With regard to the prolongation of the alteration in the bass, it is not done for the reasons that prevent all those of the same kind, and which have been previously discussed.

191. The prolongation of the descending alteration of the same degree produces only a retardation of the minor ninth on the tonic, in the major mode, and analogous harmonies in the inversions (see examples 1, 2, 3, 4, below); one may also prolong the entire chords thus altered (see examples 5, 6, 7):[27]

192. The prolongation of the ascending alteration of the second degree, and that of the substituted note of the diminished seventh chord, on the perfect chord of the tonic, resolves with a natural movement of each note, and produces an excellent harmony of fine effect, but which is not predisposed to inversion. Here is this harmony:

EXAMPLE

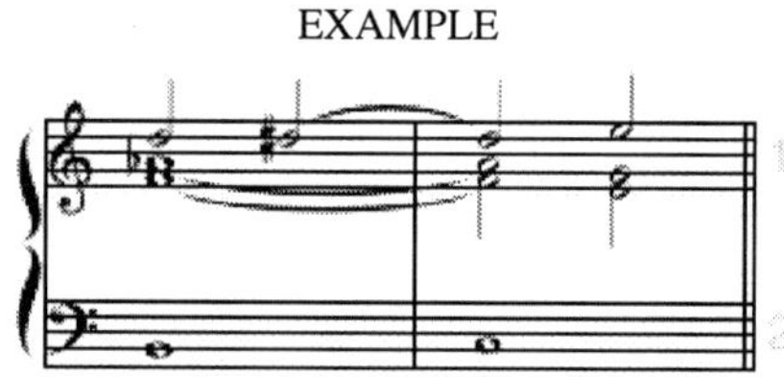

However, if the same alteration is made in the chord of the tritone with minor third, it may be prolonged conjointly with the substituted note and the leading tone, by causing the bass to immediately descend.

DEMONSTRATION

[27]The preceding observation applies in the case of this example. The prolongation of the entire chord on the stationary dominant would be pointless.

193. The double alterations of the ascending second degree and descending sixth, in the six-five chord of the fourth degree, are the only ones that may be prolonged in the chords affected by substitution and prolongation; they resolve on the six-four chord of the dominant.

DEMONSTRATION

If one wishes to prolong the inversion of the same harmony, the immediate descent of the alteration of the bass onto the dominant must be made, and the prolongation of the ascending alteration of the fourth degree with that of the second.

DEMONSTRATION

194. The prolongation of the augmented octave of the perfect chord onto the dominant seventh chord produces an ascending attraction analogous to all the preceding ones, and is good only in the upper voice in the fundamental chord, as in the inversions.

DEMONSTRATION

195. The same prolongation cannot be made in chords with the substitution of the major mode, because this substitution must be placed in the upper part, as I have shown, and because there is a similar requirement for the prolongation of the altered note; but it is very good with the substitution of the minor mode, which may be placed in the inner parts.

DEMONSTRATION

196. The same prolongation of the alteration may combine with the prolongation of the octave of the tonic, descending onto the seventh degree.

DEMONSTRATION

197. Finally, the same alteration may be prolonged and combine with the same prolongation of the unaltered tonic and the substitution of the minor mode.

DEMONSTRATION

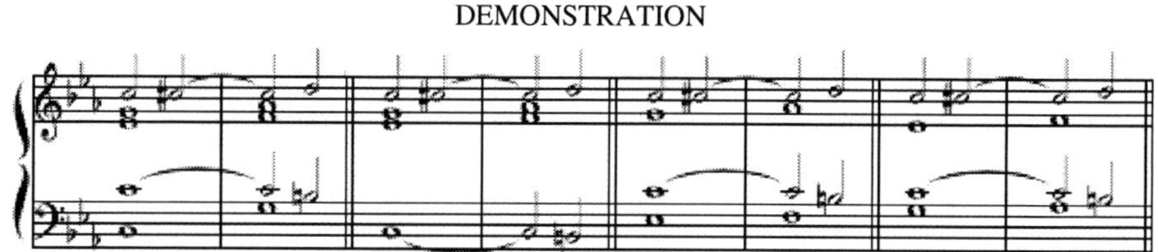

198. This ends the series of harmonies that are constituted regularly, and which may be reduced to the four fundamental and symmetrical modes of the formation of chords, namely: (1) the natural order; (2) the substitution of one interval for another; (3) the prolongation of one or more notes; (4) finally, their ascending and descending alterations.

But the principle and mechanics of this immense variety of harmonic combinations can be grasped only by means of the law of tonality, which governs the successions from which they originate. If one disregards this law and isolates the chords, not only their formation and employment become unintelligible, but the majority no longer present the musical sense with anything but a monstrous association of tones, in which the mind does not perceive the point of contact.[28]

In some of the combinations that I have just analyzed, I go beyond the point where composers until now have stopped, and these harmonies may seem strange, because they are not customary, and because they are still in the domain of future art; but with the continuous practice of developing tonal feeling, and the analysis of the normal formation of chords coming to its aid, not only will one no longer feel repugnance on hearing these harmonies, but they will even become necessary.

[28]We know what happened to Abbé Roussier, when he proposed the use of certain uncommon harmonies of his time (*Traité des accords*, 3rd part, Paris, 1764), and which were later used. Because he presents these harmonies in isolation, they offend the taste of musicians by their strangeness, and it was only after composers, directed by their instinct, had used them in good successions, that their sense and usefulness were understood.

Such is the advantage of a theory of harmony based on tonal feeling and the law of succession, of which the complete and rational presentation is seen for the first time in this work, in whose absence there exists no certain rule to decide upon the excellence or the defects of certain complicated harmonies. By the method that I have followed, this theory is brought about; the analysis of harmonic events, whatever they are, is always easy: the composer, informed about the nature and connection of chords that he uses, cannot fall into the errors in which many have gone astray, for having ignored it. For example, by means of the method in question, it is certain that a musician of genius, such as Beethoven, would not write the bad harmony of this passage from [first movement, mm. 9-11] of his Quartet, opus 131.[29]

He would see at first glance that if the key of the first measure is C-sharp minor, this key changes at the beginning of the second, by the tritone formed by the upper part against the bass, and which gives the note of the latter the character of the fourth degree of the key of E major; consequently, that the B sharp of the inner part represents the fifth degree of this key, with an ascending alteration; now, there is no harmonic succession in which the fifth degree may have an ascending alteration in the dissonant chord, because the resolution of this alteration can be made only on the sixth degree against the leading tone, that is to say, on a non-tonal dissonance that is not prepared, and which cannot have a satisfactory resolution. Finally, a harmonist guided by tonal law will not make the false relation that is found between the A-sharp of the inner part, at the beginning of the third measure, and the second note of the bass of the same measure, because it establishes a painful succession of two keys without analogy and without point of contact. In such analyses, reasoning is only the interpreter of the musical sense, but, once again, they are only possible with the help of the theory of the formation of chords and their use, which I have set forth in this book. All other methods can only lead to isolated chords of which the mind perceives neither the origin, nor the use.

[29]The misprint of B-sharp on the third beat of the second bar of this example has been corrected to C-sharp. [PL]

Chapter X

NOTES FOREIGN TO NATURAL OR MODIFIED HARMONY
PASSING NOTES—APPOGGIATURAS—ANTICIPATIONS

199. The fleeting activity of melody does not permit each note to be accompanied by a separate harmony. A certain number of these notes are often only the ornament of a principal phrase, in which the melodic and harmonic sense remains after the suppression of this ornament. For example, in this phrase from an andante by Haydn:[30]

If one suppresses the notes which are only ornamental, the following basic form results:

In the famous rondo by Mozart (*il mio tesoro*),[31] this principal phrase,

reduces to this:

Finally, in this theme of an air from *La Gazza ladra*, by Rossini,[32]

[30]Symphony in D, No. 104, *London*, 2nd movement.

[31]*Don Giovanni*, Act 11, Ottavio aria.

[32]*La Gazza Ladra*, Act I, Cavatina, *Di piacer mi balza il cor*.

the following basic form is found:

200. The ornamental notes are either contained in the harmony, or they are foreign to it: in the latter case, they are called *passing notes*.

201. The ornamental notes that are contained in the harmony generally proceed by the intervals of natural consonant and dissonant chords, such as the third, fourth, fifth, the sixth and the seventh; the passing notes generally proceed by intervals of the second. Notes that follow each other at this interval, and which are essential to the phrase, each have their own harmony.

When the passing notes are not connected with the essential notes of the phrase by intervals of the second, there is an elision of one or more ornamental notes; for example, this passage from Haydn's andante:

represents the following:

202. One divides passing notes, or those that are purely ornamental, into two kinds, namely: (1) real passing notes; (2) *appoggiaturas*.

Real passing notes are those that are found on the weak divisions of the beats of the measure. For example, in this passage from Mozart's rondo:

A, in the first measure, and E, in the second, are passing notes.

The appoggiaturas are those that, not being in the harmony, precede those that are. For example, in this beginning of the rondo by Mozart:

B and G in the second beat of the first measure are appoggiaturas.

Sometimes two ornamental notes appear to have the same character, through the structure of the phrase, and are nevertheless different. I will cite as an example this fragment of the theme from the air from *La Gazza Ladra*:

It is clear that C of the second measure, not being in the harmony of the principal notes of the key, is an appoggiatura; but A (in the same measure) is one of the chord tones of the dominant seventh chord, which enters into every perfect cadence (and here the cadence is definite by the conclusion of the phrase), and does not have the same character: from which one may conclude that G, which follows this A, is a passing note. However, this G is harmonic with E, which is the last note of the phrase, and at the same time the tonic; moreover, these two notes follow each other at the interval of a third. This appears to contradict what I have said previously about what distinguishes the real notes of the melody from the passing notes; but if one remembers the basic reduction which I have given of this phrase, one will see that the separation of the G and the E is only the effect of an elision, and that the phrase represents:

203. The melodic phrase sometimes appears under a modification of the basic form that does not permit either the character of the passing notes, or the appoggiaturas to be recognized. Such is the following:

The modification in question is seen in the third measure: it is called an *anticipation*, because the melodic notes anticipate the harmony of the following bass notes. One finds the original form and the real harmony of this kind of modification of phrases by suppressing in thought the syncopation which gives rise to the anticipation. Through this operation, and through the suppression of the passing notes and appoggiaturas, the previous example results in the following phrase:

Descending anticipations are the opposite of retardations in harmony. If one takes as an example the preceding phrase, one may replace the anticipation with the retardation in order to modify the basic phrase, and the following form will result:

204. There are anticipations of another kind, the effect of which is to give the passing notes a longer duration than the real notes of the phrase. Here is an example:

It is clear that the real notes, as much in relation to the melodic sense as to that of the harmony, are G and B-flat in the first measure, and A and C in the third.

With reference to the B-flat of the second measure, and the C of the fourth, it is easy to see that these are appoggiaturas, such that the real phrase is the following:

205. Melody that one wishes to accompany with an appropriate harmony is set in these ornaments and modifications. This situation becomes more complicated in modern music by substitutions, retardations and alterations, which must be extricated in order to regain the real notes of the natural harmony. The composer who conceives simultaneously the melody and the harmony of his work, and who could not possibly imagine a separation of the two, cannot be uncertain in the choice of chords that must accompany each phrase; but this is not the case for the musician who is presented with a melody for which he must rediscover the harmony; for it is apparent that his first job must be to clear the basic melody of all ornaments and modifications that surround it: without this preliminary operation, he could not accomplish his task. Therefore, it is necessary to make use of certain special procedures in order to distinguish the real

notes from those that are only ornaments and modifications. These procedures become easy and straightforward when one grows accustomed to recognize what characterizes the various kinds of ornaments analyzed above. Here are some points regarding this subject:

(1) Knowing the principal key, one must find out if an accidental of a foreign key appears, and by the nature of this accidental, be it the leading tone or the fourth degree, find the tonic of the new key. This operation carried out from one end of the melody to the other, will indicate all the keys to which it modulates.

(2) All harmony, freed from its various modifications, is composed only of natural or perfect chords and the dominant seventh of each key. It is the same with the basic melody that contains only the notes of these chords; for the law of tonality is no different here. One must therefore examine which notes of the melody enter into the formation of the perfect chords of the tonic and fourth degree, and proceed by disjunct intervals, as well as those that belong to the seventh chord, or to the perfect chord of the dominant, and which proceed by the same intervals: one will be convinced that these are real, and each will be accompanied by the harmony of which it is a part.

(3) In parts of a melody where two notes succeed each other by movement of a second, one belongs to the harmony, the other is ornamental. The second note is passing when the first is real; it is real when the first is an appoggiatura. It is therefore only a matter of recognizing the nature of the first of two consecutive notes. On this point, a rule may be generally applied, or at least very often, namely: that when the first of two consecutive notes is in harmony with the preceding note, it is real, and the following is a passing note; if, on the contrary, the second of the two notes is in harmony the note that precedes the first, it is the real note, and the first one is an appoggiatura.

(4) Every note that has been heard at the end of a beat or measure and which is repeated in the beat or measure that follows, in order to then descend a degree, is an appoggiatura.

The application of these rules to all melody will result in good harmony that is natural and tonal, when some practice in this type of analysis has been acquired. Let us take as an example the introduction to the air from *La Gazza*, mentioned above.

The first four notes leave no doubt, for they compose the entire perfect chord of the tonic. The two last notes of the second measure belong to the harmony of the perfect chord of the dominant or of the seventh chord. Of these two chords, the seventh is preferable, because it gives a better feeling of the cadence that ends on the first note of the third measure. This entire measure belongs to the perfect chord of the tonic; for, according to the rules previously set forth, the D that ends it can be considered only as a passing note.

Following rule No. 4, the first note of the fourth measure is an appoggiatura, from which it follows that D represents C; now C naturally belongs only to the perfect chord of the fourth degree, or to the sixth chord of the same note. If one wishes to vary the harmony, these two chords may therefore be used in turn throughout the measure, considering, as I have, that the notes found are representing C and A.

The F at the beginning of the fifth measure is an incidental note of repose; now, repose on this note is only possible in the perfect chord of the dominant.

All that follows, up to the end of the seventh measure, presents identical circumstances to those of the beginning; there can be no doubt about the appropriate harmony. The G that begins the eighth measure belongs to the perfect chord of the tonic, like the preceding measure; but the final cadence is approaching and prepares itself on this note; now, I said (§94) that the best harmonic formula for the preparation of this cadence consists of the six-four chord preceding the dominant seventh: it is therefore this inversion of the perfect chord that must accompany the first note of the eighth measure. With regard to the ornamental notes that complete the rest of this measure, I have explained their nature (§203).

The result of this analysis gives the following basic harmony:

206. Taste, development of tonal feeling, and experience, teach how to substitute, in the most advantageous manner for effect, the inversions of fundamental chords, and to modify the natural harmony of a melody thus analyzed through prolongations and alterations; finally, to replace the

simple chords decorated with varied forms in the bass and other parts of the accompaniment.

207. The forms of the accompaniment also have their passing notes and appoggiaturas. We see an example of this in the passage of the Mozart Quartet that I have cited (§150, note 1). This is the bass of the passage:

One easily understands that the B of the first measure, and the C sharp of the second, not being of the harmony, can be considered only as passing notes, and that the passage reduces to the following:

The basic notes of this passage are clearly the following:

208. The variety of forms, in the accompaniment of melody, is one of the most essential requirements in music. The choice of these forms belongs to the imagination of the composer; nevertheless, there are certain formulae in use, even in the most original compositions, because they have the double advantage of marking the rhythm and allowing the mind to focus on the melody, through the regularity of movements. Here are some examples:

The scales of the accompaniment, as in example No. 5, represent only their first notes.

Chapter XI

THE PEDAL

209. A note sustained by a voice or instrument, particularly by the bass, during the succession of several chords, is called a *pedal*. This term was given to notes of this kind because they are heard on the organ in the foot keyboard, called *pedal*, while the hands play the harmony on the other keyboards.

210. The purpose of the pedal is, originally, a more or less prolonged suspension of the cadence, through a sustained note on the dominant, or the affirmation of the key, through a sustained note on the tonic, after harmonic successions that have weakened it, or caused it to be lost. It will be seen below that it has had another use in the music of recent times.

211. The pedal is often foreign to the harmony that accompanies it; consequently, when it is the lowest note, there are many cases where it cannot be considered as the true bass of this harmony, and the bass must be sought in the lowest voice of the chords that occur over the pedal note.

212. In order that the low pedal may be considered as the bass of the harmony, the chords that make up this harmony must not tend toward keys other than the one where the pedal is a principal note, and all this harmony must be contained in the perfect chords and the dominant seventh of this key, in the retardations of their intervals, and in the substitution.

Here is an example of a pedal of this type:

The analysis of this harmony shows that the first chord of the first measure is a perfect chord of the dominant; the second, a six-four chord of the tonic; the first chord of the second measure, a retardation of the third by the fourth in the perfect chord of the dominant, resolving on the second beat of the measure.

The third measure is composed only of the six-four chord, derived from the perfect chord of the tonic.

The first beat of the fourth measure is a dominant seventh chord; and the second, the same chord with substitution, which produces a dominant major ninth chord.

The first chord of the fifth measure is that of the seventh, and the second, a six-four chord.

In the sixth measure, we see, on the first beat, the retardation of the third of the seventh chord; and, in the second, the resolution of this retardation.

The first beat of the seventh measure is a retardation of the fourth by the fifth in the six-four chord; and the second beat, the resolution of this retardation, with passing notes in the inner part.

The eighth measure is like the sixth, but with a different arrangement of the parts.

The first beat of the ninth measure is a retardation of the fourth by the fifth in the six-four chord, in the upper part, while the non-retarded fourth is in the lower part (see §144).

The tenth measure presents the same retardation as the sixth and eighth measures, but with a new arrangement of the parts.

213. When the pedal cannot be considered as the real bass of the harmony that accompanies it, because this harmony contains chords that are foreign to it in tonality, there is a real bass in the lower voice of this harmony, and it must have, in its relations and movements, all the regularity that an ordinary bass would have.

Although foreign to some of the chords that succeed each other during its passage, the pedal can satisfy the musical sense only when it relates to the tonality of the harmony right from the start, and when this relation reestablishes itself from time to time until its termination, for a pedal that would be entirely foreign to the chords that accompany it would be an harmonic absurdity:

Here is an example of a pedal on chordal successions in foreign tonalities.

This example shows: (1) that at the second beat of the second measure the tonality of A major is established by the chord of the *tritone* with substitution and alteration; (2) that the harmony then passes to D minor, by the suppression of the G-sharp, at the end of the third measure: these two modulations are foreign to the key of the pedal; but the relation reestablishes itself at the second beat of the fourth measure, by the chord of the *tritone* of the key of G, with substitution and alteration, and this relation continues until the end of the sixth measure; (3) that the harmony of the seventh measure is foreign to the pedal, since it gives to the first beat a six-five chord on the fourth degree of the key of C, with alteration of the sixth; but that the minor fifth and sixth chord of the second beat prepares the return of the tonal relation of the pedal with the harmony, and that this relation is evident during the entire duration of the eighth measure; (4) that the second beat of this eighth measure leads to the key of F minor (foreign to the pedal), on the first beat of the ninth measure; but that the return of the tonal relation is heard on the second beat of this measure, by the leading tone of the key of G, and that this relation persists until the end of the pedal.

214. The pedal, which satisfies the musical intellect through the fluctuation of the tonal relation of the sustained note with the harmony, and momentary incompatibilities with the tonality of this harmony, would become intolerable if this incompatibility were to establish itself in an absolute and persistent manner, through a cadence in the harmony, in a key absolutely foreign to the sustained note. Imagine a case such as the following:

It is clear that the key of A establishes itself so well, from the second beat of the second measure to the end of the fifth, that the tonality of the pedal is completely forgotten, and the sustained note unpleasantly takes on the mood of the idea of incompatibility, and that when the relation is reestablished, in the seventh measure, it does not immediately dissipate the memory of the painful impression which was produced. It follows that modulations foreign to the tonality of the pedal should only be implied, and not entirely completed through the cadence.

215. I have said (§213) that the pedal can only satisfy the mind when its tonality is in relation to the harmony, from its very beginning. One notices in fact that the infractions of this rule create a bad impression on the musical sense. I find a remarkable example of this in the introduction to the last movement of Beethoven's *Pastoral Symphony*. The composer, after having established the key of C on the pedal of this key, suddenly gives the basses, silent until then, a pedal on F, while the principal parts continue to develop the feeling of the tonality of C. Here is this passage:

The first time that the *Pastoral Symphony* was played by the best orchestras, there was astonishment, hesitation, a kind of painful feeling to this passage; one subsequently became accustomed to it, and the beauty of thought that develops throughout the piece caused one to forget the first unpleasant impression that results from the entry of the horn in the key of C over a pedal in the key of F.

It is not that the combination of these two keys, thus characterized, is inadmissible in a pedal harmony; but it is necessary, in order that the feeling of tonality not be harmed, that a tonal harmony of the pedal would have been previously heard. For example, if what precedes had led Beethoven to begin in F, in this manner:

The entrance of the horn would have been excellent, and the ear would not have experienced any unpleasant sensation. But the thought of what precedes having led the composer to the key of C, it was necessary, in order that the tonal feeling not be offended, that the entrance of the horn be made, like that of the clarinet, on the pedal of this key, as in the following example, and above all that the second violin, violas and basses, not strike the key of F in the eighth measure with the complete perfect chord, while the horn continues to go forward in the key of C, as Beethoven did:

I know everything that can be said to excuse, or if one wishes, to explain this fault of a great artist: after the admirable thunderstorm that follows the *scherzo* come the calm, the return of the good weather, a feeling of joy. This joy is poured out through the sound of the instruments in the mountains: here a shepherd plays his bagpipe in one key; there, it is the Alpine horn which resounds in another key; this is in nature, and Beethoven, seizing this truth, completes his picture. I know all this; but nature is one thing, art another. The latter can only completely satisfy the mind elevated to its highest aesthetic development by resting on its principal foundation, which in music is none other but tonality, that is to say, the general law of the relations of sounds. Now, what proves that Beethoven has sacrificed this to a minor circumstance, is that the passage in question has always produced in musicians an unpleasant impression upon first hearing, and that no less than the charm of what follows was necessary to cause it to be forgotten. I do not believe I am able to give a theory of the pedal, without analyzing the particular case, because the authority of a great man could validate an error in contradiction of a fundamental law of the art, as is too often seen.

216. The rule that requires the lower part of the harmony, accompanied by a pedal, to have in its progression the regularity of a real bass, is also taken from tonal law, which submits the succession of chords to regular movements in which the bass is the support, since every chord necessarily has a low note as a foundation, considered relatively to the others; whether the harmony is in three parts, or in four, independently of the pedal, the lower part must therefore have the same purity, the same regularity in its movements, than if there were no sustained note below it. The two examples that I have given, in §212 and §213, prove that in suppressing the pedal, there is a perfectly regular harmony:

217. In the music of our time, the pedal is no longer limited to certain forms of endings that were formerly used only in the style of the convention termed the *fugue*: the host of diverse keys, in which the resolutions are often avoided, cause the most famous modern composers to use the pedal in fragments in the accompaniment of their melodies. Below are some examples from an air in Rossini's *Guillaume Tell*; they provide an understanding of what this harmonic contrivance consists:[33]

[33]Act II, No. 9, Recitative and Romance, taken from the 1829 French edition. [PL]

An opening pedal, on the tonic, accompanies the entire ritornello of the air. The harmony placed over this pedal is a succession of thirds and sixths, which appears in this form by suppressing the appoggiaturas:

The pedals often present these successions of incomplete harmonies, which one would take at first sight for complicated successions, and which are reduced, in fact, to alternating successions of thirds and sixths. Such is the following passage, which is found in the ritornello of a chorus in the same opera [Act Two, Finale]:

If we suppress the pedal, we will see that there remains, between the upper and inner parts, only thirds and sixths.

Sometimes the harmony of sixth chords is complete over the pedal, in ascending or descending progressions. In this case, the chords are in an alternately harmonic and inharmonic relation with the sustained tone; but the lower part of the progression is the true basis of the harmony. The following is an example of such a progression from *La Muette de Portici* by Auber [Act One, Chorus, *O Dieu puissant*]; it is remarkably elegant:

I return to the examination of the pedals from the air from *Guillaume Tell*, which I had begun to analyze. After the tonic pedal of the ritornello, there also begins a tonic pedal above the melody until the end of the tenth measure of the air. The violin and viola parts, which are of interest for the form, are not of interest with respect to the harmony, because they play only successively the notes contained in the chords formed by the horns and bassoons. In the first two measures of the accompaniment of these latter instruments of the melody, they alternately play the perfect chord of the tonic, and the natural dissonant harmony of the dominant. On the last beat of the third measure of the melody, a striking harmony is seen, the origin of which may cause some difficulty for musicians who are not used to analysis. The F-flat of the melody is an alteration of the F-natural, which provides an accent for the expression of a *sad and cruel* character. The original note of this melody is therefore F-natural; now, this note belongs to the minor fifth and sixth chord,

for which one substitutes the diminished seventh chord:

Furthermore, the above-mentioned melodic alteration changes the F-natural to F-flat, and produces the harmony of the diminished seventh with altered third:

This harmony is all the more remarkable in that the dominant, having momentarily had the character of a new tonic, regains the character of the dominant in the next chord. These harmonic circumstances, combined with the pedal, further add to the effect of the chord thus altered.

At the eleventh measure of the piece begins a dominant pedal, which is prolonged until the first beat of the fourteenth measure. The harmony of the eleventh and twelfth measures is composed only of successions of thirds with the pedal doubled above. On the third beat of the thirteenth measure there is a harmony similar to that of the ninth measure, but transferred to the fifth. A modulation is established at the end of the fourteenth measure, to arrive in C minor, and a new pedal begins in this key at the fifteenth measure: it concludes with an interrupted cadence at the eighteenth measure.

Such is the system of pedals often used by composers of the present day for the accompaniment of melodies.

218. The sounds sustained in the pedal are also sometimes used in the inner or upper parts. In these kinds of pedals, the conditions are not the same as in those where the sustained tone is in the bass; for if the pedal note becomes a dissonance of retardation against one or another of the parts, in the succession of chords, it must change at once, and resolve, like any dissonance, by descending a degree. The ambiguity that results from the six-five chord alone permits the suspension of the resolution. Moreover, the upper or inner pedal note must always be in the harmony of the chords; the following example will clarify any difficulty that students may have with this theory:

In this example there is only a succession of sixths and thirds between the bass and the inner part; but the pedal note is contained in all the harmonies formed by these parts, and produces with them the chords of the fifth and sixth, fourth and sixth, major and minor third and sixth, and finally the major and minor perfect chord. On the first beat of the next to last measure (marked with the sign *), the pedal becomes a dissonance of the seventh by the retardation against the inner part: from this moment it must cease to be heard, and resolve by descending a degree.

219. The preceding rule, based on the most fundamental laws of harmony, proves that Beethoven made a mistake in a passage from the *Andante* of the Symphony in C Minor, but as a great man is mistaken, and

compensates for a fault with beauties of the first order. Here is the passage in which it occurs:

At the third measure, the E-flat in the clarinet, which forms the upper pedal, becomes an interval of the ninth against the D-flat of the bass, and a dissonance of the seventh with respect to the F of the cello (*): from this moment the resolution becomes necessary. However, not only does Beethoven continue the pedal in the following measure, but as a result of the transformation of the dissonance in the fourth measure, he ends the pedal by ascending, by means of a change of key. There are in this respect a number of observations to be made: first, the melody of the cello, being a variation of the previously heard theme, shares the attention of the ear with the upper pedal, and weakens the unpleasant sensation of a dissonance which does not have a resolution; second, the painful sensation for the ear of a dissonance that does not descend, being dissipated toward the end of the fourth measure, where the dissonance is passed to the inner parts, the musical feeling is now occupied only with the melancholy character, full of grandeur, of this clarinet voice which rises by degrees, and developing into melody, out of the harmony that it had been. Only men of genius know how to thus transform a fault into a sublime beauty.

220. Sometimes the pedal of an inner or upper part ends without it being necessary for the sustained note to resolve downward, because it is not in a dissonance relation. Auber wrote a pedal of this kind in the first

act of *La Muette de Portici*. Here is the passage where the pedal is in the viola part:

221. I believe that the preceding analyses of various circumstances surrounding the use of tones sustained as pedals are sufficient to give an understanding of the principle and mechanism of this harmonic device.

This concludes all the theory of the science concerning the immediate relations of the constituent tones of chords, and their particular relations, once the tonality is given.

Chapter XII

CHORD SYMBOLS, AND THE FIGURED BASS

222. When melody began to form into continuous and cadenced phrases, for a single voice or for many voices, which no longer formed amongst themselves an uninterrupted harmony, it became necessary to replace this vocal harmony with that of an instrument such as the organ, harpsichord, or theorbo; now the bass of this obbligato accompaniment, no longer being subject to the interruptions previously noted in the vocal basses of masses, motets and madrigals, was called the *basso continuo*.

223. This bass, and the harmony of which it was the support, had at first only the objective to produce the simple chords under the melody, without adding the varied forms of modern instrumentation. Now, the chords from which all harmony was composed contained only consonant intervals, or retardations of these intervals by the dissonances of prolongation. It was considered pointless to notate such a simple harmony, and one was limited to writing out the bass, the notes of which were supposed to be always accompanied by the perfect chord, that is by the third, when the symbol of another chord was not placed above the bass note. The sixth chord was designated by the figure 6; that of the six-four, by $\substack{6\\4}$. The retardation of the sixth was marked by the figure 7, and that of the third, by 4. Later, the symbols of natural dissonant chords were added.

224. This is not the place to treat historically the invention of the figured bass; I have written elsewhere on this subject:[34] I will only say that the oldest printed composition where a bass of this kind is found is the drama of Emilio de' Cavalieri, entitled: *Rappresentazione di anima e di corpo*, published by Alexander Guidotti.[35] One sees there the harmony of the sixth represented by 6, when the interval is in fact only a sixth with respect to the bass; but if the sixth is found in the second octave above this bass, the composer, or his editor, mark it with the figure 13, because six and seven indeed equal this number. Likewise, the doubled fifth is indicated by 12, and the doubled fourth by 11. Here is a figured bass passage in this system, as is found on page three of the work by Emilio de' Cavalieri.

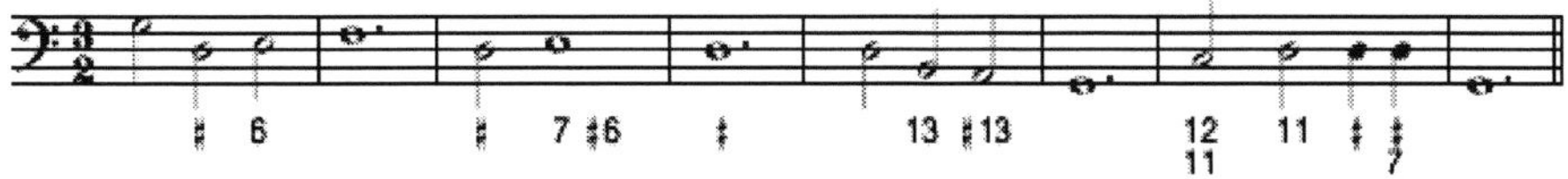

The harmony of the parts that accompany this bass is arranged thus:

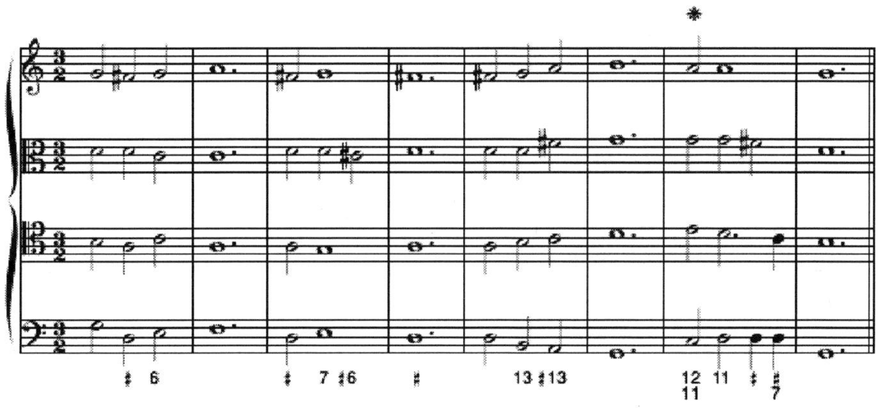

*I shall explain in Book Three what led Emilio de' Cavalieri and some older writers to make use of the six-five chord.

I should add that the minor third is often marked by a flat, even when it is produced by a note which is not altered by this sign.

It is in this system, and with the figures that have just been seen, that the *basso continuo* is figured in *Euridice*, by Jacobo Peri,[36] in *Le nuove musiche*, by Caccini,[37] in *Le musiche*, by Sigismondo d'India,[38] and in

---

[34]*Esquisse de l'histoire de l'harmonie*. Paris, 1840, 46-52.

[35]Rome, Nic. Mutii, 1600.

[36]*Le Musiche,* by Jacobo Peri, a Florentine noble, on *l'Euridice,* by Ottavio Rinuccini, published in Venice by Alessandro Raverii, 1608.

[37]Published in Florence by J. Marescotti, 1601.

many other anthologies of compositions published at the beginning of the seventeenth century.

It follows from the above, that the first musicians who made use of the figured bass not only indicated the quality of the intervals and chords, but the position of the notes with respect to the bass, in the upper octaves. This fact must be understood in order to accompany their works well.

225. The distinction of the octaves of the intervals by the figures was not generally accepted; Crüger explains very well, in the little treatise on the *basso continuo* found at the end of the second edition of his *Synopsis musica* (page 218), that the third is the foundation of the tenth, and the fifth that of the twelfth. It is through the simple figures that he represents these intervals in the examples (pages 227 and following).[39]

Nevertheless, the reform in this regard was not as complete in Italy as it was in Germany, for although one sees in the *Primi albori musicali,* by Father Lorenzo Penna,[40] examples where the intervals are reduced to their simplest numerical expression, such as the following (Book Three, 170-171):[41]

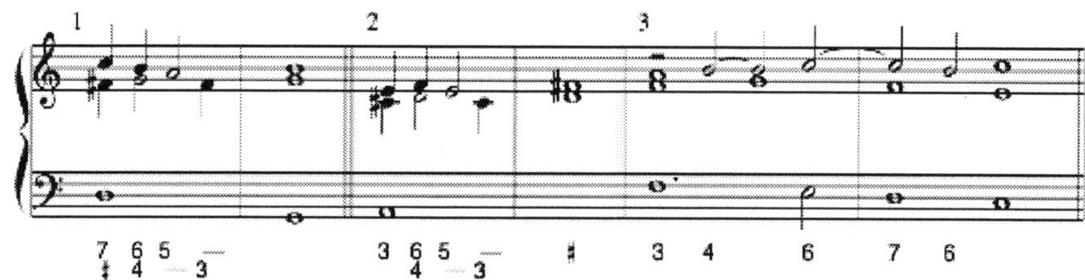

one also finds there the figures 10 and 11 for the third and fourth, when the author wishes to indicate clearly a harmonic movement above the octave, as for example, in this passage (*Primi albori musicali*, 171):

[38]*Le musiche,* by Sigismondo d'India, a noble from Palerno, to be played alone on the harpsichord, lute, double harp and other similar instruments. Published in Milan by the descendants of Simon Tini and Filippe Lomazzo, 1609.

[39]Johannes Crüger (1598-1662) wrote several theoretical works, of which the most influential was the *Synopsis musica* (1630, 1654). [PL]

[40]The third book of this work, which contains a treatise on the *basso continuo*, was published in Bologna, in 1679.

[41]Lorenzo Penna's (1613-1693) well-known theoretical work, *Li primi albori musicali per li principianti della musica figurata*, first appeared in 1672. [PL]

226. A great confusion reigned at this time in the minds of composers and theorists, concerning the representation of chords by figures; for sometimes one sees the retardation of the octave by the prolongation of the ninth represented by 2, and sometimes the same retardation is expressed by 9. Here are some examples taken from Lorenzo Penna's book (page 172):

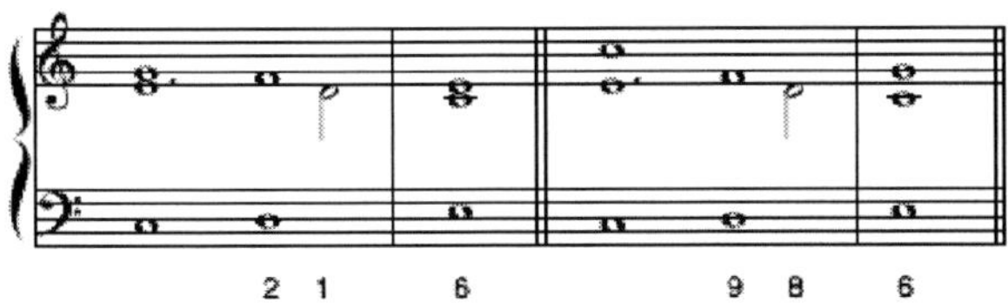

Sometimes the retardation of the third by the second, in the bass, was figured by 9, as in this example (*Primi albori musicali*, 172):

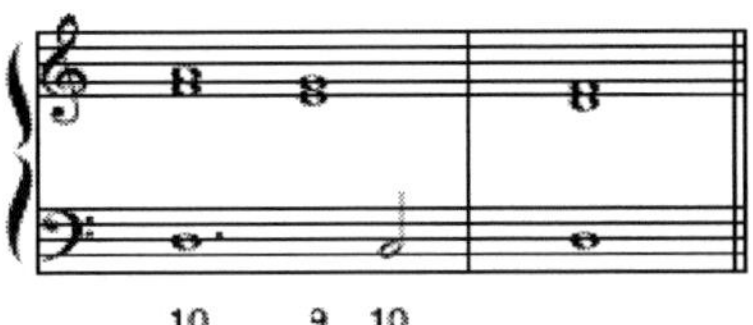

The error of musicians who thus figured the *basso continuo* is evident, for a note which is greater than the octave and retards it can only form an interval of the ninth; from which it follows that 9 must indicate the prolongation of the upper part, while the bass, retarding the third by a lesser interval, can only form a second, and that this interval should be figured by 2. The error in question is encountered frequently in figured basses in seventeenth-century compositions; it is therefore necessary that accompanists be informed in order to execute these works.

227. Toward the end of the seventeenth century the use of double figures became almost generally accepted, especially in Italy. One sees many examples of them in Gasparini's treatise on accompaniment, especially at cadences.[42] Here are some of these (pp. 24-25):

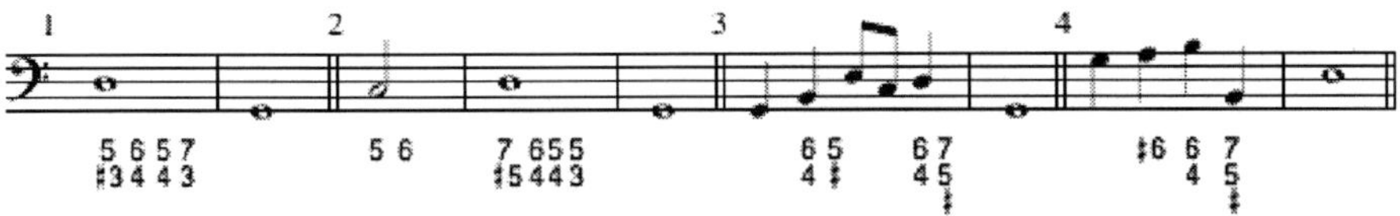

[42] *L'armonico pratico al Cembalo*, etc. (Venice, 1683).*

*Francesco Gasparini's (1661-1727) introductory manual on figured bass accompaniment and widely used throughout the eighteenth century. [PL]

The harmonies indicated by the figures in these examples are as follows:

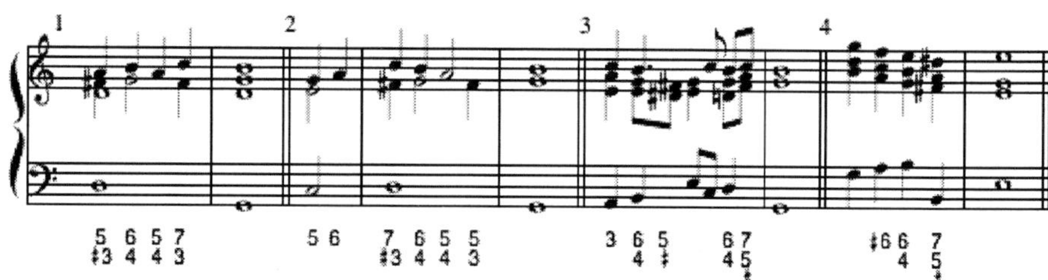

228. The use of the flat instead of the natural, in order to indicate minor intervals, was almost without exception at the time Gasparini was writing: he gives some examples of this in a series of avoided cadences which he calls *false cadences*. Sometimes the flat was placed after the figure. I believe I must give here Gasparini's examples, with their harmonic realization, in order to make accompanists understand the manner of executing these kinds of cadences, so frequent in old Italian music.

The fourth measure of this example proves that Gasparini did not correctly present the progression of parts in the succession of chords; for, in three or four parts, it is impossible that the fourth of the third beat be a regular prolongation according to what precedes it, without making two awkward and disagreeable fifths between two of the upper parts.

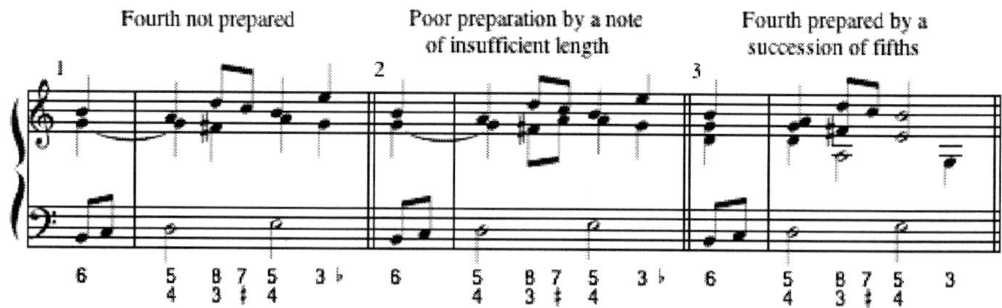

This fact being established, here is the harmony of the entire example given by Gasparini:

229. Simpler in the school of Naples in the same era, and more rational, the manner of figuring the bass had, however, peculiarities that must be explained. Alessandro Scarlatti, illustrious master and director of this school, provides us with the most remarkable examples in his cantatas. The style of his students and immediate successors, [Nicola Antonio] Porpora [1686-1768] and [Francesco] Durante [1684-1755], offer analogous harmonic forms, and the same system of figured bass.

But I must speak of certain very particular closing formulae, and very much in use amongst Neapolitan composers until the middle of the eighteenth century. The first consists of placing the leading tone on the chord of the tritone, and of raising its bass onto the dominant, to end with a kind of melody that gives the feeling of the six-four chord without a cadence. Here is an example taken from a cantata by Scarlatti:

It would be impossible to explain how such a harmonic peculiarity, always rejected by the Roman school, became a habitual formula in that of Naples, unless it was a necessity of the form of the song; for nothing would be easier than to accompany this recitative in a regular manner:

Nevertheless, it is certain that there are many closing formulae constructed on the feeling of the bass of the chord of the tritone which rises, and which could not be accompanied by any regular harmony. Such is this passage from a cantata by Porpora:

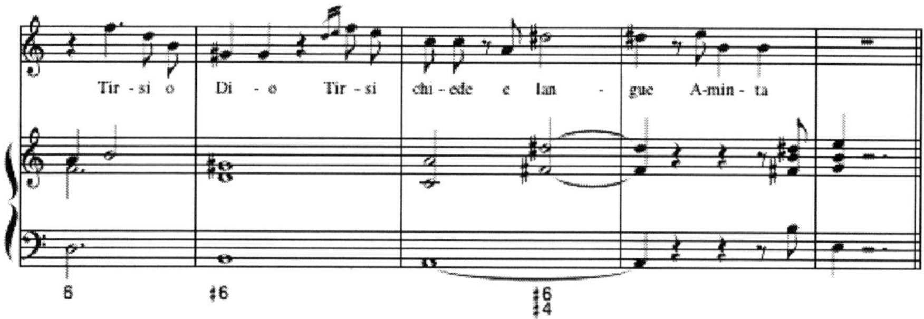

The only means that one may use to weaken the bad effect of this harmony is to suppress the interval of the second in the chord of the tritone, as I have done.

Another formula, no less peculiar, and yet no less habitual in the works of Neapolitan composers, consists in placing the final note of the piece on a fourth, often preceded by a diminished seventh chord that appears to remain unresolved. Such is this passage from the same cantata by Scarlatti:

This ending appears unacceptable, especially with the chords indicated at the end by the figured bass; for while the melody gives the feeling of the final on the tonic, the harmony sounds the perfect chord of the dominant, such that there is a clear contradiction between the melody and its accompaniment, as the realization of the figured chords proves, in the following example:

The *appoggiatura*, on the next to last note, far from remedying the faults of this harmonic construction, further adds to them; for it results in two successive intervals of a second between the melody and its accompaniment.

Cherubini, with whom I one day discussed this peculiarity, told me that he believed that tradition was for singers of old to give a double value to the appoggiatura, such that the ending had become regular, as in this example:

I nevertheless do not feel that this explanation is admissible, for the following passage from a duo by Durante proves that the ending on the fourth, without resolving the diminished seventh chord, was in the thinking of masters of this school:

The meeting of two contrary harmonies in the endings of these phrases certainly shows a lack of taste and reason; but it must be accepted as a fact that the accompanist must know, in order to perform according to the thinking of the composers.

230. As I have said (§229), the system of signs of chords was very simple in the school of Naples, at the end of the seventeenth century and the beginning of the eighteenth. The perfect chord is not figured; it is assumed on all the notes where no other chord is indicated, unless it becomes either major or minor, with signs that are not beside the clef; in this case, its quality is indicated either by the sharp or the flat, or by the natural, with or without the figure.

The sixth chord is figured by 6, with the sign that indicates its quality. The six-four chord is designated by $\begin{smallmatrix}6\\4\end{smallmatrix}$, and that of the fifth and sixth by $\begin{smallmatrix}6\\5\end{smallmatrix}$.

Sometimes one finds in the scores of the Neapolitan masters the double figure $\begin{smallmatrix}\sharp 6\\ \natural 4\end{smallmatrix}$: it indicates the chord of the tritone.

The dominant seventh chord is figured by $\begin{smallmatrix}\sharp\\7\end{smallmatrix}$ or $\begin{smallmatrix}\natural\\7\end{smallmatrix}$; the chord of the simple seventh retarding the sixth, by 7; finally, that of the diminished seventh, by $\begin{smallmatrix}7\\5\end{smallmatrix}$, or $\begin{smallmatrix}\flat 7\\5\end{smallmatrix}$.

It should be noted that Scarlatti and his students often wrote their instrumentation in three parts, and that the accompaniment of the organ or harpsichord was done in the same manner in the Neapolitan school until the end of the eighteenth century. The harmonist accompanist, who wishes to render the thought of these authors, must therefore not only know the meaning of their figures, but also choose the best intervals of the chords to accompany in three parts. The result of this system is a melodious form that is not found in chordal accompaniment in four parts.

The following fragment from an air by Alessandro Scarlatti, of which the composer wrote only the melody and the figured bass, will serve as a model for all music of this school.

231. Durante and [Leonardo] Leo [1694-1744], great composers of the school of Naples, who succeeded Scarlatti and became the masters of the conservatories of this city, completed the system of the figured bass of this school; a system which did not undergo any further change, and which is still taught, even though it is no longer in keeping with the present state of harmony.

Summarizing this system overall, it may be reduced to these facts:

(1) The perfect chord is not figured on the notes that belong to its tonality. If it becomes major in a minor key, it is figured with 3♯ or 3♮, or simply by the ♯, or by the ♮ suppressing a flat. If it becomes minor in a major key, it is figured with ♭3 or ♮3, or simply by the ♭ or ♮ alone.

(2) If the perfect chord succeeds a retardation of the third by the fourth, it is figured with a 3; if it succeeds a retardation of the octave by a ninth, it is designated by an 8. When it precedes the sixth chord on the same note, or when it follows it, it is indicated with a 5.

(3) The chord of the simple sixth, derived from the perfect chord, is figured by 6. If it becomes major in a minor key, it is figured by ♯6 or ♮6; if it becomes minor in a major key, it is indicated by ♭6 or ♮6. The augmented sixth is also designated by ♯6 or ♮6.

(4) The six-four chord is figured by $\genfrac{}{}{0pt}{}{6}{4}$.

(5) All seventh chords, whatever their quality, are figured simply with a 7, when no circumstance foreign to the key is manifested in the harmony. It is this figure which, in the works of Neapolitan composers, indicates the dominant seventh chord, the retardation of the sixth by the seventh, the minor seventh chord on the second degree, produced by the joining of the prolongation with the substitution, and even the diminished seventh chord. The latter is also sometimes figured by $\genfrac{}{}{0pt}{}{7}{5}$.

If there is a change of key, the major third of the dominant seventh is indicated by a sharp or a natural, as $\genfrac{}{}{0pt}{}{7}{\sharp}$ or $\genfrac{}{}{0pt}{}{7}{\natural}$.

If the minor third of the seventh chord of the second degree is the result of a change of key, the symbol of this chord is $\genfrac{}{}{0pt}{}{7}{\flat}$ or $\genfrac{}{}{0pt}{}{7}{\natural}$.

(6) The minor fifth and sixth chord, the first derivative of the dominant seventh chord, is indicated by $\genfrac{}{}{0pt}{}{6}{5}$, as is the six-five chord on the fourth degree. The accompanist knows the difference between these two chords only because the first has the leading tone as its bass.

(7) The leading-tone sixth chord, the second derivative of the dominant seventh chord, is figured by 6♯ or 6♮. It is also indicated, according to the circumstances, by $\genfrac{}{}{0pt}{}{\sharp}{6}$ or $\genfrac{}{}{0pt}{}{\natural}{6}$. The sharp and the natural, placed after the 6, or above, indicate the difference between this chord and the simple major sixth, where the sign precedes the figure.

(8) The tritone chord, the third derivative of the dominant seventh chord, is figured by $\genfrac{}{}{0pt}{}{4}{2}$, or 4, in the major mode, when there is no other circumstance foreign to the key; and by $\genfrac{}{}{0pt}{}{4\sharp}{2}$, 4♯, $\genfrac{}{}{0pt}{}{6\sharp}{4\sharp}$, or $\genfrac{}{}{0pt}{}{4\natural}{2}$, when the fourth becomes major with a new sharp, or by the suppression of a flat. In the minor mode, the sharp or the natural are always placed at the side of the figure.

(9) The retardation of the third by the fourth, in the perfect chord, is simply figured by 4; the same retardation, in the seventh chord is figured

by $\substack{7\\4}$. This last figure is used to indicate the retardation of the sixth by the seventh in the six-four chord.

(10) The retardation of the octave by the ninth is figured by $\substack{+\\9}$. The sign +, the usefulness of which one hardly understands, appears intended to indicate the necessity of the third to accompany the retardation; for when the third is minor, it is figured by $\substack{\flat+\\9}$.

(11) The retardation of the third by the bass, in the sixth chord, producing the second and fifth, is figured by $\substack{5\\2}$. The same retardation, with the substitution producing the second, fourth and sixth, is figured by $\substack{4\\2}$.[43]

An example of a figured bass, according to the preceding rules, will illustrate their application: I am choosing this one from the *Partimenti* of Fenaroli:[44]

[43]These rules concerning the figured bass, are the summary of the work of Fenaroli, director of the Conservatory of *la Pietà*, entitled: *Regole musicali per i principianti di Cembalo, o sia partimenti per il Cembalo* (Naples, 1795).

[44]Fenaroli was highly regarded for his teaching system that was influential well into the middle of the nineteenth century. When the Santa-Maria di Loreto and Turchini Conservatories amalgamated in 1806 he collaborated on the development of a new curriculum with Giovanni Paisiello (1740-1816) and Giacomo Tritto (1733-1824). Fétis praised Fenaroli's *Partimenti* for reducing the science to a small number rules that could be easily grasped, and illustrating them with numerous examples. [PL]

The accompanist must realize the harmony represented by the figures of this bass in the following manner:

232. The above noted system of figures is more or less the same in all the Italian schools: the only differences are that the boundaries by which the Neapolitan harmonists limited themselves become even more confining for the Roman composers of the eighteenth century, who, faithful to the traditions of their old school as to the choice of harmonies, did not use the substitution in natural dissonant chords, and whose works do not provide examples of the leading-tone seventh, or of the diminished seventh. The figures of the other chords are more or less the same; but it should be noted, for the use of accompanists, that the dissonance of the dominant seventh chord is always prepared by composers of the Roman school, as are those of seventh chords by prolongation.

The masters of the school of Bologna followed more or less the same traditions as the Romans, both in the choice of harmonies and in the figures. Clari, one of these masters who played the greatest part in perfecting the forms of music at the beginning of the eighteenth century, simply put more richness and variety into the modulations of his wonderful duos and trios.[45] The original copies of these beautiful pieces are figured with care; but there is much negligence in this respect in modern copies.

Amongst the most illustrious Venetian composers of the first half of the eighteenth century, one notes above all Lotti and Marcello. Their figured basses are not very different from Gasparini's system, and have fewer figures than the basses of the Neapolitan composers; one may even say that the principal harmonic circumstances are not sufficiently indicated, particularly in the psalms of Marcello. This master only figured with care certain movements of the bass in which the harmonic progressions were not in common use in his time. Such is a passage from the psalm: *Beato l'uom, che dietro a'rei consigli de' scelerati.*

---

[45]Giovanni Carlo Maria Clari (1677-1754), an Italian composer and *maestro di capella* at cathedrals in Pisa and Florence, is best known for his vocal chamber duets and trios. Fétis praises them for their pure taste, profound learning, and above all, for replacing real answers with tonal answers in fugal genres, which resulted in a 'modern' form of modulation. *FétisB*, 1:154. [PL]

Although Marcello figured some of the chords which precede the progression of chords of the seventh and sixth, there is an insufficiency in these figures for some chords where the accompanist cannot determine through examination the presence of the bass progression: I have indicated these cases by the figures placed below the notes of this bass.

233. The system of figures for the basso continuo, the origin of which had been similar in Italy and in Germany, soon became different in the two countries, due as much to the harmonic tendencies of the two peoples, as to their choice of symbols.

In connection with the choice of harmonies, one sees already more boldness in the Germans than in the Italians, at the end of the seventeenth century. I believe that there is not to be found in the works of the boldest Neapolitan composers, contemporaries or immediate successors of Alessandro Scarlatti, a single example of a high pedal similar to this passage from a cantata by Keiser,[46] entitled: *Der glücklich Fischer*.[47]

[46]Fétis praises Reinhard Keiser (1674-1739) for his profound expressivity, original use of forms, and strong, penetrating harmony. He notes that Johann Mattheson (1681-1764), Johann Adolpe Scheibe (1709-1776), and Charles Burney (1726-1814) considered Keiser the most important composer of his era, especially of dramatic music. *FétisB*, 5:311. [PL]

[47]*R. Keizer's Gemüths Ergoetzung, bestehend in einigen Sing-gedichten, mit einer Stimme und unterschiedlichen Instrumenten*. Hamburg, Nic. Spieringk, 1698.

234. German music would often create uncertainty in the mind of the accompanist, if it were not accompanied by more figures than the Italian music of the same period,[48] because of the multiplicity of key changes. The beginning of a cantata, reported by [Johann David] Heinichen [1683-1729],[49] of which he was probably the author, proves that the penchant of German composers for frequent modulations was already very developed in his time.

235. As can be seen in the preceding examples, the symbols of the chords of the minor fifth and sixth, the leading-tone sixth, and the tritone, are different here than those found for the same chords in the Italian system. In the German method, the six-five chord of the fourth degree is the only one indicated by $\genfrac{}{}{0pt}{}{6}{5}$, without any sign of modification of intervals; the symbol for the minor fifth and sixth chord is 5♭, whatever the note which produces the minor fifth from the bass note: the flat is, in all cases, the symbol of the minor quality of the fifth. The sharp and the natural, placed after the 6, to designate the leading-tone sixth chord, in the works of Italian composers, are replaced by the figure $\not 6$. This is the same for the chord of the tritone, marked by the symbol 4+. Sometimes this same chord of the tritone is marked by the figures for all its intervals.

[48]The beginning of the eighteenth century.

[49]*Der General-Bass der Composition* (798 onward) (Dresden, 1728).

The following example, taken from the book by [Friedrich] Niedt [1674-1717],[50] along with its figures, will provide an understanding of the manner of accompaniment of the figured basses of German music at the beginning of the eighteenth century, in chorded harmony.

236. There is little difference in the manner of figuring the bass of German composers who wrote towards the end of the eighteenth century; one only notes that for the figures $\substack{7\\5\flat}$, they substituted the $\not{7}$ for the diminished seventh chord.

237. The French harmonists followed the system of Italian composers of the seventeenth century in their manner of figured bass until Rameau. The accompaniment of the music of [Jean-Baptiste] Lully [1632-1687] and his followers therefore offers no difficulty to anyone who is familiar with the symbols of the chords used by [Giacomo] Carissimi, [1605-1674], [Alessandro] Stradella [1645-1682], Gasparini, and Alessandro Scarlatti.

238. Rameau sought to simplify the system of figuring chords, by getting rid of as many double figures as possible, and by giving the secondary signs the analogy for the base.

Thus, in his method of figured bass, the retardation of the third of the perfect chord is always figured simply by **4**; that of the octave of the same

[50]*Musikalishe Handleitung oder gründlicher Unterricht* etc., (Hamburg, 1710).

chord, by 9. For modifications of the major or minor third, he places above the notes of the bass only the ♯, the ♮, or the ♭, without the figure.

Rameau was the first to use the + to indicate the leading tone. It is through this sign that he distinguishes the dominant seventh from other seventh chords, in placing the + below the 7, in this way, $\overset{7}{+}$; but, by a peculiar contradiction, he figures the leading-tone sixth chord by a crossed 6, such as, 6̸, while he had adopted the cross in the figures as a symbol of diminution, for the fifth and seventh.

239. Rameau was also the first to use the lines going from one note to another above the bass, to indicate the prolongation of one of the notes of the harmony, whatever the movement of the bass on this prolonged note; and he established in the progressions the regular forms of these lines of prolongation, as in the following example:

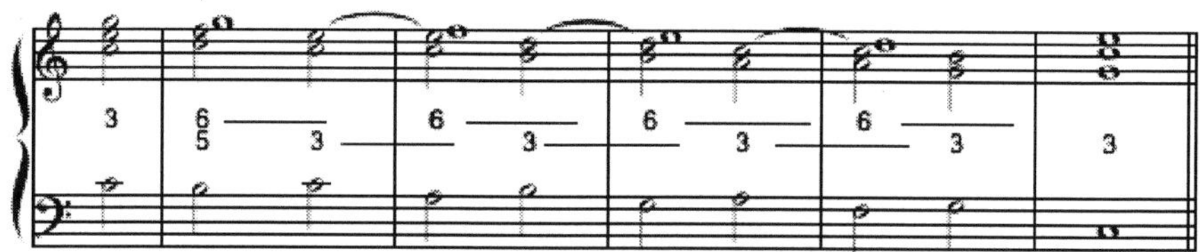

This system has the inconvenience of not making immediately visible the chord of each note, and of requiring an operation of the mind to understand the effect of the prolongations of the notes of these chords. It is therefore more natural to figure the above passage as follows:

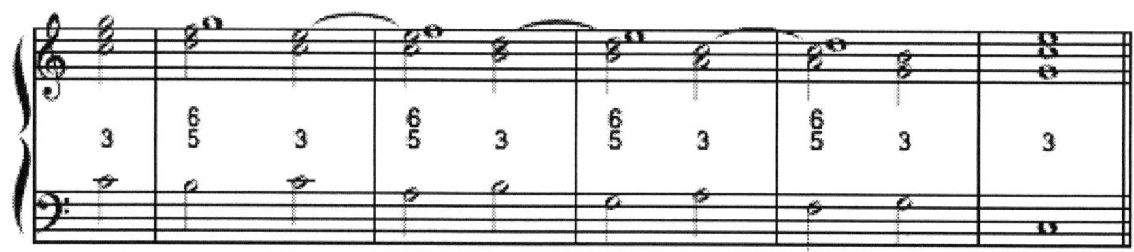

The lines of prolongation are nevertheless sometimes very useful, when they indicate entire held chords above a movement in the bass, because they avoid the use of a multitude of figures through which it would be necessary to represent the results of the prolongations, and render immediately perceptible to the eye the effect of the harmony.

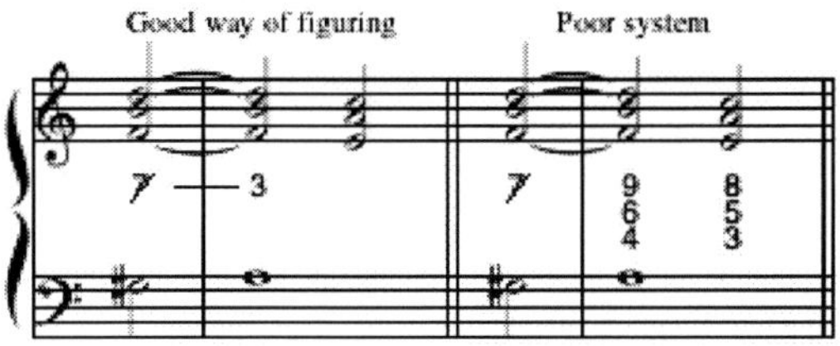

Good way of figuring Poor system

240. Since the frequent use of chords of prolongation, accompanied by altered intervals, was introduced into harmony, great difficulties were presented to the art of figuring basses, because it was necessary to multiply the figures and the accessory symbols to excess.

But at the same time, the usefulness of figured basses for accompaniment gradually faded; for while instrumentation gradually acquired more importance, its forms became inherent in the music, and made the simple harmonic accompaniment of the piano or organ disappear. When these instruments are substituted for the orchestra, they must not only play the chords that are linked to the melody, but also the forms of instrumentation that create a whole with this melody and harmony.

A simple figured bass therefore no longer represents the accompaniment of current music; it is the total score that the accompanist must translate onto the keyboard, be it with or without preparation. I have treated elsewhere this other part of the art that a good accompanist must possess;[51] I will not repeat here what I have said there.

As a result of what I have just said, the accompaniment of the figured bass being applicable only to old music, the figures of the chords which student harmonists place over a bass where they are assigned to find and write the chords, are only an exercise serving to see if they have grasped *a priori* the progression of the modulation of this bass, with all its harmonic circumstances. From that moment on, simplicity is no longer necessary in the combination of symbols, as it was when these symbols had to guide an accompanist. The only rule that one must follow in this exercise is to render perceptible, through the arrangement of the figures, the nature of the intervals and their movements.

Here are some examples of complicated cases, through combinations of prolongations and alterations of intervals, which may illustrate how to group the symbols above the bass:

[51]*Traité de lAccompagnement de la Partition sur le Piano ou l'Orgue*, 47 pp, (Paris, Schesinger).

These examples appear to me sufficient for understanding the system of representation by figures of the movement of prolonged and altered intervals in the succession of chords.

END OF THE SECOND BOOK

BOOK THREE

OF TONALITY, AND OF MODULATION IN HARMONY

Chapter I

CONSONANT CHORDS AND THEIR MODIFICATIONS BY THE RETARDATION OF THEIR INTERVALS CONSTITUTE ONLY THE OLD *UNITONIC* TONALITY – THE IMPOSSIBILITY OF ESTABLISHING ACTUAL MODULATION WITH THEM, THAT IS, THE NECESSARY CONNECTION OF ONE KEY TO ANOTHER

241. The second section of the second book of this work provided the demonstration of an important truth, namely, that the consonant chords, in their primitive form, have absolutely no attractive character which points to the transition from one key to another.

242. On the other hand, one finds in the third section of this book clear proof (chapter VII) that the retardation of the natural intervals of these chords changes neither their characteristic tonal unity, nor the destination, since this kind of modification of consonant chords must resolve onto the natural chords that have been retarded.

243. One understands, therefore, that if there is a period in the art where these chords, either original, or modified by the retardation of their intervals, were the only ones in use, the products of this time must have consisted of a music of a single key, or *unitonic*, that is, which had no necessary transition from one key to another.

Now, this period did exist: it is the one that preceded the introduction of natural dissonant harmony in the art. The tonality then in use was that of plainchant. This period continued until the end of the sixteenth century.

The greatest composers, whose genius was governed by the nature of the harmonic elements which they had at their disposal, could not avoid the rigorous tyranny of this tonal unity. Before examining the efforts made by the imagination of a few composers to break free from its iron yoke, I will analyze fragments of this unitonic music, chosen from the works of the most illustrious of these masters.

244. Nevertheless, the examination that I will make of the products of a harmony with so little variety must be preceded by an observation concerning the incomplete aspect in which this harmony often appears in these venerable works of another time. Reduced to two combinations of consonant intervals (the perfect chord and that of the sixth), and to the retardations of these intervals, the music resulting from such elements would have caused repulsion because of its monotony, if the composers had always given the complete harmony, and if, through artful forms, they had not occupied the attention of the ear.[1] In order to catch the spirit of the harmony, often incomplete, of the works of these composers, it is necessary to take the point of view of their authors.

FIRST EXAMPLE
OF UNITONIC TONALITY IN HARMONY

Benedictus from the Mass *De Beata Virgine* by Pierluigi de Palestrina

[1]These devices, which only constitute a style of application of the harmony, are the subject of a special part of the art, the exposition of which is found in some treatises on composition, and particularly in the book which I have published under the title: *Traité du Contrepoint et de la Fugue* (Paris, Troupenas), two parts. A new edition of this work is in preparation.*

*The new edition was published in 1846. [PL]

245. The key of this piece is the sixth of plainchant, which has analogy with the key of F in modern tonality. Note, however, that this analogy is very inaccurate, for there not being in the tonality of plainchant either tonic or dominant in the modern sense of these words,[2] the character of repose and of conclusion, inherent in these notes in modern music, does not exist in music created in the old tonality. Thus one often sees used on the first and fifth notes of the scale in a plainchant key the harmony of the sixth chord, as in measures 2 and 6 of the preceding piece, and that the perfect chord is placed on the second and third notes, as in measures 6, 9, 11, 13, 18, 19, 26, 29, 34, and 35 of this example. Now, these harmonies are precisely in direct opposition with what was said in Book One, chapter IV of this work, concerning the special properties of each note of a scale in modern tonality, and the harmonies that devolve to them.

Furthermore, there not being any leading tone in the music created on this bygone unitonic tonality, since this note only acquires its character through its harmonic relations with the fourth degree and the dominant, in natural dissonant chords, the actual *cadence*, that is to say, the rhythmic termination of the phrase, did not exist, or at least was never obligatory in this old music, where, on the contrary, the elegance consisted in making a perpetual sequence of entering parts, while others rested.[3] See, for example, the harmonic sequences in the seventeenth and eighteenth measures of the preceding example; if the tonality were established, as in modern music, there would be a perfect cadence on the dominant, by means of a natural accidental on the B, in this manner:

But the B-natural would be antipathetic at the re-entry of the bass, where the phrase requires the B-flat; there is therefore no cadence, and this B-flat forms a perfect minor chord on the second note of the key, followed by a perfect minor chord on the third; from then on, any distinguishing characteristic disappears, and the harmony remains in the vague tonality of the entire piece.

[2]See my *Traité élémentaire de Plain-chant* (Paris, 1843) (§ VI, 13 and following).

[3]Optional cadences were known in Palestrina's time, and even long before; but were only used at final endings.

This lack of tonal determination is precisely the cause of the absence of modulation. The most scrupulous examination of this piece would not uncover the slightest tendency toward any key foreign to the unitonic and monotonous tonality upon which it is created.

Such is the character of all music that preceded the seventeenth century. I have figured all the chords of this piece, and even the simple intervals, in order to show that one could not find any other harmony than that of perfect and sixth chords, with some retardations of the third by the fourth, and the octave by the ninth.

When one imagines that with so few harmonic resources, an invariable tonality, voices which do not leave the compass of an octave or a ninth, and which, from the lowest bass note to the highest in the soprano, do not extend more than two and a half octaves, one is seized with admiration, not only for the calm and religious character which reigns in this piece, but also by the easy and natural manner with which all the voices sing, and by the multitude of elegant forms which the immortal author of this composition was able to find under such unfavorable conditions.

246. Let us continue the demonstration of the impossibility of leaving the system of a single tonality and of using modulation with consonant harmony, natural or retarded, by taking an example in a key that has a kind of analogy with a minor mode of modern music. I am taking this example from the *Kyrie* of Palestrina's mass *O regem coeli*. This piece, which is from the second transposed key, approaches in some ways our key of G minor, and in others, that of D minor.

247. The observations concerning the vague unitonic tonality of the first example are applicable here: there is nothing distinctive enough about it to ascertain a complete analogy with D minor or G minor, and in this way the harmony of Palestrina is in keeping with the true tonality of plainchant. We note, nevertheless, that we find here concluding cadences in measures 21 and 29: in this way the first, second, third and fourth keys of plainchant, which have an analogy with our minor mode, differ from the fifth, sixth, seventh and eighth, which approach the major mode. In the former, the cadence was used in order to raise by a semitone the lower note in the endings of phrases, to make them sweeter, and after this note thus modified, a repose was needed to avoid false relations. Furthermore, there are no more traces of modulation in this example than in the first, or in any which I might mention, belonging to the same period.

248. I must anticipate here objections which could be made, or rather respond to those which have been against the theory I am developing in this third part of my work, after I presented the principles of these in 1832, in my course on the philosophy of music. Some erudite musicians from Germany and Italy, admirers, and rightly so, of Palestrina, believed to have found in the works of this great artist the dominant seventh chord, and, with this chord, the principle of modulation.

If such were the case, if, directed by his instinct in some particular cases, the illustrious master had really used the complete dominant seventh chord, with the fifth and without preparation, and if this chord had allowed him to form some unforeseen transition, there would be nothing to conclude from this isolated fact, lost in the immensity of the works of this master of the Roman school, since this fact would not have been revealed to him as the key to a new order of things, and would not even have been noticed. In this case, Palestrina would have done in an unconscious manner, and in a way without his knowing, what he did in a very few cases where he used the seventh retarding the sixth with the fifth, or the six-five chord, although these harmonies are certainly not the simple product of the retardation in a consonant chord, and even though he ignored their real origin.

But this is not what Palestrina did, for in a very few circumstances where he used the interval of the minor seventh with the major third he wrote this harmony only as the retardation of the sixth chord, in fact, with the resolution of the dissonance followed by a six-four chord in order to prepare the harmony of the fourth and fifth retarding the perfect chord.

Here is an example of this so-called seventh chord that appeared to contradict my historical classification of systems of tonality: it is from the first *Lamentation of Jeremiah*, from *Holy Wednesday*, by Palestrina.[4]

[4]Fétis has here accidentally misattributed this example to Palestrina. It is listed in the catalogue of works contained in his private collection of scores as being from the *Lamentation of Jeremiah, Holy Thursday*, by Allegri. I am grateful to Professor Brian Power for identifying this example. [PL]

The minor seventh chord with major third, without fifth, in the eighth measure, which has been labeled as a the dominant seventh chord, is the product of a prolongation which retards the sixth chord: it is not, as one sees, a true dominant seventh chord, existing on its own, sounded without preparation, and characterizing a tonality.

As for the seventh chord through retardation with the fifth, which one sees in the second measure, I have proven in the second book of this work (ch. VII) that it is not the product of a simple prolongation, and that it derives from another order of facts unknown to composers of the sixteenth century. Palestrina and a few masters of his time, who used it often, could not account for the origin of this harmony, and only used it by instinct, or as a harmonic license somewhat similar to the *changing note* which one sees in the nineteenth measure of the *Benedictus* of the *Beata Virgine* mass, and in many other places.

248. *bis*. To summarize these analyses, I will say that the rare exceptions to cases similar to those we have just seen, were they to have the significance that one had wanted to give them, would prove nothing against the authority of some thousands of compositions emanating from all of the schools from the fourteenth to the end of the sixteenth century, which demonstrate that the tonality of this entire period was unitonic, or non-modulating; finally, that dissonant harmony does not appear here, and that in its absence, there is no true modulation.

249. Among the number of objections which have been made against the theory of the unitonic tonality of all music in which the harmony is composed only of consonant chords, I find the following: "Church music, in which the themes were taken from plainchant, could very well have conformed to the nature of this chant and not modulate; but was this the case for all music, especially instrumental music? That is rather unlikely."[5]

The doubt expressed by this critic could have some value if no monument of instrumental music of the sixteenth century had reached us: It will suffice for me to relate here a fragment of a piece for organ, composed by Claudio Merulo [1553-1604], a celebrated musician of his time, to refute the objection, and demonstrate that this instrumental music was also unitonic and non-modulating. This piece is taken from the first book of *Toccate d'intavolatura d'Organo*, Rome, 1598 (7th toccata, 27).

---

[5]*Account of a new musical System set forth by M. Fétis in his lectures on musical philosophy* (London, 1834), 17.*

*The above footnote appears in the original English, which indicates that the critic to whom Fétis refers is probably British. [PL]

With the exception of some inaccuracies inherent in the genre, one finds in this music only what is found in all music of the same time, that is, a consonant harmony or dissonant harmony through retardation, and an unvarying tonality.

250. During my stay in Rome (in 1841), a learned musician, discussing these important questions with me, said that he considered as true modulating music the introduction to Palestrina's *Stabat Mater*, shown here:

Here is certainly a most singular piece for the time in which it was composed. It does not belong to any given tonality, for it does not partake of any key of plainchant, and does not give any more the feeling of modern tonality. Its purpose was to express the extreme pain of the mother of Christ, at the sight of the cross to which he is nailed: Palestrina, being a man of genius, understood that he must find other means than those of the art of his time to depict this heart-wrenching scene; he imagined the three perfect major chords which descend one degree increase the sensation of different keys without connection, and cause the ear to experience a painful effect, due to the succession of false relations.

Having then to express the word *dolorosa*, he returns to the point of departure by an inverse succession of ascending perfect chords, but by making the second chord minor; then the second choir takes up the three perfect major chords on the words *juxta crucem*, and also returns to the point of departure with a perfect minor chord, to express Mary's tears.

The 8th and 9th measures lead, through a succession of perfect minor chords, from the major chord of A to the perfect minor chord of the same note; then returning immediately with the perfect major chord of this note, Palestrina alternately touches upon, and several times, the keys of D and F major, from the 10th measure to the 19th, and finally ends with a cadence on the first of these keys in measures 19 and 20.

Is there throughout this whole beautiful introduction the least relation with our tonality, with what we call the *transition*? No, the transition results from the tendency of one key toward another, and from the point of contact that exists between them. Now, with perfect chords and a few rare sixth chords, there is neither tendency, nor point of contact between any given two keys; for they always leave the harmony at rest. The imagination of the composer may well cause the perfect chord of one key to be followed by the perfect chord of another key, as Palestrina did in the piece the beginning of which I have just analyzed; but in this succession, there is neither connection, nor necessity, nor, therefore, any transition.

251. Modern music itself offers fine examples, by their simplicity, of these successions of keys which are not hinted at beforehand, and which come about through the free succession of two perfect chords. One of the most remarkable examples of this genre, and I think the first of its kind, is in the charming canzona, *Voi che sapete,* from *The Marriage of Figaro*, second act, by Mozart. Here is this passage:

The effect as simple as it is striking of change of key is in the succession from the fourth to fifth measure. This effect has been often repeated following Mozart.

252. The simple changes of key are also sometimes made without harmony by a unison or by a single voice: the simplicity of this means is the most remarkable kind of beauty.

In this way Mozart, who endowed art with so many new things, passed from the key of D major to that of F, in the most beautiful manner, in this passage from *Don Giovanni* [Act Two, Finale]:

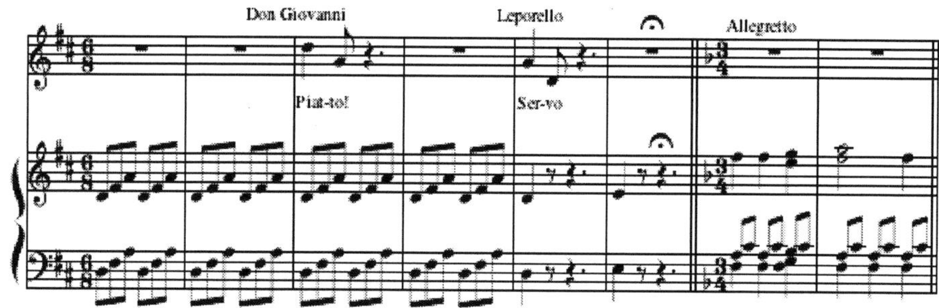

Haydn repeated exactly the same effect in the second part of the first movement of his 74th Quartet.

Through a similar means Rossini also made a change of key of a most beautiful effect in the following passage from a duet from *Guillaume Tell* [Act One, Recitative and Duet, *Where so fast?*]:

But once again, although the works from which these passages are taken belong to the most modern tonal system, the changes of key which I point out were not obligatory for their authors; the element of transition is not found here, and nothing prepares one for the new key before it is heard.

253. The theory that I set forth in this book, concerning the influence of harmony with regard to the tonality, a new theory, although intimately connected to the history of art, does not permit me to leave aside a single one of the objections which could be made against me, and which would have all the more weight, since they have the authority of musicians justly renowned for their wisdom and their erudition.

Pietro Aaron[6] said that Spataro,[7] director of music in Bologna, at the beginning of the sixteenth century, had tried to revive the chromatic and enharmonic genres of the Greeks in some of his compositions, and that he had trained his students to perform these pieces well.

About forty years later, Nicolo Vicentino, director of music for the Duke of Ferrara, published a book in which he claimed to have rediscovered these chromatic and enharmonic genres of antiquity.[8] In this book he gave as an example of the first of these genres a motet, of which the following is the beginning:[9]

---

[6]*De Institutione harmonica,* trans. J. Anton. Flaminio, bk. 2, ch. 9.*

*Pietro Aaron (c1450-1545), who was weak in Latin, called upon the humanist Giovanni Antonio Flaminio (1456-1536) to translate the *Libri tres de institutione harmonica* (Bologna, 1516). Fétis notes that although Aaron's treatises are essentially derived from the theories of Johannes Tinctoris (c1435-1511), they are valuable for their methodical organization and clarity. *FétisB*, 1:1. [PL]

[7]Giovanni Spataro (1458-1541), Italian theorist and composer known mostly for his correspondence, often polemical, with theorists Franchinus Gaffurius (1451-1522), Pietro Aaron, and Giovanni Del Lago (c1490-1544). [PL]

[8]*L'antica Musica ridotta alla moderna prattica,* published by Ant. Barre, Rome 1555.

[9]Ibid., 62

One cannot deny that the notes, which proceed by intervals of a semitone, belong to the chromatic scale; but in harmony, the chromatic genre consists of the tendencies of different keys where these progressions of semitones find their use. In the above example, the chords, which belong to these different keys, are placed close together, but without any connection. Moreover, one does not find there any melodic significance, and the progression of the four parts is most incorrect.[10] Father Baini[11] admits that he has little regard for the pieces that Vicentino used as examples to support of his system; however, he appears to accept that the piece, a fragment of which we have just seen, represents the chromatic genre in harmony; now this is a fundamental error.

254. Toward the end of the sixteenth century, many composers of merit instinctively understood that the reign of unitonic music was completed, and that after Palestrina, there remained nothing more to do in its domain. They had begun the search for new means of expression, and

[10]I do not examine here the question of the impossibility of the exact intonation of the chromatic and enharmonic intervals of the Greeks and Romans, according to Vicentino's system, nor that of the necessary modification of these intervals in performance, according to the equal temperament adopted by Bottrigari* and Doni** for their attempts in applying the chromatic and enharmonic genres to their times. These questions are not of a nature to be discussed in this work. I will limit myself to recalling the very sensible opinion of Padre Martini, who considers it a useless enterprise to reconcile the genres of Greek music with the practice of modern art (*Storia della Musica*, vl. 1, 126, n. 57.)

*Ercole Bottrigari (1531-1612), an Italian music theorist, composer, poet and Greek scholar, wrote widely on aspects of Greek music theory and contemporary musical practice.

**Fétis praises Giovanni Battista Doni (1595-1647) for his immense erudition, but is critical of his preference for the music of the ancients. In his *Compendio del trattato de' generi e modi della musica* (1635) Doni advocated infusing the Greek musical system into modern music, a notion that Fétis evidently strongly opposed. *FétisB*, 3:324. [PL]

[11]*Memorie storico-critiche della vita e della opere di G.Pierluigi da Palestrina,* (vl. 1, 348, n. 426.*

*Giuseppe Baini's (1775-1844) *Memorie storico-critiche* was the first critical study of Palestrina. His many students included Adrien de La Fage (1801-1862), and Ferdinand Hiller (1811-1885). [PL]

tonal transition, of which they foresaw possibility, without having discovered the principle. This resulted in the efforts of [Luca] Marenzio [c.1553-1599], Giovanni Gabrieli [c.1554-1612], [Don Carlo] Gesualdo [1561-1613], prince of Venice, and many others, for the creation of a modulated music; efforts that have undoubtedly given their works a different character than that of the music of their time, but which did not reach the goal they had set themselves, because, as I have said many times, consonant harmony cannot lead to true chromatic music, which is that of harmonic transition, let alone enharmonic music.

M. de Winterfeld[12] was thus given to illusion when he presented, as an enharmonic period, this fragment of a madrigal by Marenzio.[13]

Enharmony, as it relates to modern music, does not consist simply of a childish changing of a sharpened note to a unison flattened note, and vice versa; but in a multiple tendency toward diverse keys.[14] Now, if one examines the fragment by Marenzio, one finds only a succession of perfect chords independent of one another, and in which no attraction is evident, because every perfect chord is a harmony of repose. The so-called enharmonies of this fragment therefore represent only a progression of perfect chords, descending in the bass and rising in the other parts, in which the unneeded accidentals must be removed.

---

[12]Fétis criticizes Carl George Winterfeld (1784-1852), a German judge and musicologist, for numerous errors in his theory of the old tonality and of the introduction of modulation in music. Winterfeld's *Johannes Gabrieli und sein Zeitalter* (*Johaness Gabrieli and his Times*), 1834, also traces the development of music in the city of Venice. *FétisB*, 8:577. [PL]

[13]*Johannes Gabrieli und sein Zeitalter*, 2nd part, 88.*

* The excerpt is from the madrigal *O voi che sospirate*, mm. 13-17. [PL]

[14]This will be demonstrated in the third chapter of this third book.

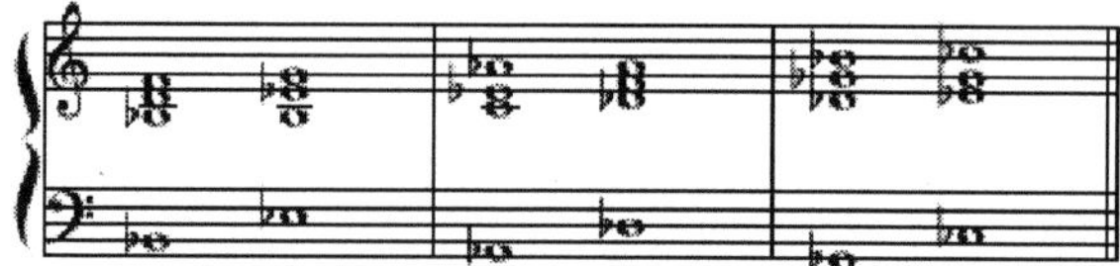

There is every indication that enharmony does not exist in these successions. With respect to the change of key which is made immediately following the progression, one cannot consider it as a transition, for there is no point of contact between the last chord of the third measure and the first chord of the fourth measure: their succession is harsh and unpleasant to the ear.

255. Through the analyses contained in this chapter, I believe to have demonstrated incontestably the propositions of its heading: *Consonant chords and their modifications by the retardation of their intervals, constitute only the old unitonic tonality. It is impossible to establish with these chords modulation properly speaking, that is, the necessary connection of one key to another.*

Chapter II

THE NATURAL DISSONANT CHORD OF THE DOMINANT SEVENTH AND ITS DERIVATIVES GIVE RISE TO MODERN TONALITY AND ITS ATTRACTIONS. —THEY PROVIDE THE ELEMENT OF TRANSITION FROM ONE KEY TO ANOTHER. *TRANSITONIC ORDER,* OR THE SECOND PHASE OF HARMONY

256. After Monteverdi, a Venetian composer, had instinctively found the harmony of the dominant seventh chord, during the first years of the seventeenth century[15], and had extracted from it the origin of modern tonality as well as the element of modulation, he first used this natural dissonant harmony temperately and with a kind of timidity, the legitimacy of which was only guaranteed by the approval of his ear, and there were against it the prejudices arising from the usage of a different harmony and tonality for over three centuries.

Here is the first example that he gave of the use of these natural dissonances without preparation, in a madrigal from his fifth book:

[15]See the entry under Monteverdi in my *Biographie universelle des Musiciens*, vl. VI, 482-484, 2nd edition.

If we compare this music with the pieces by Palestrina in the preceding chapter, we see that art has changed the elements and the object. In place of the common end of perfect and sixth chords on all degrees of the scale which one sees in the music of the illustrious Roman composer; instead of the vague unitonic tonality which is the result; finally, instead of the incessant connection of phrases, and of the absence, or at least the extreme rarity of final cadences, one sees, in the passage here presented of Monteverdi's madrigal, a tonality determined by the particular quality of the perfect chord on the tonic, by the sixth chord attributed to the third and seventh degrees, by the optional choice of the perfect chord or of the sixth chord on the sixth degree; finally, by the perfect chord, and especially by that of the seventh without preparation, with the major third, on the dominant. With this harmony, the cadences become frequent and regular, and when there is modulation, this is achieved by a new leading tone placed in relation to the fourth degree, which alone may give it its character, as can be seen on the last beat of the second measure.

257. The character of the new tonality created by Monteverdi's harmonic innovations also results from periodic phrases, where the changes of key are always determined by the relationships of the leading tone to the fourth degree, or by the dominant seventh chord. Such is the following passage of the same madrigal:[16]

258. I have said that there remained a kind of timidity in Monteverdi's mind concerning the use of the dissonant harmony of the dominant; either he could not free himself completely from the habits of his youth, or attacks on his innovations inspired this reserve. However, in many places in his *Orfeo* and in his *Arianna*, he used this harmony without preparation,

[16]One sees here an example of the negligence which abounds in Monteverdi's notation where the B sustained by the tenor in the third measure, while the contralto and bass sound the third, A-C, is a false harmony which would have been easy to avoid in the following manner:

as a means of transition. Here is an example taken from *Orfeo,*[17] an opera presented in 1607 [Act Two, *Due Pastori*]:

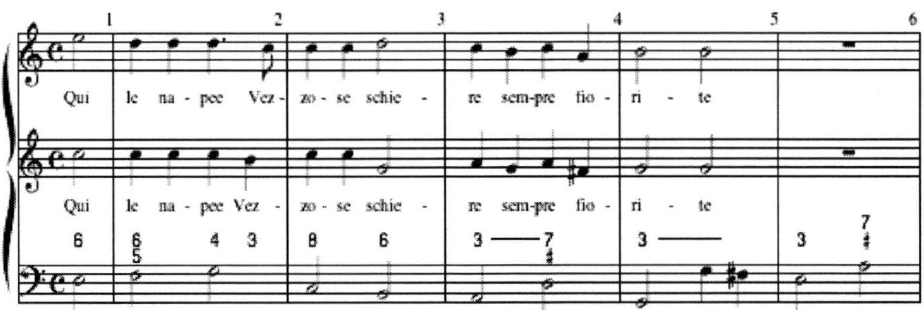

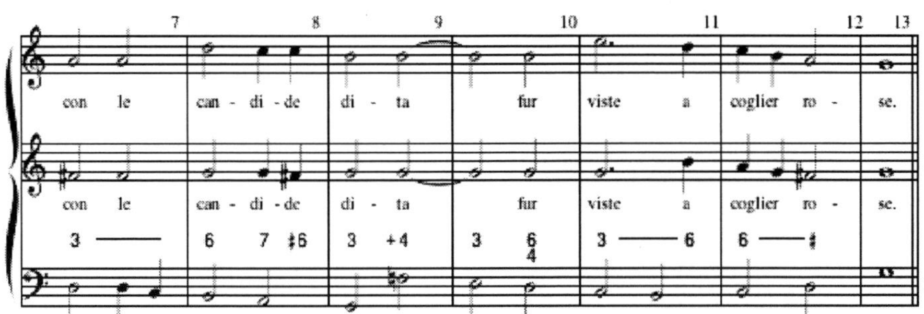

In this example, the modern key of C is established up to the first beat of the third measure; the key of G is only vaguely indicated by what follows; but, on the second beat of the fourth measure, the dominant seventh chord of this key leaves no further doubt as to the modulation. Then comes a transition to D in the basso continuo, and the return of G becomes obvious with the relationship between fourth degree of this key with the leading tone, on the last beat of the eighth measure. Finally, the return to the original key of C is the direct result of the chord of the tritone on the F-natural of the basso continuo. The perfect major chord of this key, on the dominant, then establishes a passing modulation to G.

259. The creation of modern tonality and modulation, by the facts that I have just pointed out; this creation, which, when brought together with the music produced by the preceding tonality, becomes as clear as day, had another result; namely, the formation of the regular rhythm of the periodic phrase, by the frequency of cadences. But this subject cannot be treated here: I am mentioning it only to point out that an absolutely new art began with the use of natural dissonant harmony in music.

260. There was uncertainty at first and a lack of skill in the manner of using the new natural dissonant harmony: for this reason the collections of

[17]*Orfeo*, a musical fable by Claudio Monteverdi, choirmaster of the Most Serene Republic, premiered in Mantua, in 1607, and recently reprinted (Venice, Ricciardo Amandino, 1615), 30.

songs, airs and duos, composed in Italy during the first twenty years of the seventeenth century, and in the new forms, with basso continuo accompaniment, are full of dubious modulations. No one had yet formed a correct and true opinion of the change that was coming about in tonality. The appeal of the novelty drove certain musicians to make use of some of its characteristic successions; but, accustomed as they were to the forms of the old tonality, they made a mixture of these two incompatible things.

Other composers tried to resist the revolution which the art was undergoing, although they had abandoned the old type of madrigals in four, five, or six voices for that of airs and canzonets for solo voice, with basso continuo accompaniment on the harpsichord, lute or harp.

However, one finds here and there modulations determined by the use of natural dissonances in the very compositions that remain full of tonal uncertainties. Here is a remarkable example that I have taken from the *Grazie ed affetti di musica moderna,*[18] published by J. S. Pietro de'Negri, in 1613. In the piece entitled *l'Armida in stilo recitativo* (page 5), this composer made use of this modulating progression:

The harmony indicated by the figures must translate as follows:

261. The uncertainties of which I have just spoken with respect to the determination of modern tonality had ceased toward the middle of the seventeenth century. The compositions of this period prove that this tonality was from this time onward formed and perfectly understood. Here is an example taken from *l'Orontea*, an opera by Cesti, performed in Venice in 1649. One sees here that not only the natural dissonant chords fulfill their functions for the transition from one key to another, but also the substitutions of the minor mode are very well employed.

[18]*Grace and feeling in modern music in one, two, and three voices. To be accompanied by harpsichord, double harp, and other similar instruments,* by Giulio S. Pietro de' Negri. Recently discovered. Edited by Filippo Lomazzo (Milan, 1613).

262. In instrumental music the determination of modern tonality and transition by natural dissonant chords was much more advanced than in vocal music; for, while one still saw in the latter composers uncertain about the use of the new chords, [Girolamo] Frescobaldi [1583-1643], the great organist of St. Peter's, in Rome, had boldly entered into the tonality created by them, seen in the beginning of a fugue from the second book of his pieces for organ and harpsichord, published in 1627.[19] The comparison of this piece with the one by Merulo, which I gave as an example in the

[19]This example does not appear in Frescobaldi's works. I have so far not identified the source. [PL]

preceding chapter, shows incontestably the reality of tonal transformation that I attribute to the introduction of natural dissonant chords in music.

263. Before the first years of the eighteenth century, the need for frequent modulations had taken much development, and composers had exhausted all the resources that natural dissonant chords could offer in this regard, to increase the expressive accents in their works and to give their music a dramatic and impassioned character. Without resorting to the instrumental style of this period I believe to be able to affirm that it was impossible to go further in modulation through the dissonant natural chords and their substitutes than did Alessandro Scarlatti [1660-1725] in

this air from the oratorio *il Sacrifizio d'Abramo*, where the mother of Isaac looks for her son.

264. Having arrived at this point, we believe:

(1) That the introduction of natural dissonant chords in music dates from the early years of the seventeenth century;

(2) That these chords, by placing in harmonic relation the fourth degree, the dominant and the seventh degree, have characterized the leading tone, have imparted to it the necessity of the ascending resolution, and have in this way founded modern tonality, and have substituted it for the old tonality of plainchant;

(3) That the effect of the attraction of the leading tone toward the tonic, through natural dissonant harmony, has been to formulate all the keys of modern music on the same model, each one of them divided into two modes, namely, major and minor; while the keys of plainchant differ only through the position of the semitones of a single scale beginning on

various degrees;[20] a difference hardly perceptible in harmony, and from which results the vague character of the old tonality;

(4) That, through the special character of each degree of the scales of modern tonality, each note also has its special harmony, which does not exist in the old tonality, and which establishes a radical difference between the degrees of the scale;

(5) Finally, that all the keys of modern tonality being characterized by the harmonic relations of the fourth degree, the dominant and the leading tone, the passage from one key to another always manifests itself in a clear manner, and that the key is immediately recognized by the harmony of these three notes;

(6) From which it follows that the natural dissonant harmony of the fourth degree, the dominant and the leading tone, is the means of transition, that is, of the passage from one key to another, and that its introduction into music resulted in the passing from the *unitonic order* to the *transitonic order*.

So as to leave no doubt concerning this last fact, it will be sufficient to provide here a series of harmonic transitions, apart from any melodic considerations.

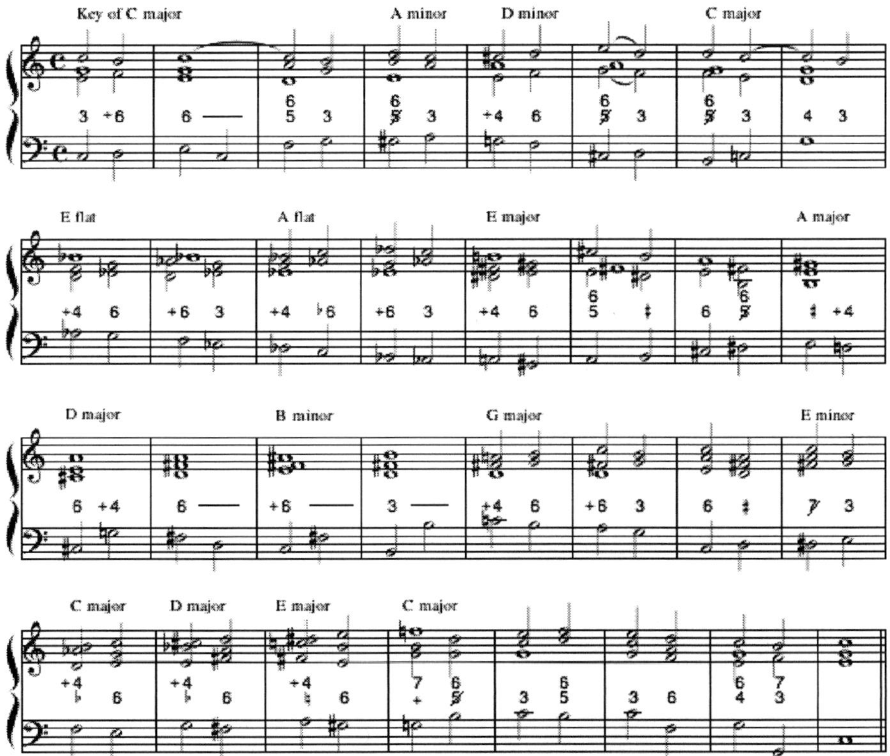

[20]See my *Traité élémentaire de Plain-Chant*, pages 3 and 12-16.

Chapter III

THE NATURAL DISSONANT CHORDS, MODIFIED BY THE SUBSTITUTION OF THE MINOR MODE, PLACE SIMULTANEOUSLY MANY KEYS IN RELATION—*PLURITONIC ORDER*.

265. Harmony, tonality and modulation, having arrived at the point where we left them at the end of the last chapter, remained in this state for more than seventy-five years, that is, for approximately the first three quarters of the eighteenth century. A more or less often use of the alteration of natural intervals of chords, especially in Germany, was the only harmonic innovation which one saw appear during this time, almost entirely devoted to the perfection of melodic and tangible forms of music.

266. The eighteenth century, a great era in modern music with respect to dramatic and instrumental conception and instrumentation, was much more preoccupied with this conception, and particularly with the distribution of ideas and their periodic return than in the search for new tonal attractions. It is not therefore in the discovery of these new attractions, but in the perfection of all melodic, harmonic, and rhythmic forms, resulting from modern tonality, that one must consider the merit of Marcello, Clari, Handel, J. S. Bach, Leo, Durante, Pergolesi, Jomelli, Gluck, and many other great musicians of the eighteenth century.

267. Mozart appears to have been the first to understand that there was a new source of expression, and an expansion of the realm of art, in the property of natural dissonant chords modified by substitutions of the minor mode; a property which consists of establishing multiple relations of tonality, that is, the tendencies of a single chord toward different keys. The works of this great master are at least those in which I found the oldest traces of these chords, in the sense spoken of here.

I have said previously (§ 253), that the enharmony attempted by some musicians of the sixteenth century was only a puerile game of changing the designations of the notes, without true harmonic results. It is not in this way that enharmony is characterized in natural dissonant chords modified by the substitution of the minor mode, for the difference in the designations of the notes of these chords is only the result of their tendency toward one key or another.

Suppose for example, that the chord is the diminished seventh on the leading tone of the key of C, in the minor mode, composed of the notes B-natural-D-F-A-flat. There is no doubt that a chord thus arranged, that is composed of the notes which form amongst themselves three intervals of minor thirds, must resolve onto the tonic of the key of C, so that each note accomplishes its natural destination.

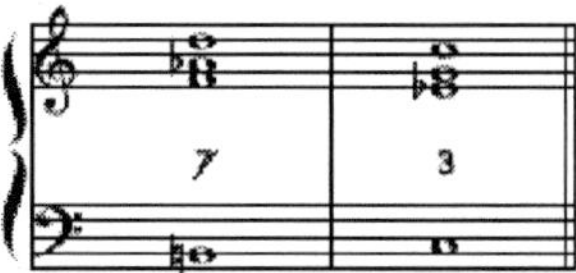

But any minor third sounds to the ear analogous to the augmented second, except for the almost imperceptible raising or lowering of one of the notes of the interval, because of their ascending or descending destination. Thus, the first minor third of the diminished seventh chord

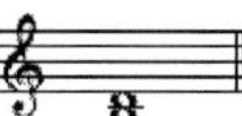

has the same effect on the ear as the augmented second:

The second minor third

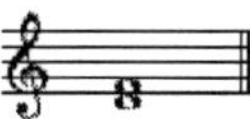

sounds like the augmented second:

Finally, the third minor third

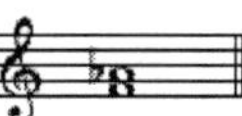

produces an identical effect to the other minor third

and with the augmented second:

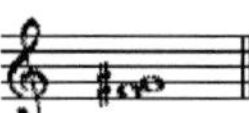

Now, each of these intervals has, as I have just said, a different tendency, due to the notation of accidentals that constitute them, and the performer characterizes this tendency, by slightly raising or lowering the intonation without his being aware, according to the ascending or descending destination of the note. For example, in the diminished seventh interval, the lower note has an ascending tendency, and the upper note a descending attraction, due to the tonality of which we are aware:

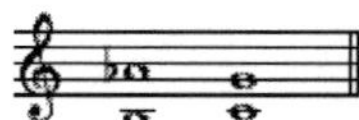

But with the major sixth, which is homophonic with the diminished seventh, it is the opposite, for the upper note has an ascending tendency, and the movement of the lower note is optional.

DEMONSTRATION

Likewise, with the interval of the minor fifth, the lower note has an ascending tendency, and the upper note a descending attraction.

DEMONSTRATION

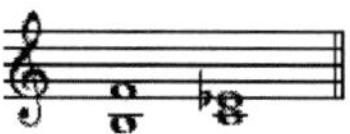

While with the major fourth, which, considered alone, sounds exactly identical to the ear, the upper note has an ascending attraction, and the lower note a descending tendency.

DEMONSTRATION

It follows from this that the dissonant chords with substitution of the minor mode have the property of resolving in many keys and in the two modes, due to the tendencies of the tonality that the composer gives them. Thus, the diminished seventh chord, which has just been analyzed, can be transformed at will, and according to the thought of the artist, into the minor fifth and sixth chord, the tritone with minor third, and the augmented second chord. Now, this transformation may produce many different cadences, and many more are possible by changing the major mode to the minor, or the minor mode to major.

DEMONSTRATION

This example proves beyond a doubt that the chords

DEMONSTRATION

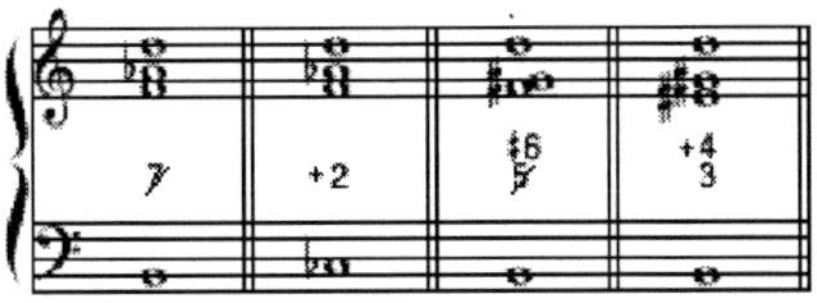

are identical to the ear, considered alone, but not in their tonal destination.

268. Once it was observed that certain notes of the chord had the ability to change their destination, one began to search for analogous effects in other harmonies, and soon found that the alterations of intervals of natural chords share the same property. For example, in the chord of the augmented sixth with fifth, the interval of the augmented sixth sounds to the ear like that of the minor seventh: this results in the possibility of changing an augmented sixth chord into a dominant seventh chord, and *vice versa*; from which result tendencies of totally different tonal resolutions.

DEMONSTRATION

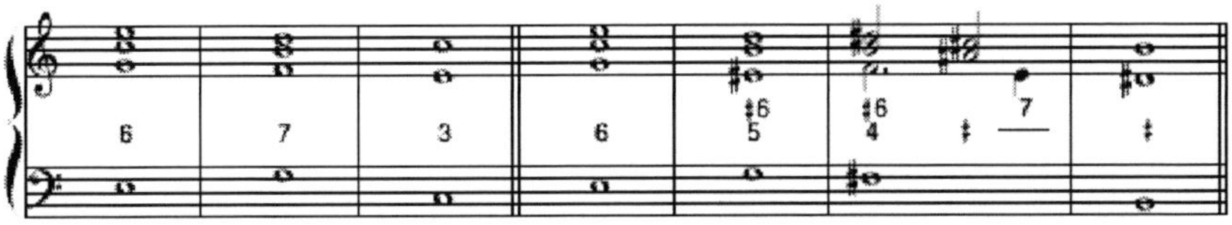

It seems to me that Mozart was the first composer who used this enharmony, by substituting, for the chord determined by the tonality, its enharmonic equivalent, and thereby making an unexpected modulation. This is how in the first duo of the first act of *Don Giovanni*, after an enharmonic modulation, by a substituted chord of the minor mode, he returns to the original key by the enharmony of the augmented sixth. Here is this passage, the effect of which was absolutely unknown when Mozart wrote his opera.

In the grand sextet of the second act of the same opera, one finds another example of enharmony with the augmented sixth, where the effect is even more perceptible, because the enharmony going toward the major mode is absolutely unexpected. Here is this passage.

269. By extending the principle of enharmony, that is, of the plurality of the tonal tendencies of certain notes of the chords, I found that the consonant chords themselves are susceptible to these tendencies, through the connection of one of their notes with those of the dissonant chord from another key, and consequently, that they may serve as enharmonic transitions. Here is an example taken from the *Requiem Mass* that I composed in 1833, for the funeral service of the victims of the revolution, in Brussels.

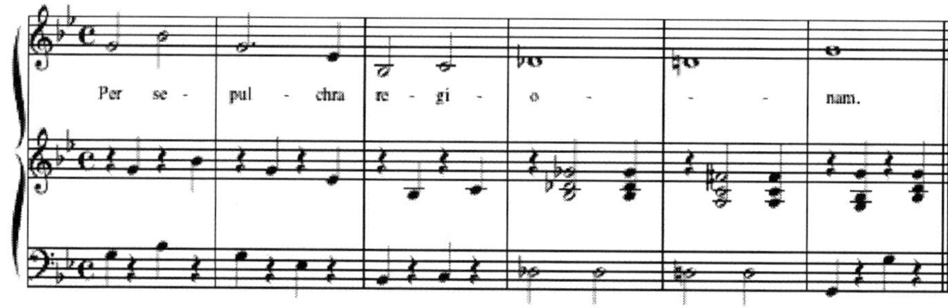

270. Generalizing more and more the notion of enharmony by considering it as a sound which has many kinds of tonal tendencies, one arrives at the conviction that these tendencies may manifest themselves through an intuitive attraction, even though the sound in question is not accompanied by the transition chord, because the musical sense compensates for this implied harmony at the moment of the change of key. An adagio from Haydn's Quartet [Op. 76, No. 2, in E-flat major], offers a quite remarkable example of an enharmonic transition occurring on a bass note alone without the accompaniment of a chord. Here is this unique passage, which has a most charming effect.

It is clear that the sudden change of key without any element of transition would be more painful than pleasant, if through a mental operation the person who heard this music did not establish the point of contact between such different tonalities in the eleventh and twelfth measures. Now, the pivot of enharmonic transition can only be found by changing in thought the B-flat, the last note of the eleventh measure, to an A-sharp, and assuming that it be accompanied by the minor fifth and sixth chord; in such a way the musical sense is struck by this transition.

271. The introduction in music of the multiplicity of tonal tendencies or attractions of apparently identical notes, created for this art a new order of harmonic and melodic events to which I have given the name of *pluritonic order*. This is the third period of the art. Independently of the strength of expression that this new medium has introduced, it has added to the other emotions expressed by music the sensation of surprise; a sensation all the more sought after in the present state of society, since one of the maladies of the human species, in our time, is the satiation of simple emotions.

God forbid that I consider as a cause of the degradation of the art this multiplicity of tonal tendencies, from which arises the sensation of surprise for which our contemporaries have proven to be so avid: it is, on the contrary, its natural and necessary development. I only rebuke the misuse, the formula turned custom; for any formula coarsens and degrades the most noble procedures of art.

Chapter IV

THE ALTERATIONS OF INTERVALS OF NATURAL CHORDS MODIFIED BY SUBSTITUTION ESTABLISH MULITIPLE RELATIONS BETWEEN DIVERSE KEYS, AND COMPLETE THE SYSTEM OF MODULATION. — THROUGH THESE MULITPLE RELATIONS, ALL MELODY MAY BE ACCOMPANIED BY MANY DIFFERENT HARMONIES. — *OMNITONIC ORDER*. ANNIHILATION OF TONAL UNITY. — THE FINAL PERIOD OF THE RELATIONS OF TONES.[21]

272. After having seen music restrained within the limits of tonal unity by consonant chords; after having seen it emerge from this unity through transition, by means of natural dissonant chords; finally, after having observed it in the creation of multiple relations of tonalities, through the diversity of enharmonic tendencies of certain notes of chords, it remains for us to consider this art in the latest period of its harmonic career, namely, the universality of the tonal relations of melody, through

[21]Mr. [Félicité Robert] de Lamennais [1782-1854] has done me the honor of borrowing my theory of tonalities that I set forth in my Course on the Philosophy of Music, in 1832. He has sought to add it to his philosophical system, in *l'Esquisse d'une philosophie* (Paris, 1840, 3 vols.); but he has forgotten to mention me as the author of this theory.

the joining of the simple transition to simple enharmony, and to the transcendent enharmony of the alterations of the intervals of chords.

This final phase of the art, with respect to harmony, is the one I call the *omnitonic order*. It is toward this last term of its career that art has progressively directed itself for half a century; it is now arriving at its goal.

273. I call *transcendent enharmonies* those that are the result of multiple alterations of the intervals of chords, in order to distinguish them from *simple enharmony*, in which one of the tones of a chord is alternately considered as the point of contact between diverse keys.

I beg the reader to give me his complete attention here, for this is the most delicate point of the absolutely new theory that is contained in this third part of my work.

274. The analysis of all instances of tonal attractions in the omnitonic order would alone provide the material for a large volume, and would be as tiring for the mind as it would be useless in the practice of the art. This analysis, applied to a single example, is sufficient to illustrate what distinguishes transcendent enharmony from simple enharmony, and to give directions for the use of this analysis in all cases of the same kind; for every chord modified by multiple alterations is in connection with diverse and collective enharmonies.

275. Suppose, as a simple harmonic example, the succession of the chord of the minor fifth and sixth and of the perfect chord, arranged in this way:

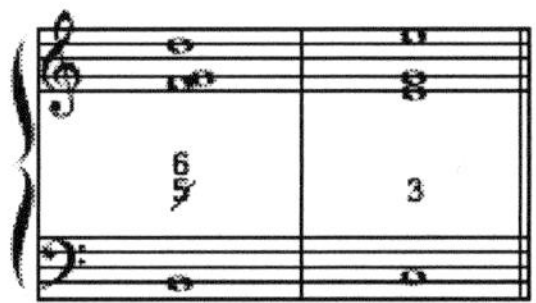

Suppose also that the key characterized by this harmony is perfectly established in the ear; for if this were not the case, the greater part of the successions to which I shall give the omnitonic formulae would offend the musical sense, the alterations which are their foundations not being adequately conceived.

It has been seen (Book II, ch. VIII, §162) that the ascending movement by one note, in the succession of two chords, when it takes place in the upper part, may be altered, and that the alteration may be prolonged onto the following chord, and resolve ascending, due to its attraction (ch. IX, §184), as in the following example:

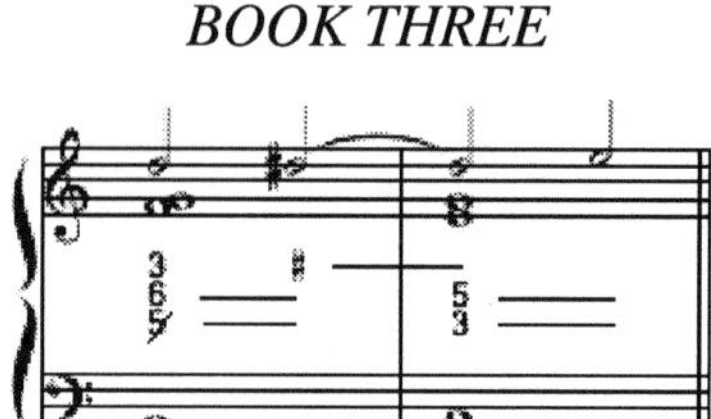

This succession is analogous to that of the same harmony modified by the substitution of the minor mode:

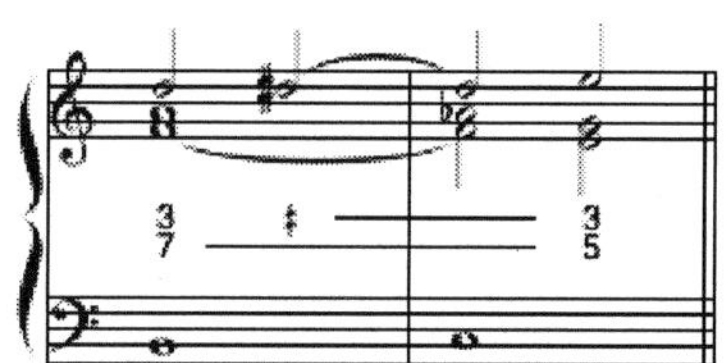

There is also an analogy between the successions of these altered harmonies and that of the seventh chord in the key of E minor, making an interrupted cadence on the sixth degree, with altered fifth:

276. We must now examine how these various alterations open the path to enharmonic transitions touching all keys, and how these transitions differ from the other means of modulation. First, I will begin with the simple alteration of the third of the minor fifth and sixth chord.

Now, the prolongation of D-sharp produces an attractive transitional note, the power of which sufficiently absorbs the character of the leading tone of the principal key, such that this note is dispensed from resolving upwards, providing that the double attraction of the fourth degree and the altered note has its resolution. In this case, the leading tone in the bass changes to the dominant of the key of E.

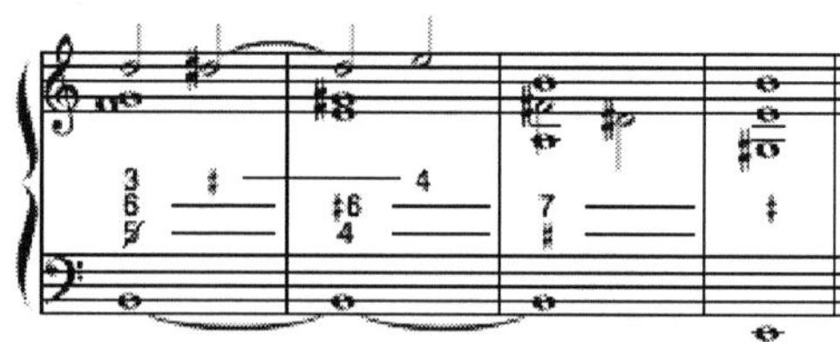

If the ascending alteration is accompanied by the substitution of the minor mode, this substitution may take, at the moment of resolution, the characteristic of a prolonged ascending alteration, and changing from A-flat to G-sharp, will lead directly to the key of A minor.

An analogous modulation, but even more immediate, will lead to the same key, if it results from the prolonged alteration of a [dominant] seventh chord, avoiding the interrupted cadence.

Another transcendent enharmonic transition results just as directly from the same prolongations of alterations, if the tonic of the bass transforms itself into the leading tone of the key of C-sharp minor.

The effect of this transformation will be even more striking if the resolution of the new leading tone changes the tonic which belongs to it into the third degree of another key.

The same double enharmony may also lead directly to the key of D.

The enharmony of the substituted note, accompanied by the transformation of the tonic of the bass into the sixth degree altered by another key, gives rise to this striking modulation, analogous to the one obtained without substitution.

277. The transcendent enharmonies in which the attractive notes preserve their regular movements, ascending and descending, are those that are the most pleasing to the musical sense. However, their natural destination is sometimes avoided during the prolongation of the notes, through the new tendencies created by means of alterations of the other notes of the harmony. Such are the enharmonic transitions in which the ascending alteration of the second degree transforms itself into a descending note of various other keys.

For example, during the enharmony of the altered note, if the dominant takes an ascending alteration, one will have the following unexpected transition.

If, in the resolution of this enharmony, the tonic of the bass, rather than transforming itself into the second degree of a lower key, changes into the sixth degree of a higher key, we have this transition.

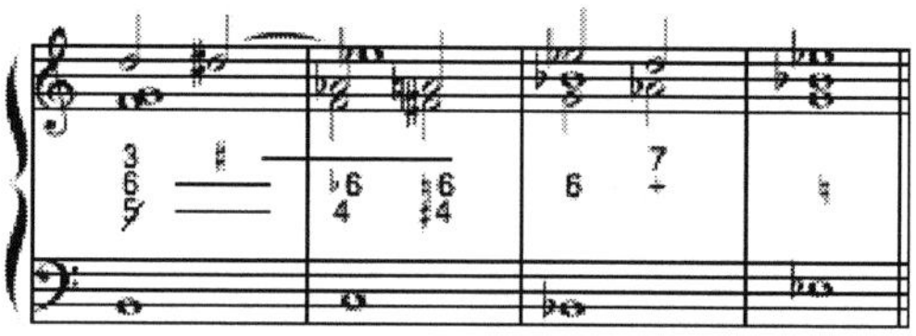

If, on the same enharmony, the tonic transforms into the fourth degree of a lower key, the modulation will be as follows:

But if, during the enharmony, the bass note changes to the third degree of a lower key, the modulation will be as follows:

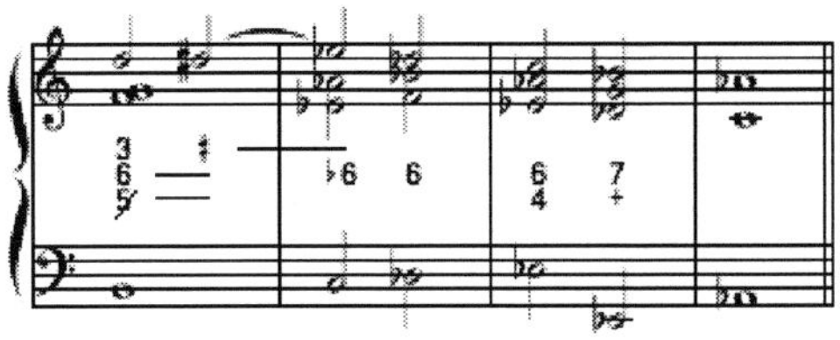

The modulation will be analogous, but sweeter if the enharmony results from the seventh degree, destined to make an interrupted cadence; in this case, there will be a double enharmony.

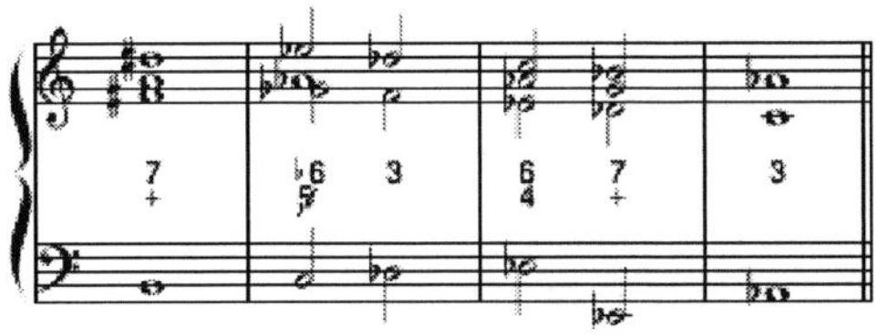

If, finally, during the enharmony of the alteration, the fourth degree transforms into the leading tone of another key, this striking modulation will result.

278. Such is the mechanism of transcendent enharmony; a mechanism applicable not only to the inverted combinations of the successions just seen, but to all alteration of dissonant harmony, and which quite truly constitutes the *omnitonic order* in music; for all harmony of this kind may resolve directly into any key whatsoever. In the preceding examples, one sees in fact a single altered harmony pass without intermediary from the key of C major to that of C-sharp major and minor, to D, E-flat, E major, G-flat or F-sharp, G, A-flat, A major and minor, and B-flat; now the combinations are by no means exhausted.

279. But, one will say, it is also possible to modulate to all the major and minor keys through the natural dissonant chords, and the substitutions open the path for enharmony. In what way do these other enharmonies, which you call transcendent, differ from the other means of modulation?

Here is my answer. The natural chords provide, it is true, means of modulation to all keys, but without allowing the possibility for resolving at will into one key or another. For example, it may be that the original key is F, and the music modulates to A minor through a seventh chord of this latter key; in this case there is no doubt concerning the modulation, for it is immediately recognized through the natural dissonant harmony of the seventh chord.

In vain would the composer avoid making a cadence in the key of A, by means of another modulation, this key of A would remain no less in the mind, after hearing the seventh chord.

DEMONSTRATION

Moreover, natural chords can open only a single path of modulation; for each new key, a new chord is needed.

With regard to the enharmony of chords modified by the substitution of the minor mode, it is certainly a source of multiple modulations; nevertheless, its tendencies are contained within the limits of change of four forms of the same chord. Now, the attraction of the notes of this chord cannot change once the form is determined, while the tendencies of enharmony produced by the alterations are only determined after the resolution of the altered notes, and the modulations to which they give rise lead to all the keys.

One should not be mistaken; the principle and the forms that I have just described are the path of a new world of events in tonality open to artists. It is the last period of the art, with respect to harmony.

280. It is not only in the accomplishment of the modulations that the music touches all tonalities, but also in the transitions that it indicates without their being realized. It is, moreover, in this latter device that present day music most frequently derives its means of effect. Mozart is once more the name that I will cite concerning this subject, for he is the first composer to use it. One must not confuse the harmonies with which he tricked the ear's expectations, as early as 1780, with *inganno* cadences known by Italian musicians long before then, of which here is an example taken from the *Madrigali e duetti* by Clari [*Poi disse in brevi accenti*, mm. 26-31].

The ingenuity of these *inganno* cadences consists in avoiding the final cadence with a new modulation, as one sees in the passage from the third to the fourth measure in the preceding example; but the modulation has already taken place, and the key is known, although the conclusion is not heard.

Nor must one confuse the modulations that are indicated, but not realized, of which Mozart gave the first examples, with very dense modulations full of dissonances, which one finds in the works of J. S. Bach, the most advanced musician of his time in this regard. Let us take one of these examples from the *St. Matthew Passion* oratorio, where the strength of mind of this great musician was developed with all its power.

Reduced to the fundamental harmony, this rich combination presents the following successions:

One sees by this analysis that the harmony of Bach's composition, like that of all music that does not admit of enharmony, presents only modulations achieved solely by the appearance of natural dissonant chords or their substitutes.

This is not the case with this passage from a Mozart Quintet, composed in 1787.

In the first beat of the fourth measure, there is no doubt that the modulation has been made in the key of C-flat, and that the cadence will be accomplished; but the enharmony changes the dominant of this key into the sixth degree of B-flat minor; this latter key is affirmed in the following measure, the cadence takes place, but the conclusion happens in the major mode instead of the minor, and completes the effect. Nothing like this previously existed.[22]

281. The collective enharmony of substituted chords of the minor mode, with alterations, and accompanied by the pedal, provides the most complete means to indicate a modulation that does not complete itself and resolves in the original key. The effect of this harmony is to be identical, considered by itself, with the natural dissonant chords of another key: the uncertainty on the resolution is therefore the result of the use of these harmonies.

Let us take the chord of the tritone of the key of G (example 1), with substitution of the minor mode (example 2), and with altered sixth (example 3): the isolated effect of the chord thus arranged will be that of the minor fifth and sixth of the key of D-flat (example 4). The natural resolution, as a substituted and altered chord, will be that of example 3; but just as one resolves the augmented sixth chord on the dominant of a key other than the one to which it seems to belong (see §168), one resolves this chord of the tritone with substitution and alteration, in the original key of C (example 5), thus tricking the ear on two tonalities which have been indicated, and neither of which is realized.

[22]Mozart, String Quintet in G minor, K 516, 3rd movement. [PL]

Rossini used this last resolution of the chord brilliantly in the air from *Guillaume Tell* which begins with the words: *sombre forêt*, and in the duet *Li Marinari*, from his collection entitled: *Soirées musicales*.

282. The tendency toward multiplicity, or even the universality of the keys in a piece of music, is the final stage of the development of harmonic combinations; beyond this, there is nothing more for these combinations.

The education of musicians has been slow along this path of the connections between diverse tonalities; but as is the case with many human affairs, after a long period of reticence, the artists have totally abandoned themselves to giving free rein to modulating music; and the formulae of this music have been so misused in recent years, that it is possible to state that tonal unity is now absolutely banished from the art. When I was foreseeing and announcing this last result of the harmonic direction of music, in my course on the philosophy of this art (in 1832), I did not believe that this result was so close at hand.

To demonstrate for us exactly the present state of harmony, with respect to the connection of tonalities, let us take a melody with little modulation, and see what difference time has made in the manner of accompanying it. This comparison appears to me to be the best way of showing what advancement has been made in the relations of keys: an important part of the art and science absolutely neglected by all the authors of harmonic systems.

The first accompaniment (example A) represents harmony in the simple transitonic system of natural dissonant chords; example B is in the *quasi omnitonic* harmonic system of our time.

B

283. In these examples, the melody holds back the harmony within certain limits which prevent it from becoming absolutely omnitonic, for this melody is by itself non-modulating; but in the present state of the art, there are melodies that break through these limits to satisfy the insatiable desire for modulations and attractive tendencies which torments the artists of our time. The melody has lost its purity and no longer has an absolute existence, independent of all external conditions, by becoming harmonic and modulating. Separate the melody from the harmony in a few compositions of recent times, and it will scarcely retain some vague meaning.

To choose an example from a very distinguished work of art from this period, I will take it from the *Serenata*, a nocturne from the collection by Rossini entitled: *les Soirées musicales*.

The first phrase of the cantilena is as follows:

This phrase is beautiful and significant; although Rossini has accompanied it with a harmony full of attractive tendencies, it does not in itself indicate a modulation. But the second phrase:

is clearly dependent upon the harmony, for this succession of notes

has no proper meaning, and acquires it only through the accompanying harmony. Here is this harmony with the entire phrase:

The collection from which this example is taken contains many phrases of the same kind, in which the principal effect resides in the choice of harmony and the multitude of elegant details scattered there by Rossini.

It was foremost in his mind, when he composed this work, to give his music a picturesque character, and to multiply the modulating sensations through the attractive tendencies, or even through successions of keys without contact, in the manner of some masters at the end of the sixteenth century, an example of which one sees in this passage from the duet *Li Mariani*:

The dual objective that I have just indicated has led the composer, particularly in this last piece, to disregard all melodic sentiment, as much in the voices as in the accompaniment, in order to portray the effects of the sea, and the emotions and cries of the sailors. Belonging to an era where modulating harmony became, as it were, the main objective of music, this most excellent author of beautiful melodies of the nineteenth century arrived at the absence of all cantilena that one sees in this piece.

Nevertheless, it is important to point out that Rossini and those who imitated the final transformation of his talent did not have knowledge of the principal of transcendent enharmony, the consequences of which I have analyzed in this chapter, and did not attain the objective of *omnitonic music* toward which this principal leads. The formulae I have taken from it remain to be exploited by the generation of artists that are emerging at this moment.

284. I have said many times over in this and other works, that any means of art reduced to a repeated formula is a degradation of that same art. This maxim is especially applicable to the incessant progression of tendencies to modulation. No doubt it was the destiny of harmony to attain the final limits of these tendencies, in order to realize all that is possible in it and through it; but there is also no doubt that the frequent use of multiple attractions of tonalities has the serious drawback of incessantly exciting nervous emotions, and removing from music the simple character and purity of idea, in order to transform it into a sensual art.

Besides, how composers make use of these attractions and impassioned accents often constitutes a *contre-sens*, for they proliferate these nervous elements in the accompaniment of melodies where the words indicate a calm and sweet subject. These modulating harmonies are today used like a lavish instrumentation; their effect most often produces fatigue in the mind and senses rather than satisfaction.

I submit these important remarks for the consideration of present-day composers, and especially to artists of the future.

END OF THE THIRD BOOK

BOOK FOUR

A CRITICAL EXAMINATION OF THE PRINCIPAL SYSTEMS OF THE GENERATION AND CLASSIFICATION OF CHORDS[1]

Chapter I

SYSTEMS BASED ON ACOUSTICAL PHENOMENA, HARMONIC PROGRESSION, AND THE MECHANICAL AGGREGATIONS OF INTERVALS

285. Previously, harmonists, much more preoccupied with the care of perfecting the art, or rather with practicing it than with seeking a theory of it, had not noticed the many ways that chords may be linked together; they were even less preoccupied with a generative principle of the aggregation of tones.

286. Rameau, a French musician who at nearly forty years of age was still living in obscurity as a provincial organist, was the first to glimpse the possibility of a general theory of the generation of chords, and had sufficient genius to organize the various elements into a coherent whole. He set forth these principles in a book published in 1722, under the title: *Traité de l'harmonie réduit à ses principes naturels*.[2]

This book had little impact when it appeared: the novelty of its subject, and the obscure and verbose style of the author made it intelligible to only a few readers; it could even be said that no one understood exactly its importance. The creation of a new science of harmony undoubtedly

---

[1]Most of this book is taken from my *Esquisse de l'Histoire de l'harmonie considéré comme art et comme science systématique (Outline of the History of Harmony Considered as Art and Systematic Science)* (Paris, 1841), 178 pages, with only 50 copies circulated amongst my friends, and not available commercially.*

*Although most of Book Four is indeed taken from the *Esquisse*, large sections of the latter are omitted, in particular those dealing with music theory up to Rameau. Moreover, Fétis makes several additions and modifications to the wording of the *Esquisse*, and the material is considerably reordered. [PL]

[2]Paris, J. B. Christ. Ballard, 1722.

merited the attention of informed musicians; but where could these be found, in an age when artists lacked education, and when all their learning was contained in the knowledge of the mechanical techniques of their art? If they could have known that Rameau's work would at least lay down the basis for a philosophical study of music, the idea would have seemed to them so ridiculous that it would certainly have incurred their derision.

There was a great distance between this state of mind and that which would have been necessary to embrace the *Traité de l'harmonie* with the interest it was worthy of inspiring. It was not until twenty years after the publication of this book that the public began to pay attention to the author's system; but from that point on the indifference was replaced with a kind of fanatical admiration, and the popularity of Rameau's theory did not flag until the beginning of the nineteenth century.

287. [Gioseffo] Zarlino [1517-1627], [Marin] Mersenne [1588-1648] and [René] Descartes [1596-1650] had introduced the author of this theory to the knowledge of numbers applied to the science of sounds: his eager soul was impassioned by this science, which was revealing to him the possibility of giving music theory a sure foundation. From that moment on it appeared to him that the regular divisions of the monochord must be the point of departure of the system of harmony, and all his attention turned toward the development of the logical consequences of facts revealed by these divisions. From the beginning of his book, he established that the identity of the results of the science of numbers, whether applied to the divisions of a single string, or concerned with the length of strings corresponding to these divisions, the dimensions of pipes in wind instruments, or the speed of vibrations, demonstrates beyond a doubt the usefulness and infallibility of this science with respect to music. His efforts then have the purpose of establishing that the sound of the full length of the string, represented by 1, is identical to the ear with the divisions of the same string corresponding to the numbers 2, 4, 8, which produce the octaves of this entire string. This identity of octaves, to which he returned later in his other works, notably in a short treatise of which it is the particular subject,[3] appeared to him, and rightly so, to be the foundation of the system of the fundamental bass that he wished to establish, and of which he will later speak.

288. On the other hand, a proposition from Descartes' *Compendium musicae* became for him the criterion of the generation of chords. It is as follows: "I may again divide the line AB (the monochord) into 4, 5, or 6 parts, but no further, because the ear is incapable of further distinguishing

[3]Taken from a response of M. Rameau to M. Euler, on the identity of octaves, from which result in all the more curious truths, because they have not yet been suspected (Paris, 1753), 41 pages.

the differences in pitch without a considerable effort."[4] Now, the numbers 1, 2, 3, 4, 5, 6 provide the perfect chord, doubled and arranged on the monochord as follows:

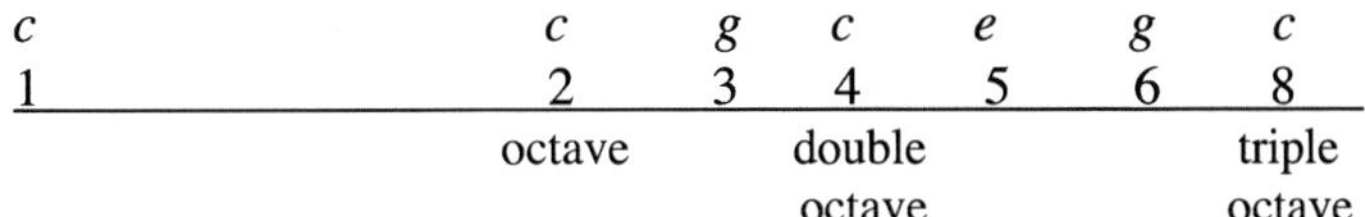

After having developed at length the demonstration of the principle of the existence of the perfect chord in the laws of numbers applied to the divisions of a resonant string, Rameau conceived a theory from which all the other chords are generated by the supposition or superposition of a certain number of major or minor thirds,[5] or derived by the inversion of these original aggregations of thirds.[6]

289. A difficulty arises, however, in the result of the division of the monochord taken as the basis of consonant harmony: this being that it gives only the perfect major chord. Rameau understood that it was serious enough to overturn his system, if he were tied to this general result; he evaded it by drawing only on the proportions of the major third 4:5, and the minor third 5:6, given by the notes C, E, and E, G, in order to form all his combinations of thirds. These combinations became his point of departure. "Indeed," he says, "to form the perfect chord, one must add one third to the other, and to form all the dissonant chords, one must add three or four thirds to each other, the differences between these dissonant chords arising only in the different position of these thirds. This is why we can attribute to them all the power of harmony by reducing it to these first degrees. This can be proved by adding a proportional fourth to each perfect chord, from which result two seventh chords; and by adding a proportional fifth to one of the these seventh chords, from which results a ninth chord that contains in its construction the four preceding chords."[7]

According to this theory, Rameau establishes that there are two perfect chords, one major, the other minor, and that each of these chords generates through inversion a sixth chord and a six-four chord.[8] To the perfect major chord which he transposes on the dominant of the key, without stating why, he adds a minor third above, and this forms the dominant seventh chord, which through inversion, gives the chords of the

[4]Rursus possum dividere lineam AB in 4 partes vel in 5 vel in 6, nec ulterius fit divisio: quia scilicet aurium imbecillitas sine labore majores sonorum differentias non posset distinguere. (*Compendium musicae,* 12, 13, edit. Trajecti ad Rhenum, 1650).

[5]*Traité de l'harmonie*, 33.

[6]Ibid., 34ff.

[7]Ibid., 33.

[8]Ibid., 34ff.

false fifth (minor fifth and sixth), the *small sixth* (leading-note sixth), and the *tritone*.[9]

Example

290. By the addition of a minor third to the perfect minor chord, Rameau forms the minor seventh chord, from which are derived, through inversion, the chords of the *large sixth* (fifth and sixth), the *small minor sixth* (third and fourth), and the *second*.[10]

Example

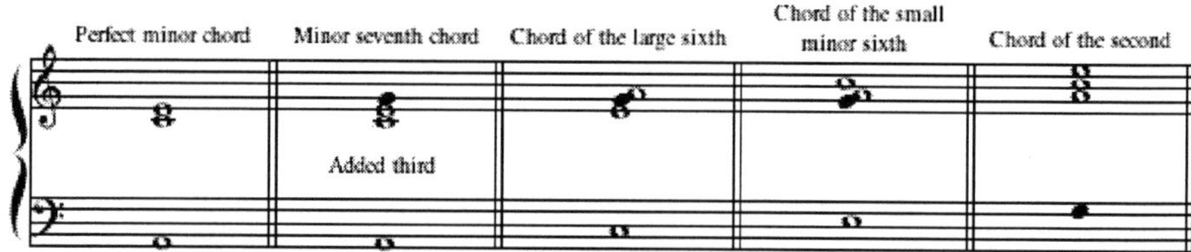

291. The addition of a major third to the perfect major chord gives Rameau the *major seventh chord*, which has its derivatives by inversion.[11]

Example

292. A minor third added below the perfect minor chord produces that of the seventh with false fifth (*leading-tone seventh chord*) and its derivatives by inversion.[12]

---

[9]Ibid., 37.

[10]Ibid., 39.

[11]Ibid., 40.

[12]Ibid., 41.

EXAMPLE

Perfect minor chord | Seventh chord with false fifth | 1st derivation | 2nd derivation | 3rd derivation

Added third

293. By the aggregation of two minor thirds, Rameau creates the chord of the *false fifth* (minor third and minor fifth or perfect diminished chord).

EXAMPLE

And the one with two major thirds gave him the chord of the chord of the *superfluous fifth* (augmented fifth chord).

EXAMPLE

294. Rameau finds the origin of the diminished seventh chord in the addition of a minor third below the *false fifth* chord, as well as its derivatives through inversion.

EXAMPLE

False fifth chord | Diminished seventh chord | 1st derivation | 2nd derivation | 3rd derivation

Added third

295. He calls *chords by supposition* those which, exceeding the limits of the octave, are formed, according to him, by the addition of one or more thirds below a given seventh chord. This is how he explains the origin of the *ninth* and *eleventh* chords, which we now consider as retardations of the octave by a ninth and of the third by a fourth. In his ignorance of the

mechanism of the prolongation, he shows a rare insight in finding a reasonable explication for the difference of this *dissonant fourth*, the object of such embarassment for previous harmonists.[13]

296. If we place ourselves in the position in which Rameau found himself, that is, in the absolute absence of any system of harmony in the period in which he wrote, we cannot help but admire the power of intellect necessary for the creation of what he invented and of which I have just given a summary, even though this system is essentially false. Captivated by certain properties of combinations of intervals used in the make-up of chords, this genius used them to form the basis of his theory. At the time when he published his *Traité de l'harmonie*, he had not yet focused his attention on the phenomenon of the production of harmonics in the resonance of a sonorous body, which later caused him to modify his ideas, and which, in turn, led to the publication of his *Nouveau système de musique théorique* and of his other works.[14] It was therefore only the principle of the superposition and subposition of thirds, which guided him in his system at the time his first book on harmony appeared. Now, to apply this principle to all chords, he was obliged to abandon any idea of tonality, because he did not always find the thirds arranged the way he needed them in his system for each dissonant chord, on the notes where these chords are placed following the tonal principle. For example, the minor seventh chord with minor third, the eternal pitfall of all false harmonic systems, this chord, I say, which is commonly called *the seventh chord of the second degree*, because it is built on the second note of the major scale (D-F-A-C), he could not create from the perfect minor chord of this second note, because he knew very well that, in the system of modern tonality, this chord does not belong to the note in question; he was therefore obliged to take, as the origin of this *minor seventh chord with minor third*, the perfect minor chord of the sixth degree (A-C-E), such that his seventh chord (A-C-E-G) appears to belong to this latter note.

By operating in this way for most dissonant chords, Rameau was obliged to consider these chords as isolated events, and to discard all the rules of succession and tonal resolution established by the earlier treatises of accompaniment and composition; for these rules, conforming to the natural laws of tonality, assign certain positions to chords, incompatible

---

[13]Ibid., 73.

[14]*Nouveau système de musique théorique*, où l'on découvre le principe de toutes les règles necessaries à la pratique, pour servir d'introduction au *Traité de l'harmonie* (Paris, Ballard, 1726).
Génération harmonic, ou *Traité de musique théorique et pratique* (Paris, 1737).
Démonstration du principe de l'harmonie, servant de base à tout l'art musical théorique et pratique (Paris, 1750).
Nouvelles reflections sur la demonstration du principe de l'harmonie (Paris, 1752).

with the doctrine of the generation of chords by the superposition or subposition of thirds. Such was the drastic fault of the harmonic system conceived by Rameau: it consisted of shattering the rules of connection based on aural impression, even though he qualified them as *arbitrary*, in order to substitute a certain order of generation, appealing because of its consistent aspect, but had the affect of which was to leave all the harmonic groups isolated and unconnected.

297. Too good a musician not to understand that after having rejected the rules of succession and resolution of chords incompatible with his system, he had to supply new rules which were not conflicting, Rameau conceived his theory of the *fundamental bass*, the system of which he set forth in the second article of chapter 18 of his *Traité de l'harmonie*, entitled: *How to Compose a Fundamental Bass Below Any Kind of Music*.[15]

In Rameau's system the fundamental bass is only a way of verifying the harmonic regularity, and not a real bass; this is why he points out that one must not stop while writing consecutive successions of octaves and fifths.[16] The main rules of this bass are: (1) that it can only form with the harmony of the other parts perfect chords on the tonic, fourth degree, dominant, and sixth degree, and seventh chords on the dominant and second degree. Certain fundamental bass successions, however, sometimes made it necessary for this bass to cadence with a six-five chord on the fourth degree to the tonic. This difficulty led Rameau to consider this chord as a perfect chord on the fourth degree, to which the sixth is added optionally, and he called it the *added sixth* chord. But considering the exact identity of this chord with the six-five chord derived from the minor seventh on the second degree, which he calls the *large sixth*, he also called it the chord of double employment, and assumed that when it resolves on the perfect chord of the dominant, it is the chord of the *large sixth*, and is derived from the minor seventh chord:

EXAMPLE

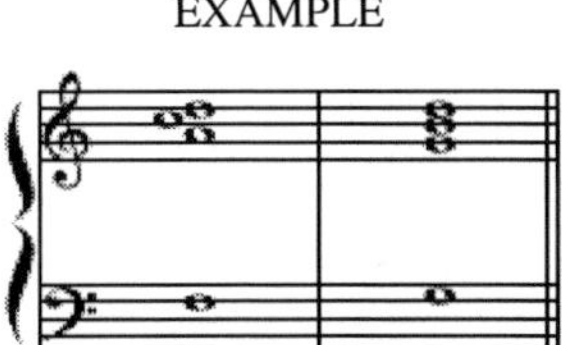

and that when it is followed by a cadence toward the tonic, it is a fundamental chord of the *added sixth*.

[15]*Traité de l'harmonie*, 134.

[16]Ibid., 135, no. 7.

EXAMPLE

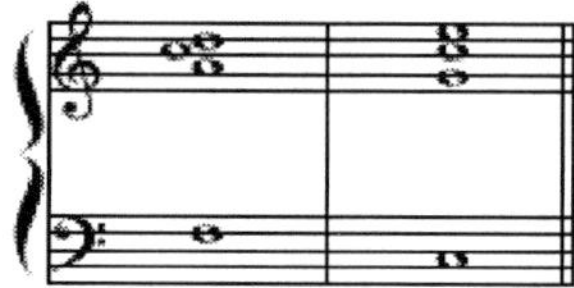

Now, it is obvious that this so-called fundamental chord, not formed by *superposed* or *subposed* thirds, completely destroys the economy of Rameau's system; but such is the effect of predisposition, that the inventor of the fundamental bass system was under complete illusion with respect to this crucial error, and his followers did not even notice it.

The other rules for the verification of the harmony by the fundamental bass were:[17] (3) in each perfect chord of the tonic or dominant, at least one of the notes of these chords should be found in the preceding chord; (4) the dissonance of a dominant seventh chord should also have been heard in the preceding chord; (5) in the six-five chord, or *added sixth*, the bass, its third, or its fifth, must be prepared by the preceding chord, *but the dissonance produced by the sixth against the fifth progresses freely*; (6) whenever the dominant is found as the fundamental bass, it must descend a fifth or ascend a fourth; (7) when the fourth degree is the fundamental bass, it must rise a fifth or descend a fourth.

These rules, given by Rameau for the formation of a bass that differs from the actual bass of the music, and for the verification of the proper use of chords, he could only have established in an arbitrary manner: it would have been impossible for him to set forth a rational theory based on the real nature of harmony. They have in addition many essential errors that the inventor with all his shrewdness could not make disappear. One was the inadequacy of these rules for a number of circumstances, which has become much more apparent since a large number of harmonic combinations, unknown in Rameau's time, have been introduced into music. But it is not only through their inadequacy that the rules of the fundamental bass are flawed; it is also through their opposition to tonal attractions and to the judgment of the ear in most successions. According to this doctrine, many of these successions are rejected, despite musical instinct and the laws of tonality; thus, according to the fourth rule, the dissonance of a dominant seventh chord or of its derivatives must be prepared by the preceding chord, while what distinguishes these natural dissonant chords from dissonances of prolongation is precisely that they can be approached without preparation. According to the fifth rule the bass, the third, or the fifth must be prepared, while the dissonant sixth is free in its approach; now, it is not the sixth which is dissonant in this

[17]Fétis omits point number two. [PL]

chord, but the fifth, and the particular characteristic of this dissonant fifth is precisely that it can be used only with the preparation, while the bass and the third are free. Moreover, the specified succession of this six-five chord to the perfect chord of the tonic is not good, and although it has been used recently by Beethoven and by other musicians of the present school, it is no less a harmonic contrary-sense, since the dissonance has no resolution.

298. The fundamental bass doctrine was, from the beginning of Rameau's ideas, only an accessory, or, if you will, a supplement to his harmonic system. Later, having become preoccupied by an acoustical phenomenon pointed out by Mersenne[18] and analyzed by Sauveur,[19] a phenomenon in which one observes that a long vibrating string, adequately tightened, causes one to hear, when it resonates, apart from the principal tone, the harmonic tones which form with it the perfect major chord, Rameau saw there the confirmation of his system, namely, that this is the only chord given by nature, and that the others stem from it by the addition of thirds. However, he felt some embarrassment regarding the perfect minor chord, which he needed for this system to be complete. Some self-satisfaction for his theory of the fundamental bass had led him to formulate the *double employment* of the six-five chord; a disdain corresponding to his new ideas led him to discover, in certain vibrations of the aliquot parts of the resonating string, this same perfect minor chord, but with a lesser degree of intensity than the major. In fact, he could have found many other resonances in various sonorous bodies of certain forms and dimensions; but I will later show that these phenomena have nothing in common with the true system of harmony. Be that as it may, it was clear that from this point on that Rameau attached less importance than before to his doctrine of the generation of chords through combinations of thirds, whereas his fundamental bass system grew more satisfying to him every day. It was also this part of what he called *his discoveries* that had the most success. Many people, who did not understand the theory of the generation of chords set forth in the *Traité de l'harmonie*, were enthusiastic about the fundamental bass, through which they believed to learn *composition* through brief formulae.

One observation escaped all the critics who have spoken of the fundamental bass system: it is that even in accepting its rules as infallible, and conforming to what the laws of tonality and our musical

[18]Marin Mersenne (1588-1648) *Harmonie universelle contenant la théorie et la pratique de la musique* (Paris, 1636). Reprint edition (Paris, 1963).

[19]Joseph Sauveur (1653-1716) demonstrated that a string can vibrate in several ways at the same time. For a detailed discussion on the influence of Mersenne and Sauveur on Rameau's theories, see Thomas Christensen's study, *Rameau and Musical Thought in the Enlightenment* (Cambridge: Cambridge University Press, 1993). [PL]

consciousness teach us, they could not have taken the place of the old practical rules, because the use of the latter gives immediate results, whereas the fundamental bass was only a way to check for mistakes that one might have had made.

299. Notwithstanding the radical shortcomings of various parts of Rameau's system, it is nonetheless true that this system could only be the work of an exceptional man, and that it will always be cited in the history of art as a creation of genius. There is as well in this system an idea that alone would immortalize its author, had he not any other claim to fame: I wish to speak of the concept of the inversion of chords which belongs to him, and which has abundant good results. Without it, no system of harmony is possible: it is a general idea that applies to any good theory, and which one may consider as the first foundation of the science.

SYSTEMS DERIVED FROM THAT OF RAMEAU

300. Rameau's works, reaching Germany, made a profound impression on the mind of Marpurg, a learned theorist, critic, and music historian.[20] A journey that he made to Paris in 1746 had shown him the enthusiasm that the theory contained in these works aroused amongst musicians. On returning to Berlin, he devoted himself to the study of this theory, upon which his *Handbuch bey dem Generalbasse und der Composition* was based.[21] He reintroduced therein the principal of the generation of chords by the addition of thirds, a principle whose inevitable consequence is to isolate all chords, and to remove their true construction in the laws of tonality and succession.

301. With respect to the modifications Marpurg introduced into Rameau's system, they consist of the following:

Taking as he did the five-three chord, major or minor, diminished or augmented, as the basis for dissonant chords of four and five notes, he forms the major seventh chord by adding a major third above the perfect major chord (see below, example 1); the dominant seventh chord, by the addition of a minor third above a perfect major chord (ex. 2); the minor seventh chord on the second degree, by the addition of a minor third above a perfect minor chord (ex. 3); the leading-tone seventh chord, by the addition of a major third above the chord of the minor third and fifth (ex.

[20]Fétis asserts that Friedrich Wilhelm Marpurg's (1718-95) high reputation in Germany as a theorist is well founded, although he criticizes his presentation and ordering of facts. It is in Marpurg's critical works that Fétis sets him above his contemporaries in Germany. *FétisB,* 6:279. [PL]

[21]*Handbuch bey dem Generalbasse und der Composition* etc. (Berlin, 1755-1758, 2nd edition, Berlin, 1762).

4); finally, the diminished seventh chord, by the addition of a minor third above the same chord (ex. 5).[22]

EXAMPLE

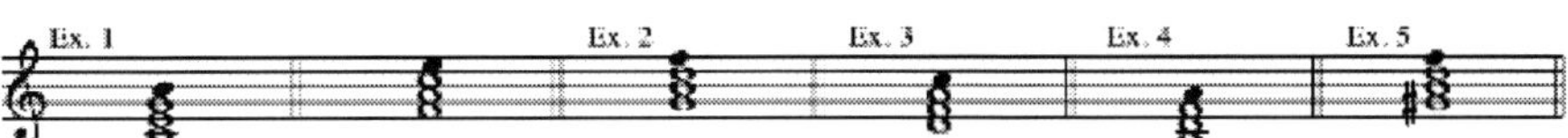

All the derivatives of these chords are obtained by inversion in Marpurg's theory, just as in Rameau's.

Marpurg derives the formation of altered seventh chords from the addition of thirds above perfect chords or the third and fifth, thus altered. In this way, a major third placed above the augmented fifth chord gives him a major seventh chord with augmented fifth (ex. 1); and a major third above the chord of a minor fifth and major third produces a leading-tone seventh chord with altered third (ex. 2), etc.[23]

EXAMPLE

In Marpurg's system, the addition of thirds below seventh chords, which one finds in Rameau's theory, disappears; it is replaced by the addition of two or three thirds above the perfect chords. Thus, two thirds placed above the perfect major chord give the chord of the seventh and major ninth (ex. 1); two thirds above the perfect major chord of the dominant produce the chord of the major ninth with minor seventh (ex. 2); finally, two thirds placed above the perfect major chord of the dominant of a minor key produce the dominant minor ninth (ex. 3), etc.

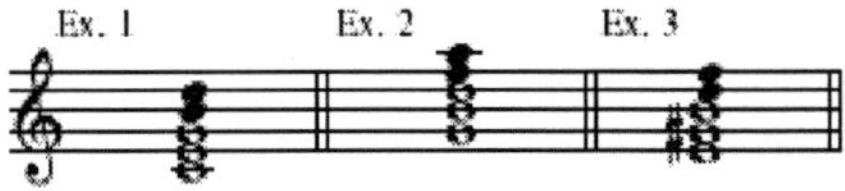

Without going into greater detail, it is easy to understand the nature of this system. Its advantage over that of Rameau is to keep harmonies in the place they should occupy on the degrees of the scale, instead of seeking to form them on arbitrary notes. Marpurg removes from his theory considerations of numerical proportion and acoustical phenomena; he replaces them with that of tonality, retaining from his predecessor's system only the mechanical formation of dissonant chords by the addition of thirds; for this reason he describes his system as *eclectic* in his preface.

---

[22]*Handbuch bey dem Generalbasse,* first part, 52.

[23]Ibid., 53.

But like Rameau, he confuses through this process natural dissonant chords with those that can only arise under circumstances of succession, and makes so many isolated facts that it is impossible to perceive their application *a priori*. This mechanical construction of dissonances is absolutely arbitrary, and has no connection with the processes of art.

302. This is the same theory that has been recently reproduced by Choron and Adrien de Lafage in their *Nouveau manuel complet de musique vocale et instrmentale*.[24] It is also the same system that Choron had taken as the basis for his classification of chords in his *Principes d'accompagnement des écoles d'Italie*,[25] with a few modifications borrowed from Padre Sabbatini, whose book he did not fully understand;[26] he later completely abandoned it in the treatise on harmony in his *Principes de composition des écoles d'Italie*, published four years later, to move closer to Catel's theory; and finally he returned in the end to Marpurg's system, which we have just examined, for his *Manuel de musique*, which he was preparing for publication at the time of his death.[27]

The system of the formation of chords by the addition of thirds has also been recently reproduced in France by Mr. Gérard, an elderly professor at the Paris Conservatory.[28]

303. In Italy, Testori[29] was the only harmonist who fully adopted Rameau's system.[30] Calegari, Vallotti and Sabbatini borrowed from this system only what Marpurg had taken, from which they made a new system that I will examine later.

303. *bis*. It would be as tedious as it would be unavailing to cite here all the treatises on the science of harmony whose authors had taken Rameau's principles as a basis. Most of them have been hardly noteworthy, and have not established particular schools.

I cannot, however, neglect to say a few words about one of his followers who founded a distinct school: I speak of Abbé Roussier, author

---

[24]Paris, 1838, vol. 1, part two.

[25]Paris, Imbault, 1804.

[26]*La vera idea delle musicali numeriche segnature* (Venice, 1799), vol. 1.

[27]The *Manuel complet* was completed by Choron's student, the composer and theorist Adrien de La Fage (1801-1862). [PL]

[28]*Traité méthodique d'harmonie* (Paris, Launer, 1833).*

* Fétis notes that although this treatise by Henri-Philippe Gerard (1763-?) was of little consequence for current music theory, its author had an excellent practical knowledge of the subject. *FétisB*, 4:301. [PL]

[29]Carlo-Giovanni Testori (1714-1782), Italian composer and theorist. Fétis did not think highly of his compositions, now lost. *FétisB*, 8:347. [PL]

[30]*La Musica ragionata espressa in dodici passegiate a dialogo famigliarmente,* etc. 4 parts. Vercelli, published by G. Panialis, 1767-1782.

of *Traité des accords et de leurs succession, selon le système de la basse fondamental* (Paris, 1764). This book is divided into three parts. There is little to say about the first two, for they contain only a classification and analysis of chords according to the principles of Rameau. I will only point out that even though he was barely skilled in the art of writing, and his basic education as a musician was undisciplined, Roussier is much more methodical than the inventor of the system, and was the first, in France, to explain his views on the notion, so important, of the succession of harmonies. But the third part is astonishing, if we consider the time of its publication, for Abbé Roussier proposes the introduction into music of a certain number of chords not then known.

It was surprising that, guided by analogy and by musical feeling, in which he was weak, Roussier had foreseen the possibility of the proper use of certain harmonies that the genius of Mozart and a few of his successors were later able to implement. It was thus that the chord of the *augmented sixth*, or *superflue*, as it was then called, led him through the law of inversion to the chord of the diminished third and perfect fifth, and that of the minor sixth with major fourth; that is also how, in passing from the chord of the diminished third and perfect fifth to that of the dominant seventh, he conceived the possibility of altering its third as in the perfect chord.

If he had limited himself to alterations of the intervals of chords, whether original or modified through prolongation or substitution, he would have rendered the greatest service to the advancement of the art and the science, and we would have formed a most favorable opinion of his instinct, taste, and experience; but such is not the case, for the crudeness of his ear led him to imagine other intolerable harmonies where all feeling of tonality is ruined.

In spite of these faults, the *Traité des accords,* and the complement of this work, which Roussier published under the title *L'harmonie pratique, ou Exemples pour le Traité des accords* (Paris, 1775), would have rendered outstanding service in France to the theory of harmony, in calling to the attention of musicians the consideration of the succession of chords that Rameau's system had forgotten, if Roussier himself had not contributed to having his practical works drop out of sight by a return to a theory of numbers applied to music, of which he gave the first evidence in the notes of his *Observations sur différents points d'harmonie* (Paris, 1765, 217-225), and which he developed since then in other works. A vague conception of the music of the ancient Greeks and Chinese led him to consider these numbers from a mysterious point of view. He convinced himself that harmonic and arithmetic progressions are each as mistaken as the other, and, admitting of the first as only the proportion of the fifth ⅓, he conceived a triple progression of fifth to descending fifth, represented by these numbers:

1. 3. 9. 27. 81. 243. 729. etc.

This progression, taken to the twelfth fifth, or thirteenth term, gives the figure 531:441, an expression, according to him, of the comma of C-flat to B-natural, which is his point of departure. This progression may be represented in music by the following:

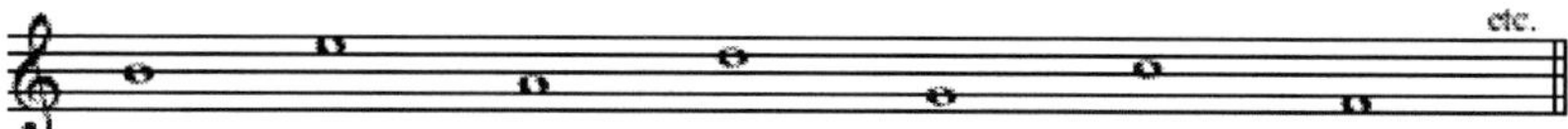

From this Roussier takes the following scale which he considers as fundamental:

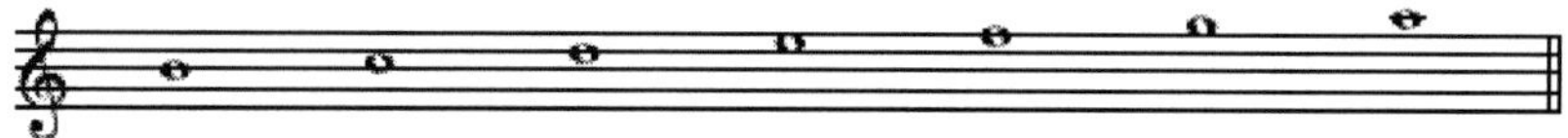

The system of the triple progression has had in France many advocates, amongst whom one notes La Borde, author of *l'Essai sur la musique*.[31]

304. Rameau, d'Alembert, who explained his system,[32] and all of the followers of the theory of the fundamental bass, were convinced that this theory was drawn from nature, because it takes its principle from the perfect chord, and this chord is the product of the resonance of an extended vibrating string sufficiently tightened. From its inception, the idea of the necessity of finding in acoustical phenomena the *criterion* of the science of harmony had become an article of faith.

At the same time as Rameau was taking the starting point of his theory in the multiple resonance of harmonics in a sonorous body, Tartini was following an opposite direction in Italy, having noted that two high notes, of perfectly just thirds exactly a third apart, being played on his violin, gave a third sound, which formed with them the perfect chord. This phenomenon was also found in nature: it served as the basis for Tartini to formulate a theory opposite to that of Rameau, even though it led him to certain results identical to those found by the French musician. Tartini's system being almost exclusively speculative and presenting only insignificant practical applications, did not create an actual school and is

---

[31]Jean-Benjamin Laborde (1734-1794) studied composition with Rameau and achieved considerable success as a composer of dramatic music. His four-volume *Essai sur la musique ancienne et moderne* (Paris, 4 vols., 1780) is still an important source of information on 18th century music. [PL]

[32]*Eléments de Musique théorique et pratique suivant les principes de M. Rameau*. Paris, 1752.

not of the kind to be analyzed here. Those of my readers who wish to know it will find this analysis in my *Esquisse de l'histoire de l'harmonie*.[33]

305. After the work of various German and French harmonists at the end of the eighteenth century and beginning of the nineteenth, it was thought that the idea of a theory of harmony taken from acoustical phenomena had been abandoned; but we have seen its resurgence in recent times, and the authors of systems of this kind, having discovered, or believing to have to discovered in sonorous bodies of diverse forms and dimensions, harmonic relations different from those observed in the resonance of a vibrating string, were convinced that they had found the means to complete nature's system, of which only one of the elements was formerly known.

Thus, recently, Baron Blein,[34] author of *Principe de mélodie et d'harmonie déduits de la théorie des vibrations*[35] did not hesitate to declare as illusory all the theories of harmony and composition which rest only on the evidence of musical sense and consciousness. He explains it clearly in his introduction and in many parts of his book, "Fux's method," he says, "which seemed to me the best, the teachings of Bemetzrieder,[36] summarized by Diderot, Rameau's principles, analyzed by d'Alembert, and many other works I have come across, have not satisfied me in this

---

[33]Paris, 1841, 94-102, and *Gazette musicale de Paris,* 1840, No. 63, 535-538.

[34]In the entry under Baron Blein (1767-1845) Fétis notes that his theory is based in part on the phenomena of the "third sound," already present in Tartini's theory of harmony, and on the two phenomena of the resonance of a cylinder and of a square metallic plate, the former providing him with the sixth derived from the perfect minor chord, and the latter with the tritone, which is the "constitutive interval of the dissonant dominant seventh, and the principle of modern tonality." Fétis goes on to say, however, that Blein ignores other intervals that may be produced by the same means, and, most importantly, "the science of harmony and the art of writing is based less on isolated chords or groups of sounds than on the laws of succession established by the relationships of affinity and repulsion." *FétisB*, 2:220. [PL]

[35]Paris, Bachelier, 1832.

[36]In the entry under Anton Bemetzrieder (1739-1808) in the *FétisB* (2:122), Fétis claims that he is completely ignorant of music, and that his extended list of publications presents a multitude of obscure ideas on the theory of harmony and tonality. Fétis' disdain, however, is almost certainly disingenuous. As Thomas Christensen points out, Bemetzrieder elaborates an intuitive approach to harmonic theory in which the student senses the imperative for unstable dissonant digressions to return to a state of consonance, a process he calls the *loi des appels*. This clearly anticipates Fétis' notion of the appellative consonance and the fundamental tenet of his theory that "all music is based on the character of repose in certain intervals, the absence of this character in certain others, and finally of the appellative affinities of some" (14). See Thomas Christensen, "Bemetzrieder's Dream: Diderot and the Pathology of Tonal Sensibility," in *Music, Sensation, and Sensibility*, ed. Linda Phyllis Austern (New York and London: Routledge, 2002), 39-56. [PL]

regard (the rules of harmony and counterpoint), and *I have looked for more solid principles in the phenomena produced by sonorous bodies of various forms and dimensions*." Now, he did not lack the elements; for, with the metal string tightened and plucked, he had the perfect chord of the major mode; the striking of an iron cylinder a meter long and fifteen millimeters in diameter, gave him the sound of the six-four chord derived from the perfect chord of the minor mode; the vibration of an equilateral triangular glass or metal plate, provided him with the dissonance of the second; finally, in striking various points of a square plate, he found the relation of two sounds which give the tritone. Indeed, here are all the elements of consonant and dissonant natural harmony.

Subjecting these facts to calculation, Baron Blein derived a new theory of vibrations that I cannot examine here, for my investigations are concerned only with systems of generation and classification of chords. I will only say that this theory does not lead its author to the formation of a scale and a tonality, the pitfall of all systems based on calculation and acoustical experiments, but to a chromatic scale, the negation of all keys and all tonality.

Blein's account of the system of chord formation, deduced from his theory of vibrations, is impossible to analyze; to get an idea of it, it must be seen in the context of the book itself of which it is the subject. It will suffice, in order to demonstrate to what errors the nature of this system led the author of this book, to present some examples of what he calls harmonic successions. I have selected them from his Table D, particularly in the successions that Blein calls *rescued dissonances*.[37]

[37]I beg the reader to believe that the book from which I take these examples of chords and modulations is serious, and I hope that he will not doubt the accuracy of my citations. It should also be noted that Blein is not only a former principal engineer, who studied mathematics at *L'Ecole des Ponts et Chaussées de Paris*, but that he is a musician, and plays the violin.

Such is the music that Blein found in nature, and which he has deduced from calculations based on acoustical facts. One is not surprised, according to this, by the deep disdain he professes for the art taught by the harmonists.

Chapter II

SYSTEMS BASED ON ARITHMETIC PROGRESSION AND THE CHROMATIC SCALE

306. At the time when French musicians began to be preoccupied with the science of harmony and the fundamental bass, another theory, at first hardly noticed, but later reproduced in various forms, also saw the light of day in France. Levens, Master of Music at Bordeaux Cathedral, was first to introduce it in a book entitled: *Abrégé des règles de l'harmonie pour apprendre la composition, avec un nouveau projet sur un système de musique sans temperament, ni chordes mobiles* (Bordeaux, 1743, 92 pages).[38] In the first part of this work Levens shows that he was a good musician and that he wrote more correctly than most of the authors of treatises on music. This first part relates to the practice of harmony, such as it was known in his time in France, and according to Rameau's doctrine, which the author does not always understand, and sometimes contradicts. The second part of the book is more interesting because of a plan for a new system of which Levens is the inventor, as he himself says; for he is the first to substitute the arithmetic progression for the harmonic progression used up to this point for the generation of intervals.

He had observed that the harmonic progression cannot generate a complete scale, the fourth note not being necessarily produced; for, he says, no numbers of this progression could find another which together would form a 4:3 ratio, which is that of the fourth. This consideration leads him to suggest resorting to the arithmetic progression, together with the harmonic progression taken to its tenth term, this one ascending, the other descending. He divides two strings according to this progression; the first gives him an ascending series of which the intervals are the natural tones of the horn and trumpet.

Example of the ascending progression:

C,	C,	G,	C,	E,	G,	B-flat,	C,	D,	E.
1,	1/2,	1/3,	1/4,	1/5,	1/6,	1/7,	1/8,	1/9,	1/10.

[38]Fétis asserts that the writings of Charles Levens (1689-1764) deserve more attention. He notes that Ballière and Jamard, who later developed a theory of music based on the harmonic and arithmetic progression, fail to acknowledge Levens' previous work. *FétisB*, 6:130. [PL]

Proceeding in an inverse manner for the second string, by means of the arithmetic progression, he finds a descending series that gives him the fourth degree and the sixth lowered by a semitone.

Example of the descending progression:

C,	C,	F,	C,	A-flat,	F,	D,	C,	B-flat,	A-flat
1,	2,	3,	4,	5,	6,	7,	8,	9,	10.

Levens finds three different tones in his system, namely the *major tone*, in the proportion 7:8; the *perfect tone*, in that of 8:9; finally, the *minor tone,* as 9:10. As a result of this experiment that he performed, he says, there resulted from this diversity of tones a most pleasant variety. To complete the chromatic scale, he had only to divide the major tone into two unequal tones, in the proportions 14:15, and 15:16; the perfect tone into two other semitones of which the proportions are 16:17, and 17:18; finally, the minor tone into two small semitones as 18:19, and 19:20.

The main fault of this system, a fault which collapses its foundation, is, on the one hand, that it does not conform to the make-up of any tonality, and, on the other, that the intervals' proportions do not correspond with the various octaves and consequently affect the ear with false sensations; for example, at the two extremes of the scale one finds on one side the distance of C to D represented by a *major tone*, and on the other by a *perfect tone*. But these difficulties do not stop Levens and do not prevent him from constructing, with the harmonic progression, a minor seventh chord (C-E-G-B-flat) on the tonic, although the note which forms the seventh is not of the key; a six-five chord (C-E-G-A) on the same note, although this chord is never found here; a dominant seventh chord (G-B-D-F), forgetting that this last note does not exist in the first ten terms of the harmonic progression, and that the one he substitutes for it is not the true fourth degree of the key; the six-five chord (F-A-C-D), although the first two notes of this chord are equally lacking in the first ten terms of the harmonic progression; finally, the dominant seventh chord through the harmonic progression, although the third of this dominant is formed by a lower note than the true leading tone.

307. Ballière, a geometrician of the Rouen academy, and Jamard, a Canon at Sainte-Geneviève in Paris, later took hold of Levens' ideas, the former developing them in a book entitled *Théorie de la musique*,[39] the latter in *Recherches sur la théorie de la musique*;[40] but the works of these two scholars being of a completely speculative nature, and not having led

[39]Paris, Didot, 1764.

[40]Paris, 1769.

to a practical theory of harmony, I need not deal with them here. Readers interested in an analysis will find it in my *Esquisse de l'histoire de l'harmonie*.[41]

SORGE'S THEORY

308. Two years after Levens' work appeared, Sorge, the organist at Lobenstein, a learned mathematician and distinguished musician, also published a theory based on the arithmetic progression; but he was superior in that in his calculations he did not lose sight of the principal subject, that is, the construction of a science in accordance with the art. He was the first German harmonist to join in Rameau's thought about the necessity of a scientific base for the processes of art. Euler had preceded him to the truth in this undertaking; but his theory is so foreign to the art, it is considered today as the mistake of a great man.[42] The book in which Sorge sets forth his system is entitled *Vorgemach der musikalischen Composition*, that is, *Introduction to Musical Composition*, or detailed instruction, well ordered and sufficient for the current practice of the *basso continuo*.[43]

Dividing, like all musicians, chords into consonant and dissonant, he considers as consonant any chord which is made up of only three notes, of intervals of the third, the fourth, the fifth or the sixth of various kinds. Many of these intervals not being the product of the pure harmonic progression, he resorts to the arithmetic progression, in which he finds the expressions that resemble these same chords; but he pushed it much further than the tenth term where Levens had stopped; the relations 4:5:6 gave him the perfect major chord, and he states (ch. VI, 14) that various kinds of experimentation prove that this chord exists in the resonance of many sonorous bodies. The arithmetic progression provides him with the perfect minor chord (ch. VII, 16), and in the natural tones of the trumpet

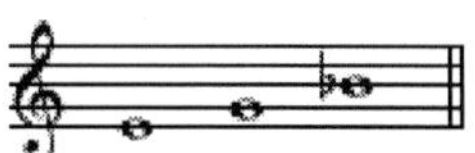

he finds the chord of the third and minor fifth (perfect diminished chord), which he calls *trias deficiens* (ch. VIII, 18). The arithmetic progression, stretched to its highest terms, provides Sorge with perfect chords with augmented fifth (ch. IX, 20), and diminished third.

[41]Pages 105-110.

[42]See the analysis of this theory in my *Esquisse de l'histoire de l'harmonie,* 74-91, and in the *Gazette Musicale de Paris* (1840, no. 52).

[43]Lobenstein, 1745.

309. In the second part of his book, he deals with the chords of the sixth and six-four chord, derived from the preceding chords, which he calls *fundamental* (*Haupt-Akkords*): but in this distinction between fundamental and derived chords, he does not mention Rameau, to whom it belongs, and does not call to his readers' attention that which is important in the consideration of inversion.

310. The third part of Sorge's book is devoted to dissonant chords. The notes of the trumpet and the geometric progression provide him with the chord of the minor seventh

that is not, it is true, the dominant seventh chord, but which he considers as such through transposition. He forms the other seventh chords by adding this dissonance (1) to the perfect minor chord, (2) to the chord of minor third and fifth, (3) to the perfect chord with augmented fifth, (4) to the perfect chord with diminished third. The arithmetic progression provides him with the figures for all the intervals of these harmonies.

310 *bis*. All these chords and those derived from them are considered by Sorge among those where the dissonance is natural, that is, approached without preparation: as for the other dissonances, they appear to him to fit into the category of passing notes or prolongations. Note this well, for we have arrived at one of the most important events in the history of harmony: it is the second period of real discovery made in this science, and the glory for this discovery belongs to the humble organist of Lobenstein, neglected by all historians of music until this day. For the first time, he established that a dissonant chord exists by itself, apart from any modification by another harmony: he further notes that this chord is completely different from other dissonant harmonies. It is true that he is wrong in according the same character to the minor seventh chord, where the dissonance is, according to him, added to the perfect minor chord, although this chord is only formed and used as a product of prolongation and of another kind of modification that will be discussed later. But if the aspect of consistency in the formation of chords led Sorge astray, he grasped, nevertheless, the fundamental character of the dominant seventh chord and modern tonality: for this he deserves a place in the history of the science of harmony immediately after Rameau who was the first to see the bases of this science and had posited them in considering the inversion of chords. With regard to his mistakes concerning the fact of the arithmetic progression for the formation of fundamental harmonies, we need only take into account the formation of the same chords by Rameau's addition of thirds.

BOOK FOUR

VALLOTTI'S SYSTEM AND THE SCHOOL OF PADUA

311. Rejected by all the supporters of the fundamental bass system, the arithmetic progression was also considered by the geometricians as incapable of producing a valid theory of harmony. They even denied it the quality of true progression, because it proceeds through a series of numbers in which the differences are equal, which do not constitute a true proportion.

Undoubtedly struck by the apparent consistency of Levens' system, which he nevertheless does not cite, Padre Vallotti, learned master of the chapel of Saint Anthony of Padua, formulated a general theory of harmony and composition, in which the arithmetic progression became a constitutive element. In the first part of his work, the only part that was published,[44] he set out to defend this progression against its critics (ch. x, 33), and established that it is as valid as the harmonic progression, that it is the inverse of the latter, and that their outermost terms are the same.[45]

312. Rameau had established in his *Traité de l'harmonie* that the dissonances that are not contained within the boundaries of the octave are not susceptible to inversion: by this he had only accepted the principles of the schools and practices of the best composers. But Vallotti rightly criticizes him for having himself misunderstood this principle by creating chords of the ninth and eleventh, by means of one or two thirds beyond the boundaries which he had marked out. He asserts in fact that there are really no inversions of chords, but the complements of octaves and inversions of numerical relations by the double harmonic and arithmetic progression (ch. xxxix, 117). No matter what he says about it, this distinction cannot justify inversions of the ninth by the seventh, examples of which he offers in many combinations, such as the following:

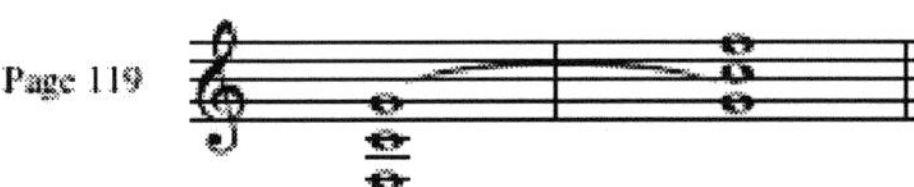

[44]*Della scienza teorica, e protica della moderna musica, libro primo* (Padua, 1779).

[45]The two proportions, harmonic and mathematical, are in inverse relation to one another since we can see, between both extremes, the same ratios expressed inversely; that is, in harmonic proportion the major (mode) is in the lower notes and the minor (mode) in the higher notes, while in mathematical proportion it is the opposite, with the lower notes in the minor (mode) and the higher notes in the major (mode). We, therefore, have three consonant terms in harmonic proportion; since even in inverse and in mathematical proportion, they are nonetheless, consonant. We must, therefore, deal with this proportion, since it too pertains to music, and not in one respect only. As we shall later see when we discuss modes, cadences, and relationships that some proportions share.*

* I am grateful to Professor Corrado Federici for the translation of this paragraph from Italian into English. [PL]

This erroneous theory leads him to a false inversion of the seventh chord by the nine-four chord in the following example:

instead of this true inversion:

Such is the bizarre system, contrary to all fine harmonic feeling and to the practice of all schools, which Vallotti had developed in treatises on harmony and counterpoint; but his death, which followed closely the publication of his first book, did not leave him the time to bring the others to light.

313. It should not be thought, however, that Vallotti did not admit in harmony the different arrangements of notes of a direct dissonant chord in the derivatives, but he considered them precisely as changes of arrangement, and believed in absolute inversion only in the form just seen.

314. Padre Sabbatini, his successor, had been a pupil of Padre Martini. But later he became Vallotti's student and adopted his system, at least in part, for he also proposes that the ninth inverted produces the seventh, in a book entitled *la vera idea delle musicali numeriche segnature* (ch. V1, 78). The method set forth in this book being purely empirical, it is not necessary to seek a general view of systematic construction; the facts are ascertained by their existence, but without research into their origin. Thus Sabbatini finds the perfect major chord on the tonic, the perfect minor chord on the sixth degree, and a progression of these chords by a series of bass movements descending a fifth and rising a fourth, leads him to the chord of the minor third and minor fifth on the seventh degree. With respect to this last chord, he has shown more sagacity than all his predecessors; for they considered it as a natural chord in the place it occupies, whereas Sabbatini, or rather Vallotti, saw very clearly that this chord, which does not answer to any tonal condition of the major or minor modes, occurs only by analogy in a progression of nonmodulatory perfect chords. It is surprising that more modern harmonists have shown themselves less advanced on this point. With respect to harmony derived from the fundamental, Vallotti and Sabbatini were following the doctrine of Rameau.

315. Considering the chromatic scale as a true scale, these authors do not present as alterations the natural intervals of the perfect major, minor and diminished, augmented fifth, and diminished third chords, nor the

other modified intervals of the consonant chords, but as an arbitrary use of intervals which all have their place in this chromatic scale.

316. Moving on to dissonant chords, Sabbatini constructs them by the addition of intervals to the perfect major, minor, and diminished chords. Thus the addition of a major third above the perfect major chord of the tonic gives him a major seventh chord C-E-G-B, which he considers to be the first in order. Likewise, the addition of a minor third above the perfect minor chord on the sixth degree creates a minor seventh chord, A-C-E-G. From these two fundamental chords he gets, by inversion, the six-five, the third, the six-four, and second chords. Finally, a major third added above the minor third and minor fifth chord creates the chord of the leading-tone seventh, B-D-F-A. Sabbatini then says (*la vera idea delle musicali numeriche segnature*, art. V, 32) that there is another minor seventh chord that is made on the fifth of the principal note of the key, and which consists of the major third, perfect fifth and minor seventh, as G-B-D-F. This one, he says, differs from the others in that it does not need to be prepared, whereas the dissonance of the others must always be heard in a prior state of consonance.

We see that the absence of a proper classification of primary chords throws the author of this system into a great confusion of ideas, and that the logical order that we have seen in authors of the most flawed systems is no longer found here. For, what is this seventh chord that is found placed outside of the system of practical generation adopted by this author, which has different conditions for its use, and which resembles them only in the necessity of downward resolution of dissonance? And how is it that having found through practice that this dissonant chord did not need preparation, Vallotti and Sabbatini did not conclude that it was a chord belonging to tonality, as well as the perfect major and minor chords? How, finally, did the necessity of preparing the dissonances of the other seventh chords not make it clear that these chords had a different origin than the additions of thirds to perfect chords? Many other imperfections result from this system; but I hasten to arrive at the peculiarities that caused this system to be rejected by the purist Italian schools, with respect to practice.

The addition of a minor third above the perfect diminished chord of the minor mode leads Vallotti and Sabbatini to the diminished seventh chord; the same addition to the same chord with a chromatic or diminished third produces the diminished seventh chord with diminished third (D-sharp-F-A-C); finally, the addition of a minor third above the perfect augmented chord gives rise to the major seventh chord with augmented fifth (C-E-G-sharp-B). All the harmonies derived from these chords are formed through inversion.

317. Up to that point, if the theory is unsatisfactory, the harmonic practical examples in Sabbatini's book conform to what is being done in the modern school; but here is an unusual new part where the ear is

offended by unfamiliar associations of sounds where the movements are unable to give a sense of resolving dissonances, considering that the notes on which the resolutions happen are already heard in the chord. Thus, in the perfect chord C-E-G-C, in which he even doubles intervals, Sabbatini says that the ninth is added, so that the chord that it presents is in the following form.

Following the principles of his teacher, he presents the derivatives under the following forms, and makes the complete inversion with a seven-four-two chord.

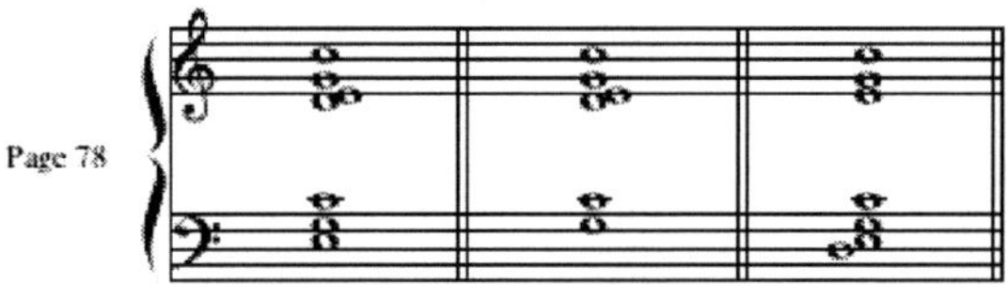

It is thus again that Sabbatini, following Vallotti, adds a dissonance of the eleventh to the perfect major or minor chord in which the intervals are doubled; the chord, thus composed, appears in these forms in its original configuration, in its derivatives, and in its complete inversion:

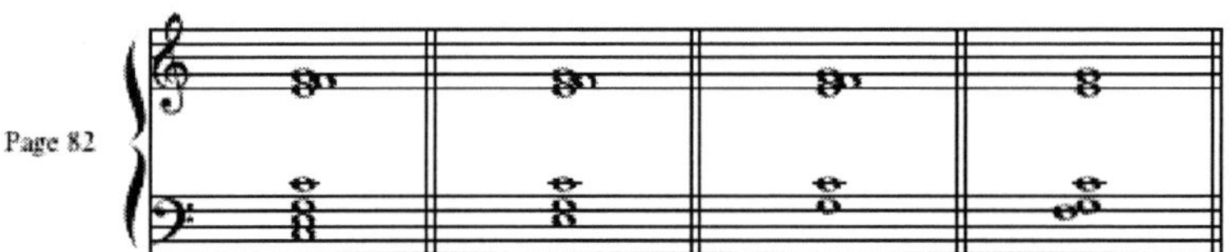

Lastly, stretching the system to its outer limits through the addition of the ninth, the eleventh, the thirteenth, which he calls the *dissonant sixth*, and the fourteenth, or doubled seventh, to the perfect chord, with the derivatives and the inversions of the three dissonances, conforming to Vallotti's theory, Sabbatini presents these chords in the following forms:

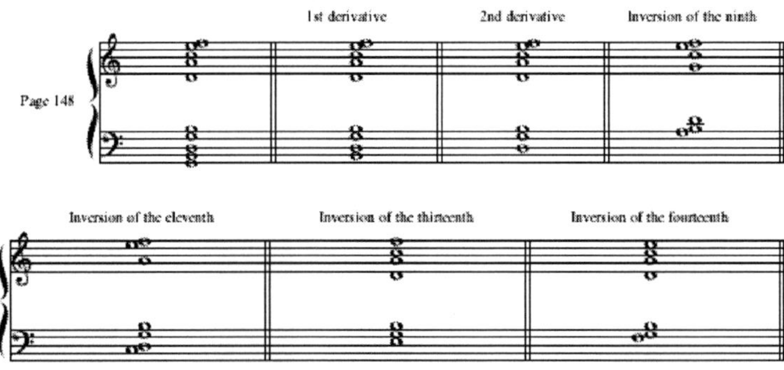

These harmonies, so harsh, so incapable of proper resolution, were not conceived by a learned musician, raised in purer principles, than by the spirit of the system, and because he did not understand the mechanism of the prolongation which retards the natural intervals of the chords. If he had followed the theory of this mechanism, he would have seen by this alone that when a note is retarded in a chord, it cannot be heard at the same time as the retardation, and consequently, instead of composing the ninth chord of C-E-G-C-D, he should have formed it as C-E-G-D, retarding C-E-G-C. Hence, he would have avoided all the harmonic horrors that he presents as derivatives of his primary harmony. Likewise, the principal of retardation would have enabled him to see that his so-called eleventh is only a fourth; that this fourth retards the third, and consequently, that the third and the fourth cannot be heard together. Thus, instead of having a chord composed of C-E-F-G-C, which is not found in well-written piece of music, he would have had C-F-G-C, retarding C-E-G-C, and its derivative harmonies would have had the same regularity. It is also in the latter example that all the most intolerable aggregations are gathered.

I do not need to proceed further with the examination of this bizarre theory to explain the opposition it faced from every composer of distinction in Italy, when Vallotti's students began to disseminate it. It had this in particular, that it was the only one to have presumed to reform the art of writing; for all the other systems aspired only to provide more or less incorrect explanations of the facts, more or less close to the truth, or to create simple speculative hypotheses.

The System of Abbé Vogler and his School

318. The author of this system had traveled to Italy in his youth, and took from Vallotti the substance of this learned musician's system. Without adopting it entirely, he shared the master's ideas concerning the usefulness of the inverse progression, harmonic and arithmetic, and from it deduced the effect of a chromatic scale, as the basis of melody and harmony. Having instituted a school of music in Mannheim in 1776, he published in the same year a sort of manifesto of the principles that he taught there, in a book entitled: *Tonwissenschaft und Tonsetzkunst* (*La science de la musique et de la composition*), followed by a sort of commentary on these principles, which appeared under the title *Kuhrpfälzische Tonschule* (*École de musique du Palatinat),* Mannheim, 1778, and the progress of the school through a new method, entitled: *Betrachtungen der Mannheimer Tonschule* (*Examen de l'école de musique de Mannheim*). Here is the content of the system Vogler envisioned.

319. Taking a string that he divides harmonically on the one hand, and in an arithmetic progression on the other, he derives the harmonic and diatonic intervals from the low and middle notes, corresponding to the acoustic construction of the trumpet and horn, and the chromatic intervals

in the high notes. Like Levens, he establishes three tones in which the proportions are different, namely, a major tone from B-flat to C, with the proportion 7:8; a middle tone from C to D, with the proportion 8:9, and a minor tone from D to E, with the proportion 9:10 (*Tonwissenschaft,* 122-23). The arithmetic progression taken to its thirty-second term, gives Vogler a chromatic scale, a major scale with the notes C, D, E, F, G, A B; a minor scale, and finally an enharmonic scale of C-sharp and D-flat, D-sharp and E-flat, E-sharp and F-natural, etc.

320. Similarly, Vogler draws from the division of his chord, through the arithmetic progression, the perfect major chord C-E-G; the perfect minor chord G-B-flat-D; the chord of the minor third and minor fifth E-G-B-flat; the minor seventh chord with major third C-E-G-B-flat; the major ninth chord C-E-G-B-flat-D; the minor seventh chord with minor fifth E-G-B-flat-D; finally, all harmonies, without excluding those in which the intervals are generally designated by the term *alterations*. It is therefore no longer a matter, according to the author of this system, of putting each of these harmonies on its most appropriate degree. This would undoubtedly be enormously difficult with respect to tonality, if Vogler accepted formulae of tonality which determined expressly the place of each one, because of certain functions of successions; but he does not forget that the arithmetic progression did not give him a key, but a chromatic scale, and, faithful to his principle, he establishes that all the possible chords, fundamental or derived, are made on all the notes of this scale; and, although he is obliged to conform to usage, and establish the keys of C, D, E-flat, F, etc., he wants each note and each harmony that did not appear to belong or was foreign to these keys, to be able to find a place, without resulting in true modulations, unless an act of cadencing constitutes a new key.

321. Based on this account, we see that Abbé Vogler placed the perfect chord on each degree of the major and minor scales.

Examples

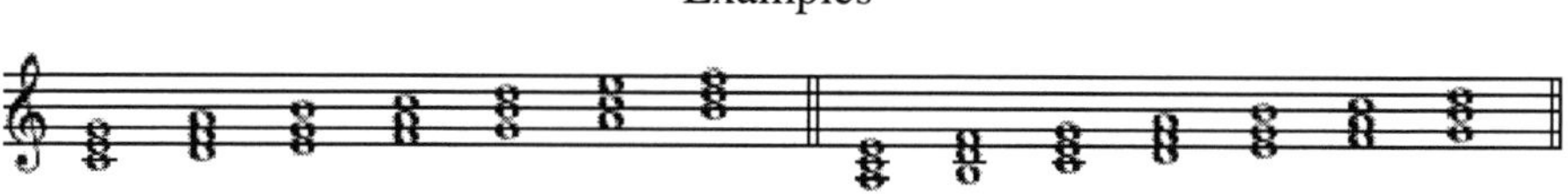

In the chromatic scales he finds the perfect chord with augmented fifth (ex. 1), the diminished third and diminished fifth chord (ex. 2), finally the major third and diminished fifth chord (ex. 3).

322. The seventh added to each of the three-note chords in the two scales gives, on each of the degrees of these scales, seventh chords in which the nature of the intervals depends on the degrees where they are found.

Examples

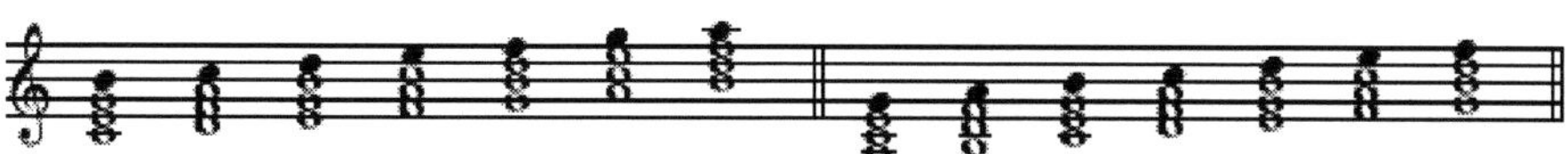

The chromatic scale gives Vogler the minor seventh with augmented fifth chord (ex. 1), the major seventh with augmented fifth chord (ex. 2), the diminished seventh with diminished third chord (ex. 3), and finally the chord of the minor seventh with major third and diminished fifth (ex. 4).

Each of these chords has derivatives and inversions according to the nature of its intervals.

323. The seventh and the ninth added to each of these five-three chords in the two major and minor scales give on each degree complete ninth chords, where the nature of the intervals depends on the degrees on which they are found.

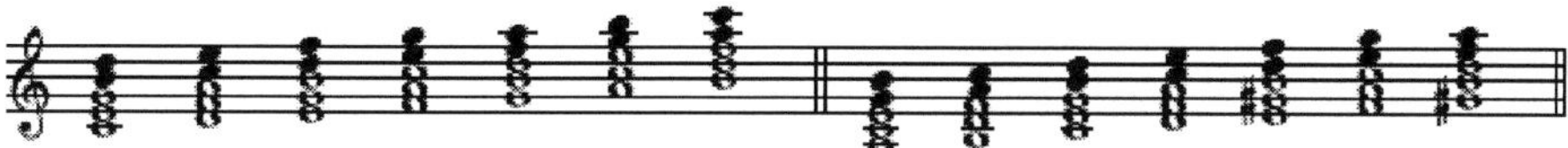

These chords have derivatives and inversions according to Vallotti's and Sabbatini's theory, that is, the ninth by the seventh.

The chromatic scale produces the chord of the major ninth with augmented fifth:

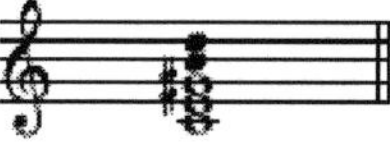

I do not understand what trepidation prevented Vogler from adding the ninth to the altered seventh chords in examples 1, 3, 4 of §321.

324. The addition of a dissonance of the eleventh to each of the five-three chords, which he places under each note of the scale, provide Vogler with as many dissonant chords which manifest themselves in these forms:

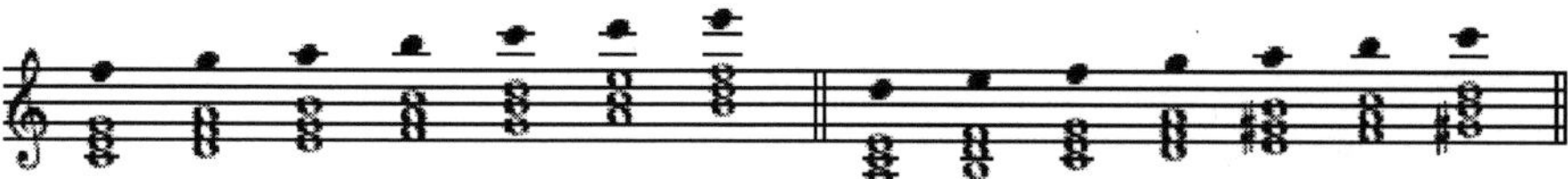

These false chords, which originally result only from the retardation of the third by the fourth, and in which the third should not consequently be retained, Vogler inverts into these dreadful harmonies, according to Vallotti's doctrine:

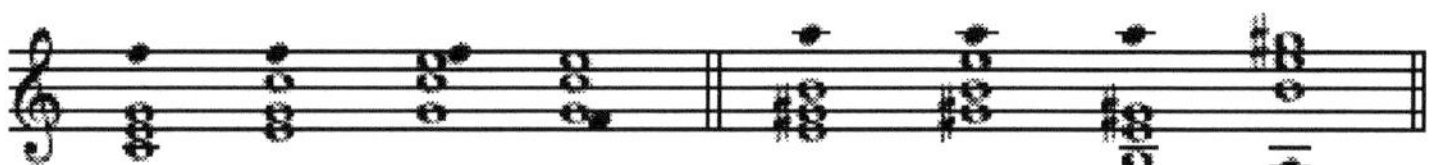

The joining of the ninth to the eleventh on complete consonant chords produces these even more offensive chords:

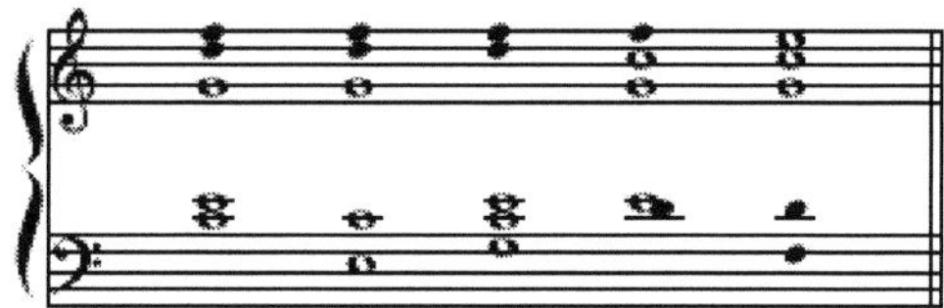

325. Such a theory is the negation of any true theory, for it reduces the art and the science to a collection of absurd facts, without connection, and opposed to the feeling of a fine harmony. The laws of harmonic creation are destroyed in this maze of diverse chords. Knecht, Vogler's student, tried in vain to establish these laws, without contradicting his master's system, in his book entitled *Elementarwerk der Harmonie und des Generalbasses (Traité élémentaire de l'harmonie et de la basse continue)*; but he was unable to do so.[46]

Some harmonic systems published today seem to have taken their origin in Vogler's system, even though their authors have discarded any consideration of numerical progression, and have rejected the inversions of the ninth and eleventh chords which he had borrowed from Vallotti.

Among these systems, I point out especially those of Friedrich Schneider,[47] choirmaster of the court of Dessau, and Jelensperger, professor of harmony at the Paris Conservatory, who died in the flower of his youth.

---

[46]*Elementarwerk der Harmonie und des Generalbasses* (Augsburg, 1792-98; Munich, 1814).*

*The full title of this work is: *Elementary Treatise on Harmony and the Basso Continuo, that is, a true method for teaching and learning the art of accompanying with a perfect knowledge of all harmony, following the principles of Vogler, with many tables of chords and practical examples.* In his article on Justin Heinrich Knecht (1752-1817) Fétis recognizes his importance as an organist and composer, but complains that his theoretical doctrine is unconvincing, lacking in logic, and inconsequential for the advancement of the science of harmony. *FétisB*, 5:358. [PL]

[47]Fétis also makes special mention of Schneider's *Handbuch des Organisten* (1829-30) which he considers to be one of the most important of its kind. *FétisB*, 8:122. [PL]

325. *bis*. Schneider presented his theory in a book entitled: *Elementarbuch der Harmonie* (*Traité élémentaire de l'harmonie*).[48] According to the basic principal of this doctrine, the perfect chord and the seventh chord are found on each note of the scale. They happen there, with regard to the nature of their intervals, conforming to the nature of the key and the mode, and have, depending on the note on which they are placed, either a major or minor third, the perfect or diminished (minor) fifth, the major or minor seventh. It is the same for the ninth chord. To complete the nomenclature of the chords it is only a question of altering various intervals.

326. Although simpler in appearance and more natural than Vogler's theory, it is nevertheless one of those eccentric ideas where there is not only a false classification of chords, but the use of these chords contrary to the true feeling for harmony, to the traditions of pure art. By admitting in the most absolute sense, that the seventh and ninth chords are only consonant chords to which one or two thirds are added, Schneider appears to be persuaded that these chords, although dissonant, have, in practice, all the freedom of the perfect chord, as can be seen in these examples that he gives of their connection (page 22).[49]

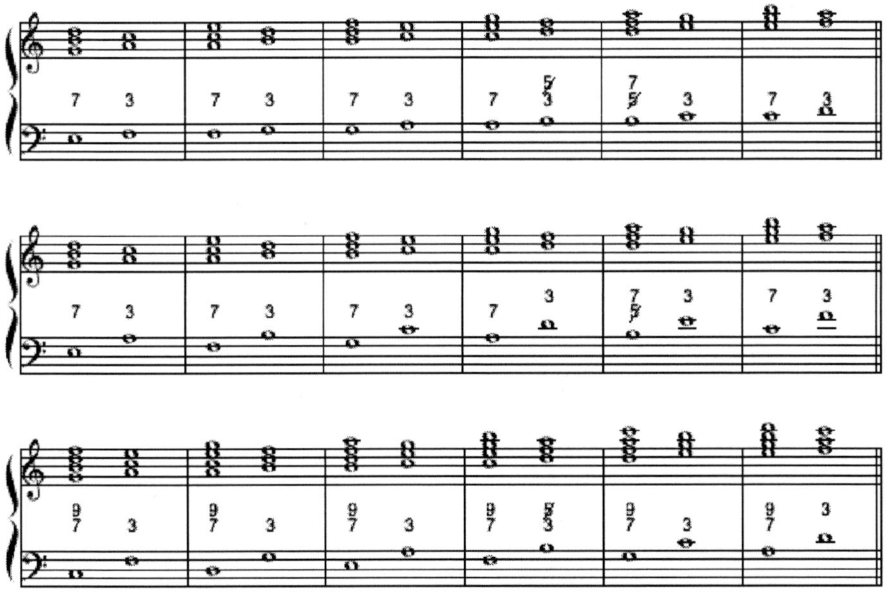

[48]*Elementarwerk der Harmonie und des Generalbasse* (Augsbourge, 1792-1798; Munich, 1814).

[49]*Elementarbuch der Harmonie und Tonsetzkunst* (Leipzig, 1820; 2nd edition, Leipzig, 1827).

In these progressions, Schneider assimilates all seventh chords as a dominant seventh, and all ninth chords as that of the ninth of the same degree; for he dispenses with the preparation, that is, the prolongation, which is the source. Consequently, not only is the classification incorrect, but the use of these chords is contrary to the true tradition of the art. Such errors are all the more disturbing in a didactic work where the authority of its author, being a very distinguished composer, may lead young harmonists in a disastrous direction.

327. Jelensperger, the author of a book entitled *L'harmonie au commencement du XIXe siecle* (Paris, 1830),[50] develops therein an eclectic system more in accordance with the traditions of the art.

A chord, he says, is the combination of two, three, four, or five different notes, taken from the same scale, and able to be arranged in thirds. For example:

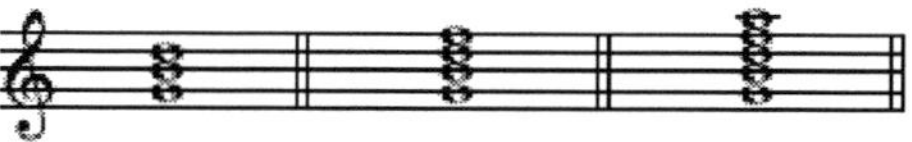

After having explained a few details from this starting point, he establishes that the three and four-note chords happen on all degrees of both the major and minor scales, and their constituent intervals are in accordance with the mode and the scale degree on which they are found. Here is his ordering of the notes of the two scales thus harmonized:

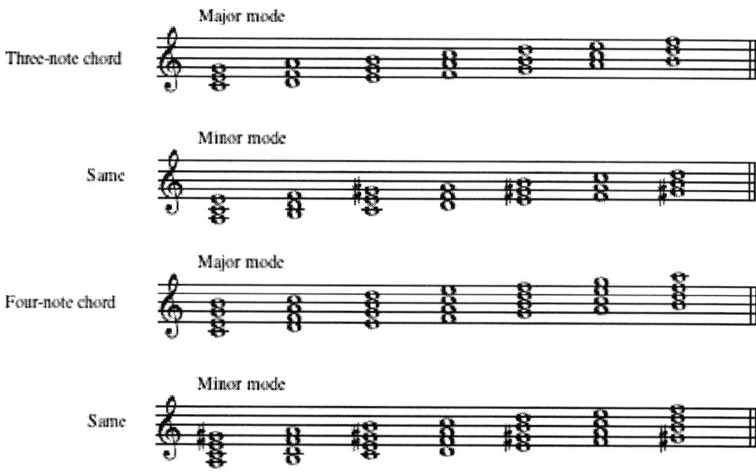

[50]Daniel Jelensperger (1787-1831) studied harmony and composition with Reicha at the Paris Conservatory, becoming Reicha's assistant and then a professor. In 1820 a group of professors at the Conservatory founded a press (Zetter & Cie) for the publication of their works, and upon Reicha's recommendation Jelensperger was appointed editor, in which position he edited Reicha's *Traité de haute composition. FétisB,* 5:264. [PL]

But in practice, he allows only the seventh chord of the fifth degree of the two modes and its inversions without preparation; for all the rest, he requires the preparation, which is none other than the prolongation, with the exception of the chord of the seventh degree. Now, if the preparation or the prolongation is indispensable for these seventh chords, it is because this is its source; therefore, this source is not a simple addition of a third to a consonant five-three chord; thus, these chords do not have an isolated existence as in the above table.

328. Jelensperger did not make such an error with the ninth chord, or of five tones arranged in thirds; for he does not allow it, *a priori*, and taken in isolation only on the fifth degree of the two modes. He also avoids the inversion of this chord, allowed in Vallotti's and Vogler's theory.

329. In the rest of his theory, Jelensperger treats the prolongation and alteration of the intervals of chords according to the principles of the school in which he was brought up. If he did not understand the role of the first of these kinds of modification for the creation of seventh chords, it is because he realized its inadequacy in the formation of the seventh chord on the second degree, and did not know any other kind of modification that joins with that one to create this chord. In his confusion, and not being able to separate the seventh chord of the second degree from the others, he found nothing better than Vogler's classification of chords.

Chapter III

SYSTEMS BASED ON AN ARBITRARY CHOICE OF FUNDAMENTAL CHORDS

330. Daube, a musician in the service of the Prince of Würtemburg and a contemporary of Sorge and Marpurg, was concerned as they were with the need for a systematic theory of harmony. But removing himself from any consideration of numbers and acoustical phenomena, he understood the usefulness of his theory only by making it conform to practice. As a matter of fact, what he published under the title *Generalbass in drey Accorden, gegründet in den Regeln der alt-und neunen Autoren* [Leipzig, 1756] (*L'harmonie en trois accords, d'après les règles des auteurs anciens et modernes)*[51] is less a theory than a classification of chords, by reason of their function in the tonality. Although this work only appeared in 1756, it was, however, completed two years earlier, as the preface, dated December 28, 1754 in Stuttgart, proves; Daube thus wrote it

[51]Fétis here omits the last part of the title which reads, "*with instruction on how to pass from one key to any of the twenty-three others, by means of two intermediary chords*." Fétis writes that despite Marpurg's criticism, the works of Johann Friedrich Daube (c1730-1797) are systematic and contain good ideas. *FétisB*, 3:250. [PL]

before knowing Marpurg's *Handbuch bey dem Generalbass*. Sorge's book, published nine years earlier, appears to have concerned him only in a practical sense; either he was too unfamiliar with mathematics to read it productively, or he wanted simply, as he indicated in several places, to replace the empirical and outdated works of Heinichen and Mattheson with a systematic treatise.

By the title *Generalbass in drey Accorden*, Daube means three fundamental chords, existing by themselves, as a result of the tonality, and by virtue of a law of intimate connection of their constituent intervals. These three chords are the perfect chord, the dominant seventh, and the six-five chord on the fourth degree. This is far from Rameau's single perfect chord, and the construction of the other chords by the addition of thirds and the suppression of intervals; however, it is clear that Daube borrowed his *double employment* chord of the fourth degree from the French harmonist, as he borrowed from Sorge, whom he does not mention, the idea of the primary existence of the dominant seventh chord. Finally, Rameau also provides him with the theory of the inversion of fundamental chords. Daube does not explain why he adopts the six-five chord as more fundamental than the seventh on the second degree; but, according to what he says in the second chapter about the dissonance of the second which gives rise to the seventh, and not the seventh giving rise to the second, there is reason to believe that this is why he considered the six-five chord as fundamental, because the interval of the second is found between the fifth and the sixth.

These three chords appear to the system's author to constitute all of harmony, because, he says (chapter III, 20), these and their derivatives suffice to accompany all the degrees of the ascending and descending scale. And to demonstrate it, he gives this tonal scheme with harmonies taken from these very chords; but some of these harmonies are as poor with respect to the feeling for tonality as they are in the succession of intervals. For example, Daube places the six-four-three chord on the ascending sixth degree followed by the chord of the sixth and minor fifth on the seventh; from which it follows that the dissonance of the chord on the sixth degree cannot possibly resolve. This error, and the six-four chord, placed on the dominant, which robs this degree of its chord of repose, render inadmissible the harmonic scheme of this system's author. Marpurg sharply criticized this scale and many other things in Daube's book, under the veil of anonymity, in the second volume of his *Historisch-kritische Beyträge zur Aufnahme der Musik* (page 465).[52]

[52]This work, published from 1754-78, and the *Kritische Briefe über die Tonkunst* (1760-64) included discussion on musical aesthetics, book reviews, theoretical topics, and tuning and temperament. [PL]

331. All other chords Daube considers as either complete prolongations of primary chords, or derived through cadencing, or as alterations of the natural intervals of these chords; a system in which Sorge had preceded him.

Daube's error with regard to the six-five chord on the fourth degree is not surprising, for this harmony, derived from certain modifications which will be discussed later, had been the pitfall of all harmonists up to that time. By considering it as primary any conception of a complete rational system is rendered impossible. In fact, Daube added nothing to the fundamental basis of the theories set down by Rameau and Sorge; there are, however, some good modulatory formulae in his book, which has enjoyed a certain popularity in Germany.

332. After Daube's work a remarkable book emerged, which, however, escaped Germany's attention, or at least was not fully appreciated: I wish to discuss what Schröter, the organist at Nordhausen, published under the title *Deutliche Anweisung zum Generalbass* (*Instruction claire sur la basse continue*).[53] An educated man, not only in music, but in letters and sciences, Schröter developed through meditation in the peace and quiet of a small city, his ideas on a theory of harmony, the subject of so many fruitless efforts. He had read everything that had been published on this science, carefully analyzed the work of his predecessors, and summarized his observations and analyses in a history of harmony, the manuscript of which unfortunately perished in the sacking of Nordhausen by the French army in 1761. Too old to restart such a work, Schröter limited himself to providing a summary of it in the excellent preface to his *Deutliche Anweisung zum Generalbass*.

333. In the eighth chapter of his book (page 36) he establishes that only the perfect chord exists by itself, and that all others are the result either of the inversion of this chord, the substitution of the seventh for the octave for the dominant seventh chord, the prolongation for the construction of the seventh on the second degree and the harmony deriving from it, or finally, the anticipation.

Here then is a big step for a genuine theory, in that the harmony of the minor seventh and those which are derived from it are considered from their real standpoint, that is, as a prolongation which retards the natural intervals of a consonant chord. Schröter considers only the effect of the retardation in this phenomenon, which is why he calls it *Verzöegerung* (*retardatio*). If he had been asked what this *retardation* is, he would have

[53]*Deutliche Anweisung zum Generalbass*, Halberstadt, 1772.*

*Under the entry on Christophe Gottleib Schröter (1699-1782) Fétis cites other theoretical works dealing with mathematics and music, criticism, the Sorge-Marpurg dispute, and instrumental design. A composer of significant output, all his works remained in manuscript and were lost. *FétisB*, 8:141. [PL]

been hard put to find a satisfactory answer; for it is clear that the prolongation coming to an end, for instance in the chord D-F-A-C, will have as its resolution D-F-A-B, which is not a consonant harmony. There is therefore some other circumstance that, in the chord D-F-A-C, combines with the prolongation of C; but Schröter's analysis did not dig so deeply: it stopped at the discovery of the phenomenon of retardation. It cannot be denied that this discovery was of great importance in that it provided the first element for the classification of dissonant chords that do not exist originally as consequences of tonality. This was the first attack against the incorrect theory that considers the seventh chord with minor third in the same class of harmony as that of the seventh with major third.

On this matter, Schröter took a step backwards, by considering it as the product of the substitution of the seventh for the octave in the perfect chord, for this dominant seventh chord, characteristic of modern tonality, exists on its own in this tonality of which it is the generator. This is what Euler and Sorge had so clearly understood.

334. In chapters nine to seventeen, Schröter develops the results of the theory set forth in the eighth chapter; the eighteenth deals with alterations; the nineteenth with the retardations of all natural and altered harmony; here the author shows great insight. Some of these observations are more advanced than the state of the art of his time, and he presents by instinct harmonic aggregations which Mozart, Beethoven, Weber, and Rossini later put into practice.

335. Kirnberger, a learned musician living in Berlin, brought out one year after the publication of Schröter's book a treatise on the same subject entitled *Die wahren Grundsätze zum Gebrauch der Harmonie* (*Les vrais principes concernant l'usage de l'harmonie*).[54] His starting point is the five-three chord in its three tonal forms, that is, composed of major third and perfect fifth;

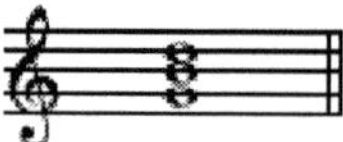

minor third and perfect fifth:

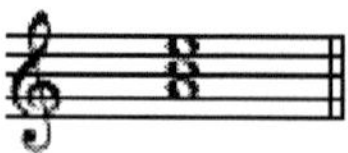

[54]*Die wahren Grundsätze zum Gebrauch der Harmonie* (Berlin and Koenigsberg, 1773).*

*In the *Esquisse* (see Arlin, 121-22) Fétis remarks that in his entry under Kirnberger in the *Biographie universelle* he gave him too much credit for the perfection of the theory of harmony, as he was not aware of the works of Sorge and Schröter at the time. Fétis earlier declared Kirnberger to be the only theorist to significantly advance the science of harmony between Rameau and Catel. *FétisB*, 5:340. [PL]

and minor third and diminished fifth.

Then he considers as primary dissonant chords the four seventh chords, namely: (1) the minor seventh, perfect fifth, major third chord;

(2) the minor seventh, perfect fifth, minor third chord;

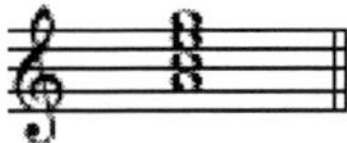

(3) the minor seventh, minor fifth, and minor third chord;

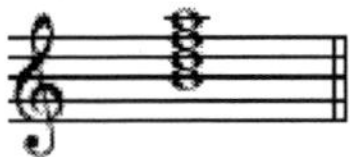

(4) the major seventh, perfect fifth, major third chord.

These forms, Kirnberger says, differ only in the quality of intervals; but the quality of intervals is precisely what establishes the difference in the natural or artificial existence of chords with respect to tonality; if this difficulty were not there, there would be nothing in it. Furthermore, in his use of these chords, he himself showed clearly that there is an essential difference between them that results from the various quality of intervals; he uses the first and third examples without preparation, and prepares the dissonance of the second and fourth. Now, the preparation is, as I have shown in many places, only identical to the prolongation; the necessity of the latter for the chords in which it arises proves a different origin than the other two, and something other than a difference between accidentals.

336. As for the seventh chord on the second degree, Kirnberger obtains it from the retardation of the sixth in the sixth chord on the same degree, derived from the chord of the third and minor fifth; for example:

Sometimes the fifth is inserted, he says, to complete the harmony, as in this example:

But by virtue of what law, and by what mechanism is this foreign note introduced into the chord? This is what he did not see, and does not even attempt to explain, limiting himself to pointing out a fact of experience. As I have said, this is one of the biggest problems in the whole of the systematic study of harmony: it has been the pitfall of every system (on this matter, see Book Two, chapter VII).

336 *bis*. Kirnberger's theory was developed and organized more logically by Türk in his *Anweisung zum Generalbassspielen (Instruction pour l'accompagment de la basse continue*, Halle and Leipzig, 1791).[55] This work appeared in many editions, and received high praise in Germany, although the overabundance of detail burdens the reader such that a clear and comprehensive theory cannot be sufficiently identified.

337. Gottfried Weber, who died several years ago, had for a long time in Germany a reputation as a learned musician. His reputation was founded on his *Versuch einer geordneten Theorie der Tonsetzkunst zum selbst unterricht, (Essai d'une théorie systématique de la composition)*,[56] and as editor of the periodical entitled: *Caecilia*. It is most peculiar that the title of the first of these works is in direct contradiction to the objective of the author and to the content of the book, which does not contain a theory, much less a systematic theory. Listen to Weber himself, and observe how he explains it in his preface.

"I should, however, note in particular that my *Versuch einer geordneten Theorie* is certainly not, as many have thought, a system in the scientific-philosophic sense of the word, nor a collection of truths deduced in a logical sequence from a supreme principle. On the contrary, I have established, as a characteristic trait of my point of view, that our art does not at all adopt, at least up to the present (1817), such a systematic base. The little we know about composition (harmony), consists still to this day in a certain number of experiences and observations of what sounds good or bad in this or that set of notes. To deduce these experiences logically from a fundamental principle, and to translate them into the discipline of philosophy, into a system, this has not been achieved until now, as I will often have the opportunity to point out in the course of this work. One sees everywhere evidence that theorists, up to this time, instead of beginning

[55]An enlarged edition of this work was published in 1800. Under the entry on Daniel Gottlob Türk (1750-1813) Fétis points to the large number of practical examples that aided the work's use and popularity. *FétisB*, 8:405. [PL]

[56]*Versuch einer geordneten Theorie der Tonsetzkunst zum selbst unterricht* (Mayence, Schott, 1817, 3 vols.; 2nd ed., ibid., 1824, 4 vols.; 3rd edition, ibid., 1830-32, 4 vols.).

the construction of a system only after examining in every detail the phenomena of consonance and dissonance in a given collection of sounds, hastily and without due consideration raise a structure, presenting it in the imposing form of a mathematical concept; then, when they encounter, which is inevitable, a multitude of phenomena which do not agree with the system established *a priori*, or are even in direct opposition to it, what do they do? They prefer to classify these phenomena under the categories of exceptions, licenses, ellipses, and so on, and brush them aside in this way, rather than renounce the sweet illusion of their harmonic system.

"My only claim is the merit of examining the principles of experience with more precision, of adding new observations, of drawing together things of the same kind, or which appear to belong together, of connecting and coordinating the facts according to the most logical scheme, not as the deductions from a rigidly systematic base, but simply in the most orderly way; in a word, as an attempt at a *methodical theory* to which I did not wish to consequently attach the pompous title of *system,* which to me appears too pretentious." (Preface, x-xii, 3rd edition).

After this account of his negative principles, one asks how Weber could choose a starting point for the study of harmony, whatever form it would take, although one would have to admit that after so many fruitless attempts at the formation of a philosophical theory of this science, his skepticism was in a way excusable. Nevertheless, for even a simple method of analysis, one needs at least some kind of basis, a certain number of stated and accepted facts: Weber understood this, and the necessity for this basis led him to adopt the three forms of Kirnberger's five-three chord, and his four seventh chords. In these forms, Weber says (vol. 1, 132-35, 135-36, 1st edition), are contained all the fundamental varieties of chords of three and four notes.[57]

---

[57]Fétis reports that Gottfried Weber (1779-1839) first attempted composing without any knowledge of harmony and counterpoint, and came to the realization that he needed theoretical instruction if he were to improve in the art of composition. Not being able to find a skilled teacher in his vicinity, Weber turned to reading whatever treatises were at hand. Fétis contends that this resulted in a haphazard musical training, and that without the practice that can only be obtained through study with a teacher, Weber became convinced that music theory was too full of contradictions to be of any use. The "accepted facts" of musical analysis to which Fétis refers include "the law of inversion, formulated by Rameau, the primary existence of a natural dissonant chord, established theoretically by Sorge, the formation of artificial dissonances by prolongations and alterations of intervals discovered by Schröter and Kirnberger, and finally the substitution of certain chords for certain others, examined by Catel." According to Fétis, it was in view of his skepticism that Weber undertook his *Versuch einer geordneten Theorie der Tonsetzkunst*, which, Fétis' criticism aside, he deems "commendable for its spirit of analysis," further remarking "if one cannot consider it as the exposition of a true theory, one must declare that it is an interesting collection of observations from which one may derive useful instruction." *FétisB,* 8: 519. [PL]

Do not ask Weber the origin of these chords, their primary laws with respect to tonality, nor anything else of this kind: according to his principles, he will respond that he has no system of this type, and that he knows nothing about it; but he will show you examples of the use of these chords, and will analyze their various combinations. His method is empiricism taken to its highest degree. Thus, his only demonstration of the identity of the chords, be they consonant or fundamentally dissonant, consists in the following harmonic progression:

If we were to raise the objection that the preparation by the syncopation is not necessary for the last seventh chord, because it is natural and conforms to the tonal attraction, while this preparation is indispensable for all the others; if, moreover, we were to object that these consonant and dissonant chords are placed on all the notes of the scale only with respect to the movement, and because the tonal feeling is suspended for the entire duration of the progression up to the dominant seventh chord, which reestablishes the character of the tonality, Weber would refer these explanations, as simple as they are obvious, to the category of forced exceptions of which he speaks in his preface; for such is his skepticism, that only accepting the fact that hits him in the face, he rejects any general rule, like that of non-modulating progressions, as hypothetical.

337 *bis*. In the absence of a general theory, Weber adopts for the teaching of harmony and composition the analysis of a multitude of particular facts. If he had not anticipated the objections which could be made to the drawbacks of this method, in the passage of his preface

---

Curiously, Fétis does not point out here a fundamental aspect of Weber's theory that has a particular resonance for his own, namely, that of "Multiple Meaning" (*Mehrdeutigkeit*), which applies to a number of musical parameters, including enharmonic modulation. He does, however, address the matter in his argument with Weber over his analysis of Mozart's "Dissonance" Quartet. For further discussion on this point, see the translator's introduction. [PL]

previously cited, one could have told him that the disadvantage of an overly-minute analysis of particular cases is to tire the attention of the readers, and to overload the memory with many facts that can escape at any moment, without hope of retrieving them, whereas general formulae apply to everything, and are not, as he says, sources of exceptions and contradictions.

338. The most notable of all systems which admit four fundamental seventh chords, differing through the nature of their intervals, but existing by themselves, is that which [Victor] Derode has published under the title: *Introduction à l'ètude de l'harmonie, ou exposition d'une nouvelle théorie de cette science*.[58] According to this theory, the third is the only origin of every chord.

The following series results from the arrangement of an ascending progression of thirds:

C, E, G, B-flat, D, F, A

With these notes the following chords are formed:

Perfect chord.	C	E	G.				
1st dissonant chord.	C	E	G	B-flat.			
2nd dissonant chord.		E	G	B-flat	D.		
3rd dissonant chord.			G	B-flat	D	F.	
4th dissonant chord.					D	F	A.

These, according to this system's author, are the only chords derived from successive thirds, and consequently the only ones that are found in nature. *The others are a matter of taste!*

Of these five chords, only one is consonant, the perfect major chord C-E-G. Derode does not wish that this term be assigned to the perfect minor chord, which is not given by nature; this, he says, is an *incomplete dissonant chord!* Now, if the perfect minor chord is not consonant, we understand that there cannot be a minor mode; moreover, Derode positively denies its existence.

If we examine the makeup of the above dissonant chords, we see that the first corresponds with Kirnberger's and Weber's first chord; the second, with their third chord; the third, with these same theorists' second chord, and that the fourth resembles their fourth. For the rest, in the two systems, these four fundamental dissonant chords have an equal primary existence.

But, in Kirnberger's and Weber's systems, these chords are placed on their tonal notes, while in Derode's system, we see the B-flat, that is, a

[58]Paris, Treuttel and Würtz, 1828.

note foreign to the key, appear in all of them. The reason for this peculiarity is that this system's author, taking as a starting point for his theory of the phenomenon of harmonics produced by the stretched and plucked metal string, heard (to a lesser degree than the perfect chord C–E–G) the dissonance B-flat. Now, here is Derode's reasoning: when this dissonance is heard on the tonic, it is no longer possible to remain on this tonic, because all dissonance needs a resolution; this resolution, he says, is made on the perfect chord of the lower fifth of the same tonic, that is, on F. The minor seventh chord, with major third, is therefore not (in Derode's system) that of the dominant, but that of the tonic. For him, the same chord, made up of the notes G-B-natural-D-F, does not belong to the key of C, but to the key of G.

However, B-flat does not belong to the key of C, but B-natural does! This is the most curious part of Derode's system; the scale, he says, does not exist. It is a conventional formula that is not justified by anything. Let us hear what he says on this matter:

“Does the scale, as a fixed series, present something necessary? The note, which follows or precedes another, is it directly created from the first? Does it form the second? Are these not three more or less independent events, which we choose to connect? And we know very well that this connection did not establish an essential dependency that did not previously exist. Thus, the C does not form the D that follows, since this D is the fifth of G; the E has no need of the D, which it follows, because this E comes from C, etc.[59]

As we see it, it is always the phenomenon of the harmonics of the sonorous body that guides Derode. The metaphysical law of cohesion that governs the position and the relationship of the notes of the scale is transformed in his imagination into an illusory arrangement. That this order of position results in the tonality and the connection of harmonies which it requires matters little to him, since this tonality is not his! It would be useless to argue with him about the facts of tonal attractions that result from harmonic combinations, which the generation of thirds has not given him; all this would be as if it did not exist: *these are matters of taste!* His system is logical; there is nothing to back down from; we can take it or leave it.

339. This system, published fifteen years ago, has not had, nor can have any success; for of all systems that have been undertaken to reconstruct the art on premises foreign to it, this is the most peculiar. I have presented this account only to show into what errors an educated and intelligent man may be dragged, when starting from the false hypothesis that harmony and its theory are the product of isolated physical events,

[59]See *l'Introduction à l'ètude de l'harmonie*, 344.

independent of our perceptual and intellectual organization, or rather dominating it.[60]

340. The generative principle of the succession of thirds, which we saw for the first time appear in Rameau's theory, and from which Derode drew such strange consequences, had been rigorously replicated before him by Langlé, professor and librarian at the Paris Conservatory, but, completely apart from any consideration of acoustical phenomena, and from any numerical theory. The work in which he set forth his system is entitled *Traité d'harmonie et de modulation*.[61] Langlé's stated purpose is to seek the true foundations of the science in the practice of the art. From the first words of the forward that he placed at the front of his treatise, one is given to believe that he has grasped the true principles of this science, for he protests against previously published books, where chords are considered in isolation, without regard for the laws of succession that govern them; but immediately afterward, we see him advance this curious proposition: *there is only one chord, that of the third, combinations of which produce all the others*. And to demonstrate this principle, he gives the example of the following succession of thirds: F-A-C-E-G-B-D-F; then he takes from this the perfect chord on the fourth degree, F-A-C; the perfect minor chord, A-C-E; the tonic chord, C-E-G; the relative minor chord of the dominant, E-G-B; the dominant chord, G-B-D; the major seventh chords, F-A-C-E, and C-E-G-B; the minor seventh chord with minor third, A-C-E-G; and the dominant seventh chord, G-B-D-F.[62] Now, in this classification, Langlé, like many other theorists, confuses everything by making, through his generation of thirds, classes of seventh chords, for example, of all kinds, as if these relationships existed on their own in music, aside from any consideration of the formation of chords by alteration, prolongation, and substitution. By this very notion he finds himself in clear contradiction with the beginning of his book. This fault, although not questioned by his readers, nevertheless made his system very difficult to understand, and harmed the success of the work. Moreover, shocking defects in the chord progressions that he gives as examples caused his book to be rejected by the group of professors at the

---

[60]Fétis remarks that: "it is in fact on mathematical principles that [Victor] Derode's theory rests, such that all considerations of the metaphysical connections of chords are excluded; however, by a kind of contradiction, in certain very difficult cases, the author is forced to declare that arithmetic and algebra are of no help in explaining the facts, and he must follow the rule of sensation." *FétisB*, 3:289. [PL]

[61]Paris, Naderman, 1797.

[62]In his entry under Honoré François Marie Langlé (1741-1807) Fétis remarks that this resembles Catel's use of the division of the monochord as the basis of his harmonic system, without the advantage of making a distinction between natural and artificial chords. *FétisB*, 8:43. [PL]

Conservatory, who, in 1800, were examining the various harmonic systems, and his theory was immediately forgotten.

341. [Johann-Gottfried] Schicht [1753-1823], director of the St. Thomas school in Leipzig, formulated his *Grundregeln der Harmonie* on an arbitrary choice of chords of which the dominant is the basis.[63] On this note he obtains the perfect major chord, G-B-D; the minor seventh chord, G-B-D-F; the ninth chord, G-B-D-F-A, from which he takes the leading-tone seventh chord, B-D-F-A, and the perfect minor chord, D-F-A; the eleventh chord, G-B-D-F-A-C, from which he takes the seventh chord with minor third, D-F-A-C; finally, the thirteenth chord, G-B-D-F-A-C-E, from which he takes the major seventh chord, F-A-C-E. The alteration of the intervals of these chords by accidentals completes the empirical harmonic system conceived by Schicht.

342. Upon close examination, the systems of Langlé and Schicht are identical in their principle, and differ only in the choice of the fundamental note that Langlé took, we know not why, at the fourth degree of the scale, while Schicht chose the dominant.

343. Amongst the harmonic systems based on the arbitrary choice of a certain number of fundamental chords, that of Reicha, former professor of composition at the Paris Conservatory, must be mentioned as having obtained the greatest success, and as having had ardent and devoted proponents. I am here obliged to go into greater detail than I did with the systems of Schicht and Langlé.

344. Discarding the consideration of the succession of chords which, since Sorge, had greatly advanced the science, and consequently the phenomena of harmonic construction resulting from prolongation, Reicha returns to the system of isolated chords, in which he forms an arbitrary classification, following certain considerations peculiar to him.[64] The basis of his theory consists of thirteen fundamental chords, consonant and dissonant, arranged in this order:

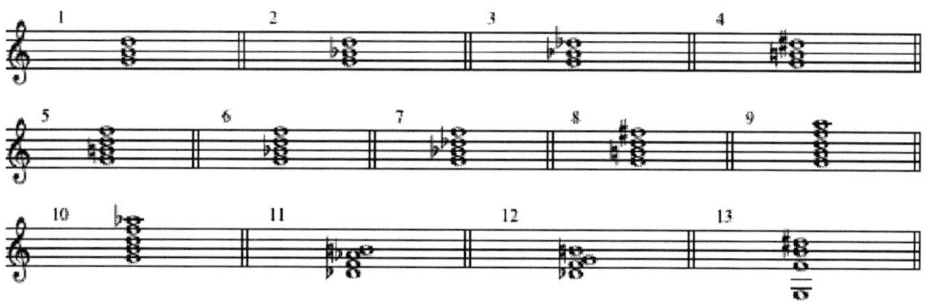

[63]*Grundregeln der Harmonie nach dem Verwechslungs Systeme* (Leipzig, Breitkopf and Haertel, 1812).

[64]**Cours de composition musicale*, or *Traité complet et raissonné d'harmonie pratique* (Paris, Gambaro).

345. From the very first steps taken by Reicha in the exposition of his principles, one sees a certain confusion in the basic ideas, which throws him into the maze of a multitude of particular facts; a most peculiar fault in a man who had taken courses in philosophy, law and mathematics in Germany.[65]

The first two chords in Reicha's classification are the perfect major and minor chords; the third is the perfect diminished chord (minor fifth and third), of which he makes a dissonant chord. In this he differs from the other authors of harmonic systems in the classification of isolated chords, who recognized as dissonant only the notes that clash at a second, or their inversions and doublings, of the seventh and ninth. What persuades Reicha to consider this chord as one of the dissonant chords is that, because of the effect of the very construction of the diminished (minor) fifth, there is a kind of attraction between the two sounds which make up this interval; but he should have seen that this attraction is not so forceful that it does not abate in a modulation following this chord, which does not happen in the case of a real dissonance, as long as it does not assume enharmonically the characteristic of a leading tone. The fourth chord in the classification is the augmented fifth; but here already is manifested the confusion of the ideas of this system's author, for in the chapter where he subsequently deals with this chord, he admits that it is only a perfect major chord with altered fifth.

346. The fifth chord is that of the dominant seventh, which he calls *first order*; then comes the sixth chord, which is this chord of the minor seventh with a minor third, the object of so many errors for all harmonists. Reicha calls it a *second order* seventh, and limits himself to saying *that it is used mainly on the second degree of a major scale* (*Cours de composition musicale*, 36), without being any more concerned about its original formation than with that of the other chords.

The seventh with minor fifth, called *third order* by Reicha, and the major seventh, or *fourth order*, the major ninth and the minor ninth, are equally considered by him to be fundamental chords of the same rank; and while chords 11, 12, and 13 are only alterations of chords derived from the

[65]It is certainly not beneath Fétis' dignity to make the occasional *ad hominum* remark against Reicha. With respect to Reicha's *Traité de mélodie* (1814), he proclaims that it is purely derivative and lacks any understanding of the principles of tonality. Fétis continues his invective: "His absolute ignorance of the history of music, and the little care that he has taken to study the monuments of this history, has, moreover, led him into serious errors." Fétis' profound distrust of empirical theoretical methods, and his fixation on the concept of tonality as the only viable approach to music of the modern era, blinded him to the significance of the emerging doctrine of the musical idea represented in the writings of theorists such as Anton Reicha and Alexandre Choron. For discussion on this point, see the translator's introduction. *FétisB*, 7:375. [PL].

augmented sixth, with fifth and fourth, and of the dominant seventh chord with augmented fifth, he nevertheless classifies them as fundamental.

It appears that Reicha arranged his thirteen chords more by chance than in a systematic order, because the thirteenth should clearly be placed after the eighth in order for his classification of chords of four tones to be similar to that of chords of three tones.

347. This theorist considers leading-tone sevenths and diminished sevenths as inversions of the two chords of the major and minor ninth (nos. 9 and 10): he presents the inversions in this form:

Although the origin of these inversions is unquestionable, how can the reader be made to understand a process of inversion where not all of the notes of the fundamental chord appear? A single consideration may explain and make clear the suppression of the fundamental note of the chord, namely, the substitution of one note for another, the true origin of these chords (see Book II, chapter 5, §117 onwards of this work). Without this consideration, the fundamental note cannot disappear in the inversions, and one could only understand the inversions of the two ninth chords in the following forms (see §124 of this work):

Fundamental chord 1st derivative 2nd derivative 3rd derivative

Fundamental chord 1st derivative 2nd derivative 3rd derivative

348. Admitting for a moment the possibility of separating the conditions of prolongation and others for the formation of seventh chords figuring in Reicha's classification, we see that to be consistent, he must classify the ninth chords in the same way, and that instead of two of these chords, he should have given five, in this order:

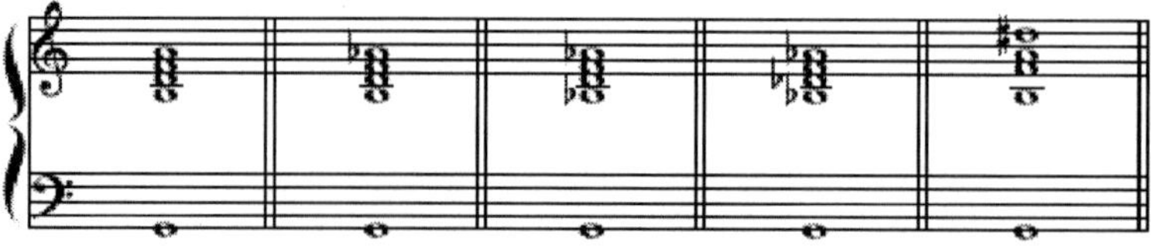

Would you say that many of these forms are only alterations (which is true)? I would ask why these alterations appear as fundamental in the seventh chords (nos. 7, 8, 13); and given that one cannot answer this question satisfactorily, I would have to say that the classification is incomplete, from the empirical point of view of Reicha's system.

349. We will complete our demonstration of the faults of this arbitrary classification. The most inexplicable element in this system is undoubtedly found in chords 11 and 12; for a chord in which the sixth is one of the constituent intervals could never be deemed as fundamental. In any form we consider it, whatever the arrangement of its notes, we can only see in such a chord an inversion of which we must find the fundamental chord. Now, the fundamental chord from which Reicha's eleventh chord is taken is that of the minor ninth of the dominant with an altered second degree:

When the substituted note is placed in the bass, the generation of this harmony appears in the following order:

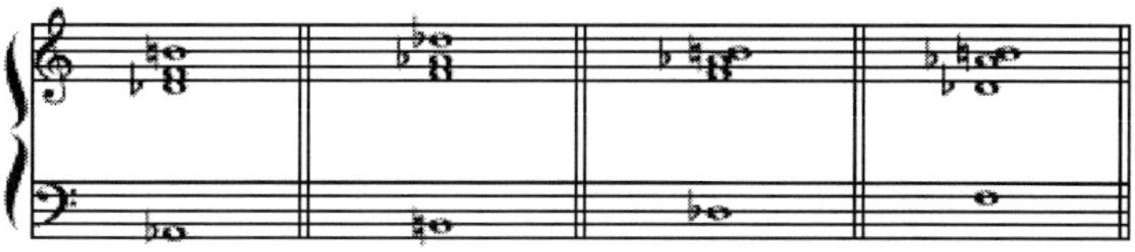

The eleventh chord of Reicha's classification is therefore not fundamental, and should not have been counted amongst those that are. Remarkably, he himself recognized it! For he says (page 10): "In the eleventh (chord), the fundamental note is suppressed, *and the chord is therefore inverted*." But, if this is so (which cannot be doubted), how can the placement of this inverted chord amongst those that are fundamental be explained?

Moreover, it is the same with the twelfth chord; for this chord, comprised of the third, fourth, and augmented sixth, is not fundamental and could not be fundamental. It is the second inversion of the dominant seventh chord, with altered fifth.

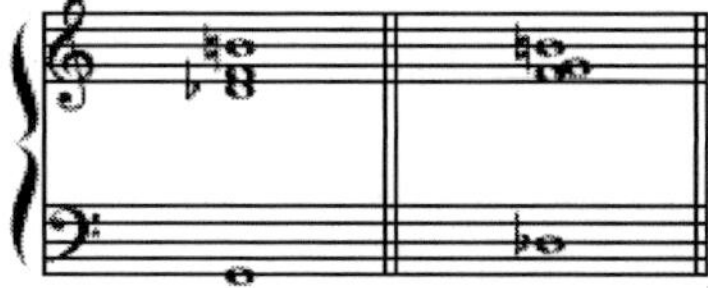

350. It is clear from the above that, even in terms of Reicha's own point of view, one is justified in declaring his classification of chords not

only incomplete, but also incorrect. This classification is all the more bewildering when one reads the following passage from the book in which it is contained:

"There are only thirteen chords in our musical system, as we have seen in the preceding table; but since these chords may be inverted and more or less altered by notes foreign to them (such as passing notes, grace notes, suspensions, etc.), it often happens that these inversions and alterations are considered as other chords that do not really exist, and which only clutter the mind and slow the students' progress (page 8)."

To read such things you would think you were dreaming. And what! Reicha admits that inverted (derived) chords, and those altered by foreign notes, suspensions, etc., should not be counted as real chords of the musical system! But, by the same account, the fourth, which is a perfect chord with an altered fifth; the sixth, seventh and eighth, which are the products of suspensions; the thirteenth, which is a natural dissonant chord with an altered fifth; finally, the eleventh and twelfth, which are inversions of altered chords, should disappear from the table of these so-called foundations of the musical system, and thus it would contain only six chords!

These observations suffice to show that Reicha's system, no less flawed than the systems previously analyzed, does not even have the benefit of their logical conception, but rests on a defective foundation. Such then is this system that has been much in vogue amongst various Parisian artists, because the professor who is the author of this work caused them to overlook his errors by his arguments and in the practical applications that he gave to his students. I repeat, this system is a conception of the least rational theory that could possibly be imagined, and the most deplorable return toward the crude empiricism of the old methods of the early eighteenth century. It ruined the good that Catel's method (which will be discussed in a moment) had done in France, and reopened the door to a multitude of false theories that were formulated in this country and elsewhere for the past few years. All the more dangerous in that it was supported by a justly respected name in other areas of the art, it again called into question what had been decided by the authority of reason and experience, and developed proponents who declared it a conception of genius, although in reality it could have led to the destruction of the science, if the science could perish.

Chapter IV

SYSTEMS BASED ON AN ARBITRARY DIVISION OF THE MONOCHORD

351. When the Paris Conservatory of Music was founded, in 1796, it brought together the most renowned professors in each branch of the art. Each taught according to his ideas and his method, because there had not

been time to prepare a set of guidelines for standardized instruction. Thus Rodolphe gave lessons in harmony according to his empirical method, devoid of all spirit of analysis;[66] Rey gave his course following the fundamental bass system; Langlé developed the results of the theory which we have already seen; and Berton used the practical method with his students, free from any consideration of system; for it was only a few years later that this well-known composer envisioned his genealogical tree of chords, and the dictionary which developed from it.[67]

The inconvenience of this diversity of method and system, however, was soon realized in a school where a unified doctrine should be the basis of instruction. A commission made up of Cherubini, Gossec, Martini, Lesueur, Méhul, Catel, Lacépède, the geometrician Prony, and the professors just mentioned, was instituted at the beginning of 1801, with the objective of debating and setting out the bases for a system of harmony. Rameau's system was the particular object of serious examination, because he still had many advocates in France; but the majority of the commission declared themselves in favor of a theory proposed by Catel, which he published shortly afterward in a book entitled: *Traité d'harmonie adopté par le Consevatoire, pour servir à l'étude dans cet établissement*.[68] The authority that the Conservatory already commanded in this period, soon caused the unquestioned acceptance of what the most renowned musicians in France declared to be the best: this was the final blow given to Rameau's system, and its abandonment was all the more complete and speedy since his remaining supporters were removed from public teaching at this time.

352. What then was this theory, so pleasing that the most informed musicians in France adopted it unquestionably, and suddenly obtained a

---

[66]*Théorie d'accompagnement et de composition, à l'usage des élèves de l'école nationale de musique* (Paris, Naderman, 1798).*

*Jean-Joseph Rodolpe (1730-1812) was appointed professor of solfége at the Conservatory in 1799. Fétis is highly critical of Rodolpe's solfége manual, attributing its success to the state of ignorance of French musicians at the time. His harmony text Fétis considers even worse. *FétisB*, 7:450. [PL]

[67]*Traité d'harmonie basé sur l'arbre généalogique des accords* (Paris, Mme Duhan, 1815); *Dictionnaire des accords*, 3 vols. (Paris, Mme Duhan, 1815).*

*Henri-Monton Berton (1767-1844) was a renowned and prolific opera composer. He was appointed professor of harmony at the Conservatory in 1795, director of music of the *Opéra italien* in 1807, elected to the Institute in 1815, and replaced Méhul as professor of composition in 1818. Fétis reports that his studies with Antonio Sacchini (1730-1786) focused more on the disposition of melodic ideas and the development and conduct of dramatic music than on formal training in harmony and counterpoint. Concerning Berton's harmony treatise, Fétis remarks that it dismisses the law of the analogy of chords through the similarity of their functions, resulting in an unnecessary multiplication of technical terms. *FétisB*, 2:175. [PL]

[68]Paris, 1802.

popularity that Rameau's works received only after thirty years of dispute and discussion? Catel expressed it in a single sentence: *In harmony there exists only one chord which contains all the others* (*Traité d'harmonie*, 5). What is this chord, and how is it formed? The following is a summary of what Catel has to say on the subject.

If we take a string tuned to the lowest G on the piano, and if we divide it in half, we find its octave; its third part gives the octave of its fifth; its fifth, the double octave of its third; its seventh, the interval of twenty-one, or double octave of its seventh; finally, its ninth, its twenty-third or double octave of its ninth. Thus, this division of the string results in a chord composed of G-B-D-F-A. In practice, this chord is called the *dominant ninth*. It contains the perfect major chord G-B-D; the perfect minor chord D-F-A; the perfect diminished chord B-D-F; the dominant seventh chord G-B-D-F, and the leading-tone seventh chord B-D-F-A. In continuing the operation of the division of the string at the third octave, that is, from the sound 1/8, one finds the notes 1/10, 1/12, 1/14 and 1/17, which produce the chord of the *minor ninth* of the dominant G-B-D-F-A-flat, and the *diminished seventh* chord B-D-F-A-flat. All these chords are fundamental and natural: by the inversion of intervals, similar natural chords are derived, and like the fundamental chords, are approached without preparation, as a result of the make-up of the tonality.

The formula from which Catel takes his theory is presented in the following way in his book:

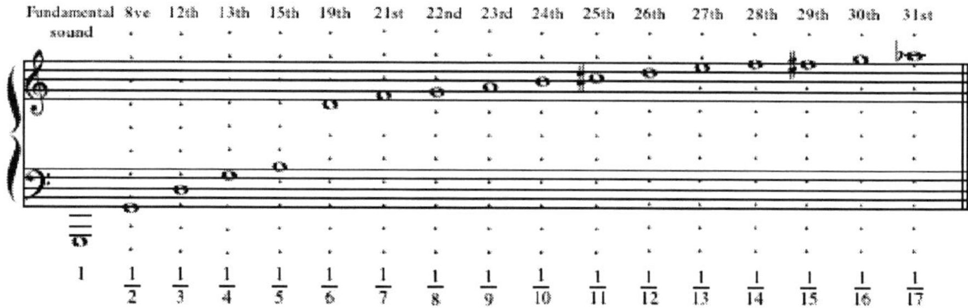

This division of the monochord is arbitrary, in that it does not represent an accurate tuning of the intervals, but an approximation. In fact, it is the expression of an inverse arithmetic progression.

353. The natural chords having been found, as we have just seen, Catel established that all other harmonic combinations are formed either by notes foreign to the chord, called *passing notes*, by prolongations that suspend or retard the natural intervals of chords, or finally by alterations of these same intervals. With regard to the substitution, Catel was not aware of it; but he had a kind of intuition about it when he said, with respect to the analogy of the use of the chord of the *diminished fifth* (minor

fifth and sixth), and those of the leading-tone seventh and the diminished seventh: *the similarity that exists between these chords proves their identity and clearly demonstrates that they have the same origin* (*Traité d'harmonie*, 14).

The results of this idea are fruitful, that is, the study of harmonies and the comparison of their destinations, conforming to the order of tonal succession. If Catel had taken this thought further, he would have left his successors nothing more to do, for he would have found the complete system of which he showed only certain parts.

354. With regard to prolongation, although he had not formulated the theory in a general way, and he was too attached to particular cases, he was well aware of the mechanics, with respect to consonant chords and some dissonant chords; but the obstacle against which other previous theories had run aground reemerges in Catel's theory, and leads to a similar wreckage. This obstacle is, as is well known, the minor seventh chord on the second degree, and the harmonies that derive from it. One must remember that in the dominant major ninth chord, produced by the division of the string, he found the perfect minor chord, D-F-A: this chord exists, therefore, for him, on the second degree of the scale, although it is not the one placed there in the determination of modern tonality. According to him, in the succession of this perfect chord to the one on the tonic, if this tonic is prolonged, it produces the seventh chord in question. But many difficulties present themselves here: (1) the perfect minor chord of the second degree does not belong at all to the tonality, while the prolongation that produces the seventh chord is tonal; (2) Catel can only demonstrate his so-called origin of the seventh chord by writing it in five parts, to make it complete, which is an exception, contrary to the principle of unity upon which must rest any true theory; (3) and finally, the principle of the artificial construction of chords by prolongation requires that the prolongation coming to a halt, the retarded chord takes place immediately. Now, all prolongation which produces a dissonance must resolve downward by one step; the application of this fundamental law has no place here, for if C, the seventh of D-F-A-C, were to descend to B, one would have a new dissonant six-five chord, D-F-A-B, which does not belong to the key, and would be the chord of the fourth degree of the relative minor key. I have proven this in many parts of this book. Catel was well aware of this difficulty; but not knowing how to deal with it, and not having been able to find the true origin of the chord, he resorted to this arbitrary rule the falsity of which is self evident, and which he states thus: "The prolongation may also be made on a chord already complete, in which the prolonged note will not have a resolution; but it must of necessity resolve downward by one step in the following chord." If Catel's views had been more general, and if he had known the device of substitution and the various combinations of collective modifications of

natural chords, he would have avoided the pitfall that shattered a part of his system.

355. If we look for what is original in Catel's system, and what he borrowed from his predecessors, or at least what he stated only after them, we will see that Sorge was the first to consider, in 1745, consonant harmony and that of the dominant seventh as forming the class of natural chords, but that he was mistaken in placing in the same category the minor seventh chord on the second degree, whereas Catel saw very clearly that he was forming an artificial harmony, although he did not discover the nature of the device. Sorge also understood clearly that some chords, notably the eleventh (of Rameau and Marpurg) were only the product of prolongations that formed artificial chords; but Schröter (in 1772) was the first to see that the seventh chord on the second degree is one of the chords in this class, even though he could not say how the prolongation operated within it. Finally, Schröter was the first to analyze clearly the elements of the alterations of intervals of natural chords and the new characteristics that these alterations give to them. If Catel had no knowledge of these authors' books, he at least reinvented what they had already published. But what is his own is the awareness of the correlation between chords of the major and minor ninth of the dominant, the leading-tone seventh, and of the diminished seventh with the dominant seventh chord; it is also the categorization that he created in various parts of his system, and finally the analysis of practical examples, where he demonstrated the ability of a great musician.

We are not surprised, therefore, with the overall success that his theory attained in France during the first fifteen years of the nineteenth century; we note, on the other hand, how many arguments seemed to oppose the backward steps that Reicha, and various other harmonists, tried to impose upon the science after the publication of this system.

356. Momigny,[69] a fervent opponent of Catel's theory, took however, as did this learned musician, the arbitrary division of the monochord as a point of departure in the science. The first work in which he set forth his ideas on this subject is titled: *Cours complet d'harmonie et de composition d'après une théorie neuve et générale de la musique, basée sur les principes incontestables puisés dans la nature, d'accord avec tous les bons ouvrages pratiques anciens et modernes, et mis par leur clarté à la*

[69]Fétis is merciless in his criticism of Jérôme-Joseph de Momigny (1762-1842), saying, "the weakness of his practical studies, and his complete ignorance of the literature and scientific study of music in foreign countries, in antiquity and in the middle ages, has given him limitless self-confidence, an arrogant air, and he has considered ideas debated for several centuries to be marvelous discoveries of his own genius." *FétisB,* 6:436. [PL]

portée de tout le monde.[70] From this period to 1834, Momigny reproduced or explained his system in polemic writings where he treats his adversaries with arrogance, and in various books that could not have made him popular.[71]

357. Taking the point of view of Levens, Ballière, Jamard and Sorge for the search for the bases of the constitution of the scale, Momigny finds them in the divisions of a sonorous string, following the arithmetic progression, which results in the scale C, D, E, F, G, A, B-flat; but considering that this scale does not conform to the music of modern Europeans, and that the B-natural is found only in the fifteenth division of the string, Momigny, instead of adopting, like Levens and his imitators, a scale of eight notes, with the B-flat and the B-natural, imagines that the string not be considered as a tonic, but as a dominant, so that its scale is G, A, B, C, D, E, F. He enumerates at length the advantages that result from the position of the tonic in the middle of the scale, like the *sun at the center of the planets*. For example, find the two semitones in the seven notes, without repeating the first at the octave, divide the scale into two perfect fourths, and have the two semitones in the same place in these fourths. For one of the most serious of Momigny's objections against the form of the scale beginning on the tonic rests with the major fourth, or *tritone*, which occurs between the fourth and seventh notes. He does not notice that it is precisely this relationship that is essential to tonality, and which leads to the final conclusion of all melody and all harmony.

358. The divisions of the string, considered as dominant, lead Momigny, with respect to harmony, to the same conclusions that Catel had obtained by the same means; but whatever his claims in this regard, he explains them much less clearly. Thus, like Catel, he arrives at the formation of perfect chords and of those of the dominant seventh and the leading-tone seventh as being the only natural chords; but as for the others, instead of explaining by what means they are formed, he calls them *chords that are not,* and labels them *major discords*, and *minor discords*,

---

[70]*Complete Course on Harmony and Composition According to a New and General Theory of Music, Based Upon Irrefutable Principles, Drawn From Nature in Accord With all the First Rate Practical Works, Old and Modern, and Placed, Because of Their Clarity, Within Everyone's Reach* (Paris, 1806), 3 vols.

[71]*La seule vrai théorie de la musique, utile à ceux qui excellent dans cette art comme à ceux qui en sont aux premiers éléments. (The Only True Theory of Music, Useful for Those Who Excel in this Art as Well as Those Who Are in the Beginning Stages)* (Paris, 1823).

Encyclopédie méthodique. Music published by Framery, Ginguené and de Momigny (Paris, 1791-1818), 2 vols.

General Music Course, for Piano, Harmony and Composition, from A to Z, for students, no matter how elementary, and for all musicians of the world, no matter how advanced. Paris, private printing at the place of the author, 1834.

so that the correct analysis of a combined harmony consisting of numerous prolongations joined with various kinds of alterations would be impossible for anyone who had read only Momigny's fastidious explanations. Besides, nearly all the examples he gives for the use of harmonies are poorly written, and prove that this writer had only confused notions about harmonic practice.

359. If one examines Momigny's claim to originality, one will realize that he borrowed the arithmetic progression from Levens, Ballière and Jamard; the carrying of the fundamental note of the scale on the dominant from Sorge; the division of this string from Catel, to derive from it the primary harmony; the combination of thirds for the formation of natural chords from Langlé, and the progressions of fourths and fifths for the formation of scales from Abbé Roussier. All that truly belongs to the one, who for thirty years spoke so confidently in favor of a system rejected by musicians, are a few insights, not lacking in accuracy, about measure and rhythm.

Chapter V

SUMMARY AND CONCLUSION

360. I must now conclude this extensive examination of what has been achieved since the beginning of the seventeenth century for the establishment of a science of harmony, and in particular from the time of its foundation as laid down by Rameau. In the final analysis we find that the principles of all systems fall into one of the following four categories: (1) the harmonic resonance of sonorous bodies, or more generally acoustical phenomena of various kinds, and the harmonic progression for which they provide the basis; (2) the arithmetic progression determined by the harmonic series of the horn or trumpet; (3) the arbitrary construction of chords by the addition and subtraction of thirds; (4) the arbitrary division of the monochord. It is therefore clear that all of these systems result more or less from sources that are not closely linked to the music itself, that is to say, to the art as it manifests itself in its immediate effects, and that in all of these it was necessary, up to a certain point, to adjust this art to the peculiar principle that was given to it.

The only thing not directly considered is to look for the principle of harmony in the music itself, that is, in *tonality*. But what is tonality? As foolish as this question may appear, it is, however, certain that few musicians could answer it in a satisfactory manner. For my part, I will say that tonality resides in the melodic and harmonic affinities of the notes in the scale, from which results the quality of necessity in their successions and aggregations. The formation of chords, the circumstances that modify them, and the laws of their succession are the necessary results of this tonality. Change the order of these sounds, invert their distances, and most of the harmonic relations will be destroyed. For example, try to apply our harmony to the major scale of the Chinese,

or to the incomplete minor scale of the Irish and the Scottish highlanders:

Our harmonic successions will become impracticable in these tonalities. How, actually, is a combined harmony like that of our music made in a major scale in which the fourth degree is a semitone higher than in our scale of the same type, and only separated from the fifth note by a semitone, so that the attraction that, in our harmonic system exists between the fourth and seventh notes, and constitutes the harmony of the dominant, is here between the tonic and the fourth degree, and thus renders any final cadence impossible? What does one make of a harmony similar to that of our minor mode in a minor scale where the sixth degree is a semitone higher than ours, and has no seventh note? It is clear that these things are not meant to go together. The Irish airs that have been published in anthologies of national airs are in the major mode, or belong to the modern era, which has allowed them to be harmonized somehow or other; the same can be said of Scottish airs and those from Wales, which, in addition, are often accompanied at the octave, or by the pedal, because their tonal character does not permit the cadences of our harmony. The unusual character that we see in these airs does not result from the fancy of their authors, but from the scale they were using.

What I call tonality is thus the order of melodic and harmonic features that result from the arrangement of sounds in our major and minor scales: if one of these distances were to be inverted, the tonality would assume another character, and the harmony would have totally different qualities. The immediate consequences of this tonality are to give certain notes a feeling of repose that does not exist in the others, and to assign to these notes the endings of cadences, that is, the perfect chord; these are the tonic, fourth, fifth and sixth degrees. The third and seventh degrees are denied this character of repose, and consequently are exclusive of the perfect chord. The relationship between the fourth and seventh degrees has a resolutive attraction that gives the dissonant harmony of the dominant seventh its particular character, and obliges it to resolve with a perfect or imperfect cadence, or be followed by a modulation; for there is no middle ground for the harmony of the dominant; it must resolve either in a cadence, or in a modulation. The rules that forbid the immediate successions of fifths and major thirds have no other origin; for two fifths in succession, ascending or descending, and two major thirds have the disadvantage of placing in immediate contact two tones that have nothing in common. All this, I repeat, is the necessary result of the form of the major and minor scales, and constitutes what are called the *laws of tonality*.

361. But, one asks, what is the principle of these scales, and who has determined the order of their notes, if they are not acoustical phenomena and laws of arithmetic? I answer that this principle is purely metaphysical. We conceive this order and the melodic and harmonic phenomena that result from it as a consequence of our customs and education. It is a fact that exists for us inherently, and independently of any external reason. And what! We would not want to admit that our instinct, combined with experience, was enough to set down in a scale the bases for enjoyment intended for our intellect, and we will search in some unknown acoustical phenomena for the secret cause of this organization of a tonality made to suit our purpose! Note, first of all, that these acoustical factors, poorly analyzed, do not have the significance that we give them without due consideration; because, for example, the production of the harmony of the perfect major chord, which one observes in the resonance of certain sonorous bodies, is accompanied by many other weaker resonances. The same is true with respect to certain other bodies that produce other harmonies. Besides, experience has proven that different types of vibration imparted onto the same bodies give rise to diverse phenomena. Troupenas has shown (*Revue musicale*, vol. XII, 125) that the interval of the *tritone* discovered by Baron Blein in the resonance of a square metal plate struck on one of its corners, is only the result of the diagonal vibration of this plate, while the vibration along one side of the plate brings about other phenomena. Let us suppose, to take the so-called natural bases of harmony to the outermost limits, that in the course of time we discover acoustical phenomena that produce every possible harmony in our system; would we then conclude that these unknown phenomena are the origin of the harmonies found *a priori* by great musicians. Truly, this would be a strange infringement of the effect alleged by certain sophists of secret influences on our decisions, and it would strike a severe blow to our philosophical freedom! Indeed, when Monteverdi found the dominant harmony that changed the character of music, and formed our tonality into uniform major and minor modes, no matter what the key, the fact of the diagonal vibration of the plate was for him nonexistent; he worked it out only by instinct and by certain analogous observations. His daring thought did not create the fact, but discovered it, and the principle that directed him is absolutely metaphysical.

Shall I speak of the acoustical phenomena of the harmonic series of the horn and trumpet, which coincides with the arithmetic progression? It provides, it is true, the elements of a scale, but of a false scale that is not ours, and we have seen what Levens, Ballière and Jamard were able to do with this.

Shall I speak of the division of the monochord, by introducing there, at the seventh term, the number recognized as necessary by Euler, as did Catel and Momigny? It contains the harmony of natural chords; but by stopping at these, there are neither all the notes of the scale, nor the elements of a tonality. To arrive at these, this division would have to be extended to all the tones, G, B, D, F, A, C, E, as Schicht has done; but then the natural and artificial chords will become confused, and the rational classification of these chords will no longer exist.

Shall I speak of the purely harmonic progression? It provides the exact measure of the unchanging intervals of the tonality of plainchant, where there is no interval endowed with attraction, but it cannot lead to the formation of a scale such as ours. Moreover, the acoustical phenomena and calculations, were they to give the elements of our tonality, would not provide the order in which they should be arranged so as to make up this tonality; and we have seen that this is where the real difficulty lies.

362. If it is recognized that the bases of these systems are illusive, that they have led astray everyone who used them as a starting point, and that they are powerless to support the edifice of tonality, it is clear that no other principle is left for the construction of the scale and of tonality than the metaphysical principle, a principle both objective and subjective, the necessary result of the sensibility that perceives the relationships of tones, and the intellect that evaluates them and deduces their effects. After so many centuries of study carried out in two totally opposite directions, we have come to recognize that the Pythagoreans were wrong in attributing to numbers a cause of tonal construction that they do not have; and that the Aristoxenians are no less incorrect in supposing that the ear possesses a faculty of comparison that it does not have. The ear perceives the sounds; the feelings find *a priori* the formulae of their associations, the mind compares their relationships, judges them, and determines the melodic and harmonic conditions of a tonality.

363. That established, the science of harmony is complete, for this science is nothing but the systematic explanation of the art. The tonic manifests itself by the feeling of absolute repose that it creates, and the dissonant harmony of the dominant rounds out this quality by giving it this character with its attractive resolution on the consonant harmony of this tonic.

The fourth, fifth and sixth degrees of the scale are also recognizable as notes of repose for the ability to conclude incidental cadences, with which these notes are provided; therefore, consonant harmony, that is the perfect chord, is also a part of their makeup. These harmonies, conforming to the key and the mode, are major or minor, because of the natural state of the notes. The third and the seventh degrees, which are separated only by a semitone from the notes immediately above them, and which therefore have an attractive tendency, can be considered neither as notes of repose, nor can they consequently carry the harmony of the perfect chord that has a quality of conclusion. Following the tonal order, only derived chords can therefore accompany them. The second degree of the scale, which can be a cadential goal only in a sequence, has only an ambiguous quality of repose. It follows that the harmony of the perfect chord does not belong to it in the ascending and descending harmonic progressions of the scale, and that this note is accompanied, in these formulae, only by a derived harmony.[72]

Therefore, only the perfect chord and the dominant seventh chord are natural fundamental chords. Following Rameau's great discovery, accepted in all harmonic systems, the other natural harmonies are derived from it through the inversion of the fundamental chords.

364. With fundamental and derived natural harmony, all harmonic tonality is established, and the possibility of modulation arises. The other harmonic groupings that can affect the ear are only modifications of these natural chords. The purpose of these modifications is to produce a variety of feelings on the one hand, and to establish a greater number of relationships between the various keys and modes on the other.

The modifications of chords consist of the *substitution* of one note for another; the *prolongation* of a note that retards an interval of the chord; the *alteration*, ascending or descending, of the natural notes of chords; *substitution combined with the prolongation; alteration combined with the substitution; alteration combined with the prolongation; ascending and descending alterations collectively; anticipations and passing notes*.

365. Substitution happens only in the dominant seventh chord and its derivatives. The substituted note is *always* the sixth degree that takes the place of the dominant. Thus, when the seventh chord is written in five parts, namely, G-B-D-F-G, if we substitute A for G in the upper part, that is, if the sixth degree takes the place of the dominant, we have the *dominant ninth* chord, which in accordance with the mode, is either major or minor. If we make a similar substitution in the first derivation (B-D-F-G), we have the *leading-tone seventh* chord B-D-F-A in the major mode, and the *diminished seventh* chord B-D-F-A-flat in the minor mode. It is the same with the other derivations. The correspondence of these chords and the origin of their formation are shown in the identical way they are used and in how they are determined tonally. Catel understood this equivalence well, and established the process of substituting a chord with its analogue; but he did not know the mechanism of the substituted note: a

[72]Fétis uses the term "derived" in two ways, as a synonym for the inversion of chords, and for the modification of chords through prolongation, substitution and alteration. [PL]

very important mechanism, since it leads to the demonstration of the origin of certain other chords which have been the pitfall of all theories.

366. In the succession of two chords, any note descending or rising a step may be prolonged into the following chord, where it retards the normal construction. If the prolongation produces a dissonance, it must resolve downward, like every dissonance that is not a leading tone; if it is a consonance, it completes its movement by rising. In this way a prolongation that retards the octave of the perfect chord produces a nine-five-three chord; one that retards the third produces a five-four chord; one that retards the sixth of the first inversion of the perfect chord produces a seven-three chord, and one that retards the sixth of the six-four chord produces a seven-four chord. In the same way, the retardation of the third of a seventh chord gives a seven-five-four chord; the retardation of the bass note, in the first inversion of this chord, produces a five-four-two chord; the retardation of the sixth, in the second inversion, brings about a seven-four-three chord. Finally, the retardation of the major fourth in the last inversion of the seventh chord produces a six-five-two chord. Note that in the seventh chord and its inversions, it is always the tonic that retards the seventh. The retardation does not affect, anymore than the substitution, the destination of natural chords, and their use remains exactly the same after the prolongation is resolved.

367. If we join the elements of substitution and prolongation, we have as a combined modification of the dominant seventh chord a nine-seven-four chord; in first derivation, a six-four-two chord; in the second derivation, a minor seven-five-minor three chord; finally, for the last derivation, a six-five-three chord. These combined modifications do not change the goal of natural chords; this goal remains the same as the resolution of the modifications. Such, therefore, is the origin of these seventh chords of the second degree, of the fifth and sixth, etc.; the origin of which has been the pitfall of all theories of harmony, because their authors ignored the mechanism of substitution and the collective modifications of chords.

368. Every note ascending or descending by the interval of a whole tone in the succession of two chords may be altered by a semitone. The ascending alterations are made with the addition of a sharp or by the removal of a flat; all descending alterations result from the addition of a flat or the removal of a sharp. All notes affected by an ascending alteration assume the character of an incidental leading tone, and must resolve upwards.

Alterations introduce a vast quantity of modifications to natural chords, and combine with simple substitution, prolongation and substitution combined with the retardation.

Ascending and descending alterations may be prolonged in the succession of two chords. When the prolongation is an ascending alteration, it must resolve upwards, although dissonant, because the character of attraction resulting from the incidental leading tone absorbs that of the dissonance.

From these complex modifications of natural chords result multiple affinities that relate all the keys and their modes, bringing to fruition the last period of harmonic development which I have called the *omnitonic order*, and providing the solution to the following problem: *For a given note, find the combinations and harmonic formulae necessary for it to resolve in any key or mode.* They also generate a large number of new chords not yet used by composers, and whose form, direction, and use, I have determined *a priori*, through analysis.

369. The anticipation is a device by which one hears in a chord one of the notes of the chord that must follow it. This device is always melodic, for it is the melodious part that uses it.

370. Passing notes are those which, either too rapid or of too little significance in the shapes of the melody or the accompaniment for each to have its own harmony, are nevertheless necessary to complete these forms. The ear allows the use of these bits of harmonic expletives, provided that they move by step, when they are foreign to the chords.

371. There are harmonic formulae called *progressions* or *sequences*, because the bass proceeds in a series of similar movements, such as rising by a second and descending a third, rising a fourth and descending a fifth, etc. In these progressions, one gives to each completed movement of the bass notes the same chords with which one accompanied the first. Some of these progressions modulate with each movement; others do not. In the latter, the mind suspends any idea of tonality and conclusion until the final cadence, so that the degrees of the scale lose their tonal character, the ear being preoccupied only with the similarity of movement. It follows that, in these non-modulating progressions, any chords may be applied to any notes. Thus, in a progression that rises a second and descends a third, one alternately places the perfect chord and the sixth chord on all the notes, with the result that the perfect chord, placed on the seventh degree, will have the minor fifth. Thus again, in a progression that rises a fourth and descends a fifth, beginning with the seventh chord on the dominant, one will place this seventh chord on all degrees, and the result of this similarity of movement and harmony will be a chord composed of a major third, perfect fifth and major seventh on the tonic and on the fourth degree, and the minor third, perfect fifth and minor seventh on the third degree and on the sixth. Such is the origin of the theories of Vogler and Schneider, who place the perfect chord and that of the seventh on all the notes of the scale, while in fact such a use of these chords would be destructive of all feeling of tonality, if it were done elsewhere than in non-modulating progressions, where the tonality is in effect destroyed until the cadence.

372. Having arrived at this point, the theory of harmony is at the concluding stage of the art and the science; it is complete, and nothing can be added to it. It is the theory that I have developed in this work. Rameau, Sorge, Schröter, Kirnberger, and Catel had in turn found the first elements, and I completed it, by placing it upon the unshakeable foundation of tonality. What demonstrates unassailably its excellence is that it is at once the history of the progress of the art, and the best analysis of the elements manifested therein.

END OF THE FOURTH AND LAST BOOK

NOTES

NOTE A
(see Book Two, chapter V)

The substitution of the sixth degree for the dominant in natural dissonant chords, for the production of the harmonic modifications of these chords, gave rise to objections from many distinguished artists and professors when I published the first edition of my *Traité de l'harmonie*. Mr. Zimmerman, my friend, a professor at the Paris Conservatory, learned musician and a declared proponent of Catel's system, attacked my doctrine on this point and many others, in the journal entitled *La France musicale*.[1] I wrote many letters on this subject which appeared in the *Revue et Gazette musicale de Paris*.[2] The first of these letters contained an in-depth discussion of the principle of substitution, the consequences of which are of the highest importance in the approach to the science: I believe I must give here an extract that will shed new light on this subject.

In the May 26, 1844 issue of *La France musicale*, Mr. Zimmerman said: *Mr. Fétis, who has founded his Theory upon the attraction between the fourth and seventh degrees of the scale, should have used common sense in the understanding of this attraction.*

Here is my response: "If I have not done that, my dear Zimmerman, in a book that had no other purpose, not only do you have the right to say that I lacked common sense, but you should add that I am the clumsiest theorist who ever undertook to formulate a system. Nevertheless, I admit

---

[1]Pierre-Joseph Guillaume Zimmerman (1785-1853) was a prominent pianist, theorist, composer, and piano pedagogue. Well versed in the theoretical orthodoxies of his time, he studied harmony with the Rameauian J-B Rey, and then with Catel. He was awarded first prize in piano (1800), the second going to Friedrich Kalkbrenner (1785-1849). In 1802 he was awarded first prize in harmony, and later studied composition with Cherubini. Fétis reports that he acquired an extensive knowledge of the art of writing. In 1816 he was appointed professor of piano at the Conservatory, and in 1821 turned down the professorship of counterpoint and fugue, which was then offered to Fétis. His students included César Franck (1822-1890), Charles-Valentin Alkan (1813-1888), Ambroise Thomas (1811-1896), Georges Bizet (1838-1875), and Charles Gounod (1818-1893), his future son-in-law. Fétis speaks highly of his *Encyclopédie du pianiste*, which contains a complete method on the art of piano playing and a treatise on harmony and counterpoint. *FétisB,* 8: 615. [PL]

[2]Year 1844, numbers 29, 32, 35, 37, 39, and 40.

that I do not see how I could have founded a theory on something that I did not adequately understand; for, either my deductions match the principle, and in this case I must have had an understanding of it in order to make them; or, the deductions do not follow the principle and from then on I would be contradicting myself, for which you have not reproached me; or, in fact the principle is false, and the consequences, rigorously deduced, are also false; now, under this assumption I would still have correctly understood the principle, only I would have erred regarding it. Let us see your opinion concerning the attraction between the fourth and seventh degrees.

"*Instead of attributing to I know not what contact between the fourth and fifth degrees the property of accepting the dominant seventh without preparation, Mr. Fétis should have recognized that this seventh, which contains the diminished fifth, owes it the privilege of being heard without preparation. It is the invigorating principle of the attraction that here manifests its power.*"

You thus glorify the attraction of two notes of the scale, which, alone, fashion it: from that moment on you are in agreement with me on what constitutes modern tonality. I formally take note of your declared opinion on this subject, for it greatly simplifies the discussion concerning the value of my theory. What you reproach me for, is to have admitted a duality of principles for natural dissonant harmony in the dominant seventh chord, that is, not only the attraction between the fourth and seventh degrees, but also, *I know not which contact between the fourth and fifth degrees*! You add, to completely clarify your thought: *Why is it that Mr. Fétis has not readily noticed that this fertile principle (the attraction of the fourth and seventh degrees) extends and transports its prerogative to the mixed and diminished sevenths that also contain this diminished fifth? The substitution has nothing to do with it. This new and pointless element only confuses and calls into question a fact henceforth accepted by the discipline.*

For the last two centuries, the diminished fifth has revealed its importance to us; let us not be ungrateful; let us not rob it of its privilege, and recognize what our art owes it.

I ask a great deal of your indulgence, friend, for the lengthy arguments into which I must enter in response to these lines. Criticism is quickly done when it attacks a principle: a few words suffice to refute it; but long analyses are necessary to justify it. And for a start I will point out that in your usual complete devotion to Catel's theory, the inevitable result of your education in harmony by this theory, did not find it necessary to discuss the part of my book where I established the reality of the genre of modification of natural harmony that I call *substitution*, and you oppose only the errors of this theory that I believe to have forever settled through methodical analysis in which nothing has been forgotten. It is particularly to the devoted disciples of Catel I had addressed myself when I wrote in the introduction to the chapter in which I treated this subject: *We touch upon one of the most delicate questions in the theory of harmony, upon one of the most singular facts of the art in which science has had to give an explanation. I must here redouble my care to clearly expose the consequences of the law of tonality in the phenomena in which it is found; but I cannot hope to reach the objective that I propose, unless the reader, granting me full attention, divests himself of preoccupations of theories based on other considerations than those of tonality*. Now, it seems to me that you are not free from these preoccupations, and that you have not granted me the complete attention that I asked; for you oppose simply what I have disproved, as if I had not understood it, or as if I neglected it.

What had I established before taking up the matter of substitution, and other modifications of the natural chords? I had demonstrated that all modern tonality is made up of the perfect chord and the dominant seventh and their derivatives; that only they are necessary; that they suffice in all instances of melodic succession, and that the other harmonic combinations are only modifications of them; modifications born in the imagination and of the desire for variety which our senses enjoy. Thus, dear Zimmerman, one must begin with a clean slate before attacking what I call *substitution*. But the way, after you have granted me that Monteverdi established modern tonality by using the minor seventh chord with major third without preparation, that is, the double attractive contact of the fourth degree of the scale, the fifth and the seventh? The way, for that matter, to deny the evidence that all music may be reduced to the harmony of natural chords of which I have spoken, by stripping away the various kinds of modifications to which chords are susceptible; whereas, if one suppresses a single one of these chords, the music would be instantly destroyed? This is a truth that anyone may immediately ascertain through experience. I believe that I have already told you: I am a stubborn logician; after a principle has been conceded to me, its consequences must be accepted. Now, if modern tonality is complete with the perfect chord, the dominant seventh and their derivatives, all the other harmonies are just their modifications; all that remains is to discover what kinds of modifications these are. To use the language of philosophy, I would say that the initial chords are the general and the essential in music, and that the others are only the contingent.

According to you, or rather according to Catel, whose opinions you have adopted, the chords that you call with him *mixed seventh* and *diminished seventh*, that is, B-D-F-A, and B-D-F-A-flat, are chords that are as natural as the dominant seventh chord, G-B-D-F, since they are approached, like it, without preparation; and you think that they owe this prerogative to the attractive relationship of the fourth and seventh degrees that exists in the seventh chord that you call *mixed*, and in the diminished seventh. The *substitution*, you add, is not needed there. Let us examine these propositions.

First, let us not infer that if a chord may be heard immediately and without preparation it is fundamental (*primitif*) and necessary; for altered chords are in the same position, although one can certainly not say that they are neither necessary nor fundamental: they would even destroy the feeling of tonality if the musical understanding did not make a quick judgment on the nature of the modification, and did not reestablish through thought the altered note or notes into their normal state.

Next, you give too much importance solely to the attractive character of the relationship of the fourth and seventh degrees: this character of attraction is only complete, compelling, when these two notes are combined with the fifth degree. Remember these successions that you yourself have used a hundred times:

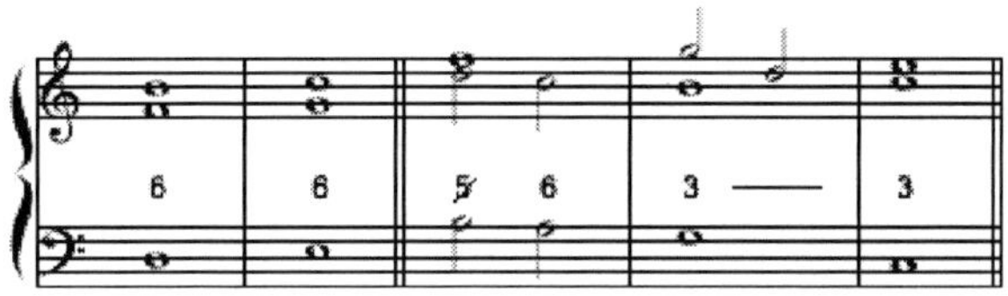

There is no attraction here: the harmonic movements are free although the fourth and seventh degrees are placed in relationship.

You say, in speaking of the relationship between the fourth and fifth degrees, that I considered necessary to determine tonal attraction: *I do not know which contact*, etc. What do you mean by that? That you do not know which law of nature established this contact? Oh! My esteemed friend, I do not know any more than you in this regard; our ignorance, everyone's, is equal; for we know the phenomena that affect our senses only by their effects; the substances and primary causes will be an eternal mystery for us. But if these words, *I do not know which contact of the fourth and fifth degrees*, have a negative meaning, I will find myself, with respect to you, in the situation of the philosopher to whom movement was denied and yet walked; I will direct you back to the phenomena itself, to the dominant seventh chord, and my answer will be triumphant; because it arises from a fact the existence of which I will prove by the fact.

Now, what is substitution, and what assurance do we have of its reality? Substitution, you have seen it in my book, is the power to sound in the dominant seventh chord and in its derivatives the sixth degree in place of the fifth, by virtue of a law that is no more known to us than other harmonic phenomena, but of which our make-up accepts the effects, and of which our intellect grasps the mechanism. When the seventh chord is accompanied by the octave of its principal sound (G-B-D-F-G, or G-B-F-G), if one substitutes the sixth degree of the major mode for the fifth, one has a dominant major ninth chord (G-B-D-F-A, or G-B-F-A). The same substitution in the first derivation of the seventh chord (B-D-F-G) gives a seventh chord (B-D-F-A), which I call *leading-tone seventh*, due to the note that serves as its root. The same substitution in the second derivation (D-B-F-G) produces a chord of the fifth and leading-tone sixth (D-B-F-A); finally, the same substitution in the third derivation (F-B-D-G) results in a chord of the tritone with third (F-B-D-A). Each of these chords thus modified has the same overall goal, and fulfils the same functions as the primary chords; for these successions:

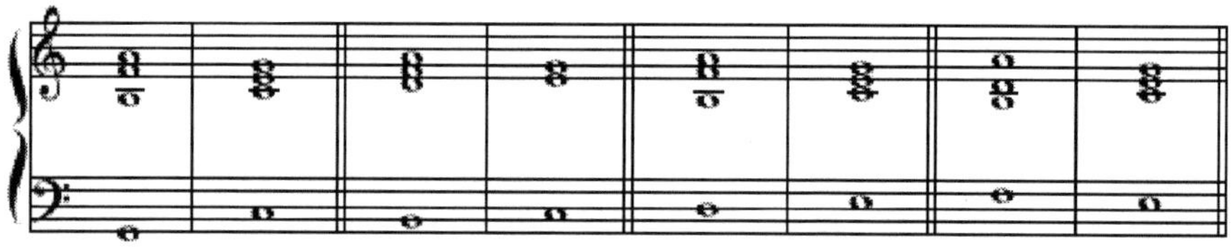

represent the following:

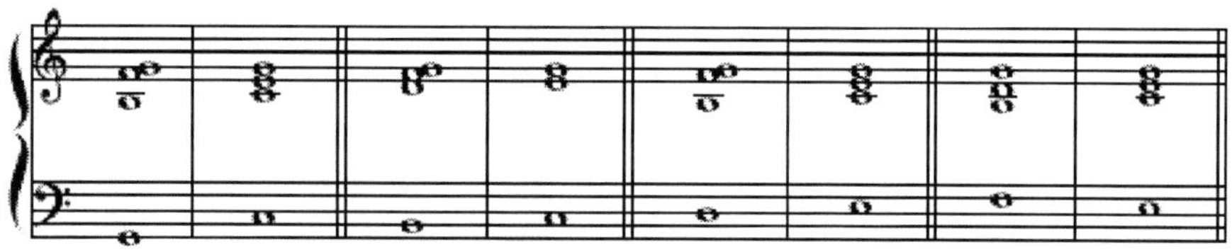

And yet a difference exists between the chords modified by substitution and the original chords; for the intervals of the latter sound pleasant in all their respective positions, and one may listen with as much satisfaction to the same chord in the forms D-F-G-B, or D-G-B-F, or D-B-F-G, while the two notes B and A in the chords modified by substitution offend the ear, if they are not held at the distance of a seventh, which permits only one form of each chord, and consequently limits the use of these modified chords to a small number of cases. For the same reason, the substitution may not be used for the lowest note of the dominant seventh chord to replace G-B-D-F, by A-B-D-F; for the two dissonant notes would be at the interval of a second.

It is here that one clearly sees the truth, the correctness of a theory of harmony based on the law of tonality, and that shortfalls and errors prove to be the natural consequences of systems established on considerations of isolated chords. Catel, not having seen that the circumstances giving rise to the dominant major ninth chord and that of the leading-tone seventh are the same, and are derived from the same principle, has made them two fundamental chords, each having their derivatives. Now, the second of these chords (B-D-F-A) has, he says, as derivatives D-F-A-B; F-A-B-D; and A-B-D-F; but too good a musician in practice not to know that these chords have, in these forms, a harsh and unpleasant harmony that does not permit their use, he establishes first of all an essential exception with these words: *In order to use the first and second derivation of this chord in a more pleasant way, the interval of the second, which is found therein, must be presented under the inversion of the seventh.* His difficulty is greater with regard to the last derivation, which, following the doctrine of the law of tonality, would result in the substitution of the sixth degree for the lowest note of the dominant seventh chord. This last derivation (A-B-D-F) is not usable, he says, without the preparation of the bottom note.[3] Thus, here is a so-called fundamental chord in which two derivations are found to be usable only by inverting their form, and in which the third does not share in the nature of the fundamental, because it must be *prepared*, and the fundamental is considered by Catel in the class of *natural chords*, that is, chords which do not need preparation! Has one ever seen such a complete absence of logic?

But we are not at the end of the confusion of ideas that can be pointed out in this part of Catel's theory, for, friend, recall this passage from his *Traité d'harmonie* (15): *The leading-tone seventh does not belong exclusively to the major mode: there are instances where one uses it without preparation on the second note of the relative minor mode. Then it is called the chord of the second note of the relative minor mode. It resolves on the dominant.*

It is because of this double employment that this chord is called a mixed seventh.

Since (considering that) *in the minor mode this chord is used much more often with prepared seventh than without preparation, it is now only a diminished fifth chord* (minor fifth) *that is prolonged by the seventh. Thus, it enters into the series of simple chords that are prolonged by a foreign note.*

What can one say? If this chord is the product of a prolongation, its use without preparation is therefore not admissible in any case; and if it does not have the same origin as the artificial leading-tone seventh chord, it is therefore not the same; and the idea of a *mixed* chord, belonging to two keys and to two different modes, having two origins and two contradictory uses, is therefore absolutely false! You see, my dear Zimmerman, that your objections to the coherent theory that I have presented of two chords that Catel has incorrectly mistaken for one, having been drawn from this notion completely lacking in logic, collapse with this unfortunate concept, of which I have shown the obvious contradictions in chapters five and six in Book Two of my *Traité de la théorie et de la pratique de l'harmonie*. One thing astonishes me, that you have been silent in your criticism of my principle of substitution, on this analysis of an important fact by which I addressed your objections in

---

[3]*Traité d'harmonie*, 14.

advance, and in such a way, it seems to me, as to not allow any possible reasonable response.

But this principle of substitution, which seems to you a *new and pointless element*, although I have demonstrated that it follows necessarily from the law of tonality, and that without it the construction of a complete and rational system of harmony, conforming to the facts of practice, is impossible, this principle, I say, has been expounded and recognized by Catel himself, though he saw neither the mechanism nor the influence; for he has said in speaking of the dominant seventh and ninth chords: *The similarity that exists between these two chords proves their identity, and clearly demonstrates that they have the same origin.* Now, if the similar use of these chords demonstrates the identity of their origin, although their form is not exactly the same, it is only a matter of discovering the circumstance that brings about the modification, and one would find none other than the substitution of the sixth degree for the dominant, in the upper note of the chord. Upon further examination, we see that the same thing happens in all the derivations of the seventh chord, and we thus find the origin of the leading-tone seventh chord and all the others of the same kind. Finally, the dominant seventh chord having in the minor mode the same make-up as in the major, we see again the same situation, that is, the substitution of the sixth degree of the minor mode for the fifth, which results in the dominant minor ninth chord, the diminished seventh on the leading tone, etc. Moreover, one comes to believe that this substitution is melodic, which amply indicates the purpose of requiring the substituted note at the top of the chord, and we avoid the anomaly into which Catel falls of a substitution in the lowest note of the chord, and the awful contradiction of a derived chord which does not have the same nature as the fundamental. In my theory, which is that of nature and art, everything is general and regular; in Catel's, which you have undertaken to defend, everything is full of contradictions, exceptions and doubtful principles.

You say that by obtaining the leading-tone seventh chord from a substitution, I give it only a conditional existence: however, you add, this chord B-D-F-A, in the major mode, and its resolution C-E-G, produce all the notes of the scale.[4] First I would point out to you that it is not I who give a conditional existence to the leading-tone seventh chord, but the nature of the chord itself along with its functions in the music. For it to have a necessary existence, independent, absolute, it should be, like the dominant seventh chord, indispensable in the context of harmonic sequence in modern tonality; that it have as the only condition its dissonance always occupying the top position, as a melodic note, be it in root position or inversions, and that its intervals may be arranged in all positions, like those of the fundamental chord of which it is the substitute.

---

[4]From the fifth letter, *Revue et Gazette musicale*, 1844, No. 40.

Now, this is not the case, and this is why the existence of the leading-tone seventh chord is only contingent or conditional.

But the absence of generality and necessity that one notices in this chord does not deprive it of its tonal character, nor of its attraction. It may even substitute for the harmony of the dominant seventh in certain cases, it represents it and completes its functions in the sphere of harmonic events where it is used; from which it follows that one must find all the notes of the scale in its make-up and resolution.

NOTE B

(See Book Two, Chapter VII)

The theory that I have set forth in Book Two, Chapter VII of this treatise, concerning the origin of certain chords by the joining of the substitution and the retardation of natural notes in dominant seventh chords and its inversions, has been the object of much criticism, notably by Mr. Zimmerman, in his letters published in *la France musicale*. I believe I recount here these criticisms with the responses that I gave to them in *la Revue et Gazette musicale de Paris*. Here we find a new source of instruction on this subject.

This is how Mr. Zimmerman expressed himself:

"Obscurity for obscurity, if it were absolutely necessary to endure the mode of substitution, I would just as well resign myself to the luxury of two substitutions than to the complication of the retardation and the substitution." He later added: "Mr. Fétis has only touched upon the mode of substitution that he proposes. We have just pointed out that, in the minor mode, it may happen that two simultaneous substitutions are devised; since the path was paved, clinging *to his substitution*, Mr. Fétis should have gone much further and drawn all the conclusions from this new doctrine; at least he would have had a complete system by obtaining the various kinds of seventh that are found on the degrees of the scale, for example:

MAJOR MODE

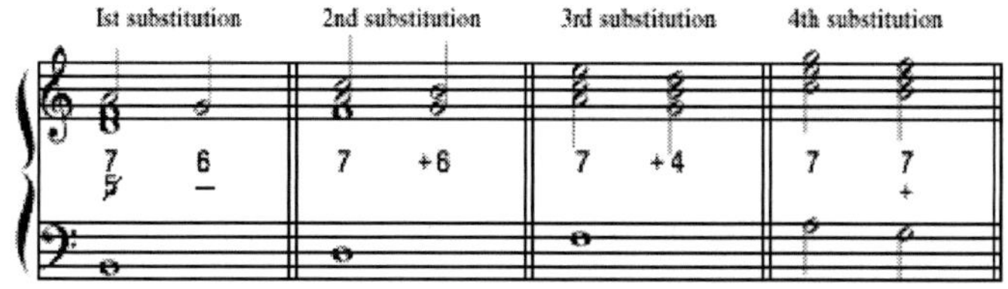

1st substitution 2nd substitution 3rd substitution 4th substitution

This was my answer:

Dear Zimmerman, the curious passages that I have just recounted throw me, I confess, into profound astonishment. You are too great a musician that I may be permitted to think that you have not understood what I have clearly established. On the other hand, you have too serious a spirit to be merely jesting. Finally, it is not possible to believe that you would wish to argue with me through a kind of irony. What then can it be, and what do you mean by this phrase: *Fétis clinging to his substitution*? Have I a substitution, myself? Have I (as you say) *proposed* this substitution? Now, my friend, there is absolutely no one who, without insulting our feeling and intelligence, can propose to insert into harmony what is not contained in it since creation. We only discover the phenomena of the relationships of sounds, and establish their identity with the operations of our faculty of understanding, through the impression of sensibility. This substitution, it is not I who wishes it: it is Catel, it is you, it is everyone; I have only discovered and analyzed its mechanism.

But if I had wished to create the chords that you give as examples of the combination of several substitutions, in your way of understanding this kind of modification of natural chords, I would have attempted the impossible; for I would have wished to establish an arbitrary system in place of reality, and universal feeling would have spurned my pretentious foolishness. You have, of course, used the chord B-D-F-A without preparation, on the seventh degree of the major mode, as you have B-D-F-G; but you have never used in the same way the chords D-F-A-C; F-A-C-E; A-C-E-G: in all of these, you have prepared the dissonance. This fact is decisive and suffices to demonstrate that these chords do not arise from the mechanism of substitution, but from certain other harmonic circumstances of which I will speak.

I have said that the second kind of modification of the natural dissonant chord is the retardation of one of its notes by the prolongation of a preceding note; this, the retarded note is *always* the leading tone by the prolongation of the tonic. Instead of these natural successions,

one therefore has these:

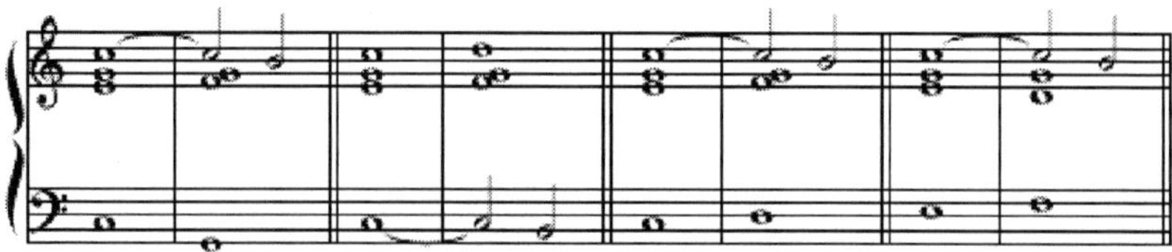

You probably do not disagree with these harmonies that are found in all music! It is impossible, for this is the requirement of tonal tendencies. Now (and notice, we have arrived here at the important point that always comes up in our discussions), I have definitely established, as much by the power of reasoning as by the persistent analysis of the facts of experience, that the various kinds of modifications introduced into natural chords are independent of each other, and that they each accomplish the purpose of their destination, without being influenced by occurrences of other modifications; wherein lies the possibility to combine them without loosing their identity. This is frequently seen in the alterations that accompany prolongations, or in double alterations, where one is ascending and the other descending. Why then, tell me, do you find the combination of substitution and prolongation so repugnant? Is there not evidence, to the contrary, that all the following successions are only one and the same tonal fact?

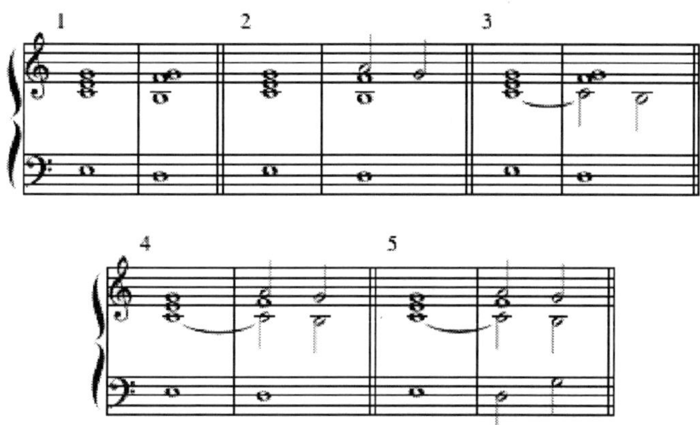

The minor seventh with minor third chord on the second degree, which is the product of substitution combined with prolongation, is presented by Catel as the result of a prolongation of the seventh on a perfect chord *already complete*. You support this theory with the following observation: *These prolongations, like all those of the same nature, find their resolution in the following chord. This circumstance brings about a great difference between the prolongation added to a chord already complete, and the retardation, the name of which alone indicates the task of retarding one of the notes of the chord that is being modified. This process of prolongation produces all the seventh chords with perfect fifths. This theory, so inspired, owes its acceptance to its admirable simplicity. This is not new; but very true.*

Something remarkable, friend, is the power of principles on the operation of our minds! What appears to you as an irrefutable given truth and of an admirable simplicity in Catel's theory, is precisely what has revealed to me the errors, and which appears to me the stumbling block on which it perishes. Therefore, let us examine carefully this difficulty.

The essential difference that one finds on this point between your theory and mine is that you bring in the chord of the minor seventh with minor third, on the second degree of the scale, from a modification of the consonant harmony, whereas I draw its origin from two modifications of the natural dissonant harmony; from which there results, following the principal of tonality that you have adopted according to my theory, that this chord, as well as all those of the seventh with perfect fifths (except that of the dominant seventh) must have preceded the introduction of the latter in music; for you recall what I have established, and what you have admitted, namely, that consonant harmony, with its modifications, makes up all music of the early tonality, and that modern tonality is the fruit of natural dissonant harmony. This being the case, we should see appearing in early music (which preceded the dominant seventh chord) the minor seventh chord of the second degree, as well as the other seventh chords with perfect fifths, and consequently the six-five chord, the six-four-three chord, and finally the six-four-two chord: now, is it not a most singular fact that these chords, born, according to Catel and you, of consonant harmony, are not encountered in the multitude of masses, motets, and madrigals written during the more than two centuries before the introduction of the dominant seventh chord in music, whereas one sees them appear after this chord had changed the tonality? And do not believe that this is the result of chance; there is no chance against the principles of things; these must exhaust all their potentiality before other principles are established.

Moreover, you, a pupil of Cherubini in the art of writing, remember his lessons, and remind yourself of his rules concerning the exclusion of the seven-five, six-five, and other harmonies of this kind in counterpoint. These rules, presented in an empirical way by Cherubini, were for him only school traditions the origins of which had not been explained in his youth, because his teacher, because all the teachers in Italy did not know more than he did in this respect; but when, guided by the law of tonality, I had demonstrated, in my *Traité du contrepoint*, that these harmonies were rejected, because they did not result from the modification of consonant harmony, Cherubini, even though he did not like new ideas in matters of doctrine, was struck by the obviousness of this deduction, and congratulated me precisely on this point, in his report to the Institute on my work. Once more, my dear Zimmerman, the principal of tonality having been established and admitted, all its consequences must be accepted. There is, there can only be, in all music based on consonant harmony and on its modifications, sevenths retarding sixths, accompanied by the third, and without the fifth; a prolongation is not possible on a perfect chord, *already complete*, except that which produces the ninth by the retardation of the octave. Finally, a prolongation that is not a retardation is absolutely incomprehensible, and has never existed but in

Catel's head. Besides, how does he make the resolution of this so-called prolongation on a complete perfect chord? Is it not on the harmony of the dominant seventh (*Traité d'harmonie*, 23)? And does this fact not demonstrate absolutely that it is this harmony that is retarded by the prolongation? Yet, my friend, here is the theory that you praise for its admirable simplicity! There is a much simpler theory, which I have analyzed in my book; it consists of placing on all the degrees of the major and minor scales the perfect chord or the third and fifth, the seventh chord and the ninth chord, as if existing on their own, and differing only in the nature of their intervals. Nothing could be simpler than this; nothing more clear! Only it is false, for most of these chords do not exist *a priori*.

I have given fitting commendation to Catel for the service he has rendered in France, by eliminating from the science of harmony the consideration of isolated chords, replacing it, for a large number of chords, by facts of succession, and bringing about in particular, in the formation of harmonious groupings, retardations and alterations. This was a large step taken toward a rational and complete theory of harmony; unfortunately, the intellectual forces of this distinguished musician failed when faced with certain difficulties, and allowed him to attain only a part of the goal that he set for himself.

These responses rest on such superior considerations, and on facts stamped with such clarity, that they have found only approval amongst artists. However, Mr. Zimmerman did not consider himself defeated, for he published in number 34 of *La France musicale* (year 1844) a retort in which he attempted to reject my arguments concerning the impossibility of taking from consonant harmony the seven-five chord, six-five etc. Concerning the absence of these chords in the works of musicians preceding Monteverdi, he says in this rejoinder:

"Reflections on what the former masters have or have not done would only bring about a more or less mellifluous jargon, but completely ineffective."

Here is my response to this passage: "I think, unlike you, that there is more than jargon in the examination of what has been drawn from a principle, when this principal was in use; and my opinion in this regard is in accordance with many justly celebrated scholars. The profound metaphysician Maine de Biran demonstrated very well, in his book *De l'influence de l'habitude sur la faculté de penser*, that the consequences of a principle are better understood and put into practice by those who are governed by it when the principle is simpler, and can be more easily exhausted.[5] Now, this is precisely the case with respect to consonant

[5]François-Pierre-Gonthier Maine de Biran (1766-1824) was awarded first prize at the Institute for his essay *Sur l'influence de l'habitude* (1803). Although his early work draws on the empiricism of Locke and Condillac, he eventually rejected the idea that

harmony, which is the only one the early masters knew. Confined by it within very narrow limits, their genius focused, as early as the end of the fourteenth century, on the search for ways to introduce variety into very restricted combinations, and discovered the existence of artificial dissonances by the retardation of consonances. From the middle of the fifteenth century, all the circumstances of these simple prolongations had been discovered; but the desire for variety in pleasure, which plagues every generation, was not yet satisfied. Not finding anything more in harmony, artists turned their attention to forms, and it was thus that they invented and gradually perfected all the kinds of imitations and canons. They even became excessively pedantic in the use of these forms, because of the impossibility of finding other means within the strict boundaries of their harmony. And would one not wish that a multitude of musicians of the first rank, such as Goudimel, Clément Jannequin, Palestrina, Roland de Lassus, and a hundred others, might have been troubled during an entire century to find new harmonic combinations, and that they would not have discovered seven-five, six-five, four-three, and six-four-two chords, if these chords could have been deduced from consonant harmony? No, no, this cannot be, for such an actuality would be a manifest contradiction with the natural and progressive development of the human mind! There is no ineffective jargon here, but reasoning based on the nature of things, and victorious, if ever it was, in the eyes of anyone who is accustomed to philosophical method.

Next you say on the same subject: "New elements were successively introduced into musical art: Is this to say that these elements can only be linked in chronological order? Alterations, appoggiaturas, etc., come together with perfect chords, as with the dominant seventh."

My friend, I will begin again here to cite authorities, before entering into my own explanations, and I will tell you to examine the seven volumes of studies given by Mr. Cousin, from 1815 to the end of his professorship.[6] There you will see this scholar, of so distinguished a mind, defend in a hundred places that the facts, the ideas, even the men who exercise the greatest influence on their contemporaries, are the necessary products of their times, that is, of the principles that are in use. Separated from the chronological order to which they are attached, these facts, these ideas, these men lose their very meaning. These propositions, to which

conscious experience is formed only from passive impressions, viewing it rather as a dynamic interaction between a self-conscious will and external conditions. [PL]

[6]The philosopher Victor Cousin (1792-1867) was influenced by Maine de Biran's ideas concerning the voluntary activity of the will in determining facts of consciousness. Fétis's notion that the history of tonality is one of transformation rather than progress may have been derived from Cousin. [PL]

Mr. Cousin's dialectic imparts the irresistible quality of inevitability, are in fact only the development of Maine de Biran's proposition.

Now, let us apply this doctrine to the questions at hand, and we will find the demonstration that the successive introduction of the new elements of which you speak into the art establishes exactly a chronological order of principles and consequences in the facts relating to harmony, and that by disconnecting them from this order, they lose their significance. See, for example, Vicentino, and later Marenzio, Croce, and Gastoldi, instinctively tired of the monotony of the tonality of their times, and attempting to break away from it by the successions of perfect chords on different notes, as I have shown in my *Traité de la théorie et de la pratique de l'harmonie* (page 159 onward). However, they cannot realize their thought, because they lack the instrument of transition. This instrument is the attraction that forces the resolution and serves as a link between the harmonies. Tonal attraction is originally found only in natural dissonant harmony, that is, in the dominant seventh chord and its derivatives, and these chords at the same time constitute tonality, by their quality of attraction and means of transition, in that they may be heard in any key that they occur, without being preceded by other chords, and because they immediately determine the new key by their tendencies. The perfect chord, on the contrary, is always at rest; thus it could not establish the necessary succession; thus it is not true, as has been said, that the musicians that I have just mentioned were the creators of chromatic harmony. This music could only have been created by the harmony of the dominant seventh: to suppose the possibility before the dominant seventh would be a fundamental error.

Here then are *some new elements introduced into music, and which can only be linked in their chronological order.*

"But, you say, *alterations, appoggiaturas, etc., group themselves with perfects chords as with the dominant seventh.*" This statement is true; but there again is the triumph of a theory into which one must factor the consideration of the chronological order of harmonic elements; for the idea of altering the notes of the chords, to increase the attractive tendencies, came to harmonists only after the existence of the fact of attraction had been demonstrated to them by natural dissonant harmony. Consonant harmony could never have revealed the possibility by itself. I would add that after the alteration had been applied to it, it lost its character of repose in the altered chords, and consequently changed its nature. Consonant harmony, having by itself no tendency, could not offer the means of leaving a given key, and therefore constituted the *unitonic* state of music; natural dissonant harmony, having provided the attractive element, and consequently the means of transition, brought the art to the *transitonic* state, and created modulation. Finally, the alterations of the natural notes of consonant and dissonant chords, having greatly increased the attractions, placed certain notes in context with several keys, such that they opened the paths of different resolutions for the same chord, and consequently created the *pluritonic* state in music. I have shown, in Chapter Five, Book Three of my *Traité de l'harmonie*, how the multiple alterations of natural dissonant chords and those affected by substitution lead to tendencies towards all keys, and constitute the *omnitonic* state, the last phase in the relations of sounds. This progression can only exist in a chronological order, and the various states of things that result from it destroy each other, if one separates this consideration from temporal succession. It is therefore clear that the elements introduced successively into musical art can only be linked in chronological order, and that the argument I have attempted to take from this line of reasoning, to corroborate my proofs that the seventh chord on the second degree and its derivatives are not the product of the modification of consonant harmony, has very real merit.

We come now to your last objection. You reproach me for not having explained four seventh chords with fifths, to which you have objected in your article of May 26, and you are persuaded that the difficulty in finding a satisfactory response is the reason for my silence. You forget once again, my dear Zimmerman, that my response had preceded the objection in my *Traité de l'harmonie* (pages 65, 66, 80, §157). Allow me to recount here extracts from my explanations; they contain responses to which there is no reasonable opposition. Here are my words:

"Modern harmonists, guided by the analogy of the dominant seventh, believed that every dominant seventh chord must have the fifth in its makeup, and introduced this interval in the retardations of the sixth, by means of a double prolongation, where one, consonant, produces the fifth, which resolves upwards. They use this combination on the degrees where the sixth chord is placed (pages 65 and 66, §139)."

Examples

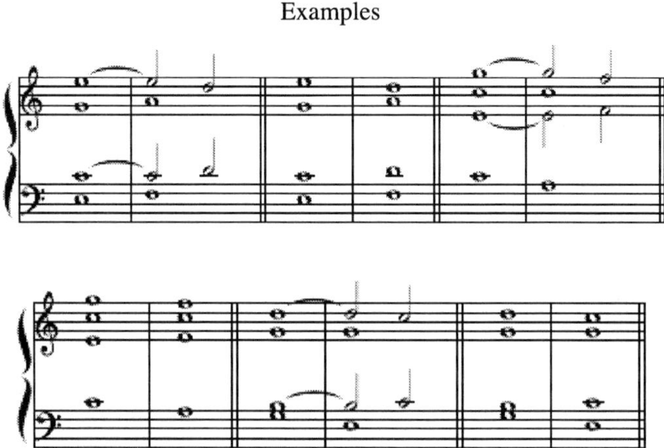

The movement of the bass which makes the minor seventh chord (on the second degree) resolve on the dominant seventh chord, produced by substitution and prolongation, has created progressions where each note is accompanied by a seventh chord, where the quality of the intervals differs by reason of the scale degree on which the chord is placed.

Just as I have said and shown (§78), the analogy of movement holds the attention in progressions of this kind, and suspends tonal feeling until the cadence; so that no scale degree is actually determined up to the moment of this cadence, which awakens the tonal feeling; we are only aware of the uniform movement of the bass and the symmetrical arrangement of the chords that accompany these its. Such is the phenomenon that is manifested in the hearing of the progression of seventh chords on the bass movements rising a fourth and descending a fifth (page 80, §157).

Here then are two very different origins of the chords of which you speak, because of the circumstances of their destination; they demonstrate that these chords have no analogy with that of the seventh on the second degree, which can only arise in one way, namely, by joining the substitution to the prolongation, and which only resolves properly on the dominant seventh chord, just as Catel has been forced to recognize by the example he gives of it in his *Traité d'harmonie* (page 23). I was therefore right to say, in speaking of this chord, which does not have an analogue in music, *that the prolonged note is always the tonic retarding the leading tone*.

Now, would you like a third origin of one of the seventh chords of which you speak? You will find it in this example:

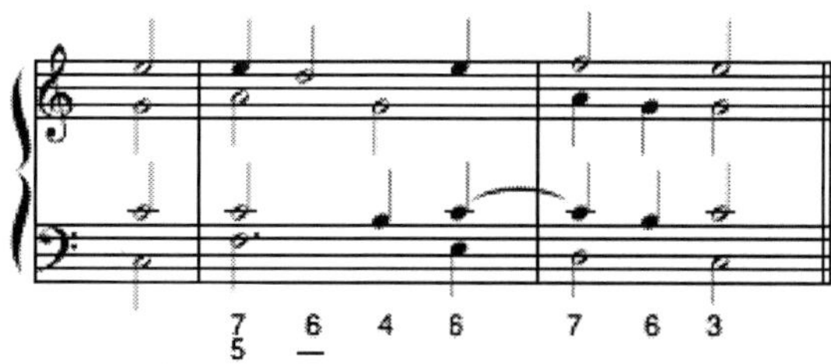

It is completely clear that the seven-five on the fourth degree is only the retardation of the sixth in the six-five chord, which is itself the result of the retardation of the leading tone by the prolongation of the tonic combined with the substitution of the sixth degree for the dominant. All these circumstances are, just as I have said, independent of each other, and are only coordinated by the supreme law of tonality. Art consists of a multitude of delicate combinations of this nature; the science that explains this art must therefore be completely analytical, and carefully distinguish the diversity of harmonic origins. You must therefore see that a theory that attempts to show the nature of all the chords of the seventh with perfect fifths, in giving as their origin a prolongation on a complete perfect chord, resolved on the following chord, is essentially only an assertion that is impossible to prove, and which has no more value than Rameau's view whereby he brings up the same chords with an added third above perfect chords on different degrees of the scale; then this theory does not stand the test of the analysis I have just made, and disappears before it.

Having refuted all Mr. Zimmerman's objections, I believe I must shed some light on the difficulties that many people have presented me, with regard to the absence of seven-five and six-five chords in the works of Monteverdi's predecessors, which I have affirmed. These people have presented me with examples of seven-five chords through prolongation in excerpts from Palestrina's works. They could also have found examples of the use of the six-five, not only in the works of the illustrious master of the Roman school, but in the works of much earlier musicians. I will explain the few very rare cases of these harmonies, which only affirm what I have said about the incompatibility of these harmonies in the old tonality.

Sometimes the voices were compressed by the old masters into a very narrow space, such that the retardation of the sixth by the seventh could not be made without doubling the third at the unison. Now, the unison was an object of horror for the old harmonists; to avoid it, in such a case, they wrote the retardation of the sixth by the seventh with third and fifth on the first beat; but this fifth quickly moved to the third at the unison, on the second beat of the measure, and the resolution was a simple retardation of the sixth chord, as if the fifth had not been heard. Here is an example of this way of writing, from the *Patrem* of Palestrina's *Sine nomine* mass.

It is clear that the harmony of the second last measure has no other tonal significance than the following:

The small number of sevenths with fifths that I have found in the works of composers of the fifteenth and sixteenth centuries are of the same kind, and the fifth is always incidental and lacking tonal significance.

With regard to the six-five, it is normally, in the works of Palestrina's contemporaries or predecessors, only a retardation of the fourth in the six-four chord at a cadence. Such is the following passage in the *Kyrie* from Palestrina's mass, *Spem in alium:*

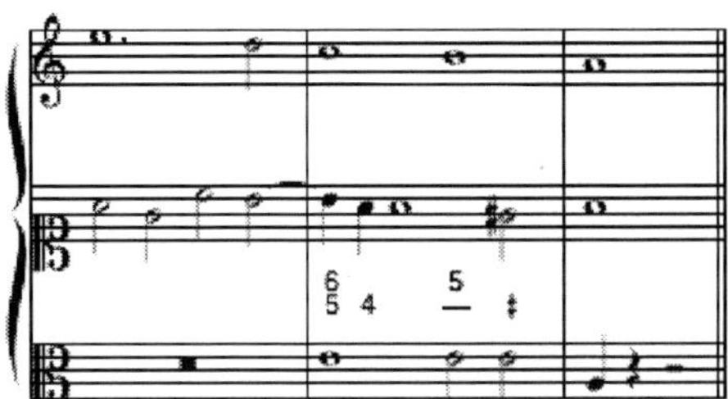

As for the true harmony of the six-five-three, on the fourth degree of the major or minor modes, it never appears in music of the old tonality. Even the bass formula that brings about this harmony in cadences is extremely rare amongst older composers; and when they used it they always accompanied it with a consonant harmony, simple or modified by retardations. Such is this cadence from the *Incarnatus est* in Palestrina's mass, *Spem in alium*.

I cannot conclude these notes without saying a few words on the errors into which the very admirable author of the *Nouvelle Biographie de Mozart*, Alexander Olïbïshev, has fallen, concerning natural dissonant harmony and its modifications.[7] In a note found in the second volume of this work (page 185 onwards), Olïbïshev casts doubt on the fact of the harmonic and tonal conception that I attribute to Monteverdi; but he knew

[7]Moscow, 1843, 3 vols*

*Alexander Olïbïshev (1794-1858), the son of a Russian diplomat posted in Dresden, was a Russian cival servant, amateur violinist, and music critic for the *Journal de St. Pétersbourg*. See the excerpt from his Mozart biography *in Musical Analysis in the Nineteenth Century: Volume I, Fugue, Form, Style*, ed. Ian Bent (Cambridge: Cambridge University Press, 1993), 281-301.

no other source of historical information, when he wrote his book, than Burney's *History of Music*, a book full of errors and mistakes, in which one does not find the monuments of the art appropriate to throw light on the question. It is necessary to have seen much music from all ages, and have made a thorough analysis of it, to distinguish what constitutes the tonalities and the harmonies to which they give rise. Many harmonists had already objected to me that one finds, in the works of composers who lived in the second half of sixteenth century, examples of the dominant seventh chord formed by passing notes; but these fleeting notes, which only happen in cadences after the perfect chord of which they are an embellishment, have had no influence on the reconstruction of harmony and tonality. None of this resembles the creation of natural dissonant harmony and modulation that one sees in the passages by Monteverdi that I have shown on pages 166-67 of this work, and even more in this fragment from the ballet *delle Ingrate*, composed by this illustrious musician, and performed at Mantua in 1608, for the wedding of Francesco Gonzague and Marguerite de Savoie.

There is nothing in this passage, of such powerful interest, that resembles either the harmony or the tonality of the sixteenth-century masters. Giovanni Gabrieli himself, despite the brilliance of his originality, does not step outside consonant harmony and its modifications. But here one sees the six-four-three chord on the sixth degree of the minor mode, the diminished seventh chord, that of the tritone with minor third, and finally, all that characterizes the tonality and expression of modern music.

A ritornello from the same work offers us the leading-tone seventh chord, the six-five on the fourth degree, in the two modes, and finally the bass formula in which this last chord is used at a cadence; a formula that has become commonplace in our music. Here is a fragment of this ritornello.

In these daring strokes of genius, we see Monteverdi develop instinctively, over a period of ten years, all the tonal and harmonic consequences of the foundations that he had laid down as early as 1598 in the third book of his madrigals, and especially in book five, published for the first time in 1604. Clearly, for anyone who is well informed about the condition of the art in former eras, it is in these acts of daring that radical transformations of art are manifested. Unfortunately, few people study the monuments of the history of the art with sufficient knowledge, and with the indispensable spirit of analysis. Olïbïshev's objections have been presented to me by literary-hack musicians who enjoy the reputation of scholars, and I have had reason to believe that the majority did not understand very clearly what characterizes the old tonality and what makes it different from that of today's music. From this results their error with regard to Monteverdi's inventions, of which they have not grasped the significance. I have dealt with this subject quite extensively in the biography of this great artist that forms part of the *Biographie universelle des musiciens*,[8] and I believe to have there completely clarified the issue. I think it necessary to reproduce here this passage for the benefit of readers who do not possess my extensive work.

"In the first two books of his madrigals, Monteverdi only showed his daring imagination by the many irregular voice movements and in the resolution of the dissonances of prolongations. In truth, one notices there more inattention than genius; it is even clear that this great artist felt a certain confusion in the placement of the parts of his harmony; for one sees there at any moment all these parts ascend or descend together in similar motion, and produce successions in which the features are as lacking in elegance as the effect is unpleasant to the ear. Let us be grateful, nonetheless, for this kind of clumsiness on the part of the composer, for it was undoubtedly the source of the audacity that he put into the exploration of a new harmony and tonality, which have become the basis of modern music.

"The genius of the master manifested itself in a larger and more distinct way in the third book of his Madrigals for five voices, published in 1598. It appears without a doubt that the ideas of Vincenzo Galilei [1520-1591], Jacopo Corsi [1561-1602], Jacopo Peri [1561-1633], and of a few other distinguished Florentine musicians, who lived towards the end of the sixteenth century, concerning the necessity of the music to express the meaning of the words, instead of making them, as did most of the old masters, a pretext for well-written counterpoint, but devoid of expression; it seems, in my opinion, that these ideas caught Monteverdi's interest, and revealed to him the scope of his genius; for, with the exception of certain harmonic inattention, one finds almost nothing of the composer of the first two madrigal books for five voices in that of the third book. Padre Martini has reproduced in his *Esemplare di Contrappunto fugato* (vol. I, 180 onward) the madrigal *Stracciami pure il core*, taken from this book; one also finds it in the third volume of the *Principes de composition des écoles*

[8]Vol. VI, page 480 onward, 2nd edition.

d'Italie, published by Choron, and in the third volume of the *History of Music*, by Burney (237 onward). This is truly an interesting idea that we have in this piece, from a historical point of view. Its rhythm has more movement, and its prosody is better than what is found in the works of most of Monteverdi's predecessors. The tonal cadence, so rare amongst the sixteenth-century masters, makes itself felt at every moment of this piece; what makes it most worthy of attention are the harmonic innovations that are found in abundance. Monteverdi does not yet approach natural dissonances without preparation, but uses the nine-six prolongation, condemned by previous composers, because it must resolve on the octave of the lower note of the semitone below that they called *mi*, and that this octave is obliged to make a passage of succession that betrays the tonality. It is, finally, in this piece that one finds, for the first time, on the words *non puo morire d'amore*, the double dissonances, by prolongation, of the nine-four, ninth, seven-four, and six-four combined with the fifth; the latter produces one of the most unpleasant effects that one could ever hear, for it results in three simultaneous notes at a distance of a second from each other. Monteverdi's audacity makes him defy all rules in this work; thus in the fourth measure of the above-mentioned madrigal, he realizes in the tenor part a passing dissonance to make a prolongation of it. Here again, as in many places, he gives notes placed at the interval of a second the character of the ninth by prolongation.

If Monteverdi did not yet approach without preparation the natural dissonances of the dominant when he wrote his third book of five-voice madrigals, he nevertheless determined the character of modern tonality by the frequent use of the harmonic relationship between the fourth and seventh degrees, and in so doing the latter constituted a true leading tone, which always found its resolution on the tonic. Now it is precisely these relationships between the fourth degree and the leading tone, and the appellative function of cadences, which distinguish modern tonality from that of plainchant, where the only necessary resolutions are those of the optional dissonances produced by prolongations.[9] In his fifth book of five-voice madrigals, Monteverdi achieved the last development of his boldness, by approaching without preparation the seventh and ninth of the dominant, the tritone, the minor fifth and sixth, and the diminished seventh. By this he completely attained the transformation of tonality, created the expressive and dramatic accent, as well as a new harmonic system. He even found, from the very first step, both the natural harmony of the dominant, as well as the principle of substitution; for we know that

---

[9]To understand what I say here about the differences between the tonality of the madrigals composed by the previous masters, and those of the same genre contained in Monteverdi's third book, it suffices to compare Palestrina's beautiful madrigal *Alla riva del Tebro* with that of the master of Cremona, *Stracciami pure il core*, in the works cited by Martini and Choron.

the dominant ninth and the diminished seventh are nothing else but substitutions. One may see in Padre Martini's *l'Esemplare*, and in the *Principes de composition des écoles d'Italie*, compiled by Choron, all these innovations combined in the madrigal *Cruda Amarilli*.

If the critics who thought they could attack the fundamental truths by which I have dissipated the darkness of the history of modern music had known Giovanni Artusi's [c. 1540-1613] book, Monterverdi's peer and principal opponent, they would have read these decisive words concerning the matter in question: *Our predecessors never taught that sevenths should be used in such an unconditional and exposed manner*.[10]

It would seem that such beautiful discoveries as those of which I have just spoken should have fulfilled the life of an artist. Yet Monteverdi produced for himself many other works to be admired by posterity. I have said in my *Résumé philosophique de l'histoire de la musique* (pages CCXVIII and CCXIX), and in the biographies of Caccini and Cavaliere, what were the beginnings of lyric drama, in the final years of the sixteenth century, and in the first of the following. Monteverdi, immediately grasping this innovation, gave it all the resources of his genius. In 1607, he wrote his opera *Arianna* for the court of Mantua. Much superior to Peri, Caccini, and even to Emilio del Cavaliere for the invention of melody, he put into these works passages in which the moving expression would still today excite the interest of artists. I will cite as an example Arianna's aria, *Lasciate mi morire*. The incorrect bass and clashing and bizarre harmony with which the composer accompanied this piece do not at all harm the quality of profound melancholy that one sees there. In his *Orfeo*, he found new forms of recitative, invented the scenic duet, and, without any model, envisaged new kinds of instrumentation, the effect of which was as striking as it was original. His dance airs, particularly in his ballet *delle Ingrate*, presented in Mantua in 1608, are filled with found forms and new and varied rhythms. It is he who was the first to introduce a modulation from fourth to fourth and from fifth to fifth, which has been used frequently since then, and of which he had made the first attempt in the madrigal *Cruda Amarilli*. Finally, the combat scene in the *Combattimento di Tancredi e Clorinda*, which was performed in 1624, in the house of Giralmo Moncenigo, in Venice, provided him the opportunity to invent accompaniments of repeated notes for all the instruments, in a more or less rapid movement; a system of instrumentation carried on by modern composers, and which was the origin of the tremolo.

Such was this predestined artist who contributed more than any other to the transformation of music, as well as to the creation of the elements of the modern art. A prolific genius, whose importance was not understood

[10]Le nostri vecchi non insegnarono mai che le settime si doveresso usare cosi assolute e scoperte. (*L'Artusi, overo delle imperfettioni della moderna musica*, 44.)

by his contemporaries, nor perhaps by he himself, for what he says of his inventions, in the prefaces to some of his works, does not indicate that he had seen that he introduced into harmony, and into melodic resolutions, a new system of tonality, completely different from that of plainchant, and that he had found the true element of modulation. What he rightly attributed to himself was the invention of the animated and expressive genre (*concitato*); no one, in fact, can deny him the creation of this immense order of splendor from which all modern music is derived, but which led to the annihilation of true church music by the introduction of drama. It is remarkable that this creation of modern tonality and all its consequences, owing to Monteverdi, has not been noticed by any music historian.